BASIC STATISTICAL FORMULAE

DESCRIPTIVE STATISTICS

Variance (s^2)

$$s^2 = \frac{\Sigma X^2 - (\Sigma X)^2/N}{N-1}$$

Standard deviation (s)

$$s = \sqrt{s^2}$$

Hinge Location

$$\frac{(\text{Median Location} + 1)}{2}$$

Percentile Rank

$$\text{Lower \%} + \frac{\text{Score} + \text{RLL}}{\text{Width}} \, (\text{Interval \%})$$

Score for a Percentile (Score_p)

$$\text{RLL} + \frac{\text{Width}}{\text{Interval \%}} \, (p - \text{Lower \%})$$

General Formula for z Score

$$\frac{\text{Score} - \text{Mean}}{\text{St. Dev.}} \quad \text{or} \quad \frac{\text{Statistic} - \text{Parameter}}{\text{St. Error of Statistic}}$$

z Score for an Observation

$$z = \frac{X - \bar{X}}{s}$$

TESTS ON SAMPLE MEANS

Standard Error of the Mean ($s_{\bar{X}}$)

$$\frac{s_X}{\sqrt{N}}$$

z for X given σ

$$z = \frac{(\bar{X} - \mu)}{\sigma_{\bar{X}}}$$

t for One Sample

$$t = \frac{\bar{X} - \mu}{s_{\bar{X}}} = \frac{\bar{X} - \mu}{\dfrac{s}{\sqrt{N}}}$$

Confidence Interval on μ

$$\text{CI} = \bar{X} \pm t_{.05}(s_{\bar{X}})$$

t for Two Related Samples

$$t = \bar{D}/s_{\bar{D}} = \frac{\bar{D}}{s_D/\sqrt{N}}$$

t for Two Independent Samples (Unpooled)

$$t = \frac{\bar{X}_1 - \bar{X}_2}{s_{\bar{X}_1 - \bar{X}_2}} = \frac{\bar{X}_1 - \bar{X}_2}{\sqrt{\dfrac{s_1^2}{N_1} + \dfrac{s_2^2}{N_2}}}$$

Pooled Variance (s_p^2)

$$s_p^2 = \frac{(N_1 - 1)s_1^2 + (N_2 - 1)s_2^2}{N_1 + N_2 - 2}$$

t for Two Independent Samples (Pooled)

$$t = \frac{\bar{X}_1 - \bar{X}_2}{s_{\bar{X}_1 - \bar{X}_2}} = \frac{\bar{X}_1 - \bar{X}_2}{\sqrt{\dfrac{s_p^2}{N_1} + \dfrac{s_p^2}{N_2}}}$$

Confidence Interval on $\mu_1 - \mu_2$

$$\text{CI} = (\bar{X}_1 - \bar{X}_2) \pm t_{.05}(s_{\bar{X}_1 - \bar{X}_2})$$

THE DUXBURY SERIES IN STATISTICS AND DECISION SCIENCES

Applications, Basics, and Computing of Exploratory Data Analysis, Velleman and
 Hoaglin
Applied Regression Analysis and Other Multivariable Methods, Second Edition,
 Kleinbaum, Kupper, and Muller
Classical and Modern Regression with Applications, Myers
A Course in Business Statistics, Second Edition, Mendenhall
Elementary Statistics for Business, Second Edition, Johnson and Siskin
Elementary Statistics, Fifth Edition, Johnson
Elementary Survey Sampling, Third Edition, Scheaffer, Mendenhall, and Ott
Essential Business Statistics: A Minitab Framework, Bond and Scott
Fundamental Statistics for the Behavioral Sciences, Second Edition, Howell
Fundamentals of Biostatistics, Second Edition, Rosner
Fundamentals of Statistics in the Biological, Medical, and Health Sciences, Runyon
Introduction to Contemporary Statistical Methods, Second Edition, Koopmans
Introduction to Probability and Mathematical Statistics, Bain and Engelhardt
Introduction to Probability and Statistics, Seventh Edition, Mendenhall
An Introduction to Statistical Methods and Data Analysis, Third Edition, Ott
Introductory Statistical Methods: An Integrated Approach Using Minitab, Groeneveld
Introductory Statistics for Management and Economics, Third Edition, Kenkel
Linear Statistical Models: An Applied Approach, Bowerman, O'Connell, and Dickey
Mathematical Statistics with Applications, Third Edition, Mendenhall,
 Scheaffer, and Wackerly
Minitab Handbook, Second Edition, Ryan, Joiner, and Ryan
Minitab Handbook for Business and Economics, Miller
Operations Research: Applications and Algorithms, Winston
Probability Modeling and Computer Simulation, Matloff
Probability and Statistics for Engineers, Second Edition, Scheaffer and McClave
Probability and Statistics for Modern Engineering, Lapin
Quantitative Forecasting Methods, Farnum and Stanton
Quantitative Models for Management, Second Edition, Davis and McKeown
Statistical Experiments Using BASIC, Dowdy
Statistical Methods for Psychology, Second Edition, Howell
Statistical Thinking for Behavioral Scientists, Hildebrand
Statistical Thinking for Managers, Second Edition, Hildebrand and Ott
Statistics for Business and Economics, Bechtold and Johnson
Statistics for Management and Economics, Sixth Edition, Mendenhall, Reinmuth,
 and Beaver
Statistics: A Tool for the Social Sciences, Fourth Edition,
 Ott, Larson, and Mendenhall
Time Series Analysis, Cryer
Time Series Forecasting: Unified Concepts and Computer Implementation,
 Second Edition, Bowerman and O'Connell
Understanding Statistics, Fourth Edition, Ott and Mendenhall

Fundamental Statistics
for the Behavioral Sciences

second edition

David C. Howell
University of Vermont

PWS-KENT Publishing Company
Boston

PWS–KENT
Publishing Company

20 Park Plaza
Boston, Massachusetts 02116

This book is dedicated to my mother and my father.

PWS-KENT Publishing Company is a division of Wadsworth, Inc.

Library of Congress Cataloging-in-Publication Data

Howell, David C.
    Fundamental statistics for the behavioral sciences/David C.
    Howell.—2nd ed.
    p. cm.
    Bibliography: p.
    Includes index.
    ISBN 0-534-91694-5
    1. Social sciences—Statistical methods.   2. Psychometrics.
I. Title.
HA29.H78   1989   88-39574
519.5—dc 19   88-39574

Printed in the United States of America

89 90 91 92 93—10 9 8 7 6 5 4 3 2 1

Acquisitions Editor: Michael R. Payne
Production Editor: S. London
Interior and Cover Designer: S. London
Interior Illustrator: Lisa C. Sparks
Manufacturing Coordinator: Margaret Sullivan Higgins
Cover Photographer: Greg Bowl Studio
Cover Props: David Bernstein
Typesetter: Doyle Graphics
Cover Printer: New England Book Components
Printer and Binder: RR. Donnelley and Sons

This text is designed for an introductory statistics course in psychology, education, and other behavioral sciences. It does not presuppose a background in mathematics beyond high school algebra, and it emphasizes the logic of statistical procedures rather than their derivation.

I have deliberately set out to make the book both interesting and useful for students and instructors. It is written in an informal style, every data set is put in the context of an experiment that one might reasonably conduct, and many of the examples are taken from the published literature. It does not seem to me to make much sense to ask the student to learn a series of statistical procedures without supplying examples of situations in which those techniques would actually be applied.

IMPORTANT FEATURES

There are several features of the book that set it apart from other books written for the same audience. One of these was just noted: the use of examples from the research literature. A second is the use of examples of computer analyses of data, for which hand-calculated solutions also appear. In most chapters a section is devoted to an example based on Minitab. The purpose of the example is to familiarize the student with the form of computer printouts and the kinds of information they contain. Each example also includes the particular program that generated the output, and students who wish may use these as templates for designing their own solutions. The first edition of this book included homework exercises that made use of Minitab. Those have largely been removed on the advice of a number of reviewers, but instructors who wish that they had remained can simply ask students to use Minitab to solve problems that are currently intended for hand calculation.

Another feature of this book is a more extensive than normal use of techniques generally included under the heading of exploratory data analysis (EDA). The intent was not to write a textbook of EDA techniques—only stem-and-leaf displays and boxplots are developed in any depth—but to emphasize the usefulness of those procedures in all data analyses. Thus, for example, the Minitab analysis in Table 14–3 (page 199) includes stem-and-leaf displays and check for outliers, skewed distributions, and so on.

The book includes over 350 homework exercises and answers. Approximately half of these exercises involve direct calculation, and the other half require the student to think about the whole process of data analysis. In addition Chapter 21 includes a set of examples of actual research studies for which the student is asked to decide upon the appropriate method of analysis. This is an area where many students have difficulty, and these exercises are intended to help overcome this difficulty.

A number of changes have been made to this edition of the book. One of the most important as far as the student is concerned is the addition of a final worked example at the end of each chapter. The purpose of this example is to show the student each step that must be gone through to solve a problem in a logical and orderly manner. A second change is the inclusion of a number of tables and figures, especially in the early chapters, to supplement or elaborate the presentation in a visual way. A number of homework problems have been added to the book, with a particular emphasis on problems that require the student to think about the material. There is also emphasis on problems that test whether the student understood points in the text that may have been passed over quickly because they should have been apparent. Finally, in response to reviewers' suggestions, the chapters on correlation and regression have been placed earlier in the book and the Mann–Whitney test has replaced the (equivalent) Wilcoxon Rank-sum test.

MATERIAL COVERED

The first eight chapters of the book are devoted to standard descriptive statistics, including ways of displaying data, measures of central tendency and variability, percentiles, the normal distribution, and those aspects of probability that are directly applicable to what follows. Chapters 9 and 10 deal with correlation and regression. Chapter 11 on hypothesis testing and sampling distributions serves as a nontechnical introduction to inferential statistics. That chapter was specifically designed to allow the student to examine the underlying logic of hypothesis testing without simultaneously being concerned with learning a set of formulae and the intricacies of a statistical test. Chapters 12–14 are devoted to tests on means, primarily t tests. Chapter 15 is concerned with power and its calculation and serves as an easily understood and practical approach to that topic. Chapters 16–18 are concerned with the analysis of variance. I have included material on simple repeated-measures designs, but have stopped short of covering mixed designs. These chapters include consideration of basic multiple comparison procedures by way of the Scheffé test and by way of Fisher's protected t, which not only is an easily understood statistic but has also been shown to be well behaved with respect to both power and error rates. Also included are measures of magnitude of effect, a fairly extensive coverage of interactions, and procedures for testing simple effects. Chapter 19 deals with the chi-square test, although that material could very easily be covered at an earlier point if desired. Chapter 20 deals with the most prominent distribution-free tests, and Chapter 21 offers the student practice in deciding upon the most appropriate statistical procedure for use with a given experimental design.

Because students often have trouble as a result of having forgotten basic mathematical operations, a review of basic arithmetic is included in Appendix A. Also, in Appendix C is a large data set that is addressed by numerous homework examples throughout the book.

ACKNOWLEDGEMENTS

Many people have played an important role in the development of this book. My editor, Michael Payne, was extremely supportive of this revision, which wouldn't have been possible without him. Susan London, the production editor, did a wonderful job for yet a fourth time—and always with apparent good cheer. A number of reviewers made many, many helpful suggestions and three of them, Dr. Maureen Powers (Vanderbilt University), Dr. Drake Bradley (Bates college) and Dr. Dominic Zerbolio (University of Missouri–St. Louis) went well beyond the normal duties of reviewers and gave extremely valuable detailed comments on the manuscript. I want to express by thanks to Jerry Cohen (University of Rhode Island), Richard Lindley (California State University, Fullerton), David Mostofsky (Boston University), and James Sheridan (Millersville University) for their very helpful reviews of the second edition.

I owe thanks to my colleagues at the University of Vermont and at the University of Bristol, England, where part of a sabbatical leave was devoted to completing the first edition of the book. My wife, Cathy, offered criticism and suggestions on many parts of the first edition, compiled the index, typed and retyped the whole thing, and insisted that variety is not the spice of life when it comes to statistical notation. Without her contribution this book would have taken an extra year to complete and would surely not have been as good. Most of all, however, I owe a debt to all of my students who have helped me over the years to see where problems lie and how they can best be approached. Their encouragement has been invaluable. Finally, I want to thank the *Biometrika* trustees for permission to reproduce the table of Wilcoxon's W statistic.

David C. Howell

CONTENTS

INTRODUCTION

In the past, when I was asked at parties and other social situations what I did for a living, I would answer that I was a psychologist. After several years of defending myself against the remarks and weird looks that this admission produced, I finally changed tactics and started telling people that I teach statistics—an answer that is also perfectly true. This answer solved one problem—people no longer look at me with blatant suspicion—but it created another. Now they either assume that I am a walking encyclopedia of "useless" facts (such as the number of metric tons of steel shipped last year from the Common Market to the Warsaw Pact nations) or else they tell me how successful they were in avoiding ever taking a statistics course (because "I was never good in math"—*an absolutely irrelevant reason*).

The basic problem is that most people don't understand what statistics is all about and what statisticians do. For that reason let's start with some basic definitions. The word *statistics* is used in at least three different ways. As the word is used in the title of this book, it refers to a set of rules and procedures for reducing large masses of data to manageable proportions and for allowing us to draw conclusions from those data. This is essentially what this book is all about.

A second, and very common, meaning of the term is expressed by statements such as "statistics show that the number of people applying for unemployment benefits has fallen for the third month in a row." In this meaning the word *statistics* is used in place of the much better word *data*. For our purposes the word *statistics* will never be used in this sense.

A third common meaning of the term is in reference to the result of some arithmetic or algebraic manipulation applied to data. Thus the mean (average) of a set of numbers is a statistic. This is a perfectly legitimate usage and will occur repeatedly throughout the book.

We thus have two proper uses of the term: (1) a set of rules and procedures and (2) the outcome of the application of those rules and procedures to samples of data. The reader can tell from the context which of the two meanings is intended.

1-1   DESCRIPTIVE AND INFERENTIAL STATISTICS

Statistical procedures can be separated into roughly two overlapping areas—descriptive and inferential statistics. The first several chapters of this book will be concerned with descriptive statistics, and the remainder will be concerned primarily with inferential statistics.

DESCRIPTIVE STATISTICS

Whenever your purpose is merely to describe a set of data, you are employing descriptive statistics. An examination of dieting scores on the Eating Restraint Scale, crime rates as reported by the Department of Justice, and certain summary information concerning grades on an examination in a particular course are all examples of descriptive statistics.

The descriptive statistician has a wealth of statistical techniques at hand to do the job efficiently, but an exhaustive elaboration of these techniques lies outside the scope of this book. The most important techniques and measures, such as ways of plotting data, exploratory data analysis, means, standard deviations, and percentiles, will be discussed in Chapters 3 through 6, because they are essential to an understanding of inferential statistics.

INFERENTIAL STATISTICS

All of us at some time or another have been guilty of making unreasonable generalizations on the basis of very limited data. If, for example, you hear or read that tall people tend to be more graceful than short people, you may agree with that statement because you once had a very tall roommate who was particularly graceful. You conveniently tend to forget about the 6′ 4″ klutz down the hall who can't even put on his pants standing up without tripping over them and landing on his face. Similarly, the man who says that girls develop motor skills earlier than boys because his daughter walked at 10 months and his son didn't walk until 14 months is guilty of the same kind of error—generalizing from single (or too limited) observations.

Single observations may be fine when we want to study something that has very little variability. If we want to know how many legs a cow has, we can find a cow and count its legs. We don't need a whole herd—one will do. However, when what we want to measure varies from one individual to another (such as the length of cows' tails or age at first calving), then we cannot be satisfied with single observations. However, neither can we make an unlimited number of observations. If we want to know when girls usually start to walk, we must look at more than one girl, but we cannot possibly look at all girls in the world. We must do something in between.

The same thing is true if we are looking at the effects of a new treatment for alcoholism. That this treatment caused one subject to stop drinking is nice, but that fact certainly would not justify widespread use of the treatment any more than the testimonial "I lost 182 lbs in 6 months and enjoyed every minute of it" justifies a newly touted diet. On the other hand we can't treat every alcoholic or overweight person before we draw conclusions. Again we must find some middle ground. This is where inferential statistics come in.

Most of the statistical work in psychology and the other social sciences is concerned with inferential statistics. To expand on this point we must define the concepts of populations and samples, because the field of inferential statistics is concerned with using samples to infer something about populations.

Population
Complete set of events in which you are interested.

Populations, Samples, Parameters, and Statistics A **population** can be defined as the *entire* collection of events in which you are interested (e.g., U.S. high school students' scores on a measure of self-worth, individual sales of all records produced in this country in the last 20 years, and so on). Thus if we were interested in the social sensitivity scores of all preadolescent Americans, then the collection of all preadolescent American social sensitivity scores would form a population—in this case a population of more than 50 million members. If, on the other hand, we were interested only in the collection of social sensitivity scores of the second-grade class in Fairfax, Vermont (a town of approximately 1800 inhabitants), the population would contain about 30 numbers and could be obtained quite easily in its entirety. Finally, consider the set of outcomes of rolling a die. Clearly, after you have rolled a die you always can roll it again, and assuming that it never wears out it could be rolled an infinite number of times, producing an infinitely large population of outcomes (mathematicians would prefer the world *uncountable*, but the word *infinite* will do).

The point is that a population can range from a relatively small set of numbers, which is easily collected, to an infinitely large set of numbers, which can never be completely collected. Unfortunately for us, the populations in which we are interested are usually quite large. The practical consequence is that we will seldom if ever collect data on entire populations. Instead, we will be

Sample
Set of actual observations. Subset of the population.

forced to draw only a **sample** of observations from that population and to use that sample to infer something about the characteristics of the population.

Statistics
Numerical values summarizing sample data.

Parameters
Numerical values summarizing population data.

When we draw a sample of observations, we normally compute numerical values (such as averages) that summarize the data in that sample. When such values are based on the sample, they are called **statistics**. The corresponding values in the population (e.g., the population average) are called **parameters**. One major purpose of inferential statistics is to draw inferences about parameters (characteristics of populations) from statistics (characteristics of samples).†

Random sample
A sample in which each member of the population has an equal chance of inclusion.

Assuming that the sample is a truly **random sample**, meaning that each and every element of the population has an equal chance of being included in the

†The word *inference* as used by a statistician means very much what it means in normal English usage—a conclusion based on logical reasoning. If three-fourths of the people at a picnic suddenly fall ill, I am likely to draw the (possibly incorrect) inference that something is wrong with the food. Similarly if the average social sensitivity score of a random sample of fifth-grade children is very low, I am likely to draw the inference that fifth graders in general have much to learn about social sensitivity. Statistical inference is generally more precise than everyday inference, but the basic idea is the same.

sample, not only can we estimate parameters of the population, but we can also have a very good idea of the accuracy of our estimates. To the extent that the sample is not a random sample, our estimates may be meaningless, because the sample will not accurately reflect the entire population.

Let us clear up one point that tends to confuse many people. The problem is that one person's sample might be another person's population. For example, if I were to conduct a study into the effectiveness of this book as a teaching instrument, one class's scores on an examination might be considered by me to be a sample, though a nonrandom one, of the population of scores for all students using, or potentially using, this book. The class instructor, on the other hand, cares only about his own students and would regard the same set of scores as a population. In turn, someone interested in the teaching of statistics might regard my population (the scores of everyone using this book) as a nonrandom sample from a larger population (the scores of everyone using any textbook in statistics). Thus the definition of a population depends upon what you are interested in studying. Notice also that when we speak about populations, we speak about populations of *scores*, not populations of *people*. We will return to this point later.

The fact that I have used nonrandom samples here to make a point should not lead the reader to think that randomness is not important. On the contrary, it is the cornerstone of most statistical procedures. As a matter of fact, one could define the relevant population as the collection of numbers from which the sample has been randomly drawn.

Inference   We previously have defined inferential statistics as that branch of statistics dealing with inferring characteristics of populations from characteristics of samples. This statement is inadequate by itself, however, as it leaves the reader with the impression that all we care about is determining population parameters such as the average height of adult American males or the average running speed of second-grade school children. There are, of course, times when we do care about actual population parameters. For example, we often read and may be excited about the fantastic number of hours per day the average child spends in front of a television set. But if that were all there were to inferential statistics, it would be a pretty dreary subject, and the people who look at me strangely when I admit to teaching statistics would be justified.

The problem that many students have with statistics is that they do not realize until too late that when we attempt to infer the average reading speed of third-grade children taught under one method of instruction, we usually do not have any great interest in what that average is. We care only whether it is larger or smaller than some other average—for example, the average reading speed of a sample of third-grade children taught under some other method. Thus in many cases inferential statistics is a tool used to estimate parameters of two or more populations, mainly for the purpose of finding out if those parameters are different. This explains why someone might conduct a study into the running speed of hooded rats under some schedule of reinforcement. It is obviously not a matter of great national concern just how fast a rat can run. But it might be a matter of more limited interest whether rats trained under a different schedule of reinforcement will run faster.

1-2 SELECTION AMONG STATISTICAL PROCEDURES

As we have just seen, an important distinction is the one between descriptive and inferential statistics. The first part of this book will be concerned with descriptive statistics because it is necessary to describe a set of data before we can use it to draw inferences. When we come to inferential statistics, however, we need to make several additional distinctions that help us to focus the choice of an appropriate statistical procedure. On the inside front cover you can see what is known as a **decision tree** for selecting among the available statistical procedures to be presented in this book. This decision tree not only represents a rough outline of the organization of the latter part of the text, but it also points up some fundamental issues that we should address at the outset. In considering these issues, keep in mind that we are not concerned at this point with which statistical test is used for which purpose. That will come later. Rather, we are concerned with the kinds of questions that come into play when we try to do anything statistically with data—whether we are talking about descriptive or inferential procedures. These issues are listed across the top of the decision tree. The first three of these will be discussed briefly now, whereas the rest will be left to a more appropriate time.

Decision tree
Graphical representation of decisions involved in the choice of statistical procedures.

TYPES OF DATA

Numerical data generally come in two kinds, which we will designate as measurement and categorical data. By **measurement data** (sometimes called **quantitative data**) we mean the result of any sort of measurement—for example, a grade on a test, a person's weight, the speed at which a person can read this page, an individual's score on a scale of authoritarianism, and so on. In all cases some sort of instrument (in its broadest sense) has been used to measure something.

**Measurement data
(Quantitative data)**
Data obtained by measuring objects or events.

On the other hand **categorical data** (also known as **frequency data** or **count data**) consist of statements such as "One hundred fifty-eight people like chocolate bars with almonds and 26 prefer plain ones" or "There were 238 votes for the new curriculum and 118 against it." Here we are counting things, and our data consist of totals or frequencies for each category (hence the name categorical data). Several hundred faculty members might vote on a new curriculum, but the results (data) would consist of only two numbers—the number of votes for and the number against the proposal. With measurement data, however, we might measure the girths of hundreds of people. Here we would come up with hundreds of numbers—one for each person. Sometimes we can measure the same variable to produce either measurement or categorical

**Categorical data
(Frequency data)
(Count data)**
Data representing counts or number of observations in each category.

data. If we worked with the height of each person recorded to the nearest inch, we would be dealing with measurement data. However, if we simply classified people as short, medium, or tall, we would be working with categorical data. As with most distinctions, the one between measurement and categorical data can be pushed too far, but in practice the choice is almost always clear.

The two kinds of data are treated in two quite different ways. In Chapter 19 we will examine categorical data to see how we can determine whether there is or is not a reliable difference between, for example, the preferences for two different candy bars. In Chapters 9 and 10, 12 through 14, 16 through 18, and 20 we are going to be concerned chiefly with measurement data. Using measurement data, we have to make a second distinction, not in terms of the type of data, but in terms of whether we are concerned with examining differences between groups of subjects or with studying the relationship between variables.

DIFFERENCES VERSUS RELATIONSHIPS

Most statistical questions fall roughly into one of two overlapping categories— differences and relationships. For example, one experimenter might be interested primarily in whether there is a difference between smokers and nonsmokers in terms of their performance on a given task. A second experimenter might be interested in whether there is a relationship between the number of cigarettes smoked per day and scores on this same task. Although these two questions obviously overlap, they are treated by what, on the surface, appear to be quite different methods. Chapters 12 through 14 and 16 through 18 will be concerned primarily with those cases in which we ask if there are differences between two or more groups, while Chapters 9 and 10 will deal with cases in which we are interested in examining relationships between two or more variables. These seemingly different statistical techniques turn out to be basically the same fundamental procedure, although they ask somewhat different questions and phrase their answers in distinctly different ways.

NUMBERS OF GROUPS OR VARIABLES

As we will see in subsequent chapters, an obvious distinction between statistical techniques concerns the number of groups or the number of variables to which they apply. Thus, for example, we will see that what is generally referred to as an independent t test is restricted to the case of data from two groups of subjects. The analysis of variance, on the other hand, is applicable to any number of groups, not just two. The third decision in our tree concerns the number of groups or variables involved.

The three decisions we have been discussing (type of data, differences versus relationships, and number of groups or variables) are fundamental to the way we look at data and the statistical procedures we will use to help us interpret those data. One further criterion that some textbooks use for creating categories of tests and ways of describing and manipulating data involves the scale of measurement that applies to the data. We will discuss this topic further in the next chapter, as it represents an important concept with which any student should be familiar.

1-3 SUMMARY

In this chapter we examined the two major branches of statistics (descriptive and inferential statistics). We then covered the distinction between populations and samples, and defined the concept of a random sample. Lastly we dealt with several dimensions along which various statistical procedures could be distinguished. Some of the important terms in the chapter are:

□ **Population**
□ **Sample**
□ **Statistics**
□ **Parameters**

□ **Random sample**
□ **Decision tree**
□ **Measurement data**
□ **Categorical data**

1-4 EXERCISES

1-1 Under what conditions would the entire student body of your college or university be considered a population?

1-2 Under what conditions would the entire student body of your college or university be considered a sample?

1-3 If the student body of your college or university were to be considered a sample, as in Exercise 1-2, would this sample be a random or a nonrandom sample, and why?

1-4 Why would choosing names from a local telephone book not produce a random sample of the residents of that city? Who would be underrepresented and who would be overrepresented?

1-5 Can you suggest ways by which we might be able to produce a random (or more nearly random) sample of people from a small city?

1-6 Even before you began this course you were probably aware of some sample statistics. Name two.

1-7 Give an example of a study in which we would be interested in estimating the average score of a population.

1-8 Give an example of a study in which we don't care about the actual numerical value of a population average, but would wish to know whether the average of one population is greater than the average of a different population.

1-9 Give three examples of categorical data.

1-10 Give three examples of measurement data.

1-11 Give an example in which the thing we are studying could be either a measurement or a categorical variable.

1-12 Give two examples of studies in which our primary interest is in looking at relationships between variables.

1-13 Give two examples of studies in which our primary interest is in looking at group differences.

2

BASIC CONCEPTS

2-1 Scales of Measurement

2-2 Variables

2-3 Random Sampling

2-4 Notation

In the preceding chapter we dealt with a number of statistical terms (e.g., parameter, statistic, population, sample, and random sample) that are fundamental to an understanding of the statistical analysis of data. In this chapter we consider some additional concepts that you will need. We will start with the concepts of measurement and measurement scales, because everything we do begins with the measurement of whatever it is we want to study.

Measurement
The assignment of numbers to objects.

Measurement is frequently defined as the assignment of numbers to objects, where the words *numbers* and *objects* are to be interpreted very loosely. When, for example, we use a test of authoritarianism (e.g., the Adorno Authoritarianism Scale) to obtain an authoritarianism score for a person, we are measuring authoritarianism by assigning a number (a score) to an object (a person). Depending on what we are measuring and how we measure it, the numbers we obtain may have different properties, and these different properties of numbers often are discussed under the specific topic of **scales of measurement**.

Scales of measurement
Characteristics of relations among numbers assigned to objects.

2-1 SCALES OF MEASUREMENT

The topic of *scales of measurement* is one of those topics that some writers think is crucial and others think is irrelevant. Although this book will tend to side with the latter group, it is important that you have some familiarity with the general issue. (You do not have to agree with something to think that it is worth studying. After all, evangelists claim to know a great deal about sin.) An additional benefit of this discussion is that you will begin to realize that statistics as a subject is not merely a cut-and-dried set of facts, but rather a set of facts put together with a variety of interpretations and opinions.

Probably the foremost leader of those who see scales of measurement as crucially important to the choice of statistical procedures was S. S. Stevens.† Basically, Stevens defined four types of scales: nominal, ordinal, interval, and

†Chapter 1 in Stevens' *Handbook of Experimental Psychology* (1951) is an excellent reference for anyone wishing to go further into the substantial mathematical issues underlying his position.

8

ratio. These scales are distinguished on the basis of the relationships assumed to exist between items having different scale values. Later scales in this series have all the properties of earlier scales, and additional properties as well.

NOMINAL SCALES

Nominal scale
Numbers used only to distinguish among objects.

In a sense **nominal scales** are not really scales at all, because they do not scale items along any dimension, but rather label them. The classical example of a nominal scale is the set of numbers assigned to football players. Frequently these numbers have no meaning whatsoever other than as convenient labels distinguishing the players from one another. We could just as easily use letters or the pictures of animals. In fact, gender is a nominal scale that uses words (male and female) in place of numbers. Nominal scales are generally used for the purpose of classification. Categorical data, which we discussed in Chapter 1, are measured on a nominal scale, because we merely assign category labels (e.g., male or female; Republican, Democrat, or independent) to observations. Quantitative (measurement) data can be measured on any of the following three types of scales.

ORDINAL SCALES

Ordinal scale
Numbers used only to place objects in order.

The simplest true scale is an **ordinal scale**, which orders people, objects, or events along some continuum. An example of an ordinal scale might be the class standings of people graduating from high school. Here the scale tells us which person in the class had the highest average, which had the second-highest average, and so on. Another example would be the Holmes and Rahe (1967) scale of life stress. Using this scale you simply count up (sometimes with differential weightings) the number of changes (marriage, moving, new job, etc.) in the past six months of a person's life. Someone who has a score of 20 is presumed to have experienced more stress than someone with a score of 15, who in turn is presumed to have experienced more stress than someone with a score of 10. Thus we order people, in terms of stress, by the changes in their lives.

Notice that these two examples differ in the numbers that are assigned. In the first case we assign the ranks 1, 2, 3, ..., whereas in the second case the scores represent the number of changes rather than ranks. Both are examples of ordinal scales, however, because no information is given about the differences between points on the scale. This is an important characteristic of ordinal scales. We do not assume, for example, that the difference between 10 and 15 life changes represents the same increase in stress as the difference between 15 and 20 life changes. Distinctions of that sort must be left to the next type of scale.

INTERVAL SCALES

Interval scale
Scale on which equal intervals between objects represent equal differences— differences are meaningful.

With an **interval scale** we have a scale of measurement in which we can legitimately speak of differences between scale points. A common example is the Fahrenheit scale of temperature, in which a 10-point difference has the same meaning anywhere along the scale. Thus the difference in temperature between

10° and 20° is the same as the difference between 80° and 90°. Notice that this scale also satisfies the properties of the two preceding ones. What we do not have with an interval scale, however, is the ability to speak meaningfully about ratios. Thus we cannot say, for example, that 40°F is one-half as hot as 80°F, or twice as hot as 20°F, because the zero point on the scale is arbitrary. For example, 20°F and 40°F correspond to -7°C and 4°C, respectively, and the two sets of ratios are obviously quite different and arbitrary.

RATIO SCALES

Ratio scale
A scale with a true zero point—ratios are meaningful.

A **ratio scale** is one that has a *true* zero point. Notice that the zero point must be a true zero point and not an arbitrary one such as 0° Fahrenheit or even 0° Celsius. (A true zero point is the point corresponding to the absence of the thing being measured. Because 0°F and 0°C do not represent the absence of temperature, they are not true zero points; 0° kelvin is taken as a true zero point, however.) Examples of ratio scales are the common physical ones of length, volume, time, and so on. With these scales not only do we have the properties of the preceding scales but also we can speak about ratios. We can say that in physical terms 10 seconds is twice as long as 5 seconds, that 100 lbs is one-third as heavy as 300 lbs, and so on.

One might think that the kind of scale with which we are working would usually be obvious. Unfortunately, especially with the kinds of measures we collect in the social sciences, this is rarely the case. Consider for a moment the situation in which an examination is administered to a group of students. If I were foolish enough, I might argue that this is a ratio scale of knowledge of the subject matter. I would maintain that a person who received a score of zero truly knew nothing and that a score of 80 represented twice as much knowledge as a score of 40. Though most people would find this position ridiculous, with certain examinations I might be able to build a reasonable case. Someone else might argue that it is an interval scale and that while the zero point was somewhat arbitrary (the student receiving a zero knew a little bit but I did not happen to ask the right questions), equal differences in grades represent equal differences in knowledge. Finally, a more reasonable case might be made that the grades represent an ordinal scale. A 95 is better than an 85, which in turn is better than a 75, but equal differences in grades do not reflect equal differences in knowledge. For an excellent and readable discussion of scales of measurement the student is referred to Hays (1981, pages 59–65).

As an example of a measurement whose scale depends upon its use, consider the temperature of your house. We generally speak of Fahrenheit temperature as an interval scale. It was just used as an example of one, and there is no doubt that to a physicist the difference between 62° and 64° is exactly the same as the difference between 72° and 74°. *But* if we are measuring temperature as an index of comfort rather than as an index of molecular activity, the same numbers no longer form an interval scale. To a person sitting in a room at 62°, a jump to 64° would be distinctly noticeable (and welcome). The same cannot be said about the difference between room temperatures of 72° and 74°. This points up the important fact that it is the underlying variable being measured (e.g., comfort), not the numbers themselves, that defines the scale.

Because there is usually no unanimous agreement concerning the scale of measurement employed, it is up to the individual user of statistical procedures to make the best decision she can concerning the nature of the data. All that can be asked of her is that she think about the problem carefully before coming to her decision, and not simply assume that the standard answer is necessarily the best answer.

THE ROLE OF MEASUREMENT SCALES

The statement was made earlier that there is a difference of opinion as to the importance assigned to scales of measurement. Some authors have ignored the problem totally, while others have organized whole textbooks around the different scales. It seems to me that the central issue is the absolute necessity of separating in our minds the numbers we collect from the objects or events to which they refer. If one subject in a verbal learning study recalled 20 items and another subject recalled 10 items, the number of words recalled was twice as large for the first subject. However, we might not be willing to say that the first subject remembered twice as much about the material studied.

A similar argument was made for the example of room temperature, where the scale (interval or ordinal) depended on whether we were interested in measuring some physical attribute of temperature or its effect on people. A difference of 2° is the same, *physically*, anywhere on the scale, but a difference of 2° when a room is already warm may not *feel* as large as a difference of 2° when a room is relatively cool. In other words we have an interval scale of the physical units but no more than an ordinal scale of comfort.

Because statistical tests use numbers without considering the objects or events to which those numbers refer, we may carry out any of the standard mathematical operations (addition, multiplication, and so on) regardless of the nature of the underlying scale. An excellent and highly recommended reference on this point is a very entertaining paper by Lord (1953) entitled "The Statistical Treatment of Football Numbers," in which he argues that these numbers can be treated in any way you like, since "the numbers do not remember where they came from" (page 751).

The problem comes when it is time to interpret the results of some form of statistical manipulation. At that point we must ask if the statistical results bear any meaningful relationship to the objects or events in question. Here we are no longer dealing with a statistical issue, however, but with a methodological one. No *statistical* procedure can tell us whether the fact that one group received higher grades than another on a history examination reveals anything at all about group differences in underlying knowledge of the subject matter. Moreover, to be satisfied because the examination provides grades that form a ratio scale of correct items (50 correct items is twice as many as 25 correct items) is to lose sight of the fact that we set out to measure knowledge of history, which may not increase in any orderly way with increases in scores. Our statistical tests can apply only to the numbers that we obtain, and the validity of statements about the objects or events that we think we are measuring hinges primarily on our knowledge of those objects or events and not on the scale of measurement. We do our best to ensure that our measures bear as close a relationship as possible to what we want to measure, but our results are ultimately only the numbers we obtain and our faith in the *relationship* between those numbers and the underlying objects or events.

≡ 2-2 VARIABLES

Variables
Properties of objects that can take on different values.

Discrete variables
Variables that take on a small set of possible values.

Continuous variables
Variables that take on *any* value.

Independent variables
Those variables controlled by the experimenter.

Dependent variables
The variable being measured. The data or score.

Properties of objects or events that can take on different values are referred to as **variables**. Hair color, for example, is a variable because it is a property of an object (hair), and it can take on different values (brown, yellow, red, etc.). Properties such as height, length, and speed are variables for the same reason. We can further discriminate between **discrete variables** (such as sex, marital status, and the number of television sets in a private home), in which the variable can take on only one of a relatively few possible values, and **continuous variables** (such as speed, time, length of a goat's tail, and so on), in which the variable could assume—at least in theory—any value between the lowest and highest points on the scale. As we will see later in this book, this distinction plays an important role in some of our procedures.

In statistics we also distinguish between different kinds of variables in an additional way. We speak of **independent variables** (those that are manipulated by the experimenter) and **dependent variables** (those that are not under the experimenter's control—the data).† In psychological studies the experimenter is interested in measuring the effects of independent variables on dependent variables. Common examples of independent variables in psychology are schedules of reinforcement, forms of therapy, placement of electrodes, and methods of treatment. Common examples of dependent variables are running speeds, scores on a test, number of aggressive behaviors, and so on. Basically what the study is "all about" is the independent variable, and the results of the study (the data) are measurements of the dependent variable. For example, a psychologist may measure the number of aggressive behaviors in depressed and nondepressed adolescents. Here the state of depression is the independent variable and the number of aggressive acts is the dependent variable.‡ Independent variables may be either qualitative (e.g., a comparison of three different forms of psychotherapy) or quantitative (performance following 1, 3, and 5 alcoholic drinks), while dependent variables are generally—but not always—quantitative only.

> †Some readers have pointed out that some independent variables are not "manipulated" by the experimenter—for example, we cannot manipulate the subject's gender or, generally, the school that she attends. However, we do manipulate the variable in the sense that we *choose* which schools to compare, or we choose to compare males and females. In this sense we do manipulate the independent variable—that is, it is under our control.
>
> ‡*Hint:* The next time you come across the independent/dependent variable distinction on a test, just remember that both *dependent* and *data* start with *d*. You can figure out the rest from there.

2-3 RANDOM SAMPLING

In Chapter 1 a sample was said to be a random sample if each and every element of the population has an equal chance of being included in the sample. I further stated that the concept of a random sample is fundamental to the process of using statistics calculated on a sample to infer the values of parameters of a population. It should be obvious that we would be foolish to try to estimate the average level of sexual activity of all high school students on the basis of data on a group of students who happen to have a study hall at the same time, particularly if they all happen to be ninth graders. We would all agree (I hope) that the data would underestimate the average value that would have been obtained from a truly random sample of the entire population of high school students.

There are a number of ways of obtaining random samples from fairly small populations. We could assign every person a number and then use a table of random numbers (see Appendix D, Table 8) to select the numbers of those who will be included in our sample. Or, if we would be satisfied with a nearly random sample, we could put names in a hat and draw blindly. The point is that every score in the population should have an equal chance of being included.

It is often helpful to have a table of random numbers to use for drawing random samples, for assigning subjects to groups, and for other tasks. Such a table is found in Appendix D, Table 8. This table is a table of uniform random numbers. The adjective *uniform* is used to indicate that every number is equally (uniformly) likely to occur. (For example, if you counted the occurrences of the digits 1, 5, and 8 in this table, you would find that they all appear about equally often.)

The table in the appendix is quite easy to use. For example, if you wanted to draw random numbers between 0 and 9, you would simply close your eyes and put your finger on the table. You would then read down the column, recording the digits as they come. When you came to the bottom of the column, you would go on to the next column and continue the process until you had as many numbers as you needed. If you wanted numbers between 0 and 99, you would do the same thing, except that here you would read off pairs of digits. Finally, if you wanted random numbers between 1 and 65, you would again read off pairs of digits but would ignore 00 or any number between 66 and 99.

If, instead of collecting a set of random data, you wanted to use the random number table to assign subjects to two treatment groups, you could start at any place in the table and assign a subject to Group I if the random digit is odd and to Group II if the random digit is even. Common-sense extrapolations of this procedure will allow you to randomly assign subjects to any number of groups.

With large populations most of the standard techniques for ensuring randomness are no longer appropriate. We cannot put the names of all U.S. women between 21 and 30 in a hat (even if we had a very big hat). Nor could we assign all U.S. women a number and then choose women by matching numbers against a random number table. Such a procedure would be totally impractical. Unless we have substantial financial resources, about the best we can do is to eliminate as many potential sources of bias as possible (e.g., don't estimate level of sexual behavior solely on the basis of a sample of people who visit Planned Parenthood), restrict our conclusions on the basis of those sources of bias that we could not feasibly control (e.g., acknowledge that the data came only from people who were willing to complete our questionnaire), and then hope a lot. Any biases that remain will limit the degree to which the results can be generalized to the population as a whole. A large body of literature is concerned with sampling methods designed to ensure representative samples, but such methods are beyond the scope of this book.

2-4   NOTATION

Any discussion of statistical techniques requires a notational system for expressing mathematical operations. It is thus surprising that no standard notational system has been adopted. Although there have been several attempts to formulate a general policy, the fact remains that no two textbooks use exactly the same notation.

The notational systems commonly used range from the very complex to the very simple. The more complex systems gain precision at the loss of easy intelligibility, while the simpler systems gain intelligibility at the loss of precision. Because the loss of precision is usually trivial when compared with the gain in comprehension, this book will adopt an extremely simple system of notation.

NOTATION FOR VARIABLES

The general rule is that a variable as a whole will be represented by an uppercase letter, usually X or Y. An individual value of that variable will then be represented by the letter and a subscript. Suppose, for example, that we have the following five scores on the length of time (in seconds) that third-grade children can hold their breath:

$$45 \quad 42 \quad 35 \quad 23 \quad 52$$

This set of scores will be referred to as X. The first number of this set (45) can be referred to as X_1, the second (42) as X_2, and so on. When we wish to refer to a single score without specifying which one, we will refer to X_i, where i can take on any value between 1 and 5. The use of subscripts is essential to precise description of statistical procedures. However, in practice the use of subscripts is often more of a distraction than an aid. In this book subscripts will generally be omitted where the meaning is clear without them.

SUMMATION NOTATION

Sigma (Σ)
Symbol indicating summation.

One of the most common symbols in statistics is the uppercase Greek letter **sigma (Σ)**, which is the standard notation for summation. It is readily translated as "add up, or sum, what follows." Thus ΣX_i is read, "Sum the X_i's." To be perfectly correct, the notation for summing all N values of X is

$$\sum_{i=1}^{N} X_i$$

which translates to "Sum all of the X_i's from $i = 1$ to $i = N$." There is seldom any need in practice for specifying what is to be done, and in most cases all subscripts will be dropped, and the notation for the sum of the X_i will be simply ΣX. will be simply ΣX.

Several extensions of the simple case of ΣX must be noted and thoroughly understood. One of these is ΣX^2, which is read as "Sum the squared values of X" (i.e., $45^2 + 42^2 + 35^2 + 23^2 + 52^2$). Another common expression is ΣXY, which means "Sum the products of the corresponding values of X and Y." The use of these terms will be illustrated in the example that follows.

Imagine a simple experiment in which we record the running speed (X) of five rats and also record the number of reinforced trials (Y) they have received. The data and simple summation operations on them are illustrated in Table 2-1. Some of these operations have been discussed already and others will be discussed in the next few chapters. Examination of Table 2-1 reveals another set of operations involving parentheses, such as $(\Sigma X)^2$. *The general rule that always applies is to perform operations within parentheses before performing operations outside of parentheses.* Thus for $(\Sigma X)^2$ we sum the values of X and *then* we square the result, as opposed to ΣX^2, in which we square the X's before we sum. The reader should double-check that ΣX^2 is not equal to ($\neq$) $(\Sigma X)^2$ using simple numbers such as 2, 3, and 4.

TABLE 2-1
Illustration of Operations
Involving Summation Notation

	Running Speed	Number of Reinforced Trials				
	X	Y	X^2	Y^2	$X - Y$	XY
	10	3	100	9	7	30
	15	4	225	16	11	60
	12	1	144	1	11	12
	9	1	81	1	8	9
	10	3	100	9	7	30
Sum	56	12	650	36	44	141

$$\Sigma X = (10 + 15 + 12 + 9 + 10) = 56$$
$$\Sigma Y = (3 + 4 + 1 + 1 + 3) = 12$$
$$\Sigma X^2 = (10^2 + 15^2 + 12^2 + 9^2 + 10^2) = 650$$
$$\Sigma Y^2 = (3^2 + 4^2 + 1^2 + 1^2 + 3^2) = 36$$
$$\Sigma(X - Y) = (7 + 11 + 11 + 8 + 7) = 44$$
$$\Sigma XY = (10)(3) + (15)(4) + (12)(1) + (9)(1) + (10)(3) = 141$$
$$(\Sigma X)^2 = 56^2 = 3136$$
$$(\Sigma Y)^2 = 12^2 = 144$$
$$(\Sigma(X - Y))^2 = 44^2 = 1936$$
$$(\Sigma X)(\Sigma Y) = (56)(12) = 672$$

A thorough understanding of notation is essential if you are to learn even the most elementary statistical techniques. You should study Table 2-1 until you fully understand all of the procedures involved.

RULES OF SUMMATION

Three additional rules for the use of the summation sign (Σ) will be extremely helpful in following the discussion in the text, and these are given next. The demonstration of these rules is left to you, since their application can be illustrated with very simple examples.

1. $\Sigma(X - Y) = \Sigma X - \Sigma Y$

2. $\Sigma CX = C \Sigma X$ (The notation ΣCX means to multiply every value of X by the **constant** C† and then to sum the results.)

Constant
A number that does not change in value in a given situation.

3. $\displaystyle\sum_{i=1}^{N} (X + C) = \Sigma X + NC$ (Note that N represents the number of items.)

2-5 SUMMARY

In this chapter we have examined briefly the concept of measurement and have considered four different levels, or scales, of measurement that are commonly discussed. We also considered the concept of a variable, different types of variables, and the system of notation to be used throughout the book. At this point you have the basic terminology you will need to allow us to begin looking at data.

Some of the important terms in the chapter are:

□ **Measurement**   □ **Discrete variables**
□ **Scales of measurement**   □ **Continuous variables**
□ **Nominal scale**   □ **Independent variables**
□ **Ordinal scale**   □ **Dependent variables**
□ **Interval scale**   □ **Summation**
□ **Ratio scale**   □ **Constant**
□ **Variables**

2-6 EXERCISES

2-1 Give one example of each kind of scale.

2-2 Give an example of a variable that might be said to be measured on a ratio scale for some purposes and on an interval or ordinal scale for other purposes.

2-3 We trained rats to run a straight-alley maze for food reinforcement. All of a sudden one of our rats lay down and went to sleep halfway through the maze. What does this say about the scale of measurement when speed is used as an index of learning?

---

†A constant is any number that does not change its value within a given situation (as opposed to a variable, which does). Constants are most often represented by the letters C and k, but other symbols may be used as well.

2–4 What does Exercise 2-3 say about speed used as an index of motivation?

2–5 Give two examples of independent variables and two examples of dependent variables.

2–6 Write a sentence describing an experiment in terms of an independent and a dependent variable.

2–7 Give three examples of continuous variables.

2–8 Give three examples of discrete variables.

2–9 In a hypothetical experiment Harris, Peabody, and Smith (1982) rated 10 Europeans and 10 North Americans on a 12-point scale of musicality. The data for the Europeans are:

$$10 \quad 8 \quad 9 \quad 5 \quad 10 \quad 11 \quad 7 \quad 8 \quad 2 \quad 7$$

Using X for this variable,
(a) What are X_3, X_5, and X_8?
(b) Calculate ΣX.
(c) Write the summation notation for (b) in its most complex form.

2–10 With reference to the preceding exercise, the data for the North Americans are:

$$9 \quad 9 \quad 5 \quad 3 \quad 8 \quad 4 \quad 6 \quad 6 \quad 5 \quad 2$$

Using Y for this variable,
(a) What are Y_1 and Y_{10}?
(b) Calculate ΣY.

2–11 Using the data from Exercise 2-9,
(a) Calculate $(\Sigma X)^2$ and ΣX^2.
(b) Calculate $\Sigma X/N$, where N = the number of scores.
(c) What do you call what you just calculated?

2–12 Using the data from Exercise 2-10,
(a) Calculate $(\Sigma Y)^2$ and ΣY^2.

(b) Calculate

$$\frac{\Sigma Y^2 - \dfrac{(\Sigma Y)^2}{N}}{N-1}$$

(c) Calculate the square root of the answer for (b).

(d) What are the units of measurement for (b) and (c)? (You will come across these calculations again in Chapter 6.)

2–13 Using the data from Exercises 2-9 and 2-10,
(a) Calculate ΣXY.
(b) Calculate $\Sigma X \Sigma Y$.
(c) Calculate

$$\frac{\Sigma XY - \dfrac{\Sigma X \Sigma Y}{N}}{N-1}$$

(You will come across these calculations again in Chapter 9.)

2–14 Use the previous data to show that
(a) $\Sigma(X + Y) = \Sigma X + \Sigma Y$
(b) ΣXY is not equal to ($\neq$) $\Sigma X \Sigma Y$
(c) $\Sigma CX = C\Sigma X$, where C is a constant (e.g., 3)
(d) $\Sigma X^2 \neq (\Sigma X)^2$

2–15 Make up 5 data points and use the third rule of summation to show what happens to the total if you add 10 points to every person's score.

2–16 I have been (correctly) criticized for using "the number of hairs on a goat" as an example of a continuous variable in an earlier edition. Why is this really a discrete variable?

3

DISPLAYING DATA

A collection of raw data, taken by itself, is no more exciting or informative than junk mail before election day. Whether the data have been neatly arranged in rows on a data collection form or whether they have been scribbled on the back of an out-of-date announcement torn from the bulletin board because you forgot to bring the right notebook, a collection of numbers is still just a collection of numbers. If they are to be interpretable, they first must be put into some sort of logical organization.

As an illustration, consider the ratings from 200 students concerning the desirability of a proposed student center. The ratings were made on a scale from 0 to 10, with higher numbers representing greater desirability. Here we have 200 numbers, one for each student. It should be apparent that we will not learn very much by looking at a jumble of 200 numbers, other than gaining some vague subjective impression that people generally found the center desirable or undesirable. We first must organize the data and then reduce them to a few numbers that carry the most relevant information.

3-1 PLOTTING DATA

One of the simplest ways to reorganize data to make them more intelligible is to plot them in some sort of graphical form. There are several common ways in which data can be represented graphically.

FREQUENCY DISTRIBUTIONS

Frequency distribution
A distribution in which the values of the dependent variable are tabled or plotted against their frequency of occurrence.

As a first step we might wish to make a **frequency distribution** of the data. In the case of the student ratings of the desirability of a center, we would count the number of times that each of the 11 numerical ratings was given by our subjects. A possible frequency distribution for this study is shown in Table 3-1 and is presented graphically in Figure 3-1. The term *frequency distribution* often is used to represent what you see in both Table 3-1 and Figure 3-1.

TABLE 3-1
Frequency Distribution of Ratings of the Desirability of a Proposed Student Center

Rating (X)	Frequency (f)
0	0
1	0
2	0
3	6
4	19
5	40
6	49
7	45
8	30
9	11
10	0

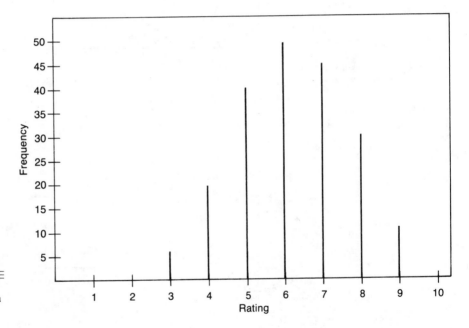

FIGURE 3-1
Frequency Distribution of 200 Ratings of the Desirability of a Proposed Student Center

From the distribution shown in Figure 3-1 it is clear that there is a wide distribution of opinion on the desirability of the center, with six people rating it as low as 3 and 11 others rating it as high as 9. There is a general tendency for the data to cluster around a point slightly above the middle of the scale—the most common value being a score of 6, which was assigned by 49 people.

An alternative way of plotting a frequency distribution is to connect the tops of the vertical bars of Figure 3-1 with lines. You can then delete the vertical bars. Such a graph is called a *frequency polygon*, and an example of one is shown in Figure 3-2.

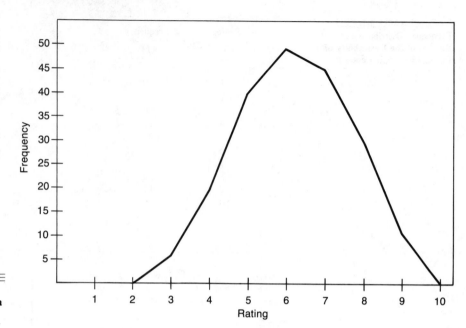

Frequency Polygon of 200
Ratings of the Desirability of a
Proposed Student Center

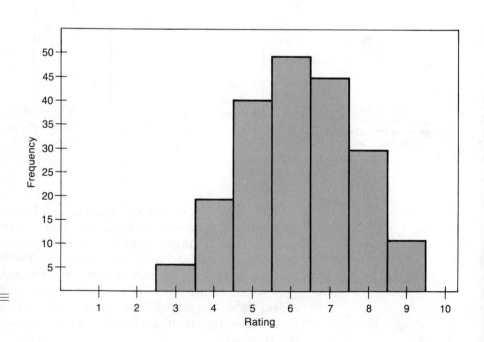

Histogram of 200 Ratings of
the Desirability of a Student
Center

HISTOGRAMS

Histogram
Graph in which rectangles are used to represent frequencies of observations within each interval.

Recognizing that forcing a subject to choose an integer value for his rating (he cannot, for example, give a rating of 3.68) forces him to assign a rating of 6 to any subjective (or personal) value between 5.5 and 6.5, we might choose to graph the data as a series of vertical bars. The width of each bar will represent the width of the interval containing the underlying subjective ratings. Such a graph is called a **histogram,** and an example of a histogram for our data is presented in Figure 3-3.

The histogram has one interesting feature that generalizes to other methods of plotting distributions. If we arbitrarily define the width of an interval to be one unit, then the *area* of any interval or set of intervals is equal to the number of scores falling within that interval or set of intervals. Furthermore the total area within the histogram is equal to N, the sample size (number of scores). The same general statement with appropriate changes in wording can be made about many distributions we plot. This is the reason that statisticians will repeatedly refer to the "area under the curve"—area and number (or percentage) of scores are interchangeable concepts. If we arbitrarily define the total area under the curve to be 1.00, then the area within a particular segment of the histogram becomes equivalent to the proportion (or percentage) of scores falling within that segment.

3-2 GROUPING DATA

In the preceding discussion of frequency distributions and histograms we have assumed that the data are presented in a discrete fashion with relatively few different values. But suppose that we were attempting to deal with data on amount of time (in minutes) that each of 100 students spends playing electronic games in a given day. With the exception of a score of zero (assigned to those students who never play electronic games), each of the individual scores will most likely be obtained by only a few, if any, students. In other words one person might play for 18 minutes, no student might play for exactly 19 minutes, another might play for 20 minutes, and so on. With data like these it would not be very instructive for us to compile and present a standard frequency distribution because it would be very flat and spread out. What might be much more useful would be for us to group the data into 10-minute intervals and to plot that distribution. An example of such a distribution is shown in Table 3-2.

In the bottom half of Table 3-2 the intervals have been listed on the left. In this case I have reported the upper and lower boundaries of the intervals as whole integers for the simple reason that it makes the table easier to read. However, you should realize that the true limits of the interval (known as the **real lower limit** and the **real upper limit**) are decimal values falling halfway between the top of one interval and the bottom of the next. The real lower limit of an interval is the smallest value that would be classified as falling into the interval. Similarly the interval's real upper limit is the largest value that would be classed as being in the interval. Thus, for example, the 20–29 interval has real

Real lower limit
Real upper limit
The points halfway between the top of one interval and the bottom of the next.

TABLE 3-2
Grouped Distribution of Time
Spent Playing Electronic
Games

Raw Data (Partial)

Minutes (X)	Frequency (f)	Minutes (X)	Frequency (f)
0	11	17	1
1	0	18	0
2	1	19	1
3	2	⋮	⋮
4	0	40	1
5	1	41	2
6	3	42	1
7	1	43	2
8	1	44	1
9	0	45	0
10	0	46	3
11	0	47	1
12	3	48	1
13	1	49	2
14	0	50	0
15	4	⋮	⋮
16	0		

Grouped Data

Interval (Minutes) (X)	Midpoint (Minutes)	Frequency (f)	Cumulative Frequency
0–9	4.5	20	20
10–19	14.5	10	30
20–29	24.5	5	35
30–39	34.5	8	43
40–49	44.5	14	57
50–59	54.5	8	65
60–69	64.5	2	67
70–79	74.5	7	74
80–89	84.5	5	79
90–99	94.5	3	82
100–109	104.5	5	87
110–119	114.5	4	91
120+	124.5†	9	100
		100	

†See text for explanation.

limits of 19.5 to 29.5, because any times falling above 19.5 or below 29.5 would be rounded up or down into that interval. (Students often become terribly worried about what we would do if a person had a score of exactly 19.500000 and therefore sat right on the breakpoint between two intervals. Don't worry about it. First, it is very unlikely to happen. Second, you can always flip a coin. Third, there are many more important things to worry about. This is one of those nonissues that makes people think the study of statistics is confusing, boring, or both.)

Midpoints
Center of interval—average of upper and lower limits.

In the second column of Table 3-2 are the **midpoints** of the intervals. They are just the average of the upper and lower limits and are presented for convenience. When we plot the data, we will plot the points as if they all fell at the midpoint of their respective intervals. The highest interval is arbitrarily given a midpoint of 124.5, although the real upper limit of that interval is left undefined.

In the third column of Table 3-2 are the frequencies with which scores fell in each interval. Thus, for example, eight people spent between 30 and 39 minutes during the day playing electronic games. The distribution tabled in Table 3-2 is shown as a histogram in Figure 3-4.

Questions often are asked about the optimal *number* of intervals to use when grouping data. Although there is no one right answer to this question, somewhere around 10 intervals is usually reasonable. In the previous example we used 13 intervals because the numbers naturally broke that way. In general it is best to use natural breaks in the number system when practical (e.g., 0–9, 10–19, ..., or 100–119, 120–139, 140–159, etc.) rather than to break up the range into exactly 10 arbitrarily defined intervals. However, if setting other kinds of limits makes the data more easily interpretable, then that method should be used. It is more important to present data clearly than to follow a predefined set of rules.

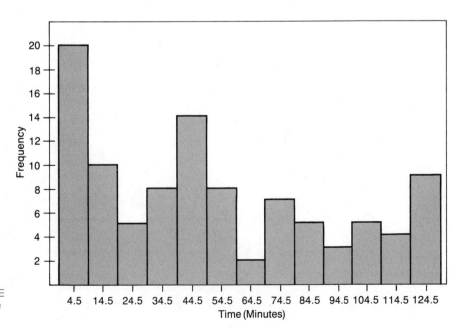

FIGURE 3-4
Histogram of Electronic Game Data

3-3   CUMULATIVE DISTRIBUTIONS

All of the distributions that we have discussed have been concerned with the frequency of observations at each score or within each interval. An alternative way of looking at data is in terms of a distribution that records the number of scores falling at *or less than* each score or interval. For example, you can see from Table 3-2 that 20 students spent 0–9 minutes playing electronic games and an additional 10 students spent 10–19 minutes. Thus $20 + 10 = 30$ students spent 19 or fewer minutes playing games. Similarly $30 + 5 = 35$ students spent 29 or fewer minutes. A distribution that plots the **cumulative frequency** is called a **cumulative distribution**, and an example of such a distribution is shown in the right-hand column of Table 3-2 and is plotted in Figure 3-5. Cumulative distributions will play an important role when we consider percentiles in Chapter 4.

Cumulative frequency
Frequency of observations at or less than a given score.

Cumulative distribution
Distribution of cumulative frequencies.

3-4   STEM-AND-LEAF DISPLAYS

Although both histograms and frequency distributions are commonly used methods of presenting data, each has its drawback. Histograms portray grouped data, thus losing the actual numerical values of the individual scores within each interval. Frequency distributions, on the other hand, retain the value of the individual observations but often are difficult to use when they do not

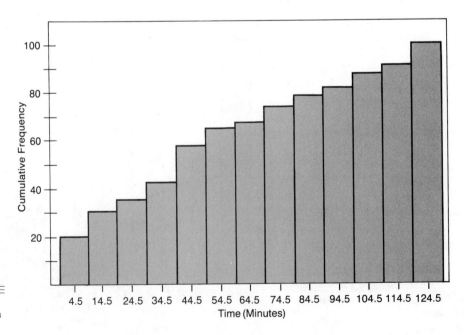

FIGURE 3-5
Cumulative Distribution of Electronic Game-Playing Data

summarize the data sufficiently. An alternative approach that avoids both of these criticisms is known as a **stem-and-leaf display**.

Stem-and-leaf display
Graphical display presenting original data arranged into a histogram.

Exploratory data analysis (EDA)
A set of techniques developed by Tukey for presenting data in visually meaningful ways.

Leading digits (most significant digits)
Left-most digits of a number.

Stem
Vertical axis of display containing the leading digits.

Trailing digits (least significant digits)
Right-most digits of a number.

Leaves
Horizontal axis of display containing the trailing digits.

As part of his general approach to data analysis, known as **exploratory data analysis (EDA)**, John Tukey (1977) developed a variety of methods for displaying data in visually meaningful ways. One of the simplest of these is a stem-and-leaf display. If you think of the previous example of amount of time spent playing electronic games, you can imagine a bunch of scores in the 40s, another in the 50s, another in the 60s, and so on. We refer to the tens' digits 4, 5, 6, ... as the **leading digits** (sometimes called the **most significant digits**) in these scores. These leading digits will form the **stem**, or vertical axis, of our display. Within that set of 14 scores that were in the 40s we had two 41s, a 42, two 43s, and so on (refer to Table 3-2). Here the units' digits 1, 2, and 3 are called the **trailing** (or **least significant**) **digits**, and they will form the **leaves** of our display— the horizontal elements. Some of the raw data on the electronic game example are presented in Figure 3-6 along with the entire stem-and-leaf display that results.†

In Figure 3-6 you can see that, for example, there was one 40, two 41s, one 42, two 43s, one 44, no 45s, three 46s, one 47, one 48, and two 49s. Thus opposite the stem 4 we find a 0, two 1s, one 2, and so on. By looking at the display we can reconstruct the original data perfectly and thus have the virtue of a full frequency distribution. On the other hand, the display itself is also just a peculiarly drawn histogram turned on its side. A comparison of Figure 3-4 and Figure 3-6 makes the last point clear.

One apparent drawback of this simplest of stem-and-leaf displays is the fact that for some data it might lead to a grouping that is too coarse for our purposes. If, for example, all the scores were between 30 and 59, we would be left

Raw Data					Stem	Leaf
					0	00000000000233566678
					1	2223555579
⋮					2	33577
40	41	41	42	43	3	22278999
43	44	46	46	46	4	01123346667899
47	48	49	49		5	24557899
52	54	55	55	57	6	37
58	59	59			7	1556689
63	67				8	34779
71	75	75	76	76	9	466
78	79				10	23677
⋮					11	3479
					12	2557899
					13	89

FIGURE 3-6
Stem-and-Leaf Display of Electronic Game Data

†It is not always true that the tens' digits form the stem and the units' digits form the leaves. For example, if the data ranged from 100 to 1000, the hundreds' digit would form the stem, the tens' digit would form the leaves, and we would ignore the units' digit.

with a stem having only three levels. Tukey solved this problem by using the stem 7* to represent the interval 70–74, and 7. to represent the interval 75–79. Likewise, 8* and 8. would represent the intervals 80–84 and 85–89, respectively. A similar system applies to the other intervals. Still other conventions handle different kinds of groupings, but we will not go into them here. The interested student will find an excellent discussion of this material in Velleman and Hoaglin (1981) or in Tukey (1977).

Stem-and-leaf displays can be particularly useful for comparing two different distributions. This is accomplished by plotting the two distributions on opposite sides of the stem. Figure 3-7 shows the actual distribution of numerical grades of males and females in a course on experimental methods that included a substantial statistics component. In this figure the 6* stem represents values between 60 and 64, and the 6. stem represents the values between 65 and 69. The code given at the bottom of the figure shows us that 4* followed by a 1 is a 41 (and not a 4.1 or 410).

3-5   ALTERNATIVE METHODS OF PLOTTING DATA

The previous sections dealt with only a few of the available ways of plotting data. There are an almost unlimited number of other ways that data could be plotted, some of which are quite ingenious and informative. A few examples are shown in Figures 3-8, 3-9, and 3-10. They were chosen as examples because they illustrate how displays can be used to reveal interesting features of the data.

In Figure 3-8 we see a comparison of the cause of death among Vermont residents in 1900 and 1981. Notice that the various causes have been ordered from bottom to top in terms of decreasing order of magnitude. From this figure it is immediately apparent that whereas almost one-third of the deaths in 1900 were attributable to a high rate of infant mortality and to tuberculosis, neither of those sources contributed noticeably to death rates in 1981. On the other hand

Male		Female
	3*	
6	3.	
	4*	1
	4.	
	5*	
	5.	
2	6*	03
	6.	568
66666632200	7*	0144
88888755	7.	555556666788899
4432221000	8*	0000011111222233444
7666666555	8.	55666666666666677888888899
422	9*	000000000133
	9.	56

Code   4*1 = 41

FIGURE 3-7
Grades (in Percent) for an Actual Course in Experimental Methods, Plotted Separately by Sex

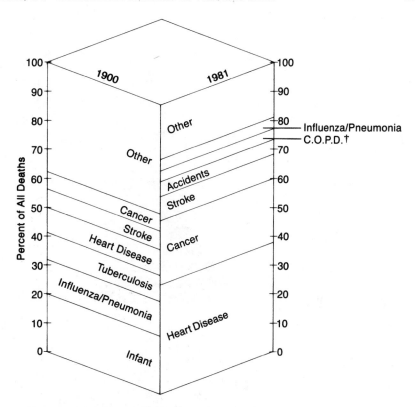

FIGURE 3-8

Major Causes of Death in
Vermont, 1900 and 1981
(From : *1981 Annual Report of
Vital Statistics in Vermont.*
Vermont Department of
Health, 1982.)

† Chronic Obstructive Pulmonary Disease

cancer and heart disease, which together accounted for 60% of all deaths in 1981, played a much reduced role in 1900, accounting for less than 15% of all deaths.

In Figure 3-9 we see the distribution by age and sex of the populations of Mexico, Spain, the United States, and Sweden. This figure clearly portrays differences between countries in terms of their age distributions. (Compare Mexico and Sweden, for example.) By having males and females plotted back to back, we can also see the effects of sex differences in life expectancy. The older age groups in all four countries contain more females than males.

Figure 3-10 is included primarily as an example of how data are sometimes presented in an accurate but misleading manner. In an attempt to illustrate in a limited space the fact that consumers in one state pay less than consumers in surrounding states for the same amount of electricity (750 kilowatts), a local utility company (which prefers to remain nameless) published a graph with the same problem as the one shown in the fictitious graph in Figure 3-10. Although the data would be accurately portrayed in such a figure, the fact that the values on the ordinate start at $40 makes it appear that customers in State C, for example, pay about seven times as much (their bar is about seven times as tall) as do customers in State A. In fact the charges were actually $41.02 and $47.11, with State C customers paying 15%, rather than 700%, more. When presenting data such as this, it is important to start the ordinate at zero or, if that is not

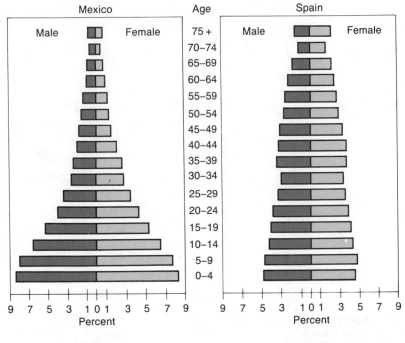

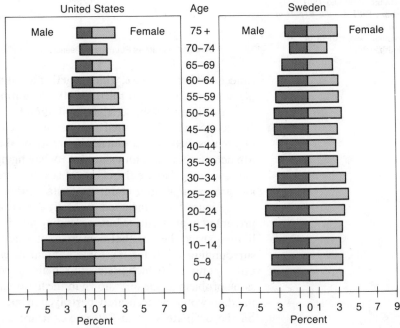

FIGURE 3-9
Population, by Sex and Age,
for Selected Countries: 1970
(From: *Social Indicators, 1976.*
U.S. Department of Commerce.
U.S. Government Printing
Office, 1977.)

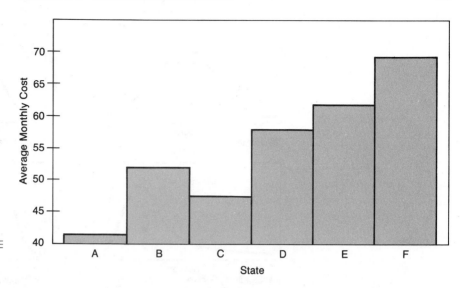

FIGURE 3-10
Average Monthly Bills for
Electricity in New England

practical, to start it at least far enough from the smallest value to avoid giving an inaccurate visual message. (If you are interested in more examples of the distorted representation of data, I would recommend the highly useful and entertaining *How to Lie with Statistics* by Huff [1954], or a more current paper by Wainer [1984].)

3-6   DESCRIBING DISTRIBUTIONS

The distribution of scores illustrated in Figure 3-1 is a more or less regularly shaped distribution, rising to a maximum and then dropping away again rather smoothly. Not all distributions are like this, however (see Figure 3-4), and it is important to understand the terms used to describe different distributions. Consider the two hypothetical distributions shown in Figures 3-11(a) and (b). Both of these distributions are called **symmetric** because they have the same shape on either side of the center. The distribution shown in Figure 3-11(a) is what we will later refer to as the normal distribution. The distribution in Figure 3-11(b) is referred to as **bimodal**, because it has two peaks. The term *bimodal* is used to refer to any distribution that has two predominant peaks, whether or not these peaks are of exactly the same height. (If a distribution has only one major peak, it is called **unimodal**.)

Next consider Figures 3-11(c) and (d). These two distributions are obviously not symmetric. The distribution in Figure 3-11(c) has a tail going out to the left, whereas that in Figure 3-11(d) has a tail going out to the right. We say that the former is **negatively skewed**, and the latter is **positively skewed**. (*Hint*: It may help to remember which is which if you notice that negatively skewed distributions point to the negative, or small, numbers, and positively skewed distributions do the reverse.) Although there are statistical measures of the

Symmetric
Having the same shape on both sides of the center.

Bimodal
A distribution having two distinct peaks.

Unimodal
A distribution having one distinct peak.

Negatively skewed
A distribution that trails off to the left.

Positively skewed
A distribution that trails off to the right.

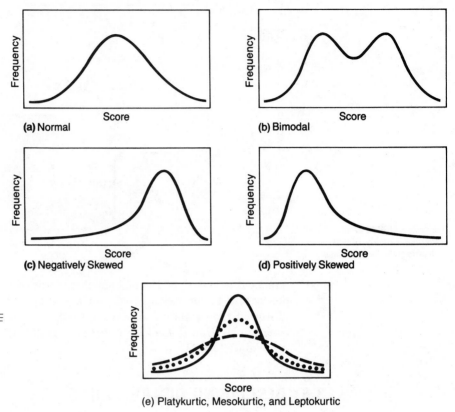

FIGURE 3-11
**Shapes of Frequency
Distributions. (a) normal, (b)
bimodal, (c) negatively skewed,
(d) positively skewed, (e)
platykurtic (dashed curve),
mesokurtic (dotted curve), and
leptokurtic (solid curve)**

Skewness
A measure of the degree to
which a distribution is
asymmetrical.

Kurtosis
A measure of the peakedness
of a distribution.

Platykurtic
A distribution that is relatively
thick in the tails.

degree of asymmetry or **skewness**, they are not commonly used in the social sciences.

An interesting example of a positively skewed bimodal distribution is shown in Figure 3-12. These data were generated by Bradley (1963), who instructed subjects to press a button as quickly as possible whenever a small light came on. You will note that most of the data points are smoothly distributed between roughly 7 and 17 hundredths of a second but that a small but noticeable cluster of points lies between 30 and 70 hundredths, trailing off to the right. This second cluster of points was obtained primarily from trials when the subject missed the button on the first try. Their inclusion in the data significantly affects the distribution's shape. An experimenter who had such a collection of data might seriously consider eliminating times greater than some maximum, on the grounds that these times are more a reflection on accuracy of a psychomotor response than they are a measure of the *speed* of the response.

The last characteristic of a distribution that we will examine is kurtosis. **Kurtosis** has a specific mathematical definition, but basically it refers to the degree to which scores congregate in the tails of the distribution. A distribution in which there are large numbers of high and low scores (relative to the mean) is referred to as a heavy-tailed (or *platykurtic*) distribution. A distribution that is

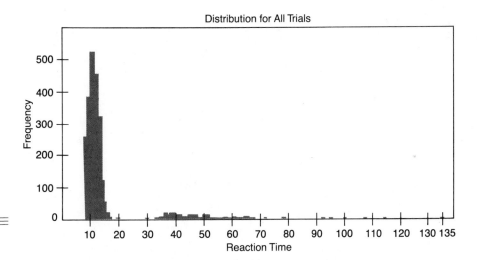

FIGURE 3-12
**Frequency Distribution of
Reaction-Time Scores**

Leptokurtic
A distribution that is relatively
thin in the tails.

Mesokurtic
A distribution with a neutral
degree of kurtosis.

relatively thin in the tails is called a **leptokurtic** distribution. Distributions, such as the normal distribution, that are neither too thick nor too thin in the tails are called **mesokurtic**. These three characteristic shapes are illustrated in Figure 3-11(e).

It is important to recognize that relatively large samples of data are needed before we can have a very good idea about the shape of a distribution—especially its kurtosis. With sample sizes of around 30 the best that we can reasonably expect to see is whether the data tend to pile up in the tails of the distribution or whether the data are markedly skewed in one direction or another.

Skewness and kurtosis, while not commonly used measures in the social sciences, are convenient verbal labels to be used in describing distributions. As an educated person, you should know what a positively skewed distribution is, even though it is unlikely that you will ever want to compute a numerical index of skewness.

3-7   USING COMPUTER PROGRAMS TO DISPLAY DATA

Almost all statistics texts—and this one is no exception—generally assume that data analyses will be carried out by hand with the help of a standard calculator. This is probably the best approach to teaching, but it is nonetheless true that more and more analyses are carried out today by computer programs. It is therefore important for you to be familiar with reading and interpreting the results of computer printouts. For that reason most chapters in this book will include samples of computer solutions for examples previously analyzed by hand. Most of these solutions will be obtained by using a program called Minitab, since it is one of the easiest general-purpose programs to use and since it is widely available. Along with the printout you will also find the instructions

═══ TABLE 3-3 ═══
Analysis of Electronic Games
Data by Minitab

```
MTB > SET THE FOLLOWING DATA IN COLUMN C1
DATA> 15 23 7 0 8 43 ....
DATA> 138 139
DATA> END
MTB > HISTOGRAM ON THE DATA IN COLUMN C1

Histogram of C1   N = 100

Midpoint    Count
       0      14   **************
      10      10   **********
      20       8   ********
      30       6   ******
      40      12   ************
      50       9   *********
      60       7   *******
      70       2   **
      80       8   ********
      90       4   ****
     100       4   ****
     110       5   *****
     120       3   ***
     130       6   ******
     140       2   **

MTB > STEM AND LEAF ON THE DATA IN COLUMN C1

Stem-and-leaf of C1        N  = 100
Leaf Unit = 1.0

      20    0  00000000000233566678
      30    1  2223555579
      35    2  33577
      43    3  22278999
     (14)   4  01123346667899
      43    5  24557899
      35    6  37
      33    7  1556689
      26    8  34779
      21    9  466
      18   10  23677
      13   11  3479
       9   12  2557899
       2   13  89

MTB > STOP
```

required to produce it. For those of you who want to explore the really powerful features of Minitab, an excellent reference is Ryan, Joiner, and Ryan (1985).

In Table 3-3 are examples of a histogram and a stem-and-leaf display for the electronic games data as produced by Minitab. Note that the raw data (number of minutes for each subject) are entered first, in any order, using the SET command. (The MTB⟩ and DATA⟩ are "prompts" supplied by Minitab requesting input of either a command or data.) (Only the first few scores are shown to illustrate the use of the SET command, but the full set of observations could be reconstructed from the stem-and-leaf display.) Then Minitab chooses its own intervals for the histogram (in this case −5 to +5, 5 to 10, ..., 135 to 145, which are not exactly the same intervals we chose in Figure 3-4) and lists each interval's midpoint. Since Minitab has chosen intervals that are different from ours, it produces a different (though still correct) histogram from the one shown in Figure 3-4.

Depth
Cumulative frequency counting in from the nearer end.

The stem-and-leaf display is equivalent to ours, although an additional column on the left contains cumulative frequencies (often referred to as **depth**) running inward from each end. The number in parentheses is the frequency (noncumulative) for the interval that contains the middle value. From this display we can see, for example, that 30 people had scores *less* than or equal to 19 minutes, 18 people had scores *greater* than or equal to 102 minutes, and 14 people fell in the interval containing the middle value. You can see that the distribution is positively skewed because the cumulative frequencies pile up much more quickly when we go from low scores toward the center than when we go from high scores toward the center. This is even more apparent in the stem-and-leaf display itself.

So far in our discussion almost no mention has been made of the numbers themselves. We have seen how data may be organized and presented in the form of distributions, and we have discussed a number of ways in which distributions can be characterized—symmetry or its lack (skewness), kurtosis, and modality. As useful as this information might be in certain circumstances, it is very inadequate in others. We still do not know whether the subjects generally liked or disliked the student center they rated, nor do we know the average time spent by students playing electronic games. Moreover we do not know how much agreement there was among subjects, either in their opinions or in their game-playing behavior. To obtain this knowledge we must reduce the data to a set of measures that carry the information we need. The questions to be asked refer to the location, or central tendency, and to the dispersion, or variability, of the distribution along the underlying scale. Measures of these characteristics will be considered in the next two chapters.

3-8 SUMMARY

In this chapter we have discussed ways of describing distributions. All the techniques discussed here are intended primarily to organize and reduce the information contained in a large set of data to manageable proportions and to allow us to readily communicate some of that information to others. In examining these techniques we have also looked very briefly at stem-and-leaf displays (one small part of Tukey's Exploratory Data Analysis) and have examined a number of terms that are useful in characterizing the shapes of distributions. Some of the important terms in the chapter are:

□ **Frequency distribution**   □ **Exploratory Data Analysis (EDA)**
□ **Histogram**   □ **Leading digits (most significant digits)**
□ **Real lower limit**   □ **Stem**
□ **Real upper limit**   □ **Trailing digits (least significant digits)**
□ **Midpoints**   □ **Leaves**
□ **Cumulative frequency**   □ **Symmetric**
□ **Cumulative distribution**   □ **Bimodal**
□ **Stem-and-leaf display**   □ **Unimodal**

☐ **Negatively skewed**   ☐ **Platykurtic**
☐ **Positively skewed**   ☐ **Leptokurtic**
☐ **Skewness**   ☐ **Mesokurtic**
☐ **Kurtosis**   ☐ **Depth**

3-9 EXERCISES

3–1 Children differ from adults in that they tend to recall stories in terms of a sequence of actions rather than in terms of an overall plot. This means that their descriptions of a movie are filled with the phrase "and then…." An experimenter with supreme patience has asked 50 children to tell her about a given movie. Among other variables she counted the number of "and then…" statements. The data are given here:

```
18  15  22  19  18  17  18  20  17  12  16  16
17  21  23  18  20  21  20  20  15  18  17  19
20  23  22  10  17  19  19  21  20  18  18  24
11  19  31  16  17  15  19  20  18  18  40  18
19  16
```

(a) Plot an ungrouped frequency distribution for these data.

(b) What is the general shape of the distribution?

3–2 Make a histogram for the data in Exercise 3-1 using a reasonable number of intervals.

3–3 What is the difficulty with making a stem-and-leaf display of the data in Exercise 3-1?

3–4 As part of the study described in Exercise 3-1, the experimenter obtained the same kind of data for adults. Their data are given here:

```
10  12   5   8  13  10  12   8   7  11  11  10
 9   9  11  15  12  17  14  10   9   8  15  16
10  14   7  16   9   1   4  11  12   7   9  10
 3  11  14   8  12   5  10   9   7  11  14  10
15   9
```

(a) What can you tell just by looking at these numbers? Do children and adults seem to recall stories in the same way?

(b) Plot an ungrouped frequency distribution for these data using the same scale on the axes as you used for the children's data.

(c) Overlay this frequency distribution on the one from Exercise 3-1.

3–5 Use a back-to-back histogram (see Figure 3-9) to compare the data from Exercises 3-1 and 3-4.

3–6 Make a cumulative frequency distribution for the data in Exercise 3-1.

3–7 Make a cumulative frequency distribution for the data in Exercise 3-4.

3–8 Create a positively skewed set of data and plot it.

3–9 Create a bimodal set of data and plot it.

3–10 What would you predict to be the shape of the distribution of number of cigarettes smoked per day for the next 200 people you meet?

The next two exercises refer to a large data set in Appendix C, Data Set. These data come from a real research study (Howell and Huessy, 1985), which is described at the beginning of Appendix C.

3–11 Draw a histogram for the data for GPA in Appendix C, Data Set, using reasonable intervals.

3–12 Create a stem-and-leaf display for the ADDSC score in Appendix C, Data Set.

3–13 What three interesting facts about the populations of Mexico and Spain can be seen in Figure 3-9?

3–14 In some stem-and-leaf displays with one or two high values, the last stem is often written as HI and the complete values follow in the leaf section. Why might we do this?

PERCENTILES

In the previous chapter we saw how to plot data to derive a general sense of what that collection of data looked like. We could see the overall shape of the distribution and get some idea of the magnitude of the numbers involved and the degree to which those numbers were tightly clustered or widely spread. Thus, if we were given a set of test grades, we could say a lot about them—as a set. But most people are basically egocentric. Most of us are less interested in describing how the class as a whole performed than we are in looking at how we performed relative to the rest of the class (especially if we think we did well). This chapter will be concerned with ways of characterizing the performance of individuals relative to the performance of other people.

4-1 CUMULATIVE DISTRIBUTIONS AND PERCENTILE RANK

In Chapter 3 we saw that frequency distributions could be converted to cumulative frequency distributions simply by recording the number of scores at *or less than* a given interval. As an example, suppose that we have developed a 100-point scale of "likability." An individual's score on such a scale might be derived by rating him or her on a large number of dimensions (such as cooperativeness, thoughtfulness, sincerity, honesty, etc.) and then summing across the several dimensions. The data in Table 4-1 were created by assuming that such a scale has been developed and administered to 260 people and that it yields scores that are fairly evenly distributed across the range of 0–100, with a slight tendency to cluster toward the center of the distribution.

The first column of Table 4-1 contains the class intervals into which the score might fall, and the second column contains the frequencies within each interval. In the third column we see the cumulative frequencies (*CF*). For example, entries in the table tell us that 15 people received a score in the interval 25–29 and that 35 people scored at or less than this interval. The last column contains the relative cumulative frequency (*RCF*). These values were obtained by taking the cumulative frequency for a particular interval and dividing by the total number of observations. For the interval 25–29 this means that we divided 35 by 260 to obtain 0.13. The result can be interpreted to mean that a proportion of 0.13, or 13%, of the scores lie in or less than this interval.

Class Interval	Frequency (f)	Cumulative Frequency (CF)	Relative Cumulative Frequency (RCF)
95+	5	260	1.00
90–94	1	255	.98
85–89	10	254	.98
80–84	8	244	.94
75–79	13	236	.91
70–74	16	223	.86
65–69	17	207	.80
60–64	17	190	.73
55–59	25	173	.67
50–54	30	148	.57
45–49	24	118	.45
40–44	25	94	.36
35–39	16	69	.27
30–34	18	53	.20
25–29	15	35	.13
20–24	10	20	.08
15–19	1	10	.04
10–14	5	9	.04
5– 9	1	4	.02
0– 4	3	3	.01
	260		

Suppose that you have been told what score you received on this likability index. It is reasonable to suppose that your first question would concern how your score compares to other people's scores. It is also reasonable to suppose that you would like to think that you will have been rated higher than most other people (although there are people who act as if they are fighting to be at the lower end of the scale).

One of the best ways to compare your score to others is to think in terms of **percentiles** and **percentile ranks**. *A percentile is the point on a scale at or below which a given percentage of the scores fall*. Thus, for example, the point below which 76% of the scores fall is called the 76th percentile. It is important to note that a percentile is a point on a scale. It is not a score, although it may be numerically equal to one. In other words, like means, percentiles need not be observed values. For example, with a particular set of data we might say that 90% of the scores were at or below 78.5 (the 90th percentile) even though no one received an actual score exactly equal to 78.5.

Percentile
Point on a scale at or below which a specified percentage of cases fall.

Percentile rank
Percentage of cases falling at or below a given point on a scale.

The percentile rank of a score, on the other hand, is the percentage of cases falling at or below that score. Thus in the previous example the percentile rank of 78.5 is 90. To phrase it differently, if a score of 71.2 is at the 82nd percentile, then the 82nd percentile = 71.2, and 71.2 has a percentile rank of 82. In the following sections we first will consider how to find the percentile rank corresponding to a given score. We then will turn the problem around and see how to find a score having a given percentile rank.

======= **4-2   COMPUTING PERCENTILE RANKS FROM SCORES**

To take a concrete example, suppose that your score on our likability index was 73. We can use the distribution given in Table 4-1 to help in the calculation of your percentile rank. The first thing that we will do is determine the class interval into which your score falls. For a score of 73 the interval is 70–74. The second thing that we will do is combine the data points into three categories: those falling in your interval, those in all lower intervals, and those in all higher intervals. From Table 4-1 we see from the relative cumulative frequencies that 80% fall in lower intervals. Because 86% fall in the same interval or lower and 80% fall in lower intervals, 86–80 = 6% must fall in your interval. Similarly, because 86% are at or below your interval, then the remaining 14% of the people must be above it and therefore must be more likable. (Well, who wants to be perfect?)

All higher intervals (higher %)	14%
Same interval (70–74) (interval %)	6%
All lower intervals (lower %)	80%

From these results it is apparent that at least 80% of the people were rated as less likable than you. Moreover, another 6% fell in your interval. Unless you have a terrible self-image, you probably don't assume that all 6% are really more likable than you. On the other hand you are probably not conceited enough to assume that they are all below you. Thus some of that 6% probably scored below you and some above you. Somehow we have to decide just how to apportion that 6%.

Linear interpolation
Proportional estimation of an intermediate value by assuming scores are evenly distributed across the interval.

In order to make a reasonable estimate of where you stand with respect to others who scored in the same interval, we will make use of simple **linear interpolation**. This means that the higher your score within your interval, the more people we will assume fell below you. In order to use linear interpolation we will have to make use of the real lower limit (RLL) of the interval that was discussed earlier (in Chapter 3). Although we act as if the interval runs from 70–74, the real limits are 69.5–74.5. (This is true even if we know that fractional values are not possible.)

With a RLL of 69.5 and an interval width of $74.5 - 69.5 = 5$ units, a score of 73 is $(73 - 69.5)/5 = 3.5/5 = .70 = 70\%$ of the distance up from the bottom of the interval. Thus it is reasonable to suppose that you surpass 70% of the people in your interval. Because 6% of the people are in your interval and you are assumed to exceed 70% of those, we will give you credit for exceeding an additional $(.70)(6\%) = 4.2\%$ of the total sample over and above the 80% in all lower intervals. Therefore your score of 73 is at the $80 + 4.2 = 84.2$ percentile. Put slightly differently, a score of 73 has a percentile rank of 84.2.

All of these calculations can be summarized in a fairly simple formula for those who feel lost without a formula to memorize. It is more important to understand the logic than to memorize a formula, because if you understand the logic you can arrive at the right answer whether or not you know the formula.

However, there is a certain sense of security in having a formula.

$$\text{Percentile Rank} = \text{Lower} \% + \frac{\text{Score} - \text{RLL}}{\text{Width}} \text{(Interval \%)}$$

where   Lower % = percent of scores in all lower intervals

Interval % = percent of scores in same interval

RLL = real lower limit

Width = interval width

For our example

$$\text{Percentile Rank} = 80\% + \frac{73 - 69.5}{5} \text{(6\%)}$$

$$= 80\% + 4.2\% = 84.2\%$$

Thus approximately 84% of the people to whom this scale was applied are rated as less likable than you.

An alternative way of seeing what we have just done is represented in Figure 4-1. Here you have a visual representation of the previous arithmetic process.

In the preceding example we dealt with a situation in which the data are grouped into intervals with a width of five units. The process would not have differed in any appreciable way had the data been presented in an ungrouped fashion (i.e., if the interval widths had been one unit). Our estimate of your percentile rank would have been somewhat more accurate, but the procedure would have been the same. In the case of ungrouped data the use of the procedure described here will have the effect of crediting an individual with surpassing half of those people who are tied for the same score. However, this brings up a problem that often confuses students, instructors, and textbook writers alike (and is the reason that I have long hated to deal with percentiles). It

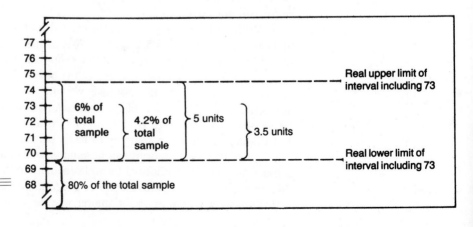

FIGURE 4-1
Visual Representation of
Likability Index Example

will be useful to address this problem head on. If you read through the chapter on percentiles in four or five different textbooks, you will discover that the authors deal with percentiles quite inconsistently (even within the same text). I have defined a percentile rank as the percentage of scores *at or below* a given point. But some books, including this, will credit half the people with whom you are tied as falling below you, while other books will count *all* scores equal to yours as being "at or below" yours. (Some authors of textbooks actually do both without appearing to realize it.) With this inconsistency it is no wonder that students become confused and develop a strong dislike for percentiles. However, there are several ways out of this problem.

First of all you should realize that much of what we do we do by convention. There is no "true" way of handling ties when computing percentile ranks. Rather there are opposing conventions on dealing with those ties. I have suggested that you assume that half of the people who are tied for a given score fall "at or below" that score. If you want to assume that *all* of those people fall "at or below" that score, you are not wrong—you are just following a different convention. (Just make sure that whoever is going to grade your assignments follows the same convention.)

A second approach to the problem is to consider that a percentile is a point (not a score or an interval); and points are infinitely small. If you think of a percentile as a point rather than a score, it is easier to justify to yourself the idea that some people with the same score will be credited with really falling above that point and others will be credited with really falling below that point. Imagine a whole bunch of angels dancing on the head of a pin that is stuck in the scale at some percentile. Some of the angels will be slightly to the left of the pin's point and some will be slightly to the right. (Exactly how many will be on each side can't be determined until I find out how many angels are on the pin—but I'm working on that.)

When all is said and done, the approach that you take to tied scores probably will not have much of a practical effect. You probably would not be appreciably happier to learn that your score has a percentile rank of 86.3 than to learn that you have a percentile rank of 84.7. If this is true, then why not just agree to adopt one convention (I prefer mine), to understand that other people might use other conventions, and to acknowledge that some people use these methods inconsistently. Students need not get hung up on the finer points of percentiles when there are many more interesting and important things to consider.

4-3 COMPUTING SCORES FOR PERCENTILE RANKS

We have seen how to compute the percentile rank corresponding to a particular score, but occasionally we want to turn things around and ask which score corresponds to a particular percentile rank. For example, you might want to know what likability score you would need in order to have a percentile rank of 95. In other words, what score would correspond to the 95th percentile?

From Table 4-1 you can see that 94% of the scores fall at or below the interval 80–84, so the score must be above 84.5 (the real upper limit of that interval and the real lower limit of the interval above). In fact you need to go one percentage point into the next interval. You can also see that 4% of the scores fall within the real interval 84.5–89.5 and that the interval is 5 units wide. If those 4 percentage points are evenly distributed across that 5-point interval, every $5/4 = 1.25$ points would account for an additional one percentage point. Thus, if 94% are at or below 84.5 and if to get the extra 1% we need to go up an additional 1.25 units, then the 95th percentile will be at $84.5 + 1.25 = 85.75$.

On those occasions when you want to assign a score to a particular percentile, the method we have used here will accomplish your purpose. We can, however, put all of this in a simple formula to make things neater and more comfortable. In this case we can define

$$\text{Score}_p = \text{RLL} + \frac{\text{Width}}{\text{Interval }\%}\,(p - \text{Lower }\%)$$

where Score_p = score corresponding to percentile p

RLL = real lower limit of critical interval

Width = interval width

Interval % = percent of scores in critical interval

p = percentile rank of interest

Lower % = percent of scores below critical interval

For our example

$$\text{Score}_p = 84.5 + \frac{5}{4\%}\,(95\% - 94\%)$$

$$= 84.5 + 1.25 = 85.75$$

REFERENCE GROUPS

It is very important to keep in mind that percentile ranks are meaningful only in the context of the reference group from which they are obtained. For example, a score at the 15th percentile on the verbal portion of the Graduate Record Exam refers to how that individual ranks relative to all other people taking the exam— most of whom are college seniors who have received all their education in English in U.S. high schools. A score at the 15th percentile from a college senior who has spoken English all her life would not be a very good score. But the same score from a freshman who has spoken English for only one year and had gone to high school in Tierra del Fuego would probably be an exceptionally good performance, and it would be unfair to take that percentile rank at face value. When interpreting percentile ranks it is important to note the reference group to which the ranks apply. The same score would have a different percentile rank when judged in relation to a different reference group.

RELATED MEASURES

Deciles
Points cutting off successive 10ths of the distribution.

Quartiles
Points cutting off successive 4ths of the distribution.

As we have seen, percentiles divide a distribution of scores into 100 equal parts. We also have a number of similar measures that divide the distribution differently (more coarsely). Thus, for example, **deciles** create ten equal-sized units while **quartiles** create four equal-sized units. Someone who is at the 8th decile has a score that equals or exceeds $8/10 = 80\%$ of all those taking the test, while a score at the 3rd quartile equals or exceeds $3/4 = 75\%$ of all scores. It is important to note that deciles and quartiles, like percentiles, are points. (The first and third quartiles are also essentially equivalent to hinges, which we will discuss in Chapter 6.) Just as we say that a person's score is at the 43rd percentile, so also do we say that a person is at the 2nd quartile or the 7th decile. We do not say that a person's score is *within* the 3rd quartile, since a score can't be within a point. This error is seldom made with percentiles (where there are many points) but is often made with quartiles. It is an error nonetheless. We could, however, say that this person's score falls between the 2nd and 3rd quartiles.

4-4   A FINAL WORKED EXAMPLE

A course I recently taught, History and Systems of Psychology, had the following distribution of scores. I want to know what percentile rank corresponded to a score of 72, and what score corresponded to the 90th percentile. The data follow:

Score	Frequency	Interval %	Cumulative %
95–99	2	1.6	100.0
90–94	10	8.0	98.4
85–89	16	12.8	90.4
80–84	21	16.8	77.6
75–79	12	9.6	60.8
70–74	26	20.8	51.2
65–69	15	12.0	30.4
60–64	16	12.8	18.4
55–59	5	4.0	5.6
50–54	1	0.8	1.6
45–49	1	0.8	0.8
	125		

The first step is to calculate the percentages in each interval. Because 10 of the 125 students fell in the interval 90–94, $10/125 = 8\%$ of the scores were in that interval. The values for all the intervals are found in the table. The cumulative percentages are also shown in the table and were obtained by adding the values in the Interval % column at or below the row in question.

To find the percentile rank corresponding to a score of 72, note that 30.4% of the scores fall at or below a RLL of 69.5. Further note that the intervals are 5 units wide (e.g., $74.5 - 69.5 = 5$) and that a 72 is 2.5 points above the RLL for that interval. Thus we will assume that $2.5/5 = 50\%$ of the 20.8% of the scores in the interval 70–74 are actually below 72. Thus the percentile rank of a score of 72 will be $30.4 + 0.5(20.8) = 30.4 + 10.4 = 40.8$. To use our formula:

$$\text{Percentile Rank} = \text{Lower }\% + \left(\frac{\text{Score} - \text{RLL}}{\text{Width}}\right)\text{Interval }\%$$

$$= 30.4 + \left(\frac{72 - 69.5}{5}\right)(20.8)$$

$$= 30.4 + \left(\frac{2.5}{5}\right)(20.8) = 30.4 + \frac{20.8}{2} = 40.8$$

To reverse the question and ask about the score corresponding to the 90th percentile, we first note that 77.6% of the scores fall below a RLL of 84.5 and 90.4% fall below an RLL of 89.5. The interval 84.5–89.5 contains 12.8% of the points. We need to go $90\% - 77.6\% = 12.4$ percentage points into this interval to round out our 90%. If the interval is 5 units wide and we need $(12.4/12.8)\%$ of it, then we need to go $5(12.4)/12.8 = 4.84$ units. Then the 90th percentile is $84.5 + 4.84 = 89.3$. Thus the 90th percentile falls at a value of 89.3 points.

To do this using our formula:

$$\text{Score}_p = \text{RLL} + \left(\frac{\text{Width}}{\text{Interval }\%}\right)(p - \text{Lower }\%)$$

$$= 84.5 + \left(\frac{5}{12.8}\right)(90 - 74.6) = 84.5 + \frac{5(12.4)}{12.8} = 89.3$$

4-5   SUMMARY

In this chapter we have examined ways of expressing individual scores relative to the scores of other people. We have seen how to compute the percentile rank corresponding to a given score and how to compute the score corresponding to a given percentile rank. In addition we have examined some of the common problems people have in fully understanding percentiles and have looked at two related measures. Some of the most important terms in the chapter are:

☐ **Percentile**   ☐ **Deciles**

☐ **Percentile rank**   ☐ **Quartiles**

☐ **Linear interpolation**

4-6 EXERCISES

4–1 If 83% of people taking a test had a score less than or equal to 74, 83 is called the _____ _____ of 74 and 74 is called the _____ _____.

4–2 Make up a simple example that clearly distinguishes between the terms *percentile* and *percentile rank*.

4–3 Using the data in Table 4-1, find the 36th percentile.

4–4 Using the data in Table 4-1, find the 50th percentile.

4–5 What is the first quartile (Q_1) for the data in Table 4-1?

4–6 What is the percentile rank of 46 for the data in Table 4-1?

Use the following data for the next five exercises:

18	13	15	14	13	14	8	12	19	13	12	18
14	14	16	16	13	13	20	21	10	16	15	13
10	12	16	14	6	3	6	12	18	15	11	11
15	11	10	8	15	10	10	12	13	9	13	12
13	7										

4–7 Draw the cumulative frequency distribution for these data.

4–8 Find the 50th percentile for these data. What is another term for the 50th percentile?

4–9 Find the 21st percentile for these data.

4–10 What is the percentile rank of a score of 20?

4–11 What is the percentile rank of a score of 13?

4–12 Some graduate schools look for applicants who have a combined Graduate Record Exam verbal and quantitative score of 1200. In October 1981 (for college seniors and nonenrolled college graduates) verbal scores of 700, 600, and 500 had percentile ranks of 94, 77, and 46, respectively. For the quantitative test the corresponding percentile ranks were 84, 59, and 20, respectively. What does this suggest about looking at combined scores?

4–13 With respect to the data in Appendix C, Data Set, Howell and Huessy (1985) classified children with a score of 66 or higher on ADDSC as exhibiting ADD-like behavior. What would be the percentile rank of a raw score of 66?

4–14 For the data in Appendix C, Data Set, what is the 80th percentile for ADDSC?

4–15 For the data in Appendix C, Data Set, what is the 75th percentile for GPA?

4–16 For the data in Appendix C, Data Set, what is the 80th percentile for ADDSC if you restrict your reference group to males?

4–17 For the data in Appendix C, Data Set, what is the 80th percentile for ADDSC if you restrict your reference group to females?

4–18 What is the 1st decile for the variable GPA in Appendix C, Data Set?

4–19 What is the 3rd quartile for the variable GPA in Appendix C, Data Set?

4–20 If a distribution is badly skewed, will the 40th and 60th percentiles be the same distance from the median?

4–21 Draw a diagram similar to the one in Figure 4-1 to illustrate the calculations in Section 4-4.

MEASURES OF CENTRAL TENDENCY

In Chapter 3 we saw how to display data in ways that will allow us to begin to draw some conclusions about how the data look. Plotting data shows us the general shape of the distribution and gives a visual sense of the general magnitude of the numbers involved.

Measures of central tendency
Numerical values referring to the center of the distribution.

In this chapter we will see several statistics that we can use to represent the "center" of the distribution. These statistics are called **measures of central tendency**, which is a fairly descriptive label. In the next chapter we will go a step further and look at measures dealing with how the observations are scattered around that central tendency, but first we must address the prior question of identifying the center of the distribution.

There are three common measures of central tendency (mode, median, and mean), and they will be discussed in turn. We will begin with what is probably the least used (and least useful) measure.

5-1 THE MODE

Mode (Mo)
The most commonly occurring score.

The **mode (Mo)** can be defined simply as the most common score—that score obtained from the largest number of subjects. Thus the mode is that value of X corresponding to the highest point on the distribution. In the example in Chapter 3 dealing with ratings of the desirability of a proposed student center (Table 3-1) this value is 6, since more people rated the center 6 than assigned it any other single numerical value.

If two *adjacent* ratings occur with equal (and greatest) frequency, a common convention is to take an average of the two values and call that the mode. If, on the other hand, two *nonadjacent* ratings occur with equal, or at least approximately equal, frequency, we would say that the distribution is bimodal, and we would most likely report both modes. Thus, for example, the electronic game data is roughly bimodal, with peaks at 0–9 and 40–49 minutes. (You might argue that it is trimodal with a peak at 120+, but since that is a catch-all interval for "all other values," it probably does not make much sense to think of it as a modal value.)

≡ 5-2 THE MEDIAN

Median (Med)
The score corresponding to the point having 50% of the observations below it when observations are arranged in numerical order.

The **median (Med)** is defined as the score corresponding to the point at or below which 50% of the scores fall when the data are arranged in numerical order. By this definition the median is also the 50th percentile. For example, consider the numbers (5 8 3 7 15). If these numbers were arranged in numerical order (3 5 7 8 15), half the scores would fall below 7 and it would be called the median. Suppose, however, that there were an even number of scores—for example, (5 11 3 7 15 14). Rearranging, we obtain (3 5 7 11 14 15), and there is no score having 50% of the values below it. That point actually falls between the 7 and the 11. In such a case the average (9) of the two middle scores (7 and 11) is commonly taken as the median.†

Median location
The location of the median in an ordered series.

A term that we shall need shortly is the **median location**. The median location of N numbers is defined as

$$\text{Median Location} = \frac{N+1}{2}$$

Thus for five numbers the median location $= (5 + 1)/2 = 3$, which means that the median is the third number in an ordered series. For 12 numbers the median location $= (12 + 1)/2 = 6.5$, and thus the median is the average of the sixth and seventh numbers.

For the student center data (see Table 3-1) the median location $= (200 + 1)/2 = 100.5$. A little work will show that if the data were arranged in order, both the 100th and 101st scores would be 6, which is thus the median. For the electronic games data there are 100 scores, and the median location is 50.5. We can tell from the stem-and-leaf display in Figure 3-6 that the 50th score is a 44 and the 51st score is a 46. The median would be 45, which is the average of these two values.

≡ 5-3 THE MEAN

Mean ($\bar{X}$)
The sum of the scores divided by the number of scores.

The most common measure of central tendency, and one that really needs little explanation, is the **mean ($\bar{X}$)**, or what is generally meant when people use the word *average*. The mean is defined as the total of the scores divided by the number of scores, and is usually designated as $\bar{X}$ (read X bar). It is defined (using

---

†The definition of the median is something over which statisticians love to argue. The definition given here, in which the median is defined as a *point* on a distribution of numbers, is the one most critics prefer. It is also in line with the statement that the median is the 50th percentile. On the other hand there are many people who are perfectly happy to say that the median is either the middle number in an ordered series (if N is odd), or the average of the middle two numbers (if N is even). I personally think that there are more interesting things to fight about.

the summation notation given in Chapter 2) as

$$\bar{X} = \frac{\Sigma X}{N}$$

where ΣX is the sum of all values of X, and N is the number of X values. As an illustration, the mean of the numbers 3, 5, 12, and 5 is

$$\frac{3 + 5 + 12 + 5}{4} = \frac{25}{4} = 6.25$$

We could calculate the mean for the electronic games data by obtaining the raw data values from the stem-and-leaf display, summing those values, and dividing by 100. For that example the mean would be 5204/100 = 52.04. Later in this chapter we will see how to use Minitab to save ourselves considerable work in calculating the mean for large data sets.

5-4 RELATIVE ADVANTAGES AND DISADVANTAGES OF THE MODE, MEDIAN, AND MEAN

Only when the distribution is symmetric will the mean and median be equal, and only when the distribution is symmetric and unimodal will all three measures be the same. In all other cases—and this includes almost all situations with which we will deal—some choice of a measure of central tendency must be made. A set of rules governing when to use a particular measure of central tendency would be very convenient. However, there are no such rules. If you are to make intelligent choices among the three measures, it is necessary to have some idea of the strengths and weaknesses of each.

THE MODE

As we have seen, the mode is the most commonly occurring score. By definition, then, it is a score that actually occurred, whereas the mean and sometimes the median may be values that never appear in the data. The mode also has the obvious advantage of representing the largest number of people. Someone who is running a small store would do well to concentrate on the mode. If 80% of your customers want the giant economy family size and 20% want the teeny-weeny, single-person size, you would probably lose many or all of your customers if you aimed for the mean and stocked only the regular size.

Related to these two advantages is the fact that, by definition, the probability that an observation drawn at random (X_i) will be equal to the mode is greater than the probability that it will be equal to any other specific score. Expressing this algebraically, we can say

$$p(X_i = \text{mode}) > p(X_i = \text{any other score})$$

Finally the mode has the advantage of being applicable to nominal data, which, if you think about it, is obviously not true of the median or the mean.

One disadvantage of the mode is that it may not be particularly representative of the entire collection of numbers. This disadvantage is illustrated in the electronics game data (Table 3-2), in which the modal interval equals 0–9, which probably reflects the fact that a number of people do not play video games. Using this interval as the mode would be to ignore all of those people who do play. A second disadvantage of the mode that arises when we group observations into intervals is the fact that the modal interval is seriously dependent on how we choose to group the data. It is quite easy to demonstrate this to yourself with fairly simple data sets.

THE MEDIAN

The major advantage of the median, which it shares with the mode, is the fact that it is unaffected by extreme scores. Thus the medians of both (5, 8, 9, 15, 16) and (0, 8, 9, 15, 206) are 9. Many experimenters find this characteristic to be very useful in studies in which extreme scores occasionally occur but have no particular significance. For example, the average trained rat can run down a short runway in approximately 1 to 2 seconds. Every once in a while this same rat will inexplicably stop halfway down, scratch himself, poke his nose at the photocells, and lie down to sleep. In this instance it is of no practical significance whether he takes 30 seconds or 10 minutes to get to the other end—it may even depend on when the experimenter gives up and pokes him with a pencil (a common practice when stamping your feet, blowing on the rat, and tapping on the runway all fail). If we ran a rat through three trials on a given day and his times were (1.2, 1.3, and 20 seconds), that would have the same meaning to us—in terms of what it tells us about the rat's knowledge of the task—as if his times were (1.2, 1.3, and 136.4 seconds). In both cases the median would be 1.3. Obviously, however, his daily *mean* would be quite different in the two cases (7.5 versus 46.3 seconds). It is this problem that frequently induces experimenters to work with the median rather than the mean time per day.

The median has another point in its favor, in contrast to the mean, which those writers who become excited over scales of measurement like to point out. The calculation of the median does not require any assumptions about the interval properties of the scale. With the numbers 5, 8, and 11, the object represented by the number 8 is in the middle, no matter how close or distant it is from objects represented by 5 and 11. When we say that the *mean* is 8, however, we may be making the implicit assumption that the underlying distance between objects 5 and 8 is the same as the underlying distance between objects 8 and 11. Whether or not this assumption is reasonable is up to the experimenter. I prefer to work on the principle that if it is an absurdly unreasonable assumption, the experimenter will realize that and take appropriate steps. If it is not absurdly unreasonable, then its practical effect on the results will most likely be negligible. This problem of scales of measurement has been discussed already in more detail in Chapter 2.

THE MEAN

Of the three principal measures of central tendency, the mean is by far the most common. It would not be too much of an exaggeration to say that for many people statistics is (unfortunately) nearly synonymous with the study of the mean.

As we have already seen, certain disadvantages are associated with the mean. It is influenced by extreme scores, its value may not actually exist in the data, and its interpretation in terms of the underlying variable being measured requires at least some faith in the interval properties of the data. You might be inclined to politely suggest that if the mean has all of the disadvantages I have just ascribed to it, then maybe it should be quietly forgotten and allowed to slip into oblivion along with statistics like the "critical ratio"—a statistical concept that hasn't been heard of for years. The mean, however, is made of sterner stuff.

The mean has several important advantages that far outweigh its disadvantages. Probably the most important of these from a historical point of view, though not necessarily from your point of view, is that the mean can be manipulated algebraically. Whatever its faults, this accounts in large part for its widespread application. The second important advantage of the mean is that it has several desirable properties with respect to its use as an estimate of the population mean. In particular, if we drew many samples from some population, the sample means would be more stable (less variable) estimates of the central tendency of that population than the sample medians or modes. The fact that the sample mean is in general a better estimate of the population mean than is the mode or the median is a major reason that it is so widely used.

5-5 OBTAINING MEASURES OF CENTRAL TENDENCY USING MINITAB

For small sets of data it is perfectly reasonable to compute measures of central tendency by hand. However, with larger sample sizes or with data sets with many variables it is much simpler to let a computer program do the work. (It is also more fun.) Minitab is ideally suited to this purpose since it is easy to use, versatile, and widely available.

Suppose that as part of a large study on teaching effectiveness we asked each of 15 students in class to record the number of different annoying mannerisms exhibited by the instructor (e.g., dropping chalk, losing chalk, excessive neatness in arranging lecture notes, pacing, alternating standing and sitting, and all of those other activities the counting of which makes the lecture bearable). These data are illustrated in Table 5-1, along with those commands that are required to produce the three common measures of central tendency. Note that we can obtain the mean and median directly, but to get the mode we need to produce a histogram (or stem-and-leaf display) and then look for the most frequently appearing interval.

TABLE 5-1

Minitab Program to Calculate Measures of Central Tendency on the Number of Annoying Mannerisms

```
MTB > SET THE FOLLOWING DATA IN COLUM C1
DATA> 12 18 19 15 18 14 17 20 18 15 17 11 23  19 10
DATA> END
MTB > MEAN OF THE DATA IN COLUMN C1
    MEAN   =      16.400
MTB > MEDIAN OF THE DATA IN COLUMN C1
    MEDIAN =      17.000
MTB > HISTOGRAM OF THE DATA IN COLUMN C1

Histogram of C1   N = 15

Midpoint   Count
     10      1   *
     11      1   *
     12      1   *
     13      0
     14      1   *
     15      2   **
     16      0
     17      2   **
     18      3   ***
     19      2   **
     20      1   *
     21      0
     22      0
     23      1   *

MTB > STOP
```

From the table you can see that the mean (16.4), median (17), and mode (18) are all about the same, and the distribution is fairly smooth but slightly negatively skewed. We can also see from the histogram that there is considerable disagreement among the students concerning the number of annoying mannerisms exhibited by the instructor. This dispersion on either side of the mean is discussed in the next chapter.

5-6 SUMMARY

In this chapter we have considered several measures used to describe the center of a distribution. Each of these measures has its own particular strengths and weaknesses. One of these, the mean, forms the basis for much of the material discussed in the remainder of this book. Some of the most important terms in the chapter are:

- **Measures of central tendency**
- **Mode (Mo)**
- **Median (Med)**
- **Median location**
- **Mean ($\bar{X}$)**

5-7 EXERCISES

5-1 Calculate the mode, median, and mean for the data in Exercise 3-1.

5-2 Calculate the mode, median, and mean for the data in Exercise 3-4.

5-3 Compare the answers in Exercises 5-1 and 5-2. What do they tell you about storytelling behavior in adults and children?

5-4 Make up a set of data for which the mean is greater than the median.

5-5 Make up a positively skewed set of data. Does the mean fall above or below the median?

5-6 Can you make up a unimodal set of data where the mean and median are equal but different from the mode?

5-7 A group of 15 rats running a straight-alley maze required the following number of trials to perform at a predetermined criterion. The frequency distribution follows.

Trials Required to Reach Criterion	18	19	20	21	22	23	24
Number of Rats (Frequency)	1	0	4	3	3	3	1

Calculate the mean and median number of trials to criterion for this group.

5-8 Given the following set of data, demonstrate that subtracting a constant (e.g., 5) from every score reduces all measures of central tendency by that constant.

$$8 \quad 7 \quad 12 \quad 14 \quad 3 \quad 7$$

5-9 Given the following data, show that multiplying each score by a constant multiplies all measures of central tendency by that constant:

$$8 \quad 3 \quad 5 \quad 5 \quad 6 \quad 2$$

5-10 Create a sample of ten numbers that has a mean of 8.6. Notice carefully how you did this—it will later help you to understand the idea of degrees of freedom.

5-11 Calculate the measures of central tendency for the data on ADDSC and GPA in Appendix C, Data Set.

5-12 Why would it not make any sense to calculate the mean for SEX or ENGL in Appendix C, Data Set? If we did go ahead and compute the mean for SEX, what would the value $(\bar{X} - 1)$ really be?

5-13 Why is the mode an acceptable measure for nominal data, and why are the mean and median not acceptable for nominal data?

$$\boxed{6}$$

MEASURES OF VARIABILITY

Dispersion
The degree to which individual data points are distributed around the mean.

In Chapter 5 we considered a number of measures related to the center of a distribution. However, an average value for a distribution (whether it be a mode, median, or mean) fails to give the whole story. We need some additional measure (or measures) to indicate the degree to which individual observations are clustered about or, equivalently, deviate from, that average value. The average may reflect the general location of most of the scores. On the other hand the scores may be distributed over a wide range of values, and the "average" may not be very representative of the full set of observations. Probably everyone has had experience with examinations on which all students received approximately the same grade and with examinations on which the scores ranged from excellent to dreadful. Measures referring to the differences between these two types of situations are what we have in mind when we speak of **dispersion** or variability around the median, mode, or any other point we wish. In general we will be referring specifically to dispersion around the mean.

As an example of a situation in which we might expect differences in variability from one group to another, consider the case in which two sections of Computer Science I are given the same exam. One section is told that the exam will account for 20% of their final grade, and the other section is told that it will account for 90%. It is probably reasonable to expect that the two sections will have roughly the same mean. However, because "pressure" has a facilitative effect on the performance of some people and a disruptive effect on the performance of others, we might expect more variability in the section for whom the exam accounts for 90% of their final grade.

As a second example, consider the following four sets of data:

(a) 4 5 6
(b) 3 5 7
(c) 2 5 8
(d) 1 5 9

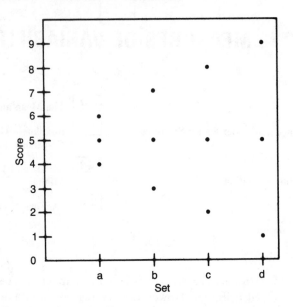

FIGURE 6-1

Plot of Four sets of Data with Different Degrees of Variability

A little calculation will show you that all four sets have the same mean (5), but that there is greater and greater variability around that mean as you move from set (a) toward set (d). This can be seen visually by plotting the values on the same graph. (See Figure 6-1).

As a final illustration, consider the following two sets of data. We have taken 20 rats from each of two strains and deposited them individually on the bottom of a circular box. The floor has been laid off in a grid, and we have counted the number of squares into which each rat stepped in a 30-second interval. This is a commonly used index of exploratory behavior (the "open field test"), and we are interested in whether animals in Strain X differ from each other (are more *variable*) in the exploratory behavior they exhibit more than do animals in Strain Y. This is not as foolish a study as you might at first suspect. Strains that show highly consistent behavior from one individual to the next (i.e., are less variable) are particularly important as sources of experimental animals because there will be less random variability floating around in our data. The mean level of exploratory behavior is of no interest to us, and in fact the two strains have the same means.

Strain X   5 4 4 6 6 4 6 4 5 6 4 4 6 5 5 6 6 4 6 4
Strain Y   5 1 8 7 4 8 8 1 5 1 5 5 7 7 7 1 5 7 5 3

We could plot the distributions of these scores to illustrate the differences between the strains. The two distributions are shown in Figure 6-2 as standard frequency distributions and as back-to-back histograms.

While it is apparent that rats of Strain Y differ from each other more than do those of Strain X, some sort of measure is needed to reflect this difference in variability. A number of measures could be used, and they will be discussed in turn, starting with the simplest.

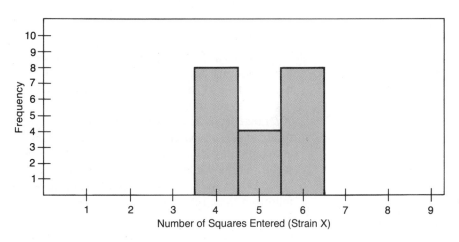

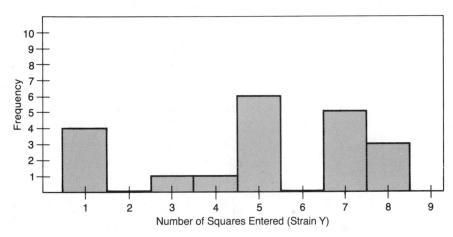

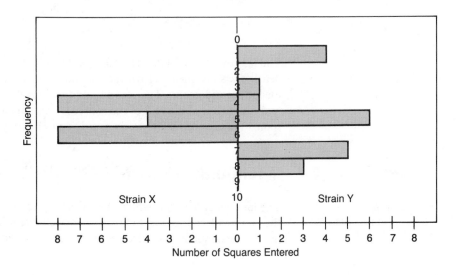

≡≡≡ FIGURE 6-2 ≡≡≡
**Distribution of Scores for
Strains X and Y in Terms of
the Number of Grid Squares
Entered**

6-1   RANGE

The **range** is a measure of distance, namely the distance from the lowest to the highest score. For our data the range for Strain X is $(6 - 4) = 2$, and for Strain Y it is $(8 - 1) = 7$. The range is an exceedingly common measure and is illustrated in everyday life by such statements as "The price of hamburger fluctuates over a 70¢ range from \$1.29 to \$1.99 per pound." The range suffers, however, by its total reliance on extreme values, or, if the values are *unusually* extreme, on what are commonly called **outliers**. As a result, the range may give a very distorted picture of the variability.

As examples of some of the difficulties with the range, consider the following three sets of data:

Group I	Group II	Group III	
8	8	6	
9	9	6	
9	9	6	
9	9	9	
9	9	9	
9	9	9	
9	9	10	
9	9	10	
9	9	10	
9	9	10	
11	11	11	
11	11	11	
11	11	11	
11	11	14	
11	11	14	
24	16	14	
10.5	10	10	= Mean
16	8	8	= Range

The first two sets of data are exactly alike except for the last score, and they have nearly the same mean. However, the range for the first group is double the range for the second group. The second and third groups have exactly the same mean and range, but almost all of the scores for Group II are 9s and 11s, whereas the scores for Group III are fairly evenly spaced from 6 to 14.

6-2   INTERQUARTILE RANGE AND OTHER RANGE STATISTICS

The **interquartile range**, which is very closely related to what we shortly will call the H-spread, represents an attempt to circumvent the problem that the range is heavily dependent on extreme scores. An interquartile range is obtained by discarding the upper and lower 25% of the distribution and taking the range of what remains. As such, it is the range of the middle 50% of the observations or the difference between the 75th percentile and the 25th percentile. We can calculate the interquartile range for the example of exploratory behavior by omitting the lowest five scores and the highest five scores and determining the range of the remainder. In this case the range for Strain X would still be $6 - 4 = 2$. For Strain Y, however, the range would now be $7 - 4 = 3$.

The interquartile range plays an important role in a very useful graphical method known as a boxplot. This method will be discussed later in this chapter.

In many ways the interquartile range suffers from problems that are just the opposite of those found with the range. Specifically, it discards too much of the data. If we want to know if one strain is more variable than another, it does not make sense to toss out those scores that are most extreme and thus vary the most from the mean.

There is nothing sacred about the idea of eliminating the upper and lower 25% of the distribution before calculating the range. In fact we could eliminate any percentage we wished, as long as we could justify to ourselves and to others what we are doing. What we really want to do is to eliminate those scores that we are likely to think of as accidents, without eliminating the variability that we seek to study. Samples that have had a certain percentage (e.g., 10%) of the values in each tail removed are called **trimmed samples**, and statistics calculated on such samples are called **trimmed statistics** (e.g., trimmed means or trimmed ranges).

Trimmed samples
Samples with a percentage of extreme scores removed.

Trimmed statistics
Statistics calculated on trimmed samples.

6-3 THE AVERAGE DEVIATION

At first glance it would seem that if we want to measure how scores are dispersed around the mean (i.e., deviate from the mean), then the most logical thing to do would be to obtain all of the deviations (i.e., $X_i - \bar{X}$) and average them. The more widely the scores are dispersed, the greater the deviations, and therefore the greater the average of the deviations—at least that is what you might think at first glance. Consider the exploratory behavior data for Strain X and Strain Y from the earlier example. These data follow on the next page, along with the deviation of each score from the mean.

You will observe that if you calculate the average of these deviations

$$\frac{\Sigma(X - \bar{X})}{N} \quad \text{or} \quad \frac{\Sigma(Y - \bar{Y})}{N}$$

the sum will be zero. The deviations below the mean are balanced by deviations above the mean. The sum of the deviations around the mean always will be zero, making the average zero. As a result this measure certainly is not going to turn out to be a satisfactory measure of dispersion.

	Strain X		Strain Y	
	X	$(X - \bar{X})$	Y	$(Y - \bar{Y})$
	5	0	5	0
	4	−1	1	−4
	4	−1	8	3
	6	1	7	2
	6	1	4	−1
	4	−1	8	3
	6	1	8	3
	4	−1	1	−4
	5	0	5	0
	6	1	1	−4
	4	−1	5	0
	4	−1	5	0
	6	1	7	2
	5	0	7	2
	5	0	7	2
	6	1	1	−4
	6	1	5	0
	4	−1	7	2
	6	1	5	0
	4	−1	3	−2
Mean Raw Score =	5		5	
Total Deviations =		0		0
Average Deviation =		0		0

6-4   THE MEAN ABSOLUTE DEVIATION

If you think about the difficulty we encountered when we tried to get something useful out of the average of the deviations, you might well be led to suggest that we could solve the whole problem by taking the absolute values of the deviations. (The absolute value of a number is the value of the number with any minus signs removed. The absolute value is indicated by vertical bars around the number. For example, $|-3| = |+3| = 3$.) The suggestion to use absolute values makes sense because we want to know *how much* scores deviate from the mean, without regard to whether they are above or below it. The measure just suggested here is a perfectly legitimate one and even has a name—the **mean absolute deviation (m.a.d.)**.

Mean absolute deviation (m.a.d.)
Mean of the absolute deviations about the mean.

$$\text{m.a.d.} = \frac{\Sigma |X - \bar{X}|}{N}$$

The sum of the absolute deviations is divided by N (the number of scores) to yield an average (mean) deviation.

For the data from the two strains of rats the mean absolute deviations are given in the following table:

	Strain X		Strain Y	
	X	$(X - \bar{X})$	Y	$(Y - \bar{Y})$
	5	0	5	0
	4	1	1	4
	4	1	8	3
	6	1	7	2
	6	1	4	1
	4	1	8	3
	6	1	8	3
	4	1	1	4
	5	0	5	0
	6	1	1	4
	4	1	5	0
	4	1	5	0
	6	1	7	2
	5	0	7	2
	5	0	7	2
	6	1	1	4
	6	1	5	0
	4	1	7	2
	6	1	5	0
	4	1	3	2
Mean Raw Score =	$\bar{5}$		$\bar{5}$	
Total Absolute Deviation =		16		38
Mean Absolute Deviation =		0.80		1.9

For Strain X the m.a.d. = 0.80, and for Strain Y it is 1.9. Thus the m.a.d. reflects the differences in dispersion, being larger with greater dispersion.

For all its simplicity and intuitive appeal, the mean absolute deviation has not played an important role in statistics. Instead, much more useful measures, the variance and the standard deviation, are normally used.

6-5 THE VARIANCE

Variance (s^2 or σ^2)
Sum of the squared deviations about the mean divided by $N - 1$.

The measure that we shall consider in this section, the sample **variance (s^2)**, represents a different approach to the problem that the deviations themselves average to zero. (When referring to the population variance we use σ^2 [lowercase sigma].) In this case we take advantage of the fact that the square of a negative number is positive. Thus we sum the *squared* deviations rather than the deviations themselves. Because we want an average, we next must divide this sum by a function of N, the number of scores. As a matter of fact we will actually divide not by N itself but by $(N - 1)$. We use $N - 1$ as a divisor *for the sample variance* because, as we will see shortly, it leaves us with a sample variance that is a better estimate of the corresponding population variance. (The population variance would be calculated by dividing the sum of the squared deviations [for each value in the population] by N rather than $N - 1$. However, we only very rarely calculate a population variance; we almost always estimate it from a sample variance.) The measure just described is called the sample variance and will be denoted s^2 or, to be more specific, s_X^2, where the subscript (X in this case) indicates the variable whose variance we are measuring.

For our example we can calculate the sample variances as follows:

Strain X:

$$s_X^2 = \frac{\Sigma(X - \bar{X})^2}{N - 1}$$

$$= \frac{(5 - 5)^2 + (4 - 5)^2 + \cdots + (4 - 5)^2}{20 - 1} = \frac{16}{20 - 1} = 0.84$$

Strain Y:

$$s_Y^2 = \frac{\Sigma(Y - \bar{Y})^2}{N - 1} = \frac{(5 - 5)^2 + (1 - 5)^2 + \cdots + (3 - 5)^2}{20 - 1} = \frac{116}{20 - 1} = 6.11$$

From the example we see that the variances reflect the difference in dispersion. Strain Y, which was much more dispersed than Strain X, has a variance of 6.11, whereas Strain X has a variance of only 0.84.

Although the variance is an exceptionally important concept and is one of the most commonly used statistics, it does not have the direct intuitive interpretation we would like. Because it is based on *squared* deviations, the result is in terms of squared units. Thus Strain Y has a mean of 5 units and a variance of 6.11 squared units. But squared units are awkward things to talk about and have little meaning with respect to the data. Fortunately the solution to this problem is simple—take the square root of the variance.

6-6 THE STANDARD DEVIATION

Standard deviation (s or σ)
Square root of the variance.

The **standard deviation (s or σ)** is defined as the positive square root of the variance and, for a sample, is symbolized as s (with a subscript identifying the variable if necessary) or, occasionally, as S.D. (The notation σ is used when referring to a *population* standard deviation.)

$$s_X = \sqrt{\frac{\Sigma(X - \bar{X})^2}{N - 1}}$$

For our example

$$s_X = \sqrt{s_X^2} = \sqrt{0.84} = 0.92$$

$$s_Y = \sqrt{s_Y^2} = \sqrt{6.11} = 2.47$$

If you look at the formula for the standard deviation, you will see that the standard deviation, like the mean absolute deviation, is basically a measure of the average of the deviations of each score from the mean. Granted, these deviations have been squared, summed, and so on, but at heart they are still deviations. And even though we have divided by $N - 1$ instead of N, we still have obtained something very much like a mean or "average" of these deviations. Thus we can say without too much distortion that subjects in Strain X deviate, on the average, 0.92 unit from the mean, and subjects in Strain Y deviate, on the average, 2.47 units from the mean. This rather loose way of thinking about the standard deviation as a sort of average deviation goes a long way toward giving it meaning without doing serious injustice to the concept. In fact, the standard deviation will be about 20% larger than the average deviation for reasonable sample sizes.

A different way of assigning meaning to the standard deviation is in terms of how many scores fall no more than a standard deviation above or below the mean. For a wide variety of reasonably symmetric and mound-shaped distributions we can say that approximately two-thirds of the observations lie within one standard deviation of the mean (for a normal distribution, to be discussed in Chapter 7, it is almost exactly two-thirds). Although there certainly are exceptions to this rule (especially for badly skewed distributions), it is still a handy rule. If I told you that for the traditional jobs the mean starting salary for college graduates this year is expected to be $15,000 with a standard deviation of $4000, you probably would not be far off to conclude that about two-thirds of the graduates who take these jobs will earn between $11,000 and $19,000.

A third characteristic to note about the standard deviation is that it is usually about one-fifth or one-sixth of the range. While this is not a particularly useful way of interpreting the standard deviation, it is a very handy way of checking your work. If a glance at the data shows that the range is about 20 and if you have just calculated $s_X = 15$, I would strongly suggest that you check your work. You may be right, but probably are not. On the other hand if you find that $s_X = 3.8$, you are justified in accepting that as at least a reasonable answer.

COMPUTATIONAL FORMULAE FOR THE VARIANCE AND STANDARD DEVIATION

The previous expressions for the variance and standard deviation, while perfectly correct, are incredibly unwieldy for any reasonable amount of data. They are also prone to rounding error, since they usually involve squaring fractional deviations. They are excellent definitional formulae, but we will now consider a more practical set of calculational formulae. To do so we will rearrange the definitional formula. The definitional formula for the sample variance is

$$s_X^2 = \frac{\Sigma (X - \bar{X})^2}{N - 1}$$

A more practical, and algebraically equivalent, computational formula is

$$s_X^2 = \frac{\sum X^2 - \dfrac{(\sum X)^2}{N}}{N-1}$$

Similarly, for the sample standard deviation

$$s_X = \sqrt{\frac{\sum (X - \bar{X})^2}{N-1}}$$

$$= \sqrt{\frac{\sum X^2 - \dfrac{(\sum X)^2}{N}}{N-1}}$$

It would be an excellent idea for you to memorize these formulae because these equations or parts of them will recur throughout this book and will crop up in the most unlikely places.

Applying the computational formula for the sample variance to our example, we obtain

$$s_X^2 = \frac{\sum X^2 - \dfrac{(\sum X)^2}{N}}{N-1}$$

$$= \frac{5^2 + 4^2 + \cdots + 6^2 + 4^2 - \dfrac{100^2}{20}}{19}$$

$$= \frac{516 - \dfrac{100^2}{20}}{19} = \frac{516 - 500}{19} = \frac{16}{19} = 0.84$$

and $$s_Y^2 = \frac{\sum Y^2 - \dfrac{(\sum Y)^2}{N}}{N-1} = \frac{5^2 + 1^2 + \cdots + 5^2 + 3^2 - \dfrac{100^2}{20}}{19}$$

$$= \frac{616 - \dfrac{100^2}{20}}{19} = \frac{616 - 500}{19} = \frac{116}{19} = 6.11$$

You will note that these answers are exactly the same as those obtained earlier. You should also note that, as pointed out in Chapter 2, $\sum X^2 = 516$ is quite different from $(\sum X)^2 = 100^2 = 10,000$.

6-7 THE MEAN AND VARIANCE AS ESTIMATORS

Mention has already been made in Chapter 1 of the fact that we generally calculate measures such as the mean and variance to use them as *estimates* of the corresponding values in the populations. Characteristics of samples are called *statistics* and are designated by Roman letters (e.g., $\bar{X}$). Characteristics of populations, on the other hand, are called *parameters* and are designated by Greek letters. Thus the population mean is symbolized by μ (mu). In general, then, we use statistics as estimates of parameters.

If the purpose of obtaining a statistic is to use it as an estimator of a parameter, then it should come as no surprise that our choice of a statistic (and even how we define it) is partly a function of how well that statistic functions as an estimator of the parameter in question. In fact the mean is usually preferred over other measures of central tendency precisely because of its performance as an estimator of μ. The variance (s^2) is defined as it is specifically because of the advantages that accrue when s^2 is used to estimate the population variance, signified by σ^2.

Three properties of estimators are of particular interest to statisticians and heavily influence the choice of the statistics we compute. These properties are sufficiency, unbiasedness, and efficiency. They are discussed here simply to give you a feel for why some measures of central tendency and variability are seen as more important than others. It is *not* critical that you have a thorough understanding of estimation and related concepts, but only that you have some general appreciation for the issues involved.

SUFFICIENCY

Sufficient statistic
A statistic that uses all of the information in a sample.

A statistic is a **sufficient statistic** if it contains (makes use of) all of the information in a sample. The mean is a sufficient statistic because we average all of the observations. The mode, however, uses only the most common observations, ignoring all others, and the median uses only the middle one, again ignoring the values of other observations. This is one of the reasons that we emphasize the mean as our measure of central tendency. Similarly, the range is not a sufficient statistic because it is based only on the two extreme values.

UNBIASEDNESS

Suppose that we have a population for which we somehow know the mean (μ)—say, for example, the heights of all basketball players in the NBA. If we were to draw one sample from that population and calculate the sample mean ($\bar{X}_1$), we would expect $\bar{X}_1$ to be reasonably close to μ, particularly if N is large, since it is an estimator of μ. So if the average height in this population is 7′ ($\mu = 7.0$), we would expect a sample of, say, 10 players to have an average height of approximately 7′ as well, although it probably would not be exactly equal to 7.0. (We can write $\bar{X}_1 \approx 7$, where the symbol $\approx$ means "approximately equal.") Now suppose that we draw another sample and obtain its mean $(\bar{X}_2)$. (The subscript is used here to differentiate the means of successive samples.) This mean would probably also be reasonably close to μ, but we would not expect it to be exactly equal to μ nor to $\bar{X}_1$. If we were to keep up this procedure and draw sample means *ad infinitum*, we would find that the *average of the sample means would be precisely equal to* μ. Thus we say that the **expected value** (i.e., the long-range average of many, many samples) of the sample mean is equal to μ, the population mean. An estimator whose expected value equals the parameter to be estimated is called an **unbiased estimator**, and this is a very important property for a statistic to possess. Both the sample mean and the sample variance are unbiased estimators of the corresponding parameters. By and large, unbiased estimators are like unbiased people—they are nicer to work with than biased ones.

EFFICIENCY

Estimators are also characterized in terms of **efficiency**. Suppose that the population is symmetric, and thus the values of the population mean and median are equal. Now suppose that we want to estimate the mean of this population (or, equivalently, its median). If we drew many samples and calculated their means, we would find that the means ($\bar{X}$'s) clustered relatively closely around μ. However, the medians of the same samples would cluster more loosely around μ. This is so even though the median is also an unbiased estimator in this situation, because the expected value of the median in this case would also equal μ. The fact that the sample means cluster more closely around μ than do the sample medians indicates that the mean is more *efficient* as an estimator (in fact it is the most efficient estimator of μ). Because the mean is more likely to be closer to μ (i.e., to be a more accurate estimate) than the median, it is a better statistic to use to estimate μ.

While it should be obvious that efficiency is a relative term (a statistic is more or less efficient than some other statistic), statements that such and such a statistic is "efficient" are common. In this usage of the term we really mean that the statistic is more efficient than all other statistics as an estimate of the parameter in question. Both the sample mean, as an estimate of μ, and the sample variance, as an estimate of σ^2, are efficient estimators in this sense. The fact that both the mean and variance are unbiased and efficient is the major reason that they play such an important role in statistics. These two statistics will form the basis for most of the procedures discussed in the remainder of this book.

THE SAMPLE VARIANCE AS AN ESTIMATOR OF THE POPULATION VARIANCE

The sample variance offers an excellent example of what was said in the discussion of unbiasedness. You may recall that I earlier sneaked in the divisor of $N - 1$ instead of N for the calculation of the variance and standard deviation. Now is the time to explain why.

There are a number of ways of explaining why sample variances require $N - 1$ as the denominator. Perhaps the simplest is in terms of what has been said already about the sample variance (s^2) as an unbiased estimate of the population variance (σ^2). Assume for the moment that we had an infinite number of samples (each containing N observations) from one population and that we knew the population variance. Suppose further that we were foolish enough to calculate sample variances as $\Sigma (X - \bar{X})^2/N$. (Note the denominator.) If we took the average of these samples' variances, we would find

$$\text{Average} \left(\frac{\Sigma (X - \bar{X})^2}{N} \right) = E \left(\frac{\Sigma (X - \bar{X})^2}{N} \right) = \frac{(N - 1)\sigma^2}{N}$$

where $E(\ )$ is read "the expected value of" whatever is in parentheses.

This last point can be illustrated by a simple example. Suppose that we had a population that consisted of only the three numbers 1, 2, and 3. Because this is the entire population, we can calculate μ and σ^2 exactly. They are $\mu = 2$ and $\sigma^2 = 0.666$. (Remember that if, *and only if*, we have the entire population instead of a sample, $\sigma^2 = (X - \mu)^2/N$.) Suppose further that we wanted to estimate the population variance on the basis of a sample of two observations. Only nine different samples of $N = 2$ could possibly be drawn from this population, and it is a simple matter in this case to list them and to compute the mean and variance of each sample. For our example we will calculate s^2 using both N and $N - 1$ as the denominator. The data and the calculations are presented in Table 6-1.

Notice that, as predicted, the mean of the sample means is exactly equal to μ and the mean of the sample variances, using $N - 1$ as the denominator, is exactly equal to σ^2. Furthermore, the average of $\Sigma (X - \bar{X})^2/N$ (the biased statistic) is

$$E \left(\frac{\Sigma (X - \bar{X})^2}{N} \right) = \frac{(N - 1)\sigma^2}{N} = \frac{1}{2} (\sigma^2) = \frac{1}{2} (0.667) = 0.333$$

Thus, the expected value of $\Sigma (X - \bar{X})^2/N$ is not σ^2, which we hoped to estimate, but instead, $\sigma^2(N - 1)/N$. Using N in the denominator we are estimating the

TABLE 6-1

The Results of Sampling from a Very Small Population

Sample		$\bar{X}$	s^2 (Using $N - 1$)	s^2 (Using N)
1	1	1.0	0.00	0.00
1	2	1.5	0.50	0.25
1	3	2.0	2.00	1.00
2	1	1.5	0.50	0.25
2	2	2.0	0.00	0.00
2	3	2.5	0.50	0.25
3	1	2.0	2.00	1.00
3	2	2.5	0.50	0.25
3	3	3.0	0.00	0.00
Average		2.0	0.667	0.333

wrong thing and have a biased estimate of σ^2. This result provides us with a basis for estimating σ^2, however. If

$$E\left(\frac{\Sigma(X - \bar{X})^2}{N}\right) = \frac{(N - 1)\sigma^2}{N}$$

then simple algebra will show that

$$E\left(\frac{\Sigma(X - \bar{X})^2}{N} \cdot \frac{N}{N - 1}\right) = \sigma^2 \quad \text{and thus} \quad E\left(\frac{\Sigma(X - \bar{X})^2}{N - 1}\right) = \sigma^2$$

This last formula is our standard definitional formula for the variance. It shows us not only how to find an estimate of σ^2, but also that this estimate is unbiased.

6-8   BOXPLOTS—GRAPHICAL REPRESENTATIONS OF DISPERSION AND EXTREME SCORES

In Chapter 3 we saw how stem-and-leaf displays can be used to represent the data in several meaningful ways at the same time. Such displays combine the data into something very much like a histogram while retaining the individual values of the observations. In addition to the stem-and-leaf display, Tukey has developed other ways of looking at data, one of which gives greater prominence to the dispersion of the data. This is the method known as **boxplots**, or, sometimes, **box-and-whisker plots**.

Boxplot (Box-and-whisker plot)
A graphical representation of the dispersion of a sample.

The data in Table 6-2 were taken from a study of normal and low-birthweight infants participating in a study at the University of Vermont, and represent preliminary data on the length of hospitalization of 38 normal-birthweight infants. Data on three infants are missing for this particular variable and are represented by an asterisk (*). (They are included to emphasize that we should not just ignore missing data.) Because the data vary from 1 to 10, with

TABLE 6-2
Data and Stem-and-Leaf Display on Length of Hospitalization of Full-Term Newborn Infants (in Days)

Data			Stem-and-Leaf	
2	1	7	1	000
1	33	2	2	000000000
2	3	4	3	00000000000
3	*	4	4	0000000
3	3	10	5	00
9	2	5	6	0
4	3	3	7	0
20	6	2	8	
4	5	2	9	0
1	*	*	10	0
3	3	4	HI	20, 33
2	3	4		
3	2	3	Missing = 3	
2	4			

two exceptions, all of the leaves are zeros. The zeros really just fill in space to produce a histogram-type distribution. Examination of the data as plotted in the stem-and-leaf display reveals that the distribution is positively skewed with a median of three days. Near the bottom of the stem you will see the entry HI and the values 20 and 33. These are extreme values (outliers) and are set off in this way to highlight their existence. Whether they are large enough to make us suspicious is one of the questions a boxplot is designed to address. The last line of the stem-and-leaf display indicates the number of missing observations.

In order to understand how a boxplot is constructed, we need to invoke a number of concepts we have already discussed and then add a few more. In Chapter 5 we defined the median location of a set of N scores as $(N + 1)/2$. When the median location is a whole number, then the median is simply the value occupying that location in an ordered arrangement of data. When the median location is a decimal number, the median is the average of the two values on either side of that location. For the data in Table 6-2 the median location is $(38 + 1)/2 = 19.5$ and the median is 3. To construct a boxplot we are going to take what amounts to the medians of each half of the display and call these points the **hinges**. Hinges are closely related to the first and third **quartiles** (often designated Q_1 and Q_3), which are the values that cut off the lowest and highest 25% of the distributions. (The difference between the hinges and the quartiles is minor and tends to vanish with large sample sizes.) To calculate the hinges we first need to obtain the **hinge location**, which is defined as

Hinges (Quartiles)
Those points that cut off the bottom and top quarter of a distribution.

Hinge location
The location of the hinge in an ordered series.

$$\text{Hinge Location} = \frac{\text{Median Location} + 1}{2}$$

If the median location is a fractional value, the fraction should be dropped in computing the hinge location. The hinge location is to the hinge what the median location is to the median. It tells us where, in an ordered series, the hinge values are to be found. For the data on hospital stay the hinge location is $(19 + 1)/2 = 10$. Thus the hinges are going to be the tenth score from the bottom and the tenth score from the top. These values are 2 and 4, respectively. For data sets without tied scores, or for large samples, the hinges will bracket the middle 50% of the scores.

To complete the concepts required for understanding boxplots we need to consider three more terms: H-spread, inner fences, and adjacent values. The **H-spread** is simply the range between the two hinges, and as such is basically just the interquartile range. For our data the H-spread is $4 - 2 = 2$. An **inner fence** is a point that falls 1.5 times the H-spread above or below the appropriate hinge. Because the H-spread is 2 for our data, the inner fence is $2 \times 1.5 = 3$ points further out than the hinges. Because our hinges are the values 2 and 4, then the inner fences will be at $2 - 3 = -1$ and $4 + 3 = 7$. Lastly we will define **adjacent values** as those values in the data that are no more extreme (no further from the median) than the inner fences. Because the smallest value we have is 1, that is the closest to the lower inner fence and is the lower adjacent value. The higher inner fence is 7, and because we have a 7 in our data, that will be the higher adjacent

H-spread
The range between the two hinges.

Inner fences
Points that are 1.5 times the H-spread above and below the appropriate hinge.

Adjacent values
Actual data points that are no more extreme than the inner fences.

Median Location $= (N + 1)/2 = (38 + 1)/2 = 19.5$
Median $= 3$
Hinge Location $=$ (Median Location$\dagger$ $+ 1)/2 = (19 + 1)/2 = 10$
Lower Hinge $=$ 10th lowest score $= 2$
Upper Hinge $=$ 10th highest score $= 4$
H-Spread $=$ Upper Hinge $-$ Lower Hinge $= 4 - 2 = 2$
H-Spread $\times$ 1.5 $= 2(1.5) = 3$
Lower Fence $=$ Lower Hinge $- 1.5$(H-Spread) $= 2 - 3 = -1$
Upper Fence $=$ Upper Hinge $+ 1.5$(H-Spread) $= 4 + 3 = 7$
Lower Adjacent Value $=$ Smallest Value $\geqslant$ Lower Fence $= 1$
Upper Adjacent Value $=$ Largest Value $\leqslant$ Upper Fence $= 7$

```
   0      5      10     15     20     25     30

   -[|]- ---   * *           *                    *
```

$\dagger$Drop any fractional values.

value. The calculations for all of the terms we have just defined are shown in the top portion of Table 6-3.

Inner fences and adjacent values cause some confusion among students. Think of a herd of cows scattered around a field (or, if you prefer, you can imagine a group of children on a playground). The fence around the field (or playground) represents the inner fence of the boxplot. The cows (or children) closest to, but inside, the fence are the adjacent values. Don't worry about the cows (or children) outside the fence. They are not involved in the calculations at this point.

Now we are ready to draw the boxplot. First we draw and label a scale that covers the whole range of the obtained values. This has been done at the bottom of Table 6-3. We then draw a rectangular box from one hinge to the other, with a vertical line representing the location of the median. Next we draw dashed lines (**whiskers**) from the hinges out to the adjacent values. Finally we plot the location of all points more extreme than the adjacent values.

Whiskers
Lines drawn in a boxplot from hinges to adjacent values.

From Table 6-3 we can see several important things. First of all the central portion of the distribution is reasonably symmetric. This is indicated by the fact that the median lies in the center of the box and also was apparent from the stem-and-leaf display. We also can see that the distribution is positively skewed, because the whisker on the right is substantially longer than the one on the left. This was apparent from the stem-and-leaf display, although not so clearly. Finally we see that we have four outliers, where an outlier is defined here as any value more extreme than the whiskers (and therefore more extreme than the adjacent values). The stem-and-leaf display did not show the position of the outliers nearly so graphically as does the boxplot.

Outliers deserve special attention. An outlier could represent an error in measurement, in data recording, or in data entry, or it could represent a legitimate value that just happens to be extreme. For example, our data represent length of hospitalization, and a full-term infant might have been born with a physical defect that required extended hospitalization. Because these are actual data, it was possible to go back to hospital records and look more closely at the four extreme cases. On examination it turned out that the two most extreme scores were attributable to errors in data entry and were readily correctable. The other two extreme scores were caused by physical problems of the infant. Here a decision was required by the project staff as to whether the problems were sufficiently severe to cause the infants to be dropped from the study. (In both cases they were retained as subjects.) The two corrected values were 3 and 5 (instead of 33 and 20, respectively), and a new boxplot on the corrected data follows:

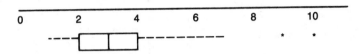

It is identical to the boxplot shown in Table 6-3 except for the spacing and the two largest values. (You should verify for yourself, now, that the corrected data set would indeed yield this boxplot.)

From what has been said, it should be evident that boxplots are extremely useful tools for examining data with respect to dispersion. I find them particularly useful for screening data for errors and for highlighting potential problems before subsequent analyses are carried out. You often will see them presented in the remainder of the book as a visual guide to the data.

6-9 OBTAINING MEASURES OF DISPERSION USING MINITAB

In Chapter 5 we saw how to use Minitab to calculate measures of central tendency. We can also use Minitab to calculate measures of dispersion, as can be seen in Table 6-4.

In the table we have the earlier data on annoying mannerisms of instructors (Table 5-1). You will note that simple commands give us the minimum and maximum values (10 and 23), from which we can obtain the range by subtraction ($23 - 10 = 13$). These values also could have been obtained from the histogram. We could obtain an estimate of the interquartile range from the histogram by deleting the top and bottom 25% of the scores and then taking the range of what remains. However, in this case, where we have only 15 scores, we can only approximate the middle 50% since 50% of the sample would be 7.5 scores. The standard deviation (3.56) is given by a simple command, and we could square this to obtain the variance (12.67). Finally the DESCRIBE command will give us N, $\bar{X}$, and s directly, and the BOXPLOT command generates a boxplot. The bottom of the boxplot tells you that the leftmost tick mark ($-$) occurs at a score of 10 and that each tick is worth 0.3 unit. (The notation .30E + 00 means 0.30 times 10^{+00}. Because any number raised to the 0th power is 1, this becomes 0.30.)

═══ TABLE 6-4 ═══
Minitab Program for Obtaining Measures of Dispersion

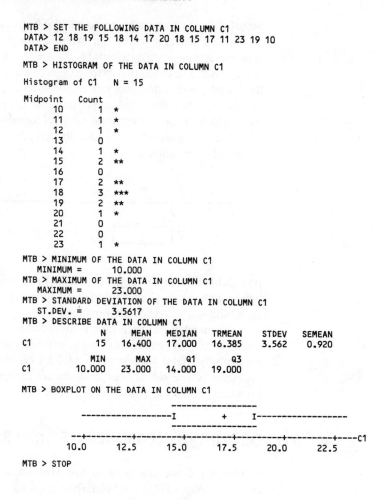

```
MTB > SET THE FOLLOWING DATA IN COLUMN C1
DATA> 12 18 19 15 18 14 17 20 18 15 17 11 23 19 10
DATA> END

MTB > HISTOGRAM OF THE DATA IN COLUMN C1

Histogram of C1   N = 15

Midpoint   Count
   10        1   *
   11        1   *
   12        1   *
   13        0
   14        1   *
   15        2   **
   16        0
   17        2   **
   18        3   ***
   19        2   **
   20        1   *
   21        0
   22        0
   23        1   *

MTB > MINIMUM OF THE DATA IN COLUMN C1
   MINIMUM =      10.000
MTB > MAXIMUM OF THE DATA IN COLUMN C1
   MAXIMUM =      23.000
MTB > STANDARD DEVIATION OF THE DATA IN COLUMN C1
   ST.DEV. =       3.5617
MTB > DESCRIBE DATA IN COLUMN C1
              N     MEAN   MEDIAN   TRMEAN    STDEV   SEMEAN
C1           15   16.400   17.000   16.385    3.562    0.920

            MIN      MAX       Q1       Q3
C1       10.000   23.000   14.000   19.000

MTB > BOXPLOT ON THE DATA IN COLUMN C1

                      -------------------
        ------------------I      +      I-------------------
                      -------------------
      --+---------+---------+---------+---------+---------+----C1
        10.0      12.5      15.0      17.5      20.0      22.5

MTB > STOP
```

═══ 6-10 A FINAL WORKED EXAMPLE

To illustrate once again the calculations of the major statistics involved in this chapter, consider the following data on a standard measure of depression for ten subjects:

X	X^2
5	25
8	64
9	81
4	16
6	36
3	9
7	49
8	64
7	49
3	9
$\Sigma X = 60$	$\Sigma X^2 = 402$

Mean:

$$\bar{X} = \frac{\Sigma X}{N} = \frac{60}{10} = 6.0$$

Variance:

$$s^2 = \frac{\Sigma X^2 - \frac{(\Sigma X)^2}{N}}{N - 1} = \frac{402 - \frac{60^2}{10}}{9} = \frac{402 - 360}{9} = 4.667$$

Standard Deviation:

$$s = \sqrt{s^2} = \sqrt{4.667} = 2.160$$

Boxplots:

First rearrange the observations in ascending order

$$3 \quad 3 \quad 4 \quad 5 \quad 6 \quad 7 \quad 7 \quad 8 \quad 8 \quad 9$$

$$\text{Median Location} = \frac{N + 1}{2} = \frac{11}{2} = 5.5$$

$$\text{Median} = \frac{6 + 7}{2} = 6.5$$

$$\text{Hinge Location} = \frac{\text{Median Location} + 1}{2} = \frac{5 + 1}{2} = 3$$

(drop fraction from median location if necessary)

Hinges are the third observations from the top and bottom of an ordered series = 4 and 8.

H-Spread = distance between upper and lower hinges = 8 − 4 = 4.

1.5 times H-Spread = 1.5(4) = 6.

Inner fences = hinges $\pm$ 1.5(H-Spread).

$$\text{Upper hinge} = 8 + 6 = 14$$

$$\text{Lower hinge} = 4 - 6 = -2$$

Adjacent values = values closest to *but not exceeding* inner fences.

$$\text{Lower adjacent value} = 3$$
$$\text{Upper adjacent value} = 9$$

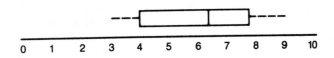

6-11   SUMMARY

In this chapter we have considered a number of measures of the degree to which scores are distributed around the mean. Of these measures the standard deviation and the variance are the most important and play a major role in the remainder of the text. We also have seen how to use boxplots to highlight the shape of the distribution and to help in identifying outliers. Some of the important terms in the chapter are:

□ **Dispersion**
□ **Range**
□ **Outliers**
□ **Trimmed samples**
□ **Variance**
□ **Standard deviation**
□ **Expected value**

□ **Unbiased estimator**
□ **Efficiency**
□ **Boxplot**
□ **Hinges**
□ **Adjacent values**
□ **Whiskers**

6-12 EXERCISES

6–1 Calculate the range, variance, and standard deviation for the data in Exercise 3-1.

6–2 Calculate the range, variance, and standard deviation for the data in Exercise 3-4.

6–3 Compare the answers to Exercises 6-1 and 6-2. Is the standard deviation for children substantially greater than the standard deviation for adults?

6–4 In Exercise 6-1 what percentage of the scores fall within two standard deviations from the mean?

6–5 In Exercise 6-2 what percentage of the scores fall within two standard deviations from the mean?

6–6 Given the following set of data, demonstrate that adding or subtracting a constant to each score does not change the standard deviation. What did we find happens to the mean when a constant is added or subtracted?

$$5 \quad 4 \quad 2 \quad 3 \quad 4 \quad 9 \quad 5$$

6–7 Given the data in Exercise 6-6, show that multiplying or dividing by a constant multiplies or divides the standard deviation by that constant. How does this relate to what happens to the mean under similar conditions?

6–8 Using the results demonstrated in Exercises 6-6 and 6-7, transform the following set of data to a new set with a standard deviation of 1.00:

$$5 \quad 8 \quad 3 \quad 8 \quad 6 \quad 9 \quad 9 \quad 7$$

6–9 Use the answers to Exercises 6-6 and 6-7 to modify the answer to Exercise 6-8 to have a mean of 0 and a standard deviation of 1.00. (*Note*: The solution to Exercises 6-8 and 6-9 will be important in Chapter 7.)

6–10 Create two sets of scores with equal ranges but different variances.

6–11 Create a boxplot for the data in Exercise 6-1.

6–12 Create a boxplot for the data in Exercise 6-2.

6–13 Create a boxplot for the variable ADDSC in Appendix C, Data Set.

6–14 (a) Calculate the variance and standard deviation for ENGG in Appendix C, Data Set.

(b) These measures should be greater than the corresponding measures on GPA. Can you explain why this should be? (We will come back to this matter in Chapter 12.)

6–15 The mean of the data used in Exercise 3-1 is 18.9. Suppose that we had an additional child who had a score of 18.9. Recalculate the variance for these data. (You can build on the intermediate steps used in Exercise 6-1.) What effect does this score have on the answers to Exercise 6-1?

6–16 Instead of adding a score equal to the mean (as in Exercise 6-15), add a score of 40 to the data used for Exercise 6-1. How does this score affect the answers to Exercise 6-1?

6–17 Repeat the computations used to generate Table 6-1, but this time let the population consist of the numbers 1, 2, 3, 4, and 5, and draw all possible samples of $N = 3$. (*Hint*: There are 10 possible unique samples.)

6–18 The discussion of an efficient statistic was phrased in terms of what would happen if we draw a very large number of samples. But we usually draw only one sample from any population. Why then do we care about the results from many samples?

6–19 Answer Exercise 6-18 with respect to unbiasedness rather than efficiency.

6–20 **(a)** Draw a boxplot for the following data:

$$
\begin{array}{cccccccc}
1 & 3 & 3 & 5 & 8 & 8 & 9 & 12 \\
13 & 16 & 17 & 17 & 18 & 20 & 21 & 30
\end{array}
$$

(b) Calculate the standard deviation of these data and divide every score by the standard deviation.

(c) Draw a boxplot for the data in (b).

(d) Compare the two boxplots.

THE NORMAL DISTRIBUTION

Normal distribution
Specific distribution having a characteristic bell-shaped form.

From what has been said in the preceding chapters, it is apparent that we are going to be very much concerned with distributions—distributions of data, hypothetical distributions of populations, and sampling distributions (which will be introduced in Chapter 11). Of all the possible forms that distributions can take, the class known as the **normal distribution** is by far the most important for our purposes.

Before elaborating on the normal distribution, however, it is worth a short digression to explain just why we are so interested in distributions in general. The critical factor is that there is an important link between distributions and probabilities. If we know something about the distribution of events (or of sample statistics) we know something about the probability that one of those events (or statistics) is likely to occur. To see the issue in its simplest form, take the lowly pie chart. (This is the only time you will see a pie chart in this book, because I find it very difficult to compare the little slices of pie to see which one is larger. There are much better ways to present data. However, the pie chart serves a useful purpose here.)

The pie chart shown in Figure 7-1 is taken from a U.S. Department of Justice report on probation and parole. It shows the current status of all individuals who have been convicted of a criminal offense. From this figure you can see that 9% were in jail, 19% were in prison, 61% were on probation, and the remaining 11% were on parole. You can also see that the percentages in each category are directly reflected in the percentage of area of the pie that each wedge occupies. The area taken up by each segment is directly proportional to the percentage of individuals in that segment. Moreover, if we declare that the total area of the pie is 1.00 unit, the area of each segment is equal to the proportion of observations falling in that segment.

It is easy to go from speaking about areas to speaking about probabilities. The concept of probability will be elaborated in Chapter 8, but even without a precise definition of probability we can make an important point about areas of a pie chart. For now simply think of probability in its common everyday usage, referring to the likelihood that some event will occur. From this perspective it is logical to conclude that, because 19% of those convicted of a federal crime are

72

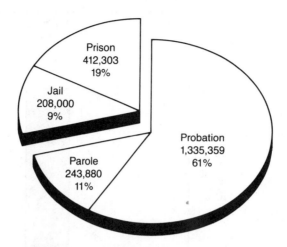

Note: The prison data are from the U.S. Department of Justice, Bureau of Justice Statistics, *Prisoners in 1982*, Bulletin NCJ-87933 (Washington, D.C.: U.S. Government Printing Office, 1983). The jail data are from the U.S. Department of Justice, Bureau of Justice Statistics, *Jail Inmates 1982*, Bulletin NCJ-87161 (Washington, D.C.: U.S. Department of Justice, February 1983). The parole data and the probation data are from the annual Uniform Parole Reports and National Probation Reports surveys.

≡ **FIGURE 7-1** ≡
Pie Chart Showing Persons under Correctional Supervision, by Type of Supervision, on December 31, 1982

currently in prison, if we were to randomly draw the name of one person from a list of convicted individuals, the probability is .19 that the individual would be in prison. To put this in slightly different terms, if 19% of the area of the pie is allocated to prison, then the probability that a person would fall in that segment is .19.

This pie chart also allows us to explore the addition of areas. It should be clear that if 19% are in prison and 9% are in jail, $19 + 9 = 28\%$ are incarcerated. In other words, we can find the percentage of individuals in one of several categories just by adding the percentages for each category. The same thing holds in terms of areas, in the sense that we can find the percentage of incarcerated individuals by adding the areas devoted to prison and to jail. And lastly, if we can find percentages by adding areas, we can also find probabilities by adding areas. Thus the probability of being incarcerated is the probability of being in one of the two segments associated with incarceration, which we can get by summing the two areas (or their associated probabilities).

There are other ways to present data besides pie charts, and one of the simplest is a histogram (discussed in Chapter 3) or its closely related cousin, the bar chart. In Figure 7-2 I have redrawn Figure 7-1 in the form of a bar chart. Although this figure does not contain any new information, it has two advantages over the pie chart. First of all it is easier to compare categories, because the only thing we need to look at is the height of the bar, rather than trying to compare the lengths of two different arcs in different orientations. The second advantage is that the bar chart is visually more like the common distributions we will deal with, in that the various levels or categories are spread out along the horizontal dimension and the percentages in each category are

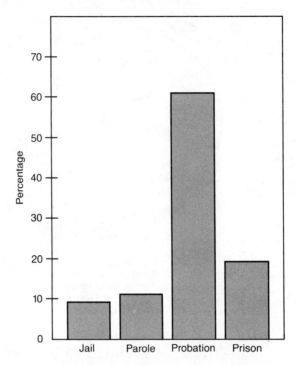

FIGURE 7-2
Bar Chart Showing Persons under Correctional Supervision by Type of Supervision

shown along the vertical dimension. Here again you can see that the various areas of the distribution are related to probabilities. Further, you can see that we can meaningfully sum areas in exactly the same way that we did in the pie chart. When we move to more common distributions, particularly when we move to the normal distribution, the principles of areas, percentages, probabilities, and the addition of areas or probabilities carry over almost without change.

I stated earlier that the normal distribution is one of the most important distributions we will encounter. There are several reasons for this:

1. Many of the dependent variables with which we deal commonly are assumed to be normally distributed in the population. That is to say that we frequently assume that if we were to obtain the whole population of observations, the resulting distribution would closely resemble the normal distribution.

2. If we assume that a variable is at least approximately normally distributed, then the techniques that are discussed in this chapter allow us to make a number of inferences (either exact or approximate) about values of that variable.

3. The theoretical distribution of the hypothetical set of sample means obtained by drawing an infinite number of samples from a specified population can be shown to be approximately normal under a wide variety of conditions. Such a distribution is called the sampling distribution of the mean and is discussed and used extensively in later chapters.

4. Most of the statistical procedures we will employ have, somewhere in their derivation, an assumption that the population of observations is normally distributed.

To introduce the normal distribution we will look at one additional data set that is approximately normal (and would be normal if we had more observations). The data we are going to look at were collected using the Achenbach Youth Self Report form (Achenbach, 1986). This is a frequently used measure of behavior problems that produces scores on a number of different dimensions. The one we are going to look at is the dimension of Total Behavior Problems, which represents the total number of behavior problems reported by the child (weighted by the severity of the problem). (Examples of Behavior Problem categories are "Argues," "Impulsive," "Shows off," and "Teases.") Figure 7-3 is a histogram of data from 309 junior high school students. A higher score represents more behavior problems. You can see that this distribution has a center very near 50 and is fairly symmetrically distributed on either side of that value, with the scores ranging between about 25 and 75. The standard deviation of this distribution is approximately 10. The distribution is not perfectly smooth—it has some bumps and valleys—but overall it is fairly smooth, rising in the center and falling off at the ends. (The actual mean and standard deviation for this particular sample are 50.98 and 10.42, respectively.)

One thing that you might note from this distribution is that if you add the frequencies of people falling in the intervals 52–53, 53–54, and 55–56 you will find that approximately 65 people obtained a score between 52 and 56. Because there are 309 observations in this sample, 65/309 = 21% of the observations fell

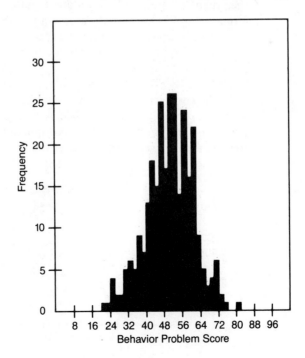

FIGURE 7-3
Histogram Showing
Distribution of Total Behavior
Problem Scores

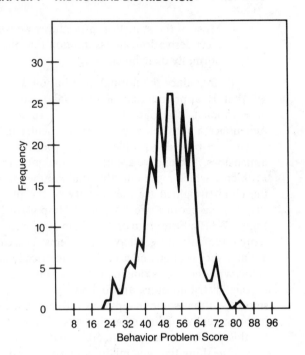

in this interval. This illustrates the comments made earlier on the addition of areas.

If we take this same set of data and represent it by a frequency polygon rather than a histogram, we obtain Figure 7-4. There is absolutely no new information in this figure that was not in Figure 7-3. I have merely connected the tops of the bars in the histogram and then erased the bars themselves. Why then waste an artist's time by putting in a figure that has nothing new to offer? The reason is simply that I want to get people to see the transition from a histogram, which you see nearly every time you open a newspaper or a magazine, to a line graph. The next transition from there to the smoothed curves you will see in the rest of the book (e.g., Figure 7-5) is straightforward. The major difference between the line graph (frequency polygon) and the smoothed curve is that the latter is a stylized version that leaves out the bumps and valleys. If you would

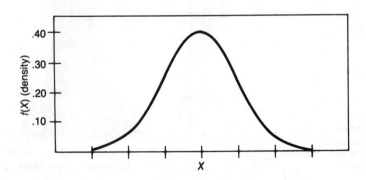

prefer, you can always think of the smoothed curve as sitting on top of an invisible histogram.

Now we are ready to go to the normal distribution. First we will consider it in the abstract, and then we will take a concrete example making use of the Achenbach Youth Self Report Total Behavior Problem scores that we saw in Figures 7-3 and 7-4.

The distribution shown in Figure 7-5 is a characteristic normal distribution. It is a symmetric, unimodal distribution, frequently referred to as "bell shaped," and has limits of $\pm\infty$. The **abscissa**, or horizontal axis, represents different possible values of X, while the **ordinate** (or vertical axis) is referred to as the density and is related to (but not the same as) the frequency or probability of occurrence of X. The concept of density will be discussed in further detail in the next chapter.

Abscissa
Horizontal axis.

Ordinate
Vertical axis.

The normal distribution has a long history. It was originally investigated by DeMoivre (1667–1754), who was interested in its use in describing the results of games of chance (gambling). The distribution was defined precisely by Laplace (1749–1827) and put in its more usual form by Gauss (1777–1855), both of whom were interested in the distribution of errors in astronomical observations. In fact the normal distribution often is referred to as the Gaussian distribution and as the "normal law of error." Adolph Quetelet (1796–1874), a Belgian astronomer, was the first to apply the distribution to social and biological data. He collected chest measurements of Scottish soldiers and heights of French soldiers. He found that both sets of measurements were approximately normally distributed. Quetelet interpreted the data to indicate that the mean of this distribution was the ideal at which nature was aiming and that observations to either side of the mean represented error (a deviation from nature's ideal). (For 5′8″ males like myself it is somehow comforting to think of a 6′2″ football player as nature's mistake.) Although we no longer think of the mean as nature's ideal, this is a useful way to conceptualize variability around the mean. In fact we still use the word *error* to refer to deviations from the mean. Francis Galton (1822–1911) carried Quetelet's ideas further and gave the normal distribution a central role in psychological theory—especially the theory of mental abilities.

Mathematically, the normal distribution is defined as

$$f(X) = \frac{1}{\sigma\sqrt{2\pi}}\,(e)^{-(X-\mu)^2/2\sigma^2}$$

where π and e are constants ($\pi = 3.1416$ and $e = 2.7183$), and μ and σ are the mean and standard deviation, respectively, of the distribution. Given that μ and σ are known, the ordinate ($f(X)$) for any value of X is obtained simply by substituting μ, σ, and X in the equation and solving the equation. This is not nearly as difficult as it looks, but in practice you are unlikely to ever have to make the calculations. The cumulative form of this distribution is tabled, and we can simply read the information we need from the table.

Those of you who have had a course in calculus may recognize that the area under the curve between any two values of X (say X_1 to X_2), and thus the probability that a randomly drawn score will fall within that interval, could be found by integrating the function over the range from X_1 to X_2. Those of you who have not had such a course can take comfort from the fact that tables are readily available in which this work has already been done for us—or by use of which we can easily do it ourselves. Such a table appears in Appendix D, Table 9.

You might be excused at this point for wondering why anyone would want to table such a distribution in the first place. Just because a distribution is common (or at least commonly assumed) doesn't automatically suggest a reason for wanting an appendix telling all about it. The reason is quite simple. By use of Appendix D, Table 9, we can readily calculate the probability that a score drawn at random from the population will have a value lying between any two specified points (X_1 and X_2). Thus by using statistical tables we can make probability statements in answer to a variety of questions.

7-1 THE STANDARD NORMAL DISTRIBUTION

A problem arises when we try to table the normal distribution, however, because the distribution depends upon the values of the mean and standard deviation (μ and σ) of the distribution. Thus to do the job right we would have to make up a different table for every possible combination of the values of μ and σ. The solution to this problem is quite simple. What we actually have in the table is what is called the **standard normal distribution**, which has a mean of 0 and a standard deviation and variance of 1. Such a distribution is often designated as $N(0, 1)$, where N refers to the fact that it is normal, 0 is the value of μ, and 1 is the value of σ^2. (Thus the more general expression is $N(\mu, \sigma^2)$.) Given the standard normal distribution in the appendix and a set of rules for transforming any normal distribution to standard form, and vice versa, we can use Appendix D, Table 9, to find the areas under any normal distribution.

Consider the distribution shown in Figure 7-6. This is a distribution with a mean of 50 and a standard deviation of 10 (variance of 100). It represents the

Standard normal distribution
A normal distribution with a mean equal to 0 and variance equal to 1. Denoted $N(0, 1)$.

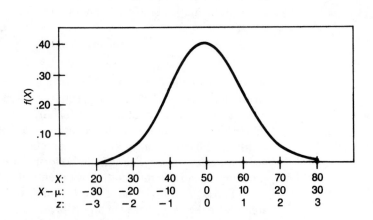

FIGURE 7-6
A Normal Distribution with Various Transformations on the Abscissa

X:	20	30	40	50	60	70	80
$X - \mu$:	−30	−20	−10	0	10	20	30
z:	−3	−2	−1	0	1	2	3

distribution of *an entire population* of Total Behavior Problem scores from the Achenbach Youth Self Report form, of which the data in Figures 7-3 and 7-4 are a sample. If we knew something about the areas under the curve in Figure 7-6 we could say something about the probability of various values of Behavior Problem scores and could identify, for example, those scores that are so high that they are obtained by only 5% or 10% of the population.

Because the only tables of the normal distribution that are readily available are those of the *standard* normal distribution, before we can answer questions about the probability that an individual will get a score above some particular value, we must first transform the distribution in Figure 7-6 (or at least specific points along it) to a standard normal distribution. That is, we want to be able to say that a score of X_i from $N(50, 100)$ (i.e., a normal distribution with a mean of 50 and a variance of 100) is comparable to a score of z_i from $N(0, 1)$. Then anything that is true of z_i is also true of X_i, and z and X are comparable variables.

From Exercise 6-6 we know that subtracting a constant from each score in a set of scores reduces the mean of the set by that constant. Thus if we subtract 50 (the mean) from all of the values for X, the new mean will be $50 - 50 = 0$. (More generally, the distribution of values of $(X - \mu)$ has a mean of 0.) The effect of this transformation is shown in the second set of values for the abscissa in Figure 7-6. We are halfway there since we now have the mean down to 0, although the standard deviation (σ) is still 10. We also know from Exercise 6-7 that if we divide all values of a variable by a constant (e.g. 10), we divide the standard deviation by that constant. Thus the standard deviation will now be $10/10 = 1$, which is just what we wanted. We will call this transformed distribution z and can define it, on the basis of what we have done, as

$$z = \frac{X - \mu}{\sigma}$$

For our particular case, where $\mu = 50$ and $\sigma = 10$,

$$z = \frac{X - \mu}{\sigma} = \frac{X - 50}{10}$$

Linear transformation
A transformation involving addition, subtraction, multiplication, or division of or by a constant.

The third set of values (labeled z) for the abscissa in Figure 7-6 shows the effect of this transformation. Note that aside from a **linear transformation**† of the numerical values, the data have not been changed in any way. The distribution has the same shape and the observations continue to stand in the same relation to each other as they did before the transformation. It should not come as a great surprise that changing the unit of measurement does not change the shape of the distribution or the relative standing of observations. Whether we measure the quantity of alcohol that people consume per week in ounces or in milliliters

†A linear transformation involves only multiplication (or division) of X by a constant and/or adding (or subtracting) a constant to X. Such a transformation leaves the relationship among the values unaffected. In other words it does not distort values at one part of the scale more than values at another part. Changing units from inches to centimeters is a good example of a linear transformation.

really makes no difference in the relative standings of people. It just changes the numerical values on the abscissa. (The town drunk is still the town drunk even if now his liquor is measured in milliliters.) It is important to realize exactly what converting X to z has accomplished. A score that used to be 60 is now 1. That is, a score that used to be one standard deviation (10 points) above the mean remains one standard deviation above the mean but now is given a new value of 1. A score of 45, which was 0.5 standard deviation *below* the mean, now is given the value of -0.5, and so on. In other words a *z* **score** represents the number of standard deviations that X_i is above or below the mean—a positive z score being above the mean and a negative z score being below the mean.

The equation for z is completely general. We can transform any distribution to a distribution of z scores simply by applying this equation. However, keep in mind the point that was just made. The *shape* of the distribution is unaffected by the transformation. That means that *if the distribution was not normal before it was transformed, it will not be normal afterward*. Some people believe that they can "normalize" (in the sense of producing a normal distribution) their data by transforming them to z. It just won't work.

USE OF THE TABLES OF THE STANDARD NORMAL DISTRIBUTION

As I have mentioned, the standard normal distribution is extensively tabled. Such a table can be found in Appendix D, Table 9, part of which is reproduced in Table 7-1. To see how we can make use of this table, consider the normal distribution represented in Figure 7-7. This might represent the standardized distribution of the Behavior Problem scores as seen in Figure 7-6. Suppose we wish to know how much of the area under the curve is above 1 standard deviation from the mean, if the total area under the curve is taken to be 1.00. (We care about areas because they translate directly to probabilities.) We already have seen that z scores represent standard deviations from the mean, and thus we know that we want to find the area above $z = 1$.

Only the positive half of the normal distribution is tabled. Because the distribution is symmetric, any information given about a positive value of z applies equally to the corresponding negative value of z. From Table 7-1 (or Appendix D, Table 9) we find the row corresponding to $z = 1.00$. Reading across that row, we can see that the area from the *mean to z* = 1 is 0.3413, that the area in the *larger portion* is 0.8413, and the area in the *smaller portion* is 0.1587. (If you visualize the distribution being divided into the segment below $z = 1$ [the unshaded part of Figure 7-7] and the segment above $z = 1$ [the shaded part], the meaning of the terms *larger portion* and *smaller portion* becomes obvious.) Thus the answer to our original question is 0.1587. Because we already have equated the terms *area* and *probability* (see Chapter 3), we now can say that if we sample a child at random from the population of children and if Behavior Problem scores are normally distributed, then the probability that the child will score more than one standard deviation above the mean of the population (i.e., above 60) is .1587. Because the distribution is symmetric we also know that the

z score
Number of standard deviations above or below the mean.

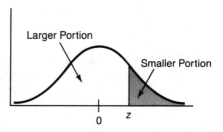

z	Mean to z	Larger Portion	Smaller Portion	z	Mean to z	Larger Portion	Smaller Portion
0.00	0.0000	0.5000	0.5000	0.45	0.1736	0.6736	0.3264
0.01	0.0040	0.5040	0.4960	0.46	0.1772	0.6772	0.3228
0.02	0.0080	0.5080	0.4920	0.47	0.1808	0.6808	0.3192
0.03	0.0120	0.5120	0.4880	0.48	0.1844	0.6844	0.3156
0.04	0.0160	0.5160	0.4840	0.49	0.1879	0.6879	0.3121
0.05	0.0199	0.5199	0.4801	0.50	0.1915	0.6915	0.3085
...	...	...	...	...	...	...	...
0.97	0.3340	0.8340	0.1660	1.42	0.4222	0.9222	0.0778
0.98	0.3365	0.8365	0.1635	1.43	0.4236	0.9236	0.0764
0.99	0.3389	0.8389	0.1611	1.44	0.4251	0.9251	0.0749
1.00	0.3413	0.8413	0.1587	1.45	0.4265	0.9265	0.0735
1.01	0.3438	0.8438	0.1562	1.46	0.4279	0.9279	0.0721
1.02	0.3461	0.8461	0.1539	1.47	0.4292	0.9292	0.0708
1.03	0.3485	0.8485	0.1515	1.48	0.4306	0.9306	0.0694
1.04	0.3508	0.8508	0.1492	1.49	0.4319	0.9319	0.0681
1.05	0.3531	0.8531	0.1469	1.50	0.4332	0.9332	0.0668
...	...	...	...	...	...	...	...
1.95	0.4744	0.9744	0.0256	2.40	0.4918	0.9918	0.0082
1.96	0.4750	0.9750	0.0250	2.41	0.4920	0.9920	0.0080
1.97	0.4756	0.9756	0.0244	2.42	0.4922	0.9922	0.0078
1.98	0.4761	0.9761	0.0239	2.43	0.4925	0.9925	0.0075
1.99	0.4767	0.9767	0.0233	2.44	0.4927	0.9927	0.0073
2.00	0.4772	0.9772	0.0228	2.45	0.4929	0.9929	0.0071
2.01	0.4778	0.9778	0.0222	2.46	0.4931	0.9931	0.0069
2.02	0.4783	0.9783	0.0217	2.47	0.4932	0.9932	0.0068
2.03	0.4788	0.9788	0.0212	2.48	0.4934	0.9934	0.0066
2.04	0.4793	0.9793	0.0207	2.49	0.4936	0.9936	0.0064
2.05	0.4798	0.9798	0.0202	2.50	0.4938	0.9938	0.0062

probability that a child will score more than one standard deviation *below* the mean of the population. is .1587.

Now suppose that we want the probability that the child will be more than one standard deviation (10 points) from the mean *in either direction*. This is a simple matter of the summation of areas. Because we know that the normal distribution is symmetric, then the area below $z = -1$ will be the same as the area above $z = +1$. This is why the table does not contain negative values of z—they are not needed. We already know that the areas in which we are interested are each 0.1587. Then the total area outside $z = \pm 1$ must be

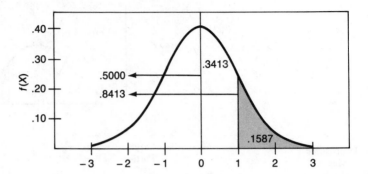

FIGURE 7-7
Illustrative Areas under the
Normal Curve

0.1587 + 0.1587 = 0.3174. The converse is also true. If the area outside $z = \pm 1$ is 0.3174, then the area between $z = +1$ and $z = -1$ is equal to $1 - 0.3174 = 0.6826$. Thus the probability that a child will score between 40 and 60 is .6826.

To extend this procedure, consider the situation in which we want to know the probability that a score will be between 30 and 40. A little arithmetic will show that this is simply the probability of falling between 1.0 standard deviation below the mean and 2.0 standard deviations below the mean. This situation is diagrammed in Figure 7-8. (*Hint:* It is always wise to draw simple diagrams such as Figure 7-8. They eliminate many errors and make clear the area(s) for which you are looking.)

From Appendix D, Table 9, we know that the area from the mean to $z = -2.0$ is 0.4772 and from the mean to $z = -1.0$ is 0.3413. The difference in these two areas must represent the area between $z = -2.0$ and $z = -1.0$. This area is $0.4772 - 0.3413 = 0.1359$. Thus the probability that Behavior Problem scores drawn at random from a normally distributed population will be between 30 and 40 is .1359.

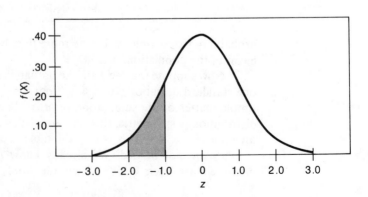

FIGURE 7-8
Area between 1.0 and 2.0
Standard Deviations below the
Mean

7-2 SETTING PROBABLE LIMITS ON AN OBSERVATION

For a final example, consider the situation in which we want to identify limits within which we have some specified degree of certainty that a given child sampled at random will fall. In other words we want to make a statement of the form "If I draw a child at random from this population, 95% of the time her score will lie between ____ and ____." From Figure 7-9 you can see the limits we want—the limits that include 95% of the scores in the population.

If we are looking for the limits within which 95% of the scores fall, we also are looking for the limits beyond which the remaining 5% of the scores fall. To rule out this remaining 5%, we want to find that value of z that cuts off 2.5% at each end ("tail") of the distribution. (We would not need to use symmetric limits, but we typically do because they usually make the most sense and produce the shortest interval.) From Appendix D, Table 9, we see that these values are $z = \pm 1.96$. Thus we can say that 95% of the time a child's score sampled at random will fall between 1.96 standard deviations above the mean and 1.96 standard deviations below the mean.

Because we generally want to express our answers in terms of raw Behavior Problem scores rather than z scores, we must do a little more work. To obtain the raw score limits we simply work the formula for z backward, solving for X instead of z. Thus if we want to state the limits within which 95% of the population falls, we want to find those scores that are 1.96 standard deviations above or below the mean of the population. This can be written as

$$z = \frac{X - \mu}{\sigma}$$

$$\pm 1.96 = \frac{X - \mu}{\sigma}$$

$$X - \mu = \pm 1.96\sigma$$

$$X = \mu \pm 1.96\sigma$$

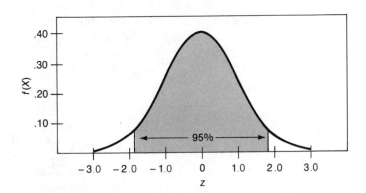

FIGURE 7-9
Values of z That Enclose 95%
of the Behavior Problem Scores

where the values of X corresponding to $(\mu + 1.96\sigma)$ and $(\mu - 1.96\sigma)$ represent the limits we seek. For our example the limits would be

$$\text{Limits} = 50 \pm (1.96)(10) = 50 \pm 19.6 = 30.4 \text{ and } 69.6$$

Thus the probability is .95 that a child's score (X) chosen at random would be between 30.4 and 69.6. We may not be very interested in low scores, because they don't represent problems. But anyone with a score of 69.6 is a problem to someone. Only 2.5% of children score that high.

What we have just discussed is closely related to, but not quite the same as, what we will later consider under the heading of confidence limits. The major difference is that here we knew the population mean and were trying to estimate where a single observation (X) would fall. When we discuss confidence limits, we will have a sample mean (or some other statistic) and will want to set limits that have a .95 probability of bracketing the population mean (or some other relevant parameter). You do not need to know anything at all about confidence limits at this point. I simply mention the issue to forestall any confusion in the future.

7-3 USING THE NORMAL DISTRIBUTION TO CALCULATE PERCENTILES

In the previous examples we have used the normal distribution to calculate areas or probabilities above, below, or between given values of X. The same procedures can be used to solve questions dealing with percentiles.

In Chapter 4 we calculated percentiles by looking at the frequency distribution of the data and almost literally counting up the scores falling below some specified point. However, if we know that the distribution is normal (or even approximately normal), we can use what we already know to approximate percentiles and percentile ranks. As an example, suppose that we want to calculate the 90th percentile for Behavior Problem scores. We might, for example, want to use this as a cutoff to identify people falling in a clinical range—that is, showing clinically severe behavior problems. We know that the 90th percentile is that point below which 90% of the scores fall. From Appendix D, Table 9, we find that 90% of the area falls below $z = 1.28$. What we need to know is what value of X (the score) corresponds to $z = 1.28$. We can obtain this value by substituting the values of μ, σ, and z in the formula for z and then solving for X.

$$z = \frac{X - \mu}{\sigma}$$

$$1.28 = \frac{X - 50}{10}$$

$$10(1.28) = X - 50$$

$$12.8 = X - 50$$

$$50 + 12.8 = X$$

$$X = 62.8$$

Thus the 90th percentile among Behavior Problem scores is 62.8.

To take another example, suppose that we wanted to find the 25th percentile. From Appendix D, Table 9, we find that a z score of -0.67 cuts off the lowest 25%. (Notice that z is negative because we are looking at a point in the lower half of the distribution.) To obtain the price corresponding to $z = -0.67$ we use the same procedure as in the previous example.

$$z = \frac{X - \mu}{\sigma}$$

$$-0.67 = \frac{X - 50}{10}$$

$$10(-0.67) = X - 50$$

$$-6.7 = X - 50$$

$$50 - 6.7 = X$$

$$X = 43.3$$

Thus the 25th percentile is at 43.3.

Now suppose that the child actually scored 75. What is the percentile rank of that child's score? Here we solve the problem in reverse. Instead of finding the z that corresponds to a particular area and then solving for X, we start with X, convert it to z, and find the area corresponding to that value of z. For our example

$$z = \frac{X - \mu}{\sigma}$$

$$= \frac{75 - 50}{10} = \frac{25}{10} = 2.5$$

From Appendix D, Table 9, we find that 99.38% of the area lies below $z = 2.5$. We would therefore conclude that a child scoring 75 has a percentile rank of 99.3%, which makes him a very problematic child relative to other children.

When using the normal distribution to deal with percentiles, it is important to keep in mind that such a procedure requires the assumption that the scores in question are at least approximately normal. If the data are badly skewed or otherwise nonnormal, obtaining percentiles by means of the normal distribution could lead to quite distorted results.

7-4 MEASURES RELATED TO z

Standard scores
Scores with a predetermined mean and standard deviation.

We already have seen that the z formula given earlier can be used to convert a distribution with any mean and variance to a distribution with a mean of 0 and a standard deviation (and variance) of 1. We frequently refer to such transformed scores as **standard scores**. There are, however, other transformational scoring systems with particular properties, some of which people use every day without realizing what they are.

A good example of such a scoring system is the common IQ. The raw scores from an IQ test are routinely transformed to a distribution with a mean of 100 and a standard deviation of 15 (or 16 in the case of the Binet). Knowing this, you can readily convert an individual's IQ (e.g., 120) to his position in terms of standard deviations above or below the mean (i.e., you can calculate his z score). Because IQ scores are more or less normally distributed, you can then convert z into a percentile measure by use of Appendix D, Table 9. (In this example a score of 120 is at approximately the 91st percentile.)

Some other very common examples are the nationally administered examinations, such as the SAT. In these cases the raw scores are transformed by the producers of the test and are reported as coming from a distribution with a mean of 500 and a standard deviation of 100 (at least when the tests were first developed). Such a scoring system is very easy to devise. We start by converting raw scores to z scores (on the basis of the raw score mean and standard deviation). We then convert the z scores to the particular scoring system we have in mind. Thus

$$\text{New score} = \text{New S.D.}(z) + \text{New mean}$$

where z represents the z score corresponding to the individual's raw score. For the SAT

$$\text{New score} = 100(z) + 500$$

7-5 SUMMARY

In this chapter we have examined the normal distribution. We have seen how to use the tables of the standard normal distribution to obtain areas under any normal distribution and have seen that areas are directly related to probabilities. We also have seen how to use the normal distribution to calculate percentiles and percentile ranks. Some of the most important terms in the chapter are:

- **Normal distribution**
- **Abscissa**
- **Ordinate**
- **Standard normal distribution**
- **Linear transformation**
- **z score**
- **Standard scores**

7-6 EXERCISES

7–1 Assume that the following data represent a population with $\mu = 4$ and $\sigma = 1.63$:

$$X = 1 \quad 2 \quad 2 \quad 3 \quad 3 \quad 3 \quad 4 \quad 4 \quad 4 \quad 4 \quad 5 \quad 5 \quad 5 \quad 6 \quad 6 \quad 7$$

(a) Plot the distribution as given.
(b) Convert the distribution in Exercise 7-1(a) to a distribution of $X - \mu$.
(c) Convert the distribution in Exercise 7-1(b) to a distribution of z.

7–2 Using the distribution in Exercise 7-1, calculate z scores for $X = 2.5$, 6.2, and 9. Interpret these results.

7–3 Suppose that we want to study the errors found in the performance of a simple task. We take a piggy bank containing approximately $10.00 in pennies and ask a large number of subjects to count the pennies. We find that the mean number of pennies reported is 975 with a standard deviation of 15. Assume that the distribution of counts is normal.
(a) What percentage of the counts will lie between 960 and 990?
(b) What percentage of the counts will lie below 975?
(c) What percentage of the counts will lie below 990?

7–4 Using the example from Exercise 7-3:
(a) What two values of X (the count) would encompass the middle 50% of the results?
(b) 75% of the counts would be less than _____.
(c) 95% of the counts would be between _____ and _____.

7–5 The chairman of my department has just finished counting the pennies, and he claims that there are only 950 pennies in the pile. Is this count a reasonable answer if he was counting conscientiously? Why or why not?

7–6 A set of reading scores for fourth-grade children has a mean of 25 and a standard deviation of 5. A set of scores for ninth-grade children has a mean of 30 and a standard deviation of 10. Assume that the distributions are normal.
(a) Draw a rough sketch of these data, putting both groups in the same figure.
(b) What percentage of fourth graders score better than the average ninth grader?
(c) What percentage of the ninth graders score worse than the average fourth grader? (We will come back to

the idea behind these calculations when we study power in Chapter 15.)

7–7 Under what conditions would the answers to (b) and (c) of Exercise 7-6 be equal?

7–8 A certain diagnostic test is indicative of problems only if a child scores at or below the 10th percentile. If the mean score is 150 with a standard deviation of 30, what would the diagnostically meaningful cutoff be?

7–9 A dean must distribute salary raises for next year. She has decided that the mean raise is to be $2000, the standard deviation of raises is to be $400, and the distribution is normal.
(a) Ten percent of the faculty will have a raise equal to or greater than $_____.
(b) The 5% of the faculty who haven't done anything useful in years will receive no more than $_____ each.

7–10 We have sent out everyone in a large introductory psychology course to check whether people use seat belts. Each has been told to look at 100 cars and to count the number of people wearing seat belts. The number found by any given student is considered that student's score. The mean score for the class is 30 with a standard deviation of 7.
(a) Diagram this distribution, assuming that the counts are normally distributed.
(b) A student who has done very little work all year has reported finding 50 users (out of 100). Do we have reason to suspect that the student just made up a number rather than actually counting?

7–11 Several years ago a friend produced a diagnostic test of language problems. A score on her scale is obtained simply by counting the number of language constructions (e.g., plural, negative, passive) that the child produces correctly in response to specific prompts from the person administering the test. The test has a mean of 48 and a standard deviation of 7. Parents have trouble understanding the meaning of a score on this scale, and my friend wants to convert the scores to a mean of 80 and a standard deviation of 10 (to make them more like the kinds of grades parents are used to). How should she go about this task?

7–12 Unfortunately the whole world is not built upon the principle of a normal distribution. In the preceding example the real distribution is badly skewed because most children do not have language problems and therefore produce all constructions correctly.

(a) Diagram how this distribution might look.

(b) How would you go about finding the cutoff for the bottom 10% if the distribution is not normal?

7–13 In October of 1981 the mean and standard deviation on the Graduate Record Exam (GRE) for all people taking the exam were 489 and 126, respectively. Use what you know about the normal distribution to find the percentile rank of a score of 600.

7–14 In Exercise 7-13 what score would correspond to the 75th percentile?

7–15 For all seniors and nonenrolled college graduates taking the GRE in October 1981 the mean and standard deviation were 507 and 118. How does this change the answers to Exercises 7-13 and 7-14?

7–16 What does the answer to Exercise 7-15 suggest about the importance of reference groups?

7–17 Using the data in Appendix C, Data Set, recalculate the answer to Exercise 4-13 using the normal approximation.

7–18 Using the normal approximation with the data in Appendix C, Data Set, calculate the 80th percentile for ADDSC.

7–19 What is the 75th percentile for GPA in Appendix C, Data Set?

7–20 How do the answers for Exercises 7-19 and 4-15 compare? Why are they not in closer agreement?

7–21 Make up sample data that are markedly skewed and demonstrate that using the normal distribution to approximate percentiles produces misleading results.

7–22 Assuming that the Behavior Problem scores discussed in this chapter come from a population with a mean of 50 and a standard deviation of 10, what would be a diagnostically meaningful cutoff if you wanted to identify those children who score in the highest 2% of the population?

BASIC CONCEPTS OF PROBABILITY

In Chapter 7 we began to make use of the concept of probability. For example, we saw that about 68% of children have Behavior Problem scores falling between 40 and 60, and we thus concluded that if we chose a child at random, the probability that he or she would score between 40 and 60 is .68. When we begin concentrating on inferential statistics in Chapter 11, we will rely heavily on statements of probability. There we will be making statements of the form "If this hypothesis is correct, the probability is only .015 that we would have obtained the data that we actually obtained." If we are to rely on statements of probability, then it is important to understand what we mean by probability and to understand a few basic rules for computing and manipulating probabilities. That is the purpose of this chapter.

The material covered in this chapter has been selected for one of two reasons. Either it is directly applicable to understanding material presented in the remainder of the book or it is intended to allow you to make very simple calculations of probabilities that are likely to be useful to you. Material that does not satisfy one of these qualifications has been deliberately omitted. Thus, for example, we will not consider such things as the probability of drawing the queen of hearts, given that 14 cards, including the four of hearts, have already been drawn. Nor will we consider the probability that your desk light will burn out in the next 25 hours of use, given that it has already lasted 250 hours. The student who is interested in these topics is encouraged to take a course in probability theory, in which such material can be covered in depth.

8-1 PROBABILITY

The concept of probability can be viewed in several different ways. There is not even general agreement as to what we mean by the word *probability*. The oldest and most common definition of a probability is what is called the **analytic view**. I have a bag of caramels hidden in the drawer of my desk. (It is hidden because I have learned not to trust my colleagues.) This bag contains 85 of the light caramels, which I like, and 15 of the dark ones, which I save for candy-grubbing

Analytic view
Definition of probability in terms of analysis of possible outcomes.

colleagues. Being hungry, I reach into the bag and grab a caramel at random. What is the probability that I will pull out a light-colored caramel? Because 85 out of 100 caramels are light and because I am sampling at random, the probability (p) of drawing a light caramel is $85/100 = .85$. This example illustrates one definition of probability.

> If an event can occur in A ways and can fail to occur in B ways and if all possible ways are equally likely (e.g., each caramel has an equal chance of being drawn), then the probability of its occurrence is $A/(A + B)$, and the probability of its failing to occur is $B/(A + B)$.

Because there were 85 ways of drawing a light caramel (one for each of the 85 light caramels) and 15 ways of selecting a dark caramel, $A = 85$, $B = 15$, and $p(A) = 85/(85 + 15) = .85$.

Relative frequency view
Definition of probability in terms of past performance.

Sample with replacement
Sampling in which the item drawn on trial N is replaced before the drawing on trial $N + 1$.

An alternative view of probability is the **relative frequency view**. Suppose that we keep drawing caramels from this bag, noting the color on each draw. In conducting this sampling study we **sample with replacement**, meaning that each caramel is replaced before the next one is drawn. If we made a very large number of draws, we would find that (approximately) 85% of the draws would result in a light caramel. Thus we might define probability as the limit† of the relative frequency of occurrence of the desired event that we approach as the number of draws increases.

Subjective probability
Definition of probability in terms of personal subjective belief in the likelihood of an outcome.

There is yet a third concept of probability that is advocated by a number of theorists. That is the concept of **subjective probability**. By this definition probability represents an individual's subjective belief in the likelihood of the occurrence of an event. Thus, for example, the statement "I think that tomorrow will be a good day" is a subjective statement of degree of belief, which probably has very little to do with the long-range relative frequency of occurrence of good days, and in fact may have no mathematical basis whatsoever. This is not to say, however, that such a view of probability has no legitimate claim for our attention. Subjective probabilities play an extremely important role in human decision making and govern all aspects of our behavior. At the same time, statistical decisions as we will make them can generally be stated with respect to more mathematical approaches, although even here the *interpretation* of these probabilities has a strong subjective component.

Although the particular definition of probability that you or I prefer may be important to each of us, any of the definitions will lead to essentially the same result in terms of hypothesis testing, which is discussed in Chapter 11 (although those who favor subjective probabilities may not agree with the general hypothesis-testing orientation). In actual fact most people use the different approaches interchangeably. When we say that the probability of losing at Russian roulette is 1/6, we are referring to the fact that one of the gun's six

---

†The word *limit* refers to the fact that as we sample more and more caramels the proportion of light will get closer and closer to some value. After 100 draws the proportion of light might be .84; after 1000 draws the proportion might be .852; after 10,000 it might be .8496, and so on. Notice that the answer is coming closer and closer to $p = .8500000\ldots$. The value that is being approached is called the limit.

cylinders has a bullet in it. When we buy a particular car because *Consumer Reports* said that it has a good repair record, we are responding to the fact that a high proportion of these cars have been relatively trouble-free. When we say that the probability of the Yankees winning the pennant is high, we are stating our subjective belief in the likelihood of that event. But when we reject some hypothesis because there is a very low probability that the data would have been obtained if the hypothesis had been true, it is not important which view of probability we hold.

8-2 BASIC TERMINOLOGY AND RULES

Event
The outcome of a trial.

The basic bit of data for a probability theorist is called an **event**. The word *event* is a term that statisticians use to cover just about anything. An event can be the occurrence of a king when dealing cards, a score of 36 on a scale of likability, a classification as "female" of the next person appointed to the Supreme Court, or the mean of a sample. Whenever you speak of the probability of something, the something is called an event. When we are dealing with something as simple as flipping a coin, the event is the outcome of that flip—either a head or a tail. When we draw caramels out of a bag, the possible events are light and dark; and when we speak of a grade in a course, the possible events are the letters A, B, C, D, and F.

Independent events
Events are independent when the occurrence of one has no effect on the probability of the occurrence of the other.

Two events are said to be **independent** when the occurrence or nonoccurrence of one event has no effect on the occurrence or nonoccurrence of the other. Thus the voting behavior of two randomly chosen subjects normally would be assumed to be independent, especially with a secret ballot, because how one person votes could not be expected to influence how the other will vote. However, the voting behavior of two members of the same family would probably not be independent events, because those people share many of the same beliefs and attitudes.

Mutually exclusive
Two events are mutually exclusive when the occurrence of one precludes the occurrence of the other.

Exhaustive
A set of events that represents all possible outcomes.

Two events are said to be **mutually exclusive** if the occurrence of one event precludes the occurrence of the other. Thus the standard college classes of first year, sophomore, junior, or senior are mutually exclusive because one person cannot be a member of more than one class. Finally a set of events is said to be **exhaustive** if it includes all possible outcomes. Thus the four college classes are exhaustive with respect to full-time undergraduates, who have to fall in one of these categories—if only to please the registrar's office. At the same time they are not exhaustive with respect to total university enrollments, which include graduate students, medical students, nonmatriculated students, hangers-on, and so forth.

As you already know—or could deduce from our definitions of probability—probabilities range between .00 and 1.00. If some event has a probability of 1.00, then it is certain to occur. If its probability is .00, it is certain not to occur. The closer the probability is to either of those extremes, the more likely or unlikely is the occurrence of the event.

BASIC LAWS OF PROBABILITY

Two very important theorems are central to any discussion of probability. They are often referred to as the additive and multiplicative rules.

The Additive Rule   To illustrate the additive rule we will complicate the earlier example by eating some of the light caramels and replacing them with wooden cubes. We now have 30 light caramels, 15 dark caramels, and 55 rather taste-less wooden cubes. Given these frequencies, we know from the analytic defini-tion of probability that $p(\text{light}) = 30/100 = .30$, $p(\text{dark}) = 15/100 = .15$, and $p(\text{wooden}) = 55/100 = .55$. But what is the probability that I will draw a caramel, either light *or* dark, rather than a wooden cube? Here we need the **additive law of probability**:

Additive law of probability
The rule giving the probability of the occurrence of one or more mutually exclusive events.

> Given a set of mutually exclusive events, the probability of occurrence of one event *or* another is equal to the sum of their separate probabilities.

Thus $p(\text{light or dark}) = p(\text{light}) + p(\text{dark}) = .30 + .15 = .45$. Notice that we have imposed the restriction that the events must be mutually exclusive, meaning that the occurrence of one event precludes the occurrence of the other. About one-half of the population of this country are female and about one-half of the population have traditionally feminine names. But the probability that a person chosen at random will be female *or* will have a feminine name is obviously not $.50 + .50 = 1.00$. The two events are not mutually exclusive. However, the probability that a girl born in Vermont in 1981 was named Sarah or Jessica equals $p(\text{Sarah}) + p(\text{Jessica}) = .047 + .039 = .086$.

The Multiplicative Rule   Now we will continue with the bag of caramels in which $p(\text{light}) = .30$ and $p(\text{dark}) = .15$, and the probability of a wooden cube $= .55$. Suppose that I draw two caramels, replacing the first before drawing the second. What is the probability that I will draw a light one the first time *and* a light one the second? Here we need to invoke the **multiplicative law of probability**:

Multiplicative law of probability
The rule giving the probability of the joint occurrence of independent events.

> The probability of the joint occurrence of two or more independent events is the product of their individual probabilities.

Thus $p(\text{light, light}) = p(\text{light}) \times p(\text{light}) = .30 \times .30 = .09$. Similarly the proba-bility of a light caramel followed by a dark one is $p(\text{light, dark}) = p(\text{light}) \times p(\text{dark}) = .30 \times .15 = .045$. Notice that we have restricted ourselves to independent events, meaning that the occurrence of one event has no effect on the occurrence or nonoccurrence of the other. Because sex and name are not independent, it is also wrong to state that $p(\text{female with feminine name}) = .50 \times .50 = .25$.

Finally we can take a simple example that illustrates both the additive and the multiplicative laws. What is the probability that over two trials (sampling with replacement) I will draw one light caramel and one dark one, *ignoring the order in which they are drawn*? First we use the multiplicative rule to calculate

$$p(\text{light, dark}) = .30 \times .15 = .045$$

$$p(\text{dark, light}) = .15 \times .30 = .045$$

Because these two outcomes satisfy our requirement (and because they are the only ones that do), we now need to know the probability that one or the other of these outcomes will occur. Here we apply the additive rule:

$$p(\text{light, dark}) + p(\text{dark, light}) = .045 + .045 = .09$$

Thus the probability of obtaining one caramel of each color over two draws is .09—that is, it will occur a little less than one-tenth of the time.

JOINT AND CONDITIONAL PROBABILITIES

It is important to define two types of probabilities that play an important role in discussions of probability. They are joint probabilities and conditional probabilities.

Joint probability
The probability of the co-occurrence of two or more events.

A **joint probability** is defined simply as the probability of the co-occurrence of two or more events. For example, the probability that both you and I are over 6' tall is a joint probability. Similarly, the probability that the next six people to enter a theater are all wearing brown shoes is also a joint probability. Given two events A and B, their joint probability is denoted $p(A, B)$. *If* those events are independent, then the probability of the joint occurrence can be obtained by using the multiplicative rule, as we saw for $p(\text{light, dark})$.

Conditional probability
The probability of one event *given* the occurrence of some other event.

A **conditional probability** is the probability that one event will occur *given* that some other event has occurred. The probability that you will have an automobile accident given that you are drunk is an example of a conditional probability. The probability of the Yankees winning the World Series given that they win the pennant is another. With two events, A and B, the conditional probability of A given B is denoted $p(A|B)$. Suppose that a radio station sampled 100 people, 20 of whom have children. They found that 30 of the people sampled used seat belts but that 15 of those with children used them. Then the probability that a person sampled at random will use a seat belt is $30/100 = .30$, and the conditional probability of using seat belts given that you have children is $15/20 = .75$.

It is important not to confuse joint and conditional probabilities. The probability that you have one child who is three and one who is six is a joint probability. On the other hand the probability that you have a six-year-old *given* that you have a three-year-old is a conditional probability. This conditional probability is higher than the joint probability, partly because if you have a three-year-old, you are at least in the right age group to also have a six-year-old. To take another example, the probability that you have been drinking and that you have an accident at night is a joint probability. This probability is not very high since relatively few people are drinking at any one time and relatively few people have accidents. However, the probability that you have been drinking *given that* you have an accident is a conditional probability. At night this conditional probability approaches .50 since nearly half of all automobile accidents at night in the United States involve alcohol. Notice that both p(drinking|accident) and p(accident|drinking) are conditional probabilities involving alcohol and highway accidents. However, these two probabilities are nowhere near equal.

8-3   DISCRETE VERSUS CONTINUOUS VARIABLES

In Chapter 2 a distinction was made between discrete and continuous variables. As mathematicians view things, a discrete variable is one that can take on a countable number of different values, whereas a continuous variable is one that can take on an infinite number of different values. For example, the number of people attending a specific movie theater for each of the next 52 weeks is a discrete variable because we literally can count the number of people entering the theater, and there is no such thing as a fractional person. However, the distance between two people in a study of personal space is a continuous variable because the distance could be 2′, or 2.8′, or 2.8173765814′. Although the distinction given here is technically correct, common usage is somewhat different.

In practice when we speak of a discrete variable, we *usually* mean a variable that takes on one of a relatively small number of possible values (e.g., years of education). A variable that can take on one of many possible values is generally treated as a continuous variable. Thus we usually think of an IQ score as a continuous variable even though we recognize that IQ scores come in whole units and you will not find someone with an IQ of 105.317.

The distinction between discrete and continuous variables was reintroduced here because the *distributions* of the two kinds of variables are treated somewhat differently in probability theory. With discrete variables we can speak of the probability of a specific outcome. With continuous variables, on the other hand, we need to speak of the probability of obtaining a value that falls within a specific *interval*.

8-4   PROBABILITY DISTRIBUTIONS FOR DISCRETE VARIABLES

An interesting example of a discrete probability distribution is seen in Figure 8-1. The data plotted in this figure come from a study by Campbell, Converse, and Rogers (1976), in which they asked 2164 respondents to rate on a 1−5 scale the importance they attach to various aspects of their lives (1 = extremely important, 5 = not at all important). Figure 8-1 presents the distribution of responses for several of these aspects. You will note that the possible values of X (the rating) are presented on the abscissa, and relative frequency (or probability) of people choosing that response is plotted on the ordinate. From this figure you

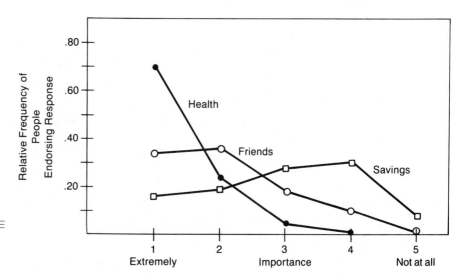

FIGURE 8-1
**Distributions of Importance
Ratings of Three Aspects of
Life**

can see that the distribution of responses to questions concerning health, friends, and savings are quite different. The probability that a person chosen at random will consider his or her health to be extremely important is .70, whereas the probability that the same person will consider a large bank account to be extremely important is only .16. (So much for stereotypic conceptions of the American Dream.)

As another example, consider the case of traffic lights. On my way to and from work every day I have to pass through four widely spaced, and therefore more or less independent, traffic lights. Having nothing better to do with my time (and needing an example for this book), I have kept track of how often I have had to stop at each light. Occasionally I have had to stop at all four lights, usually I have had to stop for one to three lights, and once in a great while I haven't had to stop for any. The data are plotted in Figure 8-2, in which once again the probability values have been computed as relative frequencies. From this figure you can see that the probability of not having to stop for any lights on my way to work tomorrow is .03, whereas the probability of stopping at all four is .11. The most likely event is having to stop for two lights, and that has a probability of .36. This distribution is asymmetric because the lights are red or yellow for a longer period of time in each cycle than they are green, and I never, never accelerate through a yellow—well, hardly ever.

8-5   PROBABILITY DISTRIBUTIONS FOR CONTINUOUS VARIABLES

When we move from discrete to continuous probability distributions, things become slightly more complicated. We dealt with a continuous distribution when we considered the normal distribution in Chapter 7. You may recall that

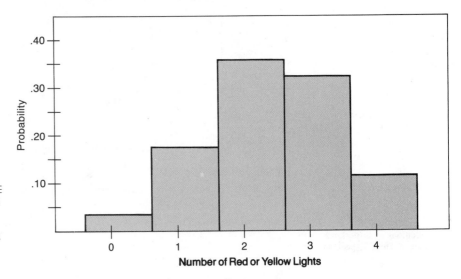

FIGURE 8-2
Probability Distribution for the Number of Traffic Lights That Are Red or Yellow. The Individual Probabilities for 0–4 Lights Are .0311, .1719, .3560, .3278, and .1132, Respectively.

in that chapter we labeled the ordinate of the distribution "density." We also spoke in terms of intervals rather than in terms of specific outcomes. Now we need to elaborate somewhat on those points.

In Figure 8-3 is the approximate distribution of the age at which children first learn to walk. (Figure 8-3 is based on data from Hindley et al., 1966.) The mean is approximately 14 months, the standard deviation is approximately three months, and the distribution is positively skewed. You will notice that in this figure the ordinate is labeled "density," whereas in Figures 8-1 and 8-2 it was labeled "probability." **Density** is not synonymous with probability, and it is probably best thought of as merely the height of the curve at different values of X. The reason for changing the label on the ordinate is that we now are dealing with a continuous distribution rather than a discrete one. If you think about it for a moment, you will realize that although the highest point of the curve is at

Density
Height of the curve for a given value of X—closely related to the probability of an observation in an interval around X.

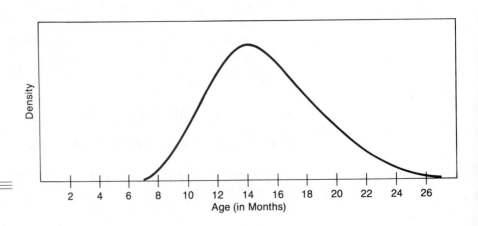

FIGURE 8-3
Age at Which a Child First Walks Unaided

14 months, the probability that a child picked at random will first walk at *exactly* 14 months (i.e., 14.000000000000 months) is infinitely small—statisticians would argue that it is in fact 0. Similarly the probability of first walking at 14.000000000001 months is also infinitely small. This suggests that it does not make any sense to speak of the probability of any *specific* outcome. On the other hand we know that many children start walking at *approximately* 14 months, and it does make sense to speak of the probability of obtaining a score falling within some specified interval. For example, we might be interested in the probability that an infant will start walking at 14 months plus or minus one-half month. Such an interval is shown in Figure 8-4. If we arbitrarily define the total area under the curve to be 1.00, then the shaded area in Figure 8-4 between points *a* and *b* will be equal to the probability that an infant chosen at random will begin walking at this time. Those of you who have had calculus will probably recognize that if we knew the form of the equation that describes this distribution (i.e., if we knew the equation for the curve), then we would simply need to integrate the function over the interval from *a* to *b*. Those of you who have not had calculus are not at any disadvantage, however, because the distributions with which we will work are adequately approximated by other distributions that already have been tabled. In this book we will never integrate functions, but we will often refer to tables of distributions. You have already had experience with this procedure with regard to the normal distribution in Chapter 7.

   We have just considered the area in Figure 8-4 between *a* and *b*, which is centered on the mean. However, the same things could be said for any interval. In Figure 8-4 you can see the area corresponding to the period that is one-half month on either side of 18 months (denoted as the shaded area between *c* and *d*). Although there is not enough information in this example for us to calculate actual probabilities, it should be clear by inspection of Figure 8-4 that the one-month interval around 14 months has a higher probability (greater shaded area) than the one-month interval around 18 months.

   A good way to get a feel for areas under a curve is to take a piece of transparent graph paper and lay it on top of the figure (or use a regular sheet of

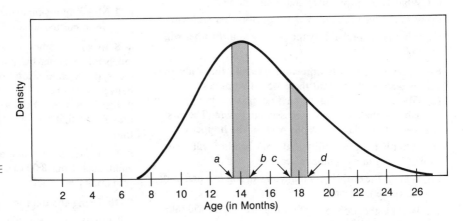

FIGURE 8-4
Probability of First Walking during One-Week Intervals Centered on 14 and 18 Months

graph paper and hold the two up to a light). If we then count the number of squares falling within a specified interval and divide by the total number of squares under the whole curve, we will approximate the probability that a randomly drawn score will fall within that interval. It should be obvious that the smaller the size of the individual squares on the graph paper, the more accurate the approximation.

8-6 SUMMARY

In this chapter we have examined the various definitions of what we mean by the term *probability* and have considered a number of fundamental concepts and rules of probability theory. We also have considered the differences between discrete and continuous variables and their distributions. Some of the most important terms in the chapter are:

□ **Analytic view**   □ **Exhaustive**
□ **Relative frequency view**   □ **Additive law of probability**
□ **Sample with replacement**   □ **Multiplicative law of probability**
□ **Subjective probability**   □ **Joint probability**
□ **Event**   □ **Conditional probability**
□ **Independent events**   □ **Density**
□ **Mutually exclusive**

8-7 EXERCISES

8-1 Give an example of an analytic, a relative frequency, and a subjective view of probability.

8-2 Assume that you have bought a ticket for the local fire department lottery and that your brother has bought two tickets. You have just read that 1000 tickets have been sold.
(a) What is the probability that you will win?
(b) What is the probability that your brother will win?
(c) What is the probability that you *or* your brother will win?

8-3 Now assume in the previous question that only 10 tickets were sold and that there were two prizes.
(a) Given that you don't win first prize, what is the probability that you will win second prize? (The first prize-winning ticket is not put back in the hopper.)
(b) What is the probability that your brother will come in first and you will come in second?
(c) What is the probability that you will come in first and he will come in second?
(d) What is the probability that the two of you will take first and second place?

8-4 Which of the parts of Exercise 8-3 dealt with joint probabilities?

8-5 Which of the parts of Exercise 8-3 dealt with conditional probabilities?

8-6 Make up a simple example of a situation in which you are interested in joint probabilities.

8-7 Make up a simple example of a situation in which you are interested in conditional probabilities.

8-8 In some homes a mother's behavior seems to be independent of her baby's, and vice versa. If the mother looks at her child a total of 2 hours each day and if the baby looks at the mother a total of 3 hours each day, and if they really do behave independently, what is the probability that they will look at each other at the same time?

8-9 In Exercise 8-8 assume that both the mother and child sleep from 8:00 P.M. to 7:00 A.M. What would the probability be now?

8-10 Using the data in Figure 8-2, what is the probability of my having to stop for *at least* three traffic lights?

8–11 Give an example of a common continuous distribution for which we have some real interest in the probability that an observation will fall within some specified interval.

8–12 Give an example of a continuous variable that we routinely treat as if it were discrete.

8–13 Give two examples of discrete variables.

8–14 A graduate admissions committee has finally come to realize that it cannot make valid distinctions between the top applicants. This year the committee rated all 1000 applicants and randomly chose ten from those at or above the 80th percentile. What is the probability that any particular applicant will be admitted (assuming you have no knowledge of her rating).

8–15 With respect to Exercise 8-14, what is the conditional probability that the person will be admitted (a) given that she has the highest rating, and (b) given that she has the lowest rating?

8–16 In Appendix C, Data Set, what is the probability that a person drawn at random will have an ADDSC score greater than 50?

8–17 In Appendix C, Data Set, what is the probability that a male will have an ADDSC score greater than 50?

8–18 In Appendix C, Data Set, what is the probability that a person will drop out of school given that he has an ADDSC score of at least 60?

8–19 How might you use conditional probabilities to determine if an ADDSC cutoff score in Appendix C, Data Set, of 66 is predictive of whether or not a person will drop out of school?

8–20 Compare the conditional probability from Exercise 8-18 with the unconditional probability of dropping out.

9
CORRELATION

The previous chapters have dealt in one way or another with describing data on a single dependent variable. We have discussed the distribution of a variable, how to find its mean and standard deviation, and so on. However, some studies are designed to deal with not one dependent variable, but with two or more. In such cases we often are interested in knowing the *relationship* between two variables rather than in knowing what each variable looks like on its own. To illustrate the kinds of studies that might involve two variables (denoted X and Y), consider the following research questions:

1. Does driving ability (Y) depend upon the amount of alcohol (X) consumed?

2. Does admission to college (Y) relate to the number of extracurricular activities (X) the student engaged in while attending high school?

3. Does rated "likability" (Y) have anything to do with physical attractiveness (X)?

4. Does degree of hoarding behavior (Y) vary as a function of level of deprivation (X) during development?

5. Does the accuracy of performance (Y) decrease as speed (X) increases?

Correlation
Relationship between variables.

Correlation coefficient
A measure of the relationship between variables.

Pearson product-moment correlation coefficient (r)
The most common correlation coefficient.

In each case we are asking if one variable (Y) is related to another variable (X). When we are dealing with the relationship between two variables, we are concerned with **correlation**, and our measure of the degree or strength of this relationship is represented by a **correlation coefficient**. There are in fact a number of different correlation coefficients, depending primarily on the underlying nature of the measurements, but we will see later that in many cases the distinctions among these different coefficients are more apparent than real. For the present we will be concerned with the most common correlation coefficient—the **Pearson product-moment correlation coefficient (r)**.

9-1 SCATTER DIAGRAMS

**Scatter diagram
(Scatter plot)
(Scattergram)**
A figure in which the individual data points are plotted in two-dimensional space.

Predictor variable
The variable from which a prediction is based.

Criterion variable
The variable to be predicted.

When we collect measures on two variables for the purpose of examining the relationship between these variables, one of the most useful techniques for gaining some insight into this relationship is the preparation of a **scatter diagram** (also called a **scatter plot** or **scattergram**). Examples of four such diagrams appear in Figure 9-1. In this figure every experimental subject in the study is represented by a point in two-dimensional space, the coordinates of this point (X_i, Y_i) being the individual's (or object's) scores on variables X and Y, respectively.

In preparing a scatter diagram the **predictor variable** is traditionally represented on the abscissa, or X axis, and the **criterion variable** on the ordinate, or Y axis. If the eventual purpose of the study is the prediction of one variable from knowledge of the other, the distinction is obvious since the criterion variable is that variable to be predicted, while the predictor is that variable from which the prediction is made. If the problem is simply one of obtaining a correlation coefficient, the distinction may be obvious (incidence of cancer would be dependent upon amount smoked rather than the reverse and thus incidence would appear on the ordinate) or it may not (neither running speed nor number of correct choices—common dependent variables in a learning study—is obviously in a dependent position relative to the other). Where the

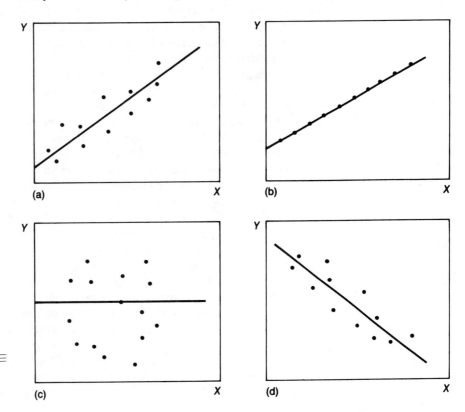

FIGURE 9-1
Scatter Diagrams Illustrating Various Degrees of Relationship

distinction is not obvious, it is irrelevant which variable is labeled X and which Y.

Consider the four hypothetical scatter diagrams in Figure 9-1. Figure 9-1(a) represents a case in which there is a relatively strong relationship between X and Y. Although the relationship is not perfect, it is generally true that as X increases Y also increases. Figure 9-1(b) illustrates the case of a **perfect relationship**. Every increase in X is accompanied by an exactly proportional increase in Y, with all of the points falling on a straight line. In Figure 9-1(c) we have a situation in which there is **no relationship** between X and Y. There is no systematic tendency for Y to vary with X, and knowing the value of X tells us nothing about the corresponding value of Y. Finally, Figure 9-1(d) represents a relatively strong **negative relationship** between X and Y. In fact the degree of relationship, though not its direction, is exactly the same as that shown in Figure 9-1(a) (the points merely have been rotated 90°). In this situation an increase in X corresponds to a general decrease in Y.

The lines that have been superimposed upon Figures 9-1(a–d) represent those straight lines that best fit the data—the way in which this line is "best" will be defined in the next chapter. These lines often are included in a scatter plot because they help to clarify the relationship. The correlation coefficient itself is a measure of how well the line fits the data. Correlation coefficients range between $+1.00$ and -1.00. In Figure 9-1(a) the points cluster reasonably closely about the line and the correlation is high ($r = .81$). In Figure 9-1(b) the points fall exactly on the line and the correlation is perfect ($r = 1.00$). In Figure 9-1(c) the points do not cluster at all around the line and the correlation is 0. And in Figure 9-1(d) the degree of clustering is the same as in Figure 9-1(a), but the relationship is negative, so the correlation is negative ($r = -.81$).

An alternative approach to interpreting scatter diagrams can be seen in Figures 9-2 and 9-3. These figures are based on data from the Achenbach Teacher Report form, which is a rating form for behavior problems similar to the Achenbach Youth Self Report form that we have seen elsewhere. This form, however, is filled out by the teacher rather than the child. (The data have been modified somewhat for purposes of this example.) In Figure 9-2 I have plotted the relationship between the teacher's rating of the degree to which the child exhibits behavior appropriate to the situation and the teacher's rating of how much the child is learning. All ratings are on 7-point scales. The dots with circles around them represent coincident points for two children. In Figure 9-3 I have plotted the degree to which the teacher rates the child as happy and the degree to which he or she shows appropriate behavior.

In these figures I have drawn vertical and horizontal grid lines to divide both axes at their means. For example, the vertical line in Figure 9-2 divides those children who were below the mean on appropriate behavior from those who were above the mean. Similarly, the horizontal line separates those children who were below the mean on the learning variable from those who were above it. In both cases that variable we would be most likely to think of as the dependent variable is plotted on the Y axis, and the likely independent variable on the X axis. Admittedly, the choice is somewhat arbitrary.

Perfect relationship

A situation in which every change in the predictor is matched by a corresponding change in the criterion.

No relationship

A situation in which the predictor and the criterion are linearly independent.

Negative relationship

A situation in which an increase in one variable is accompanied by a decrease in the other.

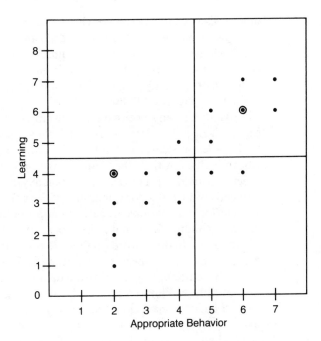

≡ **FIGURE 9-2** ≡

Relationship between Learning and Adaptive Behavior in Normal Boys, Ages 12–16

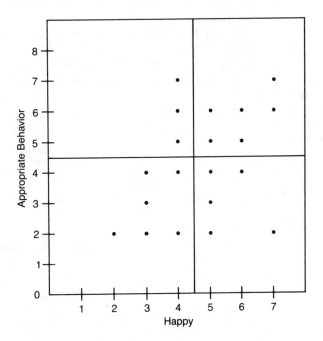

≡ **FIGURE 9-3** ≡

Relationship between Happiness and Appropriate Behavior in Normal Boys, Ages 12–16

If there were a strong positive relationship between learning and appropriate behavior, for example, we would expect that most of the children who were high (above the mean) on one variable would be high on the other. Likewise, most of those who were below the mean on one variable should be below it on the other. Such an idea can be represented by a simple table in which we count the number of children who were above the mean on both variables, the number below the mean on both variables, and the number above the mean on one and below it on the other. Such a table is shown in Table 9-1 for the data in Figures 9-2 and 9-3.

With a strong positive relationship between the two variables, we would expect most of the data points in Table 9-1 to fall in the "Above-Above" and "Below-Below" cells, with only a smattering in the "Above-Below" and "Below-Above" cells. On the other hand, if the two variables are not related to each other we would expect to see approximately equal numbers of data points in the four cells of the table (or quadrants of the scatter diagram). From Table 9-1 we see that for the relationship between appropriate behavior and learning, 17 out of the 20 children fall in the cells associated with a positive relationship between the variables. In other words, if they are below the mean on one variable they are generally below the mean on the other, and vice versa. Only 3 of the children break this pattern. However for the data plotted in Figure 9-3, Table 9-1 shows us that only 12 children are on the same side of the mean on both variables, while 5 children are below the mean on appropriate behavior but above it on happy, and 3 children show the opposite pattern.

These two examples, then, illustrate in a simple way the interpretation of scatter diagrams and the relationship between variables. In the first case there is a strong positive relationship between the variables. In the second case the relationship, although positive, is considerably weaker. This result is reflected in the correlation between the variables. For Figure 9-2 the correlation is .78, whereas the correlation among the data points in Figure 9-3 is .38. (Keep in mind that I have used small samples for the ease of discussion, and these

═══ TABLE 9-1 ═══
Examining Scatter Diagrams
by Division into Quadrants

Appropriate Behavior versus Learning
(Figure 9-2)

		Appropriate Behavior	
		Above Mean	Below Mean
Learning	Above Mean	7	1
	Below Mean	2	10

Happy versus Appropriate Behavior
(Figure 9-3)

		Happy	
		Above Mean	Below Mean
Appropriate Behavior	Above Mean	6	3
	Below Mean	5	6

correlations might well be different if we had larger samples. This is especially true because I hunted around to find somewhat extreme examples and may have managed to find unrepresentative ones. We will address the issue of the unreliability of sample results in later chapters.)

9-2 AN EXAMPLE— THE RELATIONSHIP BETWEEN SPEED AND ACCURACY

Many cognitive psychologists doing research on problem solving have been concerned with the variable of impulsivity and have suggested that impulsive subjects use less effective problem-solving strategies than nonimpulsive subjects. In a study on the relationship between impulsivity and problem-solving strategy, Knehr–McDonald (1984) assessed impulsivity by means of Jerome Kagan's Matching Familiar Figures Test (MFFT). In this task subjects are shown a simple line-drawn figure (the standard) and six similar comparison figures. The task is to identify the comparison figure that exactly matches the standard. (Subjects continue answering until they are correct.) This task is repeated with 12 different sets of figures. Two of the dependent variables are the total time to the first response (summed over all 12 figures) and the total number of errors. By plotting these two variables against each other it is possible to identify groups of subjects with different response styles. Knehr-McDonald's data on this task, slightly modified for the sake of our example, are shown in Table 9-2 and plotted in Figure 9-4. In Table 9-2 you will also see the mean and standard deviation of each variable, along with some intermediate calculations that will prove useful.

From inspection of Figure 9-4 you can see a fairly strong negative relationship between time and errors—as time increases, errors decrease, and vice versa. The relationship is slightly **curvilinear** (i.e., the best-fitting line might in fact be curved), but there is a sufficiently **linear relationship** between the two variables so that a straight line fits the data quite well as a first approximation. This line has been superimposed to make the relationship clearer. Those people whose data points fall in the upper left of the scatter diagram are what Kagan called "impulsives"—they act impulsively, with short response times and many errors. (Impulsives are always sure that "This time I'm right," but it never seems to work out that way.) In the lower right are data points from the "reflectives." These people take a lot of time to think things out, but when they finally do come to a decision, it is usually correct. Away from the line toward the upper right are data points of two or three people who take a long time to think things out and then blow it anyway. Finally, in the lower left are a few of those fast and accurate people who make the rest of us feel bad. The circled points represent multiple subjects with the same X and Y score.

Curvilinear relationship
A situation that is best represented by something other than a straight line.

Linear relationship
A situation in which the best-fitting regression line is a straight line.

TABLE 9-2

Data on Total Errors and
Total Response Time (in
Seconds) for the Matching
Familiar Figures Test

Subject #	1	2	3	4	5	6	7	8	9
Time (X)	285	599	1001	324	595	363	361	870	531
Errors (Y)	11	9	5	15	5	9	4	4	2
Subject #	10	11	12	13	14	15	16	17	18
Time	526	749	852	514	856	467	449	949	929
Errors	6	3	5	7	1	6	12	2	1
Subject #	19	20	21	22	23	24	25	26	27
Time	776	348	507	640	474	497	953	575	1253
Errors	1	10	13	5	4	11	1	7	2
Subject #	28	29	30	31	32	33	34	35	36
Time	762	827	973	571	832	1352	813	603	866
Errors	8	5	0	8	6	1	2	5	4
Subject #	37	38	39	40	41	42	43	44	45
Time	1357	1220	635	1105	242	371	951	1183	1184
Errors	2	1	7	5	15	8	1	1	7
Subject #	46	47	48	49	50	51	52	53	54
Time	977	411	989	930	519	485	434	710	708
Errors	1	12	2	1	5	9	7	3	2
Subject #	55	56	57						
Time	941	170	889						
Errors	5	10	1						

$$\Sigma X = 41{,}253 \qquad \Sigma Y = 305 \qquad \Sigma XY = 174{,}474$$
$$\Sigma X^2 = 34{,}673{,}815 \qquad \Sigma Y^2 = 2483 \qquad N = 57$$
$$\bar{X} = 723.737 \qquad \bar{Y} = 5.351$$
$$s_X = 293.30 \qquad s_Y = 3.90$$

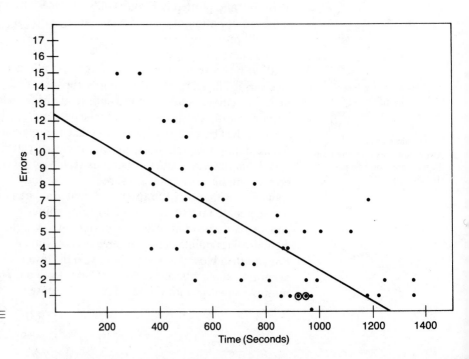

FIGURE 9-4

Scatter Diagram of Time (X)
and Errors (Y)

Errors

Time (Seconds)

THE COVARIANCE

Covariance
A statistic representing the degree to which two variables vary together.

The correlation coefficient that we seek to compute on these data is itself based upon a statistic called the **covariance**. The covariance is basically a number that reflects the degree to which two variables vary together. If, for example, high scores on one variable tend to be paired with high scores on the other, the covariance will be large and positive. If, as happens in our example, high scores on one variable are paired with low scores on the other, the covariance will be large but negative. Finally, when high scores on one variable are paired about equally often with both high and low scores on the other, the covariance will be near zero.

To define the covariance mathematically we can write

$$\text{cov}_{XY} = \frac{\Sigma(X - \bar{X})(Y - \bar{Y})}{N - 1}$$

From this equation it is apparent that the covariance is very similar in form to the variance. If we changed both of the Y's in the equation to X's, we would have s_X^2, or if we changed the X's to Y's, we would have s_Y^2. It is also apparent that the covariance is based on how an observation deviates from the mean on each variable, which is a point that was raised in Section 9-1. Some insight into the meaning of the covariance can be gained by considering what we would expect to find in the case of a high negative correlation, such as the data in Table 9-2. In this situation high times will be paired with low errors. Thus for a slow, accurate subject $(X - \bar{X})$ will be positive, $(Y - \bar{Y})$ will be negative, and their product will be negative. The same is true for a fast, inaccurate subject. Thus the sum of $(X - \bar{X})(Y - \bar{Y})$ will be large and negative, giving a large negative covariance.

Next consider the case of a strong positive relationship. Here large positive values of $(X - \bar{X})$ will most likely be paired with large positive values of $(Y - \bar{Y})$, and vice versa. Thus the sum of products of the deviations will be large and positive, indicating a high positive relationship. Such a situation was illustrated in Figure 9-2.

Finally, consider a situation in which there is no relationship between X and Y. In this case a positive value of $(X - \bar{X})$ sometimes will be paired with a positive value of $(Y - \bar{Y})$, and sometimes with a negative value. The result is that the products of the deviations will be positive about half the time and negative about half the time, producing a near-zero sum and indicating no relationship between the variables. A less extreme case of this was illustrated in Figure 9-3.

For a given set of data, it is possible to show that covariance will be at its positive maximum whenever X and Y are perfectly positively correlated $(r = 1.00)$ and at its negative maximum whenever they are perfectly negatively correlated $(r = -1.00)$. When the two variables are perfectly uncorrelated $(r = 0)$, covariance will be zero.

For computational purposes a simple expression for the covariance is given by

$$\text{cov}_{XY} = \frac{\Sigma(X - \bar{X})(Y - \bar{Y})}{N - 1} = \frac{\Sigma XY - \dfrac{\Sigma X \Sigma Y}{N}}{N - 1}$$

As you should remember from Chapter 2, ΣXY is calculated by multiplying a subject's X score times his Y score and then summing the results. Thus for the data in Table 9-2, $\Sigma XY = (285)(11) + (599)(9) + (1001)(5) + \cdots + (889)(1)$. Using the results for the data in Table 9-2, the covariance is

$$\text{cov}_{XY} = \frac{\Sigma XY - \dfrac{\Sigma X \Sigma Y}{N}}{N-1}$$

$$= \frac{174{,}474 - \dfrac{(41{,}253)(305)}{57}}{56} = -826.17$$

9-4 THE PEARSON PRODUCT-MOMENT CORRELATION COEFFICIENT (r)

What I have just said about the covariance might suggest that we could use the covariance as a measure of the degree of relationship between two variables. An immediate difficulty arises, however, in that the absolute value of cov_{XY} is also a function of the standard deviations of X and Y. Thus $\text{cov}_{XY} = 20$, for example, might reflect a high degree of correlation when the standard deviations are small but a low degree of correlation when the standard deviations are high. To resolve this difficulty we will divide the covariance by the size of the standard deviations and make this our estimate of correlation. Thus we will define

$$r = \frac{\text{cov}_{XY}}{s_X s_Y}$$

Since the maximum value of cov_{XY} turns out to be $\pm s_X s_Y$, it then follows that the limits on r are ± 1.00. One interpretation of r, then, is that it a measure of the degree to which the covariance approaches its maximum.

An equivalent way of writing the preceding equation would be to replace the variances and covariances by their computational formulae and then simplify by cancellation. If we do this, we will arrive at

$$r = \frac{N\Sigma XY - \Sigma X \Sigma Y}{\sqrt{[N\Sigma X^2 - (\Sigma X)^2][N\Sigma Y^2 - (\Sigma Y)^2]}}$$

Sum of squares
The sum of the squared deviations from the mean—
$\Sigma(X - \bar{X})^2$.

Sum of products
The sum of the products of the X and Y deviations from their own means—
$\Sigma(X - \bar{X})(Y - \bar{Y})$.

There is yet a third formula for r, which is algebraically equivalent to the other two but which has the advantage of using the same terminology we will use when we speak of regression (Chapter 10) and the analysis of variance (Chapters 16 through 18). If we define the **sum of squares** of X as $SS_X = \Sigma(X - \bar{X})^2 = \Sigma X^2 - (\Sigma X)^2/N$ and the **sum of products** of X and Y as

$$SP_{XY} = \Sigma(X - \bar{X})(Y - \bar{Y}) = \Sigma XY - \frac{\Sigma X \Sigma Y}{N}$$

then we can define r as

$$r = \frac{SP_{XY}}{\sqrt{SS_X SS_Y}}$$

A nice feature of sums of squares and products is that they lead directly to variances and covariances. Thus

$$s_X^2 = \frac{SS_X}{N-1} \quad \text{and} \quad \text{cov}_{XY} = \frac{SP_{XY}}{N-1}$$

The three equations for r will produce exactly the same answers. The choice is up to you. If your calculator automatically produces standard deviations or if you need them for other purposes anyway, then the first equation is probably most useful. If your calculator doesn't give standard deviations automatically, then the second equation is probably most useful. If you are working with regression, as in the next chapter, the approach using sums of squares and sums of products is convenient.

Applying the first equation to the data in Table 9-2, we have

$$r = \frac{\text{cov}_{XY}}{s_X s_Y} = \frac{-826.17}{(293.30)(3.90)} = -.722$$

Applying the second equation, we have

$$r = \frac{N \Sigma XY - \Sigma X \Sigma Y}{\sqrt{[N \Sigma X^2 - (\Sigma X)^2][N \Sigma Y^2 - (\Sigma Y)^2]}}$$

$$= \frac{57(174{,}474) - (41{,}253)(305)}{\sqrt{[57(34{,}673{,}815) - 41{,}253^2][57(2483) - 305^2]}}$$

$$= \frac{-2{,}637{,}147}{\sqrt{(274{,}597{,}450)(48{,}506)}} = -.722$$

Finally, in terms of sums of squares and products we have

$$SS_X = \Sigma X^2 - \frac{(\Sigma X)^2}{N} = 4{,}817{,}499.10$$

$$SS_Y = \Sigma Y^2 - \frac{(\Sigma Y)^2}{N} = 850.98$$

$$SP_{XY} = \Sigma XY - \frac{\Sigma X \Sigma Y}{N} = -46{,}265.74$$

Then $$r = \frac{SP_{XY}}{\sqrt{SS_X SS_Y}} = \frac{-46{,}265.74}{\sqrt{(4{,}817{,}499.10)(850.98)}} = -.722$$

In all three cases we see that the correlation is $-.722$.

The correlation coefficient must be interpreted cautiously so as not to attribute to it meaning that it does not possess. Specifically, $r = -.72$ should *not* be interpreted to mean that there is 72% of a relationship (whatever that might mean) between time and errors. The correlation coefficient is simply a point on the scale between -1.00 and $+1.00$, and the closer it is to either of those limits, the stronger is the relationship between the two variables. For a more specific interpretation we will prefer to speak in terms of r^2, which is discussed in the next chapter.

9-5   CORRELATIONS WITH RANKED DATA

In the previous example the data for each subject were recorded in everyday units such as time and number of errors. Often, however, we ask judges to rank a number of items on two dimensions and then want to correlate the two sets of ranks. For example we might ask one judge to rank the importance of 10 memoranda. The least important would be assigned a rank of 1, the next most important would be assigned a rank of 2, and so on. Another judge might rank the simplicity and clarity with which those same 10 memoranda were written. We could then correlate the two sets of ranks to see if memoranda that are least important are also least clear. When we have such **ranked data**, we often use what is known as **Spearman's correlation coefficient for ranked data**, denoted r_S. (This is not the only coefficient that can be calculated from ranked data, but it is one of the simplest.)

Ranked data
Data for which the observations have been replaced by their numerical ranks from lowest to highest.

Spearman's correlation coefficient for ranked data (r_S)
A correlation coefficient on ranked data.

Probably the nicest thing about Spearman's r_S from your point of view is that you don't have to learn anything new. You already know how to calculate it. Most textbooks have a nice-looking formula to produce r_S, and some even leave you with the idea that you have just learned a new statistic. In fact, however, that "simple" formula is really derived as an algebraic simplification of the original formula for r.

Spearman derived his formula for rank order correlation by noting that if we have ranked data on 10 objects, the ranks for each dependent variable are going to be the first 10 consecutive integers $(1, 2, 3, \ldots, 10)$. The sum of the first N integers (ΣX) is always $N(N + 1)/2$, and the sum of the first N squared integers (ΣX^2) is always $N(N + 1)(2N + 1)/6$. All that Spearman did was to go to Pearson's formula and replace ΣX and ΣY with $N(N + 1)/2$, and replace ΣX^2 and ΣY^2 with $N(N + 1)(2N + 1)/6$. That step was a real simplification when people did not have ready access to calculators, but now that a calculator costs less than a compact disc, such a simplification is not particularly useful. You can just use Pearson's original formula. Most people would rather do the small amount of work required to square and sum a few numbers than memorize another formula. I'll give the formula so that those who collect formulae don't feel cheated, but frankly I had to look it up myself.

When the data on both dependent variables are in the form of ranks

$$r_S = \frac{N \Sigma XY - \Sigma X \Sigma Y}{\sqrt{[N \Sigma X^2 - (\Sigma X)^2][N \Sigma Y^2 - (\Sigma Y)^2]}} = 1 - \frac{6 \Sigma D^2}{N(N^2 - 1)}$$

where D stands for the set of differences between the X and the Y ranks for each subject, as illustrated in Table 9-3.

As an example of the use of rank correlations, suppose that we asked a group of students to rank order the quality of 15 courses and also to rank order the amount of work required in each. (The students were asked to come to some sort of consensus so that each course received one rank for quality and one for work.) The data are shown in Table 9-3. Using one of the standard formulae for Pearson's r, but labeling the coefficient as r_s to remind everyone that we are working with sets of ranks, we have

$$r_s = \frac{N\Sigma XY - \Sigma X \Sigma Y}{\sqrt{[N\Sigma X^2 - (\Sigma X)^2][N\Sigma Y^2 - (\Sigma Y)^2]}}$$

$$= \frac{15(1112) - (120)(120)}{\sqrt{[15(1240) - 120^2][15(1240) - 120^2]}}$$

$$= \frac{2280}{\sqrt{(4200)(4200)}} = \frac{2280}{4200} = .543$$

Using an alternative formula,

$$r_s = 1 - \frac{6\Sigma D^2}{N(N^2 - 1)} = 1 - \frac{6(256)}{15(15^2 - 1)} = 1 - \frac{1536}{15(224)} = 1 - 0.457 = .543$$

You will note that the two answers are exactly equal, as they had to be because the formulae are algebraically equivalent. You will also note that there is a

TABLE 9-3
Rankings of Quality and Work Required for Each of 15 Courses

Course	Quality	Work	D	D^2
A	1	3	−2	4
B	2	5	−3	9
C	3	1	2	4
D	4	6	−2	4
E	5	2	3	9
F	6	8	−2	4
G	7	14	−7	49
H	8	12	−4	16
I	9	11	−2	4
J	10	9	1	1
K	11	10	1	1
L	12	7	5	25
M	13	15	−2	4
N	14	13	1	1
O	15	4	11	121

$\Sigma X = 120$ $\Sigma Y = 120$ $\Sigma D^2 = 256$

$\Sigma X^2 = 1240$ $\Sigma Y^2 = 1240$

$\Sigma XY = 1112$

Note: Low rankings indicate high quality and heavy workload.

moderately strong relationship ($r_S = .543$) between the quality of a course and the workload of that course. (One of the nice things about inventing examples for a statistics text is that you can make the data come out to fit your preconceived ideas about how the world ought to be.)

TIED RANKS

Ties are generally a source of considerable annoyance to people who work with ranked data. Tied ranks tend to invalidate our formulae and to distort the logic of our procedures. In the case of Spearman's r_S, the "simplified" formula is in error with ties because ΣX^2 no longer will be $N(N + 1)(2N + 1)/6$. However, there is no particular problem as long as you stick with Pearson's original formula. In that case you simply assign those people or objects that have the same score the average of the ranks for which they are tied and then proceed to apply the standard formula as you normally would. As an example of assigning ranks to tied scores, assume that we have the following data:

$$1 \quad 3 \quad 3 \quad 5 \quad 8 \quad 8 \quad 8$$

The ranks then would be

$$1 \quad 2.5 \quad 2.5 \quad 4 \quad 6 \quad 6 \quad 6$$

THE INTERPRETATION OF r_s

Spearman's r_S is slightly more difficult to interpret than Pearson's r, partly because of the nature of the data. In the example we have just examined, the data occurred naturally in the form of ranks because that is the task that we set our subjects. In this situation r_S is a measure of the *linear* relationship between one set of *ranks* and another.

    In other situations the data do not naturally occur in ranks but, instead, we convert raw data to ranks. For example we might measure a person's "sociability" by the number of friends he claims to have and measure his physical attractiveness by asking an independent judge to assign a rating on a 10-point scale. Having very little faith in the underlying properties of either scale, we might then simply convert the raw data on each variable to ranks and carry out our correlations with those ranks. In this case the value of r_S is a measure of the *linearity* of the relationship between the *ranks*, but it is only a measure of the **monotonic relationship** (one that is continuously rising or continuously falling) between the original variables. This should not surprise you, however. A correlation coefficient tells us directly only about the variables on which it is computed. It can hardly be expected to give us very precise information about variables on which it was not computed. As discussed in Chapter 2, it is essential to keep in mind the similar distinction between the variables that you have actually measured (e.g., number of friends) and the underlying property that you wish to examine (e.g., sociability).

Monotonic relationship
A relationship represented by a regression line that is continually increasing (or decreasing), but perhaps not in a straight line.

9-6 FACTORS THAT AFFECT THE CORRELATION

The correlation coefficient can be importantly affected by characteristics of the sample. Two of these characteristics are the restriction of the range (or variance) of X and/or Y and the use of heterogeneous subsamples.

THE EFFECT OF RANGE RESTRICTIONS

Range restrictions
Refers to cases in which the range over which X or Y varies is artificially limited.

A common problem, which arises in many instances, concerns restrictions on the range over which X and Y vary. The effect of such **range restrictions** is to alter the correlation between X and Y from what it would have been if the range had not been so restricted. Depending upon the nature of the data, the correlation may either rise or fall as a result of such restriction, although most commonly r is reduced.

With the exception of very unusual circumstances, restricting the range of X will increase r only when the restriction results in eliminating some *curvilinear* relationship. For example, if we correlated height with age, where age ran from 0 to 70, the data would be decidedly curvilinear (rising to about 17 years of age and then leveling off or even declining), and the correlation, which measures *linear* relationships, would be quite low. If, however, we restrict the range of ages to 0 to 17, the correlation would be quite high, because we have eliminated those values of Y that were not varying linearly as a function of X.

The more usual effect of restricting the range of X or Y is to reduce the correlation. This problem is especially important in the area of test construction, because in that area criterion measures (Y) may be available for only the higher values of X. Consider the hypothetical data in Figure 9-5. This figure represents

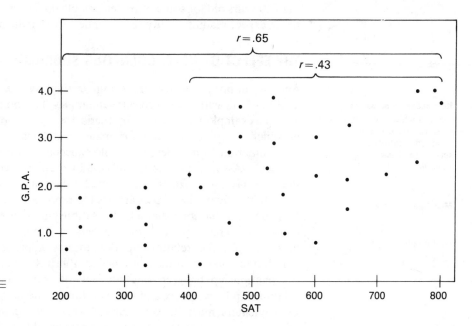

FIGURE 9-5
Hypothetical Data Illustrating the Effect of Restricted Range

the relation between college grade point average and scores on a standard achievement test (such as the SAT) for a hypothetical sample of students. In the ideal world of the test constructor all people who took the exam would then be sent to college and receive a grade point average, and the correlation between test scores and grade point averages would be computed. As can be seen from Figure 9-5, this correlation would be reasonably high. In the real world, however, not everyone is admitted to college. Colleges take only the more able students, whether this ability be measured by achievement test scores, high school performance, or whatever. This means that college grade point averages will be available mainly for students having relatively high scores on the standardized test. Suppose that this has the effect of allowing us to evaluate the relationship between X and Y for only those values of $X > 400$. From Figure 9-5 you will note that in this case the correlation will be relatively low, not because the test is worthless, but because the range has been restricted. In other words when we use the entire sample of points in Figure 9-5, the correlation is .65. However, when we restrict the sample to those students having SAT scores of at least 400, the correlation drops to only .43.

The effect of range restrictions must be taken into account whenever we see a validity coefficient based upon a restricted sample. The coefficient might be quite inappropriate for the question at hand. Essentially what we have done is to ask how well a standardized test predicts a person's suitability for college, but we have answered that question by reference only to those people who actually are admitted to college. At the same time, it is sometimes useful to deliberately restrict the range of one of the variables. For example, if we wanted to know the way in which reading ability increases linearly with age, we probably would restrict the age range by using only subjects who are at least 5 years old and less than 20 years old (or some other reasonable upper limit). We presumably would never expect reading ability to continue to rise indefinitely.

THE EFFECT OF HETEROGENEOUS SUBSAMPLES

Heterogeneous subsamples
Data in which the sample of observations could be subdivided into two distinct sets on the basis of some other variable.

Another important consideration in evaluating the results of correlational analyses deals with **heterogeneous subsamples**. This point can be illustrated with a simple example. Consider a hypothetical study of smoking and life expectancy, in which we plot the data for males and females separately to eliminate contamination from difference in life expectancy normally found between the two sexes. Assume that the results could be represented as in Figure 9-6, where the data have been exaggerated to make the point more vividly.

In this figure the ellipses are used to represent the clustering of data points. It is apparent that for males a high relationship exists between smoking and life expectancy. This is equally true for females. But if we group the data into one large sample, the relationship deteriorates appreciably. The fact that the correlation is lower for the combined sample has nothing whatsoever to do with the relationship between smoking and life expectancy, but rather with the relationship between sex and life expectancy. The point to be made here is that experimenters must be very careful when they combine data from several sources, so as not to include variance attributable to irrelevant variables.

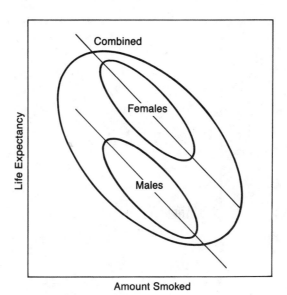

FIGURE 9-6
Illustration of the Effect of Heterogeneous Subsamples

9-7   A WORD OF CAUTION

It is important to point out two things that tend to be overlooked. The first relates to the fact that we are dealing here only with linear relationships, and the second deals with the issue of cause and effect.

The Pearson product-moment correlation coefficient deals only with *linear relationships* between two variables—that is, where the best-fitting line that can be passed through the scatter plot is a straight line. It is usually not useful to calculate r when you know that the data are markedly nonlinear. (The correlation would still be a measure of the degree of linearity of the relationship, but if the relationship is markedly curvilinear, who cares how well a straight line will do in fitting the points?) Similarly, the fact that r is near zero does not mean that no relationship exists between X and Y. It means only that no *linear* relationship exists. An example of a nonlinear relationship is presented in Figure 9-7 on the hypothetical relationship between salary and years of service among middle-level managers in a medium-sized corporation.

The second word of caution concerns the fact that the existence of a correlation between two variables does not mean that one variable causes the other. The fact that sightings of storks on chimneys is correlated with changes in birth rate is not to be taken as evidence that storks have something to do with births (or else I have been cruelly misinformed). Both of these variables vary with the season of the year, and that is what produces the correlation.

9-8   OTHER CORRELATION COEFFICIENTS

The standard correlation coefficient is Pearson's r, which applies primarily to variables that are distributed along more or less interval or ratio scales of measurement. We also have seen that the same formula will produce a statistic

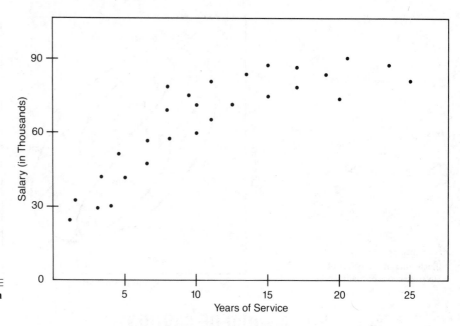

Nonlinear Relationship between Salary and Years of Service

called r_S (or Spearman's r_S) when the variables are in the form of ranks. There are two other correlation coefficients with which you should be familiar, although here again there is very little that is new.

When we have one variable that is measured on a continuous scale and one variable that is measured as a dichotomy (i.e., takes on one of only two levels), then the correlation coefficient that we produce is called the **point biserial correlation (r_{pb})**. For example we might perform an analysis of test items by correlating total score on the text (X) with "pass/fail" on a particular item (Y). In this case X values might run from roughly 60 to 100, but Y values would be either 0 (fail) or 1 (pass). Although special formulae exist for calculating r_{pb}, you can accomplish the same thing just as easily by computing r. Only we call the answer r_{pb} instead of r to point out the nature of the data on which it was computed.

A point is in order here about **dichotomous variables**. In the preceding example I scored "fail" as 0 and "pass" as 1. That makes the arithmetic simple. I could just as well have scored them 1 and 2, or even 82 and 97—just as long as all of the "pass" scores receive one number and all of the "fail" scores receive the other. The correlation will be the same no matter what numbers we use.

A slightly different correlation coefficient, **phi (ϕ)**, arises when *both* variables are measured as dichotomies. For example, in studying the relationship between sex and religiosity we might correlate sex (coded male = 1, female = 2) with regular church attendance (no = 0, yes = 1). Again it makes no difference what two values we use to code the dichotomous variables. Although ϕ has a special formula, it is just as easy and correct to use Pearson's formula, but label the answer ϕ.

There are a number of other correlation coefficients, but the ones given here are the most common. All are special cases of Pearson's r, and all can be

Point biserial correlation (r_{pb})
The correlation coefficient when one of the variables is measured as a dichotomy.

Dichotomous variables
Variables that can take on only two different values.

Phi (ϕ)
The correlation coefficient when both of the variables are measured as dichotomies.

obtained by using the formula for r discussed in this chapter. Finally these coefficients are the coefficients that usually are generated when a large set of data is entered into a computer and a correlation or regression program is run.

9-9   USING MINITAB TO OBTAIN CORRELATION COEFFICIENTS

Minitab can be used both to plot scatter diagrams and to obtain correlation coefficients. The following example (Table 9-4) examines hypothetical data for test grade, anxiety level, sex, and attendance at a review session. I have plotted

TABLE 9-4
Relationships between Test Grade, Anxiety Level, Sex, and Attendance at a Review Session

```
MTB > SET THE FOLLOWING DATA IN COLUMN C1
DATA> 58 63 65 70 72 82 89 91
DATA> END
MTB > NAME C1 'GRADE'
MTB > SET THE FOLLOWING DATA IN COLUMN C2
DATA> 42 43 35 36 28 30 20 28
DATA> END
MTB > NAME C2 'ANXIETY'
MTB > SET THE FOLLOWING DATA IN COLUMN C3
DATA> 1 2 1 1 2 2 1 2
DATA> END
MTB > NAME C3 'SEX'
MTB > SET THE FOLLOWING DATA IN COLUMN C4
DATA> 0 0 1 1 0 1 1 1
DATA> END
MTB > NAME C4 'ATTEND'
MTB > DESCRIBE C1-C4

                N      MEAN    MEDIAN   TRMEAN    STDEV   SEMEAN
GRADE           8     73.75     71.00    73.75    12.28     4.34
ANXIETY         8     32.75     32.50    32.75     7.76     2.74
SEX             8     1.500     1.500    1.500    0.535    0.189
ATTEND          8     0.625     1.000    0.625    0.518    0.183

              MIN       MAX        Q1       Q3
GRADE       58.00     91.00     63.50    87.25
ANXIETY     20.00     43.00     28.00    40.50
SEX         1.000     2.000     1.000    2.000
ATTEND      0.000     1.000     0.000    1.000

MTB > PLOT 'GRADE','ANXIETY'

      -                        *
  90+        *
      -
      -
      -
      -                            *
  80+
      -
      -
      -
      -               *
  70+                                   *
      -
      -                              *
      -                                        *
  60+
      -                                    *
      ----+---------+---------+---------+---------+---------+ANXIETY
        20.0      25.0      30.0      35.0      40.0      45.0

MTB > CORRELATE C1-C4

            GRADE   ANXIETY      SEX
ANXIETY    -0.867
SEX         0.283    -0.069
ATTEND      0.635    -0.525   -0.258

MTB > STOP
```

the relationship between the two continuously measured variables and then calculated the whole set of correlation coefficients for all the variables. Notice that some of these variables are measured dichotomously. Which correlations are point biserial correlations and which one is ϕ?

9-10   A FINAL WORKED EXAMPLE

The following set of observations are actual data on the evaluation of 15 courses, taken from a large data set on the evaluation of several hundred courses. We are using just two of the variables. Students were asked to rate the overall quality of a course that they were taking and were asked to indicate their anticipated grade in that course. In the data below are the mean ratings for each of the 15 courses on these two variables. From these data can we conclude that courses that generally give lower grades are likely to receive a lower evaluation?

Expected Grade (X)	Overall Quality (Y)
3.5	3.4
3.2	2.9
2.8	2.6
3.3	3.8
3.2	3.0
3.2	2.5
3.6	3.9
4.0	4.3
3.0	3.8
3.1	3.4
3.0	2.8
3.3	2.9
3.2	4.1
3.4	2.7
3.7	3.9
$\Sigma X = 49.5$	$\Sigma Y = 50.0$
$\Sigma X^2 = 164.65$	$\Sigma Y^2 = 171.68$
$\Sigma XY = 166.48$	

Our first step is to calculate the mean and variance of each variable. These are shown as follows:

$$\bar{X} = 49.5/15 = 3.3000 \qquad\qquad \bar{Y} = 50.0/15 = 3.3333$$

$$s_X = \sqrt{\frac{164.65 - 49.5^2/15}{14}} \qquad\qquad s_Y = \sqrt{\frac{171.68 - 50.0^2/15}{14}}$$

$$= 0.3047 \qquad\qquad\qquad = 0.5984$$

The covariance is given as

$$\text{cov}_{XY} = \frac{166.48 - (49.5)(50.0)/15}{14} = .1057$$

Finally, the correlation is given by

$$r = \frac{\text{cov}_{XY}}{(s_X)(s_Y)} = \frac{.1057}{(0.3047)(0.5984)} = .5797 \approx .58$$

This is a fairly high correlation, and is one that would lend support to the proposition that courses that have higher average grades also have higher average ratings. That does not mean that higher grades cause higher ratings. It is just as plausible that more advanced courses are rated more highly, and it is often in these courses that students do their best work. It is also possible that there really is not much of a correlation, but that we found a high correlation by chance. We will see how to test that question in Chapter 12.

9-11 SUMMARY

In this chapter we have dealt with the correlation coefficient as a measure of the relationship between two variables. We have seen how to draw a scatter plot of the variables and how to compute the correlation coefficient. We also have considered the correlation of ranked data and have seen that Pearson's original formula is appropriate for this purpose. Finally we considered factors that affect the magnitude of the correlation, some cautions concerning interpretation, and the treatment of dichotomous variables. Some of the most important terms in this chapter are:

- Correlation
- Correlation coefficient
- Pearson product-moment correlation coefficient (r)
- Scatter diagram
- Predictor variable
- Criterion variable
- Curvilinear relationship
- Linear relationship

- Covariance
- Sum of squares
- Sum of products
- Spearman's correlation coefficient for ranked data (r_S)
- Monotonic relationship
- Point biserial correlation (r_{pb})
- Dichotomous variables
- Phi (ϕ)

9-12 EXERCISES

9-1 The state of Vermont is divided into 10 Health Planning Districts—corresponding roughly to counties. The following data for 1980 represent the percentage of births under 2500 grams (Y), the fertility rate for females $\leqslant 17$ or $\geqslant 35$ years of age (X_1), and the percentage of illegitimate births (X_2) for each district.

(a) Make a scatter diagram of Y and X_1.

(b) Draw in (by eye) the line that appears to best fit the data.

9-2 Calculate the correlation between Y and X_1 in Exercise 9-1.

District	Y	X_1	X_2
1	6.1	43.0	9.2
2	7.1	55.3	12.0
3	7.4	48.5	10.4
4	6.3	38.8	9.8
5	6.5	46.2	9.8
6	5.7	39.9	7.7
7	6.6	43.1	10.9
8	8.1	48.5	9.5
9	6.3	40.0	11.6
10	6.9	56.7	11.6

9-3 Calculate the correlation between Y and X_2 in Exercise 9-1.

9-4 Draw a scatter diagram for Y and X_1 from Exercise 9-1. Divide the diagram into quadrants as in Figure 9-2 and count the observations in each quadrant.

9-5 Draw a scatter diagram for Y and X_2 from Exercise 9-1. Divide the diagram into quadrants as in Figure 9-3 and count the observations in each quadrant.

9-6 Compare the answers to Exercises 9-4 and 9-5. Do they reflect the differences between the answers to Exercises 9-2 and 9-3?

9-7 Draw scatter diagrams for the following sets of data:

1		2		3	
X	Y	X	Y	X	Y
2	2	2	4	2	8
3	4	3	2	3	6
5	6	5	8	5	4
6	8	6	6	6	2

(a) Calculate the covariance for each using the definitional formula.

(b) Calculate the covariance for each using one of the computational formulae.

9-8 Calculate the correlation for each data set in Exercise 9-7. How can the values of Y in Exercise 9-7 be rearranged to produce the smallest possible positive correlation?

9-9 The following data represent the percentage of voluntary homework problems completed by each of 20 students and their final grade at the end of the course (converted to a 100-point scale).

Problems Completed	50	60	80	70	90	40	100	85
Final Grade		75	75	90	80	85	60	98	95
Problems Completed	90	80	50	95	40	80	85	95
Final Grade		95	80	75	90	60	50	70	85
Problems Completed	70	40	80	30				
Final Grade		75	60	80	55				

(a) Plot the data points.

(b) Compute the correlation between amount of homework completed and the final grade.

(c) Interpret this correlation.

Exercises 9-10 through 9-15 involve an unusual amount of work. However, the data are real and the answers are important.

Sternglass and Bell (1983) published a controversial paper arguing that "the principal new factor in the sharp decline (of SAT scores) during the 1970s was the fallout from the massive nuclear bomb tests in the 1950s and early 1960s." As support for this hypothesis they reported a correlation of .55 between the iodine-131 levels (by state) in 1962 (when nuclear testing was briefly resumed in Nevada) and the decline from 1978 to 1979 in *verbal* SAT scores. Their argument was that exposure to I-131 early in life led to poor performance later in life. The correlations for declines in 1978 and 1977, respectively, were reported as .2956 and .3300. The raw data for math and verbal SAT scores for the years 1972-73 to 1978-79, for those states for which SAT data were reported, are shown in Table 9-5, along with the iodine-131 levels. (In these data each row represents a state. The 1972-73 score, for example, is denoted as the 1972 score because most students take the SAT exams in the fall.)

9-10 Calculate the *decline* for both math and verbal scores from 1978 to 1979, and correlate the decline with I-131 levels. Does this answer agree with the reported results?

9-11 Make a stem-and-leaf display for the variable I-131 and for the change in math scores from 1977-1979.

9-12 Draw a scatter diagram of the relation between the 1977-78 to 1978-79 decline in math SAT and I-131 level. What does this diagram suggest?

9-13 The data for the most extreme data point in the scatter diagram referred to in Exercise 9-12 was based on 4% of the high school seniors in that state (the other extreme point was based on 31% of the high school seniors). What problems does this present?

9-14 Omit the two extreme data points identified in Exercise 9-12 and rerun the correlations.

9-15 Use Minitab to generate the correlation between the 1962 I-131 level and changes in math and verbal SAT scores from year to year during the 1970s. (*Hint:* You can save yourself work by using commands of the form SUBTRACT M73 FROM M74, PUT IN COLUMN C16.)

9-16 In 1957 there was also a substantial increase in nuclear testing in Nevada as compared to the previous

===== TABLE 9-5 =====   Data on SAT Scores and Radioactive Fallout

V72	V73	V74	V75	V76	V77	V78	M72	M73	M74	M75	M76	M77	M78	I-131
464	474	461	454	459	458	452	486	495	481	485	487	485	478	104
502	501	496	491	492	492	485	534	534	525	532	531	529	524	12
478	484	482	485	480	483	478	511	512	510	518	519	514	513	37
452	450	435	430	427	427	428	485	484	473	470	470	466	473	13
485	484	479	476	469	473	469	521	522	515	521	518	516	513	15
451	452	442	439	437	438	435	482	480	471	473	468	469	465	21
447	449	439	437	438	436	433	482	479	476	476	477	477	468	32
417	420	414	409	401	398	396	481	481	478	479	473	468	467	12
484	492	493	483	489	488	480	520	518	524	519	530	521	518	25
472	471	460	464	459	463	462	509	513	510	509	507	511	511	38
429	423	418	415	412	413	412	470	469	463	460	458	457	455	33
525	526	523	523	513	516	518	565	570	568	572	563	569	567	59
441	441	437	437	431	429	430	481	477	471	476	471	467	468	22
454	452	436	432	431	431	426	488	485	471	470	469	466	464	24
444	445	434	432	429	430	428	481	477	469	469	465	465	463	22
450	458	451	453	454	459	456	491	502	498	506	508	511	508	30
506	512	506	504	500	497	497	552	556	552	557	556	550	549	43
475	475	465	464	464	465	461	509	510	500	505	506	506	504	58
505	512	500	490	493	493	487	553	558	547	545	550	549	541	40
475	476	465	456	457	457	449	501	502	497	497	498	494	486	*
459	461	449	446	443	446	444	497	496	485	488	484	486	483	20
438	436	424	422	422	419	419	469	464	454	456	455	451	452	22
482	492	486	481	481	485	486	522	525	516	522	521	524	521	21
452	452	441	437	434	431	426	495	495	484	484	479	471	469	28
458	459	456	457	459	459	457	496	500	499	504	506	504	502	35
491	492	480	482	483	483	486	528	527	514	515	525	527	522	48
445	446	440	432	432	437	434	482	475	468	469	468	469	466	27
443	442	430	431	429	427	426	479	477	470	470	468	467	464	36
442	439	432	429	424	425	424	477	471	469	469	461	463	459	23
438	439	431	427	424	425	418	474	475	467	466	464	460	456	38
528	532	516	506	515	516	507	561	560	553	545	550	564	538	87
448	445	439	435	435	434	434	483	478	476	474	475	473	472	23
484	496	489	479	480	484	481	523	528	522	522	525	525	525	43
496	502	492	483	479	479	476	548	552	544	546	545	540	535	39
516	500	506	486	501	498	488	559	547	548	545	555	542	532	55
448	454	459	466	476	484	487	498	506	507	518	533	538	538	53
401	401	386	387	376	*	381	422	418	403	403	377	*	401	23
504	510	503	496	503	*	498	545	546	540	543	550	*	541	59
477	484	470	476	480	*	*	511	517	507	517	520	*	*	29
456	455	456	464	466	*	460	491	488	491	501	505	*	495	23
426	466	477	470	466	*	468	460	493	503	499	501	*	497	23
522	519	510	504	501	*	525	568	558	554	548	561	*	570	41
398	386	367	363	354	*	*	437	430	428	417	420	*	*	14
515	528	523	515	534	*	531	552	573	561	586	586	*	570	39
473	479	462	466	459	*	461	505	514	502	510	499	*	494	19

year. If we assume that the distribution of I-131 across states would have been similar to the distribution in 1962 (and that may not be a fair assumption), what would you expect to see in the data? Use the answers to Exercise 9-15 to evaluate this expectation.

9–17 Plot and calculate the correlation for the relationship between ADDSC and GPA for the data in Appendix C, Data Set.

9–18 Rank the data in Exercise 9-1 and compute Spearman's r_S for Y and X_1 using both formulae.

9–19 Rank the data in Exercise 9-1 and compute Spearman's r_S for Y and X_2 using both formulae.

9–20 Assume that a set of data contains a slightly curvilinear relationship between X and Y (the best-fitting line is slightly curved). Would it ever be appropriate to calculate r on these data?

9–21 Several times in this chapter I have referred to the fact that a correlation based on a small sample might not be reliable.

(a) What does reliable mean in this context?

(b) We will discuss this idea in later chapters, but why do you think that a correlation based on a small sample might not be reliable?

REGRESSION

Regression
The prediction of one variable from knowledge of one or more other variables.

Linear regression
Regression in which the relationship is linear.

In many situations in which we have two variables we really only want to know whether the variables are related, and we are not particularly concerned about the exact nature of that relationship. For example, having found that the correlation between the time spent on a task and the number of errors is $-.722$, I may know as much about that relationship as I care to know. On the other hand in many situations the form of the relationship between two variables is of at least as much interest as the correlation. To put this another way, there are many situations in which we want to go beyond a correlation coefficient to write an equation that will allow us to predict a person's score on one variable from knowledge of that person's score on another variable. When we are interested in deriving an equation for predicting one variable from another, we are dealing with **regression**, which is the topic of this chapter.

Just as we did when discussing correlation, we will restrict our coverage of regression to those cases in which the best-fitting line through the scatter diagram is a straight line. This means that we will deal only with **linear regression**. This is not as serious a restriction as you might expect, however, since a surprisingly high percentage of sets of data turn out to be basically linear. And even in those cases in which the relationship is *curvilinear* (i.e., where the best-fitting line is a curve) a straight line often will provide a very good approximation—especially if we eliminate the extremes of the distribution of one of the variables.

10-1 AN EXAMPLE—FROM THE UNIVERSITY DINING HALLS

As an example consider the case of the manager of a university's food service. He is concerned with the problem of making sure there is enough food available for everyone who wants it, but he must be careful not to prepare more food than people will eat. He assumes that people generally eat more of the foods they like and less of the foods they dislike. Therefore he reasons that if he could assess the desirability of different menus, then he could collect data and write an equation predicting consumption from rated desirability. When new menus are developed in the future, all that he would have to do then is have a small sample of students rate their desirability. He then could use his equation to predict how many helpings will be eaten. To carry out this study the manager asks a group of students to rate the desirability of 30 standard menus (ranging from Tuna Surprise to the roast beef dinner served on parents' weekend). For each menu he calculates the mean rating of desirability (averaging across respondents). He also records the number of servings of each menu that were consumed the last time it was served to a dining-hall population of 550 students, where second and third helpings are free. The raw data are given in Table 10-1 and plotted in Figure 10-1.

Before considering the regression line for predicting Servings from Ratings, it is useful to calculate the correlation between the two variables. If it should turn out that they are not correlated, there would be no real point in trying to fit a regression line to predict one from the other. The information in Table 10-1 allows us to compute the correlation. In Chapter 9 I introduced the concept of sums of squares and sums of products, partly because they are quite useful for computations in regression. I will use them for computations in this chapter alongside the more traditional formulae.

The correlation between X and Y is given by

$$r = \frac{SP_{XY}}{\sqrt{SS_X SS_Y}} = \frac{15{,}770}{\sqrt{(7056.8)(85{,}250)}} = .643$$

or equivalently, $r = \dfrac{\text{cov}_{XY}}{s_X s_Y} = \dfrac{543.793}{(15.599)(54.219)} = .643$

From a method to be discussed in Chapter 12 it can be shown that this correlation is a reliable one. How much people eat does depend in part on how much they like the food (isn't science wonderful?).

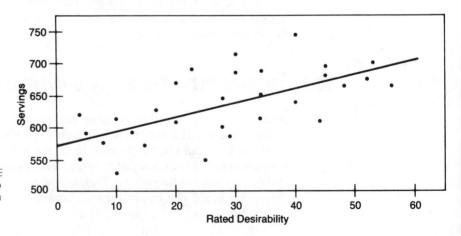

FIGURE 10-1
Scatter Plot of the Relationship between Desirability of a Menu and the Number of Servings Consumed

TABLE 10-1
Data on the Relationship
between Rated Desirability of a
Menu and the Number of
Servings Consumed

Menu	Rating (X)	Servings (Y)
1	4	550
2	4	620
3	5	590
4	8	575
5	10	530
6	10	615
7	13	590
8	15	570
9	17	630
10	20	610
11	20	670
12	23	690
13	25	550
14	28	600
15	28	645
16	29	585
17	30	685
18	30	715
19	34	615
20	34	650
21	36	690
22	40	640
23	40	745
24	44	610
25	45	680
26	45	695
27	48	665
28	52	675
29	53	700
30	56	665

$$\bar{X} = 28.2 \qquad \bar{Y} = 635$$
$$SS_X = 7056.8 \qquad SS_Y = 85{,}250$$
$$s_X = 15.599 \qquad s_Y = 54.219$$
$$SP_{XY} = 15{,}770$$
$$\text{cov}_{XY} = 543.793$$

10-2 THE REGRESSION LINE

If we wanted to know how many servings of a given menu will be consumed, a good strategy might be to compute the average consumption over the last several times that menu was served. However, if we are dealing with new menus that have not been served before, we obviously need a different approach. The one we will adopt here is to ask a sample of students to rate the desirability of that menu and then use their ratings to form a prediction. But first we need to obtain an equation, based on available data, of a line that will relate Y (Servings) to X (Rating). As many of you will remember from high school, the equation of a straight line is an equation of the form $Y = bX + a$. For our purposes we will write the equation as

$$\hat{Y} = bX + a$$

where

$\hat{Y} =$ the predicted value of Y (in our case, Servings)

$b =$ the **slope** of the regression line (the amount by which $\hat{Y}$ increases for every one unit change in X)

$a =$ the **intercept** (the value of $\hat{Y}$ when $X = 0$)

Slope
The amount of change in $\hat{Y}$ for a one unit change in X.

Intercept
The value of $\hat{Y}$ when X is 0.

The variable X is simply the value of the predictor variable (in our case, Rating). Our task will be to solve for those values of a and b that will produce the best-fitting linear function. In other words we want to use the existing data to solve for the values of a and b such that the regression line (the predicted values of $\hat{Y}$ for different values of X) will come as close as possible to the actual obtained values of Y.

But how are we to define the phrase "best fitting"? The most logical way would be in terms of **errors of prediction**—that is, in terms of the $Y - \hat{Y}$ deviations. Because $\hat{Y}$ is the value that the equation would predict and Y is a value that we actually obtained the last time the meal was served, $Y - \hat{Y}$ is an error of prediction. We want to find that line (i.e., that set of $\hat{Y}$'s) that minimizes such errors. We can't just minimize the *sum* of the errors, however, because for an infinite variety of lines that sum will always be zero. Instead we will look for that line that minimizes the sum of the squared errors—that is, the line that minimizes $\Sigma(Y - \hat{Y})^2$. (You might note that I said much the same thing in Chapter 6 when I was discussing the variance, although there I was discussing deviations from the mean and here I am discussing deviations from the regression line—something like a floating or changing mean.)

Errors of prediction
The differences between Y and $\hat{Y}$.

It is not difficult to derive the equations for the optimal values for a and b, but I will not derive them here. As long as you keep in mind that they are derived in such a way as to minimize squared errors in predicting Y, it is sufficient to state simply

$$b = \frac{SP_{XY}}{SS_X} = \frac{\text{cov}_{XY}}{s_X^2}$$

and

$$a = \bar{Y} - b\bar{X} = \frac{\Sigma Y - b\Sigma X}{N}$$

(Recall that $SP_{XY} = \Sigma XY - \Sigma X \Sigma Y/N$ and $SS_X = \Sigma X^2 - (\Sigma X)^2/N$.)

You should note that the equation for a includes the value of b, so you need to solve for b first. Also note that the equation for b resembles the equation for r except that the denominator is SS_X instead of $\sqrt{SS_X SS_Y}$ (or, equivalently, s_X^2 instead of $s_X s_Y$). (What does that tell you about the relationship between r and b when $s_X = s_Y$?)

If we apply these equations to the data, we obtain

$$b = \frac{SP_{XY}}{SS_X} = \frac{15{,}770}{7056.8} = 2.235$$

or $\quad b = \frac{\text{cov}_{XY}}{s_X^2} = \frac{543.793}{15.599^2} = \frac{543.793}{243.338} = 2.235$

$$a = \bar{Y} - b\bar{X} = 635 - 2.235(28.2) = 571.973$$

We now can write

$$\hat{Y} = 2.235X + 571.973$$

The interpretation of this equation is straightforward. Consider the intercept first. If $X = 0$ (i.e., the menu is rated as positively dreadful), the predicted value of $\hat{Y}$ is approximately 572 servings. This is probably a reasonable figure for 550 students, given that most people will eat something when they are hungry and some people will eat all they can get no matter how awful it tastes. Next consider the slope. In this example b is 2.235. This means that for every one point increase in the ratings, the dining hall will serve about 2.2 more servings. Similarly for a 10-point increase in the rating the dining hall will serve about 22 more servings. Most people think of the slope as just a numerical constant in a mathematical equation, but it really makes more sense to think of it as how much different you expect Y to be for a one unit difference in X.†

A word is in order about actually plotting the regression line. To plot the line you can simply take any two values of X (preferably at opposite ends of the scale), calculate $\hat{Y}$ for each, mark these coordinates on the figure, and connect them with a straight line. I generally use three points, just as a check for accuracy. For the data we have a regression line of

$$\hat{Y} = 2.235X + 571.973$$

When $X = 0$ $\qquad \hat{Y} = 2.235(0) + 571.973 = 571.973$

When $X = 25$ $\qquad \hat{Y} = 2.235(25) + 571.973 = 627.848$

And when $X = 50$ $\qquad \hat{Y} = 2.235(50) + 571.973 = 683.723$

Thus rounding off for convenience, we can draw a line through the points (0, 572), (25, 628), and (50, 684). This line can be seen in Figure 10-1 (page 124).

---

†A quick way to obtain a rough estimate of b is to draw a line through the data points by eye. Because b is the average difference in Y for every one unit difference in X, you can calculate the coordinates X_u, Y_u at the upper end of the line and X_l, Y_l at the lower end of the line. An approximation for b, then, is

$$b = \frac{Y_u - Y_l}{X_u - X_l}$$

Similarly an estimate of a is simply the value of $\hat{Y}$ at the point at which your line crosses the ordinate (i.e., at $X = 0$).

It is important to point out that we have constructed a line to predict Servings from Ratings and that this line was derived to minimize the sum of the squared deviations of predicted Servings from obtained Servings. If we wanted to turn things around and predict Ratings from Servings, we could not use this line—it wasn't derived for that purpose. Instead we would have to find the line that minimizes squared deviations of predicted Ratings from obtained Ratings. The simplest way to do this is just to reverse which variable is labeled X and which is labeled Y. You then can use the same formulae we have already used.

10-3   THE ACCURACY OF PREDICTION

The fact that we can fit a regression line to a set of data does not mean that our problems are solved. On the contrary, they have only begun. The important point is not whether or not a straight line can be drawn through the data (you can always do that) but whether or not that line represents a reasonable fit to the data—in other words whether our effort was worthwhile.

Before discussing errors of prediction, however, it is instructive to consider the situation in which we wish to predict Y without any knowledge of the value of X.

THE STANDARD DEVIATION AS A MEASURE OF ERROR

As mentioned earlier, the data in Table 10-1 represent the number of servings of a meal (Y) as a function of the rated quality of that meal (X). Assume that you are now given the task of predicting the number of servings that will be needed without any knowledge of what is to be served. Your best prediction in this case would be the mean servings ($\bar{Y}$) (averaged across all meals), and the error associated with your prediction would be the standard deviation of Y (s_Y), because your prediction is the mean and s_Y deals with deviations around the mean. Examining s_Y, we know that it is defined as

$$s_Y = \sqrt{\frac{\Sigma (Y - \bar{Y})^2}{N - 1}}$$

or, in terms of the variance,

$$s_Y^2 = \frac{\Sigma (Y - \bar{Y})^2}{N - 1}$$

The numerator is the sum of squared deviations from $\bar{Y}$ (the point you would have predicted in this particular example) and is what we have been referring to as the sum of squares of Y (SS_Y).

THE STANDARD ERROR OF ESTIMATE

Now suppose that we wish to make a prediction about servings for some newly designed meal that our panel of student experts tells us has a rating of 26. In this situation we know the relevant value of X (and the regression equation), and our best prediction would be $\hat{Y}$ (in this case $X = 26$ and $\hat{Y} = 630.083$). In line with our previous measure of error (the standard deviation), the error associated with the present prediction will again be a function of the deviations of Y about the predicted point, but in this case the predicted point is $\hat{Y}$ rather than $\bar{Y}$. Specifically a measure of error now can be defined as

$$s_{Y-\hat{Y}} = \sqrt{\frac{\Sigma(Y-\hat{Y})^2}{N-2}} = \sqrt{\frac{SS_{Y-\hat{Y}}}{N-2}}$$

Standard error of estimate
The average of the squared deviations about the regression line.

**Residual variance
(Error variance)**
The square of the standard error of estimate.

and again the sum is of squared deviations about the prediction ($\hat{Y}$). The numerator is again a sum of squares and is often denoted SS_{error} because it is a sum of squared errors of prediction. The statistic $s_{Y-\hat{Y}}$ is called the **standard error of estimate** and is sometimes written $s_{Y\cdot X}$ to indicate that it is the standard deviation of Y predicted from X. It is the most common (though not always the best) measure of the error of prediction. Its square, $s^2_{Y-\hat{Y}}$, is called the **residual**, or **error**, **variance**. Notice that $\Sigma(Y-\hat{Y})^2$, $SS_{Y-\hat{Y}}$, and SS_{error} are equivalent. The first term is a definition, the second says the same thing in different words, and the third makes it clear that we are discussing errors of estimation. Statisticians use these terms interchangeably, and it is important for you to be familiar with all of them and to recognize that they all mean the same thing.

Table 10-2 shows how to calculate directly the standard error of estimate. The raw data are given in columns 2 and 3, and the predicted values of $\hat{Y}$ (obtained from $\hat{Y} = 2.235X + 571.973$) are given in column 4. Column 5 contains the values of $Y - \hat{Y}$ for each observation. Note that the sum of that column ($\Sigma(Y-\hat{Y})$) is 0, as was stated previously. Column 6 shows the squared deviations ($\Sigma(Y-\hat{Y})^2$) and their sum. From this sum we can calculate

$$s_{Y-\hat{Y}} = \sqrt{\frac{\Sigma(Y-\hat{Y})^2}{N-2}} = \sqrt{\frac{50,008.403}{28}} = \sqrt{1786.014} = 42.261$$

Finding the standard error this way is hardly the most enjoyable way to spend a winter evening. Fortunately a much simpler procedure exists that not only represents a way of obtaining the standard error of estimate but also leads directly into even more important matters.

r^2 AND THE STANDARD ERROR OF ESTIMATE

We have defined the residual, or error, variance as

$$s^2_{Y-\hat{Y}} = \frac{\Sigma(Y-\hat{Y})^2}{N-2}$$

=== **TABLE 10-2** ===   Direct Calculation of Variance Estimates for Data in Table 10-1.

Menu	Rating (X)	Servings (Y)	$\hat{Y}$	$(Y - \hat{Y})$	$(Y - \hat{Y})^2$
1	4	550	580.913	−30.913	955.614
2	4	620	580.913	39.087	1527.794
3	5	590	583.148	6.852	46.950
4	8	575	589.853	−14.853	220.612
5	10	530	594.323	−64.323	4137.448
6	10	615	594.323	20.677	427.538
7	13	590	601.028	−11.028	121.617
8	15	570	605.498	−35.498	1260.108
9	17	630	609.968	20.032	401.281
10	20	610	616.673	−6.673	44.529
11	20	670	616.673	53.327	2843.769
12	23	690	623.378	66.622	4438.491
13	25	550	627.848	−77.848	6060.311
14	28	600	634.553	−34.553	1193.910
15	28	645	634.553	10.447	109.140
16	29	585	636.788	−51.788	2681.997
17	30	685	639.023	45.977	2113.884
18	30	715	639.023	75.977	5772.504
19	34	615	647.963	−32.963	1086.559
20	34	650	647.963	2.037	4.149
21	36	690	652.433	37.567	1411.280
22	40	640	661.373	−21.373	456.805
23	40	745	661.373	83.627	6993.475
24	44	610	670.313	−60.313	3637.658
25	45	680	672.548	7.452	55.532
26	45	695	672.548	22.452	504.092
27	48	665	679.253	−14.253	203.148
28	52	675	688.193	−13.193	174.055
29	53	700	690.428	9.572	91.623
30	56	665	697.133	−32.133	1032.530

Sum:	846	19,050	19,050.000	0.000	50,008.403
Sum of Squared Entries:	30,914	12,182,000	12,132,000.000		

and we know that

$$\Sigma(Y - \hat{Y})^2 = SS_{Y-\hat{Y}} = SS_{error}$$

After considerable algebraic manipulation it is possible to express SS_{error} as

$$SS_{error} = SS_Y(1 - r^2)$$

where $SS_Y = \Sigma(Y - \bar{Y})^2$. Thus the sum of squares for residual error is a function of the sum of squares for the original values of $Y(SS_Y)$ and the correlation between X and Y. This may not strike you as a great simplification, but it really is. From here a small amount of substitution and algebraic manipulation will bring us to

$$s_{Y-\hat{Y}} = s_Y\sqrt{(1 - r^2)\left(\frac{N - 1}{N - 2}\right)}$$

or, as most textbooks present it (although not quite accurately),

$$s_{Y-\hat{Y}} = s_Y\sqrt{1 - r^2}$$

This last equation is arrived at by treating the term $(N - 1)/(N - 2)$ as essentially 1.0.

From our data we now can calculate $s_{Y-\hat{Y}}$ in three different ways.

1. $s_{Y-\hat{Y}} = \sqrt{\dfrac{\Sigma(Y - \hat{Y})^2}{N - 2}}$

    $= \sqrt{\dfrac{50{,}008.403}{28}}$

    $= 42.261$

2. $s_{Y-\hat{Y}} = s_Y\sqrt{(1 - r^2)\left(\dfrac{N - 1}{N - 2}\right)}$

    $= 54.219\sqrt{(1 - .643^2)\left(\dfrac{29}{28}\right)}$

    $= 42.261$

3. $s_{Y-\hat{Y}} \simeq s_Y\sqrt{1 - r^2}$

    $= 54.219\sqrt{1 - .643^2}$

    $= 41.524$

The third solution differs from the other two because it is based on a formula that ignores the constant $\sqrt{(N - 1)/(N - 2)}$. That is why the "approximately equals" sign ($\simeq$) was used. For large sample sizes the differences will be minor, but not so for small sample sizes.

Now that we have computed the standard error of estimate we can interpret it as a form of standard deviation. Thus is is reasonable to say that the standard deviation of points about the regression line is 42.261. Because the regression line represents our set of predictions, a standard deviation of approximately 42 meals around those predictions should make us a little uneasy. Being off by about 40 meals on average in our prediction is not a particularly happy state of affairs. We run a substantial risk of either having too much food or having many hungry people standing around and hurting our feelings with unkind words. You might take some comfort, however, from the fact that had we not had a regression equation, our best guess would have been $\bar{Y}$, and in that case our measure of error would be the standard deviation of Y (54.219; see Table 10-2), which is almost 30% higher than $s_{Y-\hat{Y}}$.

I have a specific reason for pointing out the substantial errors of prediction in regression analysis. Most people seem to think that if we have a regression equation, we can make a prediction and that's that. Although it is true that a regression equation yields better predictions than predictions made without one, a substantial amount of error remains in the system (and in this case the correlation was a respectable .643!). You would do well to keep in mind all of those hungry students attacking the food service manager's office. It is an appropriately sobering thought when you become overly excited about a regression equation.

r^2 AS A MEASURE OF PREDICTABLE VARIABILITY

From the preceding equation expressing residual error in terms of r^2 it is possible to derive an extremely important interpretation of the correlation coefficient. We already have seen that

$$SS_{error} = SS_Y(1 - r^2)$$

Expanding and rearranging, we have

$$SS_{error} = SS_Y - SS_Y(r^2)$$

$$r^2 = \frac{SS_Y - SS_{error}}{SS_Y}$$

In this equation SS_Y is the sum of squares of Y and represents the total of

1. the part of the sum of squares of Y that is related to X, in other words $SS_{\hat{Y}}$, and

2. the part of the sum of squares of Y that is independent of Y, in other words $SS_{Y-\hat{Y}}$ or SS_{error}.

In the context of our example we are talking about the part of the amount of food people ate (Servings) that is related to how good the food tastes and the part that is related to other things—such as the fact that lunch was even worse and people are unusually hungry. SS_{error} is that part of the sum of squares of Y that is independent of X and is a measure of the amount of error remaining even after we use X to predict Y. These concepts can be made clearer with a second example.

Suppose that we were interested in studying the relationship between cigarette smoking (X) and age at death (Y). As we watch people die off over time we notice several things. First we see that not all die at precisely the same age— there is variability in age at death regardless of smoking behavior, and this variability is measured by $SS_Y = \Sigma(Y - \bar{Y})^2$. We also notice the obvious fact that some people smoke more than others. This is variability in smoking regardless of age at death and is measured by $SS_X = \Sigma(X - \bar{X})^2$. We further find that cigarette smokers tend to die earlier than nonsmokers, and heavy smokers earlier than light smokers. Thus we write a regression equation to predict Y from X. Because people differ in their smoking behavior, they will also differ in their *predicted* life expectancy ($\hat{Y}$), and we will label this variability $SS_{\hat{Y}} = \Sigma(\hat{Y} - \bar{\hat{Y}})^2 = \Sigma(\hat{Y} - \bar{Y})^2$. This last measure is variability in Y that is directly attributable to variability in X, since different values of $\hat{Y}$ arise from

different values of X and the same values of $\hat{Y}$ arise from the same value of X—
that is, $\hat{Y}$ does not vary unless X varies.

We have one last source of variability, and this is the variability in the life
expectancy of those people who smoke exactly the same amount. It is measured
by SS_{error} and is variability in Y that cannot be explained by variability in X,
because these people did not differ in the amount they smoked. These several
sources of variability (i.e., sums of squares) are summarized in Table 10-3.

If we consider the absurd extreme in which all the nonsmokers die at
exactly age 72 and all the smokers smoke precisely the same amount and die at
exactly age 68, then all the variability in life expectancy is directly predictable
from variability in smoking behavior. If you smoke you will die at 68 and if you
don't you will die at 72. Here $SS_{\hat{Y}} = SS_Y$, and $SS_{error} = 0$.

In a more realistic example smokers might tend to die earlier than
nonsmokers, but within each group is a certain amount of variability in life
expectancy. This is a situation in which some of SS_Y is attributable to smoking
($SS_{\hat{Y}}$) and some is not (SS_{error}). What we want to be able to do is specify the
percentage of the overall variability in life expectancy that is attributable to
variability in smoking behavior. In other words we want a measure that
represents

$$\frac{SS_{\hat{Y}}}{SS_Y} = \frac{SS_Y - SS_{error}}{SS_Y}$$

As we have seen, that measure is r^2. In other words

$$r^2 = \frac{SS_{\hat{Y}}}{SS_Y}$$

This interpretation of r^2 is extremely useful. If, for example, the correlation
between amount smoked and life expectancy were an unrealistically high .80,
we could say that $.80^2 = 64\%$ of the variability in life expectancy is directly
predictable from the variability in smoking behavior. Obviously this is a
substantial exaggeration of the real world. If the correlation were a more likely
$r = .20$, we would say that $.20^2 = 4\%$ of the variability in life expectancy is
related to smoking behavior, whereas the other 96% is related to other factors.

One of the problems associated with focusing on the squared correlation
coefficient is in maintaining an appropriate sense of perspective. If it were true
that smoking accounted for 4% of the variability in life expectancy, it might be
tempting to dismiss smoking as a minor contributor to life expectancy.
However, you have to keep in mind that there are an enormous number of
variables that contribute to life expectancy, and one that accounts for 4% of that

---

TABLE 10-3
Sources of Variance in
Regression

SS_X = variability in amount smoked = $\Sigma (X - \bar{X})^2$

SS_Y = variability in life expectancy = $\Sigma (Y - \bar{Y})^2$

$SS_{\hat{Y}}$ = variability in life expectancy directly attributable to variability in smoking
behavior = $\Sigma (\hat{Y} - \bar{Y})^2$

SS_{error} = variability in life expectancy that cannot be attributable to variability in
smoking behavior = $\Sigma (Y - \hat{Y})^2 = SS_Y - SS_{\hat{Y}}$

variability is probably one of the major predictors. In fact, it has been suggested that 30% of the cancers in the United States are caused by smoking. A variable that accounts for 4% of the variability in course grades is probably minor. But something that accounts for 4% of variability in life expectancy is not to be dismissed so easily.

It is important to note that when we use phrases such as "accountable for," "attributable to," "predictable from," and "associated with," they are not to be interpreted as statements of cause and effect. Thus you could say that pains in your shoulder account for 10% of the variability in the weather without meaning to imply that sore shoulders cause rain, or even that rain itself causes sore shoulders. For example, your shoulder might hurt when it rains because carrying your umbrella aggravates your bursitis.

10-4   MULTIPLE REGRESSION

In this chapter we have dealt with the case in which we have only one predictor variable. In this situation we have a regression equation of the form $\hat{Y} = bX + a$. There is no good reason to limit ourselves to one predictor, however. It is perfectly appropriate to ask how well some linear combination of two, three, or four predictors will predict the criterion. Here, with three predictors, we would have a regression equation of the form

$$\hat{Y} = b_1 W + b_2 X + b_3 Z + a$$

where b_1, b_2, and b_3 are the slope coefficients for predictors W, X, and Z, respectively. Again, a is the intercept. Although multiple regression solutions are usually quite awkward to compute by hand, especially with more than two predictors, they are readily computed using any of the widely available computer programs.

Several years ago I collected data on admission to graduate school. All faculty rated several hundred graduate applications on a scale from 1 to 7, where 1 equals "reject immediately" and 7 equals "offer immediate acceptance." For a random sample of 100 applications I attempted to predict the mean rating for each application on the basis of Graduate Record Exam Verbal score (GREV), a numerical rating of the combined letters of recommendation (LETTERS), and a numerical rating of the statement of purpose (PURPOSE). The obtained regression equation was

$$\hat{Y} = 0.009\text{GREV} + 0.51\text{LETTERS} + 0.43\text{PURPOSE} - 1.87$$

Multiple correlation coefficient (R)
The correlation coefficient between the criterion and several predictor variables.

and the **multiple correlation coefficient (R)** was .775. Thus the squared correlation coefficient (R^2) was .60. The interpretation of R^2 is the same as for the case of r^2 with one predictor. In other words 60% of the variability in ratings can be accounted for by variability in the three predictors considered together. Put slightly differently, using GREV, LETTERS, and PURPOSE *simultaneously* as predictors, we can account for 60% of the variability in ratings.

The regression equation is interpreted in much the same way that it was interpreted with only one predictor. For every one unit change in GREV the predicted rating will increase by .009 unit, assuming *that the other two predictors are held constant.* Similarly, for every one-unit change in the rating of the letters of recommendation there will be a .51 unit change in the ratings, again assuming that the other two predictors are held constant.

You might be tempted to conclude from the regression equation that letters and statements of purpose are more important as predictors than GREV simply because they have larger **regression coefficients** (the slopes). However, these variables are measured in entirely different units (GREV scores range from 200 to 800, whereas the other two variables range from 1.0 to 3.0). Comparisons based on the magnitude of the coefficients are not appropriate. The task of deciding on the relative importance of predictors is a difficult one (and, for predictors that are themselves highly correlated, maybe even a meaningless one). A more extensive discussion of this problem is found in Howell (1987).

An important consideration in a multiple regression problem is the degree of correlation among the predictors themselves. When the predictors are highly correlated with each other (a condition known as **multicollinearity**), the regression equation is very unstable from one sample of data to another. In other words two random samples from the same population might produce regression equations that appear to be totally different from one another. I would very strongly advise that you avoid using highly correlated predictors and even avoid moderate intercorrelations where possible.

Multiple regression is a very useful technique. However, its use and interpretation are far from simple. Excellent discussions of this technique can be found in Neter and Wasserman (1974), Overall and Klett (1972), and Younger (1985).

Regression coefficients
The slope coefficients corresponding to each of the predictor variables.

Multicollinearity
A situation in which the predictors are highly intercorrelated.

10-5 USING MINITAB TO OBTAIN REGRESSION SOLUTIONS

Minitab has a solution for regression problems that will apply to both the one-predictor and the multiple-predictor case. The analysis of the dining hall example is shown in Table 10-4. Notice that the regression command requires that you specify the criterion (the variable to be predicted), then the number of predictor variables (in this example, one), and finally the name of the predictor variable(s). The other words are unimportant and are inserted only for clarity. If you enter the command NOBRIEF before the regression command, you will be provided with considerably more printout. I have left out the NOBRIEF command to save space and because we have not discussed many of the things that would be printed out. You would be wise to examine Table 10-4 carefully and to compare the values in the table with the ones that I calculated by hand. (Ignore the section labeled "Analysis of Variance." The "*t*-ratios" for the coefficients are simply *t* tests on whether the slopes and intercept are significantly different from 0. This concept will be developed in the next few chapters.) To run a multiple regression you would simply change the number of predictor variables and the list of predictor variable names.

═══ TABLE 10-4 ═══
Minitab Analysis of Dining Hall Example

```
MTB > SET THE FOLLOWING DATA IN COLUMN C1
DATA> 4 4 5 8 10 10 13 15 17 20 20 23 25 28 28 29 30 30 34 34 36 40 40 44 45
DATA> 45 48 52 53 56
DATA> END
MTB > SET THE FOLLOWING DATA IN COLUMN C2
DATA> 550 620 590 575 530 615 590 570 630 610 670 690 550 600 645 585 685 715
DATA> 615 650 690 640 745 610 680 695 665 675 700 665
DATA> END
MTB > NAME C1 'RATING'
MTB > NAME C2 'SERVINGS'
MTB > REGRESSION 'SERVINGS' AGAINST 1 PREDICTOR 'RATING'

The regression equation is
SERVINGS = 572 + 2.23 RATING

Predictor       Coef        Stdev      t-ratio
Constant       571.98       16.15       35.42
RATING          2.2347      0.5031       4.44

s = 42.26       R-sq = 41.3%     R-sq(adj) = 39.2%

Analysis of Variance

SOURCE         DF          SS           MS
Regression      1         35242        35242
Error          28         50008         1786
Total          29         85250

Unusual Observations
Obs.  RATING  SERVINGS      Fit  Stdev.Fit  Residual  St.Resid
 23     40.0    745.00    661.37    9.74       83.63     2.03R

R denotes an obs. with a large st. resid.

MTB > SAVE 'FOOD.MIN'

MTB > STOP
```

═══ 10-6 A FINAL WORKED EXAMPLE

In Chapter 9 we obtained the correlation coefficient for the relationship between the rated quality of a course and the difficulty of that course (as reflected in the average expected grade for students in that course). The data are repeated on the next page for convenience. In this chapter we will solve for the regression equation for predicting rated Overall Quality (Y) from Expected Grade (X). We will then consider the interpretation of the coefficients in that equation.

Our first step is to calculate the mean and variance of each variable. These are shown as follows:

$$\bar{X} = 49.5/15 = 3.3000 \qquad \bar{Y} = 50.0/15 = 3.333$$

$$s_X = \sqrt{\frac{164.65 - 49.5^2/15}{14}} \qquad s_Y = \sqrt{\frac{171.68 - 50.0^2/15}{14}}$$

$$= 0.3047 \qquad\qquad = 0.5984$$

$$s_X^2 = 0.3047^2 = 0.0928 \qquad s_Y^2 = 0.5984^2 = 0.3581$$

The covariance is given as

Expected Grade (X)	Overall Quality (Y)
3.5	3.4
3.2	2.9
2.8	2.6
3.3	3.8
3.2	3.0
3.2	2.5
3.6	3.9
4.0	4.3
3.0	3.8
3.1	3.4
3.0	2.8
3.3	2.9
3.2	4.1
3.4	2.7
3.7	3.9

$$\Sigma X = 49.5 \qquad \Sigma Y = 50.0$$
$$\Sigma X^2 = 164.65 \quad \Sigma Y^2 = 171.68$$
$$\Sigma XY = 166.48$$

$$\text{cov}_{XY} = \frac{166.48 - (49.5)(50.0)/15}{14} = 0.1057$$

To calculate the slope we have

$$b = \frac{\text{cov}_{XY}}{s_X^2} = \frac{0.1057}{0.0928} = 1.1385$$

We calculate the intercept as

$$a = \bar{Y} - b(\bar{X}) = 3.3333 - (1.1390)(3.3000) = -0.4238$$

Our equation is then

$$\hat{Y} = 1.1385(X) - 0.4238$$

We can interpret our results as follows. If we had a course in which students expected a grade of 0, our best guess is that the expected course rating would be -0.42. This is not a particularly meaningful statistic as far as interpretation is concerned because it is difficult to imagine a course in which everyone would expect to fail, and because course ratings below 0.0 are not possible. In this case the intercept merely serves to anchor the regression line.

A slope of 1.1385 can be interpreted to mean that if two courses differ by one point in expected grades, their overall ratings would be expected to differ by a little over one point. Such a difference, then, would be expected between a course in which students anticipate a grade of C and a course in which students anticipate a grade of B. Keep in mind, however, the remarks in Chapter 9 about the fact that we are not making a causal statement here. We have no particular reason to conclude that lower expected grades *cause* lower ratings.

10-7 SUMMARY

In this chapter we have expanded on what we already knew about the relationship between two variables to cover the situation in which we wish to predict one variable from knowledge of the other. We saw how to calculate the equation for a regression line and looked at the standard error of estimate $(s_{Y-\hat{Y}})$ as a measure of the accuracy of the prediction. We saw that r^2 is a very important index of the percentage of variability in one variable that can be accounted for by variability in the other. The use of r^2 instead of r adds considerable meaning to the correlation coefficient, although it must be interpreted with caution. Finally we briefly examined the topic of multiple regression. Some of the most important terms in this chapter are:

- Regression
- Linear regression
- Slope
- Intercept
- Errors of prediction

- Standard error of estimate
- Residual variance (error variance)
- Multiple correlation coefficient (R)
- Regression coefficients
- Multicollinearity

10-8 EXERCISES

10–1 From the data in Exercise 9-1 compute the regression equation for predicting the percentage of births of infants weighing under 2500 grams (Y) on the basis of fertility rate for females whose ages are $\leqslant 17$ or $\geqslant 35\,(X_1)$. (X_1 is known as "high-risk fertility rate.")

10–2 Calculate the standard error of estimate for the regression equation from Exercise 10-1.

10–3 If, as a result of ongoing changes in the role of women in society, we saw a change in the age of childbearing such that the high-risk fertility rate jumped to 70 in Exercise 9-1, what would we predict for incidence of birthweight <2500 grams?

10–4 Why should you feel very uncomfortable making a prediction in Exercise 10-3 for a rate of 70?

10–5 Compute a regression equation for predicting the final grade for the data in Exercise 9-9.

10–6 Compute a regression equation for predicting the number of problems completed from the final grade for the data in Exercise 9-9.

10–7 Using the data in Table 10-1 predict the number of servings for a rating of 21.

10–8 The mean rating for the data in Table 10-1 was 28.2. What would your prediction for servings be for a rating of 28.2? How does this compare to $\bar{Y}$?

10–9 Use the data in Exercise 9-10 to fit a regression equation predicting the decline in SAT math scores from 1978 to 1979 on the basis of I-131 levels.

10–10 With regard to the previous exercise, ignore I-131 and write an equation to predict a state's mean 1978 SAT math score from the corresponding SAT verbal score.

10–11 Interpret the results of the answer to Exercise 10-10.

10–12 Substract 100 points from each 1978 verbal score in Exercise 10-9. Then run the correlation between M78 and both the old and new V78.

10–13 Generate $\hat{Y}$ and $Y - \hat{Y}$ for the data in Table 10-1.

10–14 Using the data in Appendix C, Data Set, compute the regression equation for predicting GPA from ADDSC.

10–15 Use Minitab and the data from Exercise 9-1 to obtain the multiple correlation and regression equation for predicting Y from both X_1 and X_2 simultaneously. (Ignore the part of the printout that you don't understand.)

10–16 Within a group of 200 faculty members who have been at a well-known university for less than 15 years (i.e., before the salary curve levels off) the equation relating salary (in thousands of dollars) to years of service is

$\hat{Y} = 0.9X + 15$. For 100 administrative staff at the same university the equation is $\hat{Y} = 1.5X + 10$. Assuming that all differences are significant, interpret the meaning of these two equations. How many years must pass for an administrator and a faculty member to earn roughly the same salary?

10–17 In Section 10-6 there is a reference to the question of whether the slope is significantly different from zero. This question is addressed in the next two chapters in general terms. Try to anticipate that discussion by thinking about the problem. How might the calculated value of b for a sample of faculty members differ from the one obtained here? What does it mean if the slope is, or is not, different from zero?

■ SAMPLING DISTRIBUTIONS AND HYPOTHESIS TESTING ■

In the last several chapters we examined a number of different statistics and how they might be used to describe a set of data, represent the probability of the occurrence of some event, or measure the relationship between two variables. Although the description of data is important and fundamental to any analysis, it is not sufficient to answer many of the most interesting problems we encounter. In a typical experiment we might treat one group in a special way and wish to see if their scores differ from the scores of people in general. Or we might do something to one group and have an untreated control group and wish to compare the means of the two groups on some variable. Descriptive statistics will not tell us, for example, whether the difference between a sample mean and a hypothesized population mean or the difference between two obtained sample means is small enough to be explained on the basis of chance alone or whether it represents a true difference that might be attributable to the effect of our experimental treatment(s).

Statisticians frequently use phrases such as "differ by chance" or "sampling error" and assume that you know what they mean. Probably you do, but if you don't you are headed for confusion in the remainder of the book unless we spend a minute clarifying the meaning of these phrases. We will begin with a very simple example. In Chapter 7 we considered the distribution of Total Behavior Problem scores from Achenbach's Youth Self Report form. Total Behavior Problem scores are normally distributed in the population (i.e., the complete population of such scores is normally distributed) with a population mean (μ) of 50 and a population standard deviation (σ) of 10. We know that children show different levels of problem behaviors and therefore have different scores, and that if we took a sample of children their sample mean would probably not equal exactly 50. One sample of children might have a mean of 49, while a second sample of children might have a mean of 51.3. The actual sample mean would depend on the particular children who happened to be included in it. This expected variability that we see from sample to sample is what is meant when we speak of "variability due to change." We are referring to the fact that statistics (in this case, means) obtained from samples naturally vary from one sample to another.

Sampling error
Variability of a statistic from sample to sample due to chance.

Along the same lines the phrase **sampling error** often is used in this context as a synonym for variability due to chance. It indicates that the value of a sample statistic probably will be in error (i.e., will deviate from the parameter that it is estimating) as a result of the particular observations that happened to be included in the sample. In this context "error" does not imply carelessness or mistakes. In the case of behavior problems one random sample might just happen to include an unusually obnoxious child, whereas another sample might happen to include an unusual number of relatively well-behaved children.

11-1 TWO SIMPLE EXAMPLES INVOLVING BEHAVIOR PROBLEMS AND RUDE MOTORISTS

One of the useful scales included on the Youth Self Report form is the Total Behavior Problem score, which, for a population of normal children, is known to have a mean of 50 and a standard deviation of 10. Suppose that we have a sample of five children who we know to have been under a considerable amount of stress at home due to parental divorce, and we want to study this sample to see if children who are under high levels of stress also show an elevated level of behavior problems. Suppose further that these five children filled out the Youth Self Report form, and the mean for this sample turned out to be 56, which is a full 6 points above the mean of a population of normal children. What we really want to know is whether the difference between 56 and 50 is small enough to be attributable to the chance variation we would normally expect if the scores were sampled from normal children, or whether the difference is sufficiently large to lead us to conclude that the population of children from which we sampled has a mean that is higher than the mean of a population of normal children. Put another way, we want to test the hypothesis that the mean of the population from which we sampled (μ) is 50 against the alternative hypothesis that μ is greater than 50. The answer to this specific question will be discussed in detail in the next chapter. Here we are concerned only with general issues involved in the approach to such questions.

A second example comes from a study by Doob and Gross (1968), who investigated the influence of perceived social status. They found that if an old, beat-up (low-status) car failed to start when a stoplight turned green, 84% of the time the driver of the second car in line honked the horn. However, when the stopped car was an expensive, high-status car, only 50% of the time did the following driver honk. These results could be explained in one of two ways. Either

1. the difference between 84% in one sample and 50% in a second sample is attributable to sampling error (random variability among samples),

and therefore we cannot conclude that perceived social status influences horn-honking behavior; or

2. the difference between 84% and 50% is large, a difference not to be attributable to sampling error (random variability among samples), and therefore people are less likely to honk at drivers of high-status cars.

Although the statistical calculations required to answer this question are different from those used to answer the previous one (because the first dealt with means and the second deals with proportions), the underlying logic is fundamentally the same.

These examples of behavior problems and horn-honking behavior are two of the kinds of questions that fall under the heading of **hypothesis testing**. This chapter is intended to present the theory of hypothesis testing in as general a ways as possible, without becoming involved in the specific techniques or properties of any particular test.

The theory of hypothesis testing is so important in all that follows that a thorough understanding of it is essential. Many students who have had one or more courses in statistics and know how to run a number of different statistical tests still do not have a basic knowledge of what it is they are doing. As a result they have difficulty interpreting statistical tables and must learn every new procedure in a step-by-step, rote fashion. This chapter is designed to avoid that difficulty by presenting the theory in its most general sense, without the use of any formulae. You can learn the formulae later, after you understand why you might want to use them. Professional statisticians might fuss over the looseness of the definitions, but any looseness can be set right in subsequent chapters. Others may object that we are considering hypothesis testing before we consider the statistical procedures that product the test. That is precisely the intent. The material covered here cuts across all statistical tests and can be discussed independently of them. By separating the material in this way, you are free to concentrate on the underlying principles without worrying about the mechanics of calculation.

The important issue in hypothesis testing is to find some way of deciding whether we are looking at a small chance fluctuation from a true underlying mean of 50, to use the behavior problem example, or whether the deviation from 50 is large enough to suggest that stressed children present, on average, more behavior problems that normal children. To answer this kind of question we have to use what are called **sampling distributions**, which tell us specifically what degree of sample-to-sample variability we can expect by chance as a function of sampling error.

Hypothesis testing
A process by which decisions are made concerning the values of parameters.

Sampling distributions
The distributions of a statistic over repeated sampling from a specified population.

11-2   SAMPLING DISTRIBUTIONS

The most basic concept underlying all statistical tests is that of the sampling distribution of a statistic. It is fair to say that if we did not have sampling distributions, we would not have any statistical tests. Roughly speaking, sampling distributions tell us what values we might (or might not) expect to obtain for a particular statistic under a set of predefined conditions (e.g., what the obtained mean of five children might be *if* the true mean of the population from which those children come is 50.0). As such, sampling distributions provide the opportunity to evaluate the likelihood (given the value of a sample statistic) of whether or not such predefined conditions actually exist.

Basically the sampling distribution of a statistic can be thought of as the distribution of values obtained for that statistic over repeated sampling (i.e., running the experiment, or drawing samples, an unlimited number of times). Although sampling distributions are almost always derived mathematically, it is easier to understand what they represent if we consider how they could, in theory, be derived empirically with a simple sampling experiment.

Sampling distribution of the mean

The distribution of sample means over repeated sampling from one population.

We will take as an illustration the **sampling distribution of the mean**, because it is the most easily understood and relates directly to the example of behavior problems. The sampling distribution of the mean is nothing but the distribution of the means of an infinite number of random samples drawn under certain specified conditions (for example, under the condition that the true mean of our population is 50 and the standard deviation is 10). Suppose that we have a population with a known mean ($\mu = 50$). Further suppose that we draw a very large number (theoretically an infinite number) of random samples from this population, each sample consisting of five scores. For each sample we will calculate its mean, and when we finish drawing all of the samples, we will plot the distribution of these *means*. Such a distribution would be a sampling distribution of the mean and might look like the one presented in Figure 11-1. We can see from this figure that sample means between 48 and 52, for example, are quite likely to occur when we sample five children at random. We also can see that it is extremely unlikely that we would draw from this population a sample of five observations that has a sample mean as high as 70, although there is some (quite small) probability of doing so. The fact that we know the kinds of values to expect for the mean of a sample drawn from this population is now going to allow us to turn the question around and ask if an obtained sample mean can be taken as evidence in favor of the hypothesis that we actually are sampling from this population.

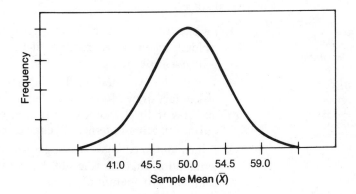

FIGURE 11-1

Distribution of Sample Means of Behavior Problems, Each Based on *n* = 5 Scores

11-3   HYPOTHESIS TESTING

We do not go around obtaining sampling distributions, either mathematically or empirically, simply because they are interesting to look at. We have important reasons for doing so. The usual reason is that we want to test some hypothesis. As mentioned previously, I have found that a random sample of five highly stressed children have a mean behavior problem score of 56. I would like to test the hypothesis that such a sample mean could reasonably have arisen had I drawn my sample from a population in which $\mu = 50$. This is another way of saying that I want to know whether the mean of stressed children is different from the mean of normal children. The only way I can test such a hypothesis is to have some idea of the probability of obtaining a sample mean of 56 *if* I were actually sampling observations from a population in which $\mu = 50$. The answer to this question is precisely what a sampling distribution is designed to provide.

Suppose that we obtained (constructed) the sampling distribution of the mean for samples of five children from a population whose mean μ is 50. (This is actually the distribution plotted in Figure 11-1.) Suppose further that we then determined from that distribution the probability of a sample mean as high as 56. For the sake of argument suppose that this probability is .15. My reasoning can then go as follows: "If I in fact did sample from a population with $\mu = 50$, the probability of obtaining a sample mean as high as 62 is .15—a fairly likely event. Because a sample mean this high is often obtained from a population with a mean of 50, I have no reason to doubt that this sample came from such a population."

On the other hand suppose that I obtained a sample mean of 62 and that I calculated from the sampling distribution that the probability of a sample mean as high as 62 was only .004. My argument can then go like this: "If I in fact did sample from a population with $\mu = 50$, the probability of obtaining a sample mean as high as 62 is only .004—an unlikely event. Because a sample mean this high is unlikely to be obtained from such a population, I can reasonably conclude that this sample probably came from some other population (one whose mean is not 50)."

It is important to realize precisely what has been done in this example, because the logic is typical of most tests of hypotheses. The actual test consisted of several stages.

Research hypothesis
The hypothesis that the experiment was designed to investigate.

1. I wished to test the hypothesis, often called the **research hypothesis**, that children under stress are more likely than normal children to exhibit behavior problems.

Null hypothesis (H_0)
The statistical hypothesis tested by the statistical procedure. Usually a hypothesis of no difference or of no relationship.

2. I set up the hypothesis (called the **null hypothesis, H_0**) that the sample was in fact drawn from a population whose mean, denoted μ_0, equals 50. This is the hypothesis that stressed children do not differ from normal children in terms of behavior problems.

3. I then obtained the sampling distribution of the mean under the assumption that H_0 (the null hypothesis) is true (i.e., I obtained the sampling distribution of the mean from a population with $\mu_0 = 50$).

4. I obtained a random sample of children under stress.

5. Given the sampling distribution, I calculated the probability of a mean *at least as large* as my actual sample mean.

6. On the basis of this probability I made a decision. I either rejected or failed to reject H_0. Because H_0 states that $\mu = 50$, rejection of H_0 represents a belief that $\mu > 50$, although the actual value of μ remains unspecified.

The preceding discussion is oversimplifed in the sense that we would generally prefer to test the research hypothesis that children under stress are *different from* (rather than just *higher than*) other children, but we will return to this point shortly. It is also oversimplified in the sense that in practice we also would need to take into account (either directly or by estimation) the value of σ^2, the population variance, and N, the sample size. However, the logic of the approach is representative of the logic of most, if not all, statistical tests. In each case we will begin with a research hypothesis, set up the null hypothesis, construct the sampling distribution of the particular statistic on the assumption that H_0 is true, collect some data, compare the sample statistic to that distribution, and reject or retain H_0 depending upon the probability, under H_0, of a sample statistic as extreme as the one we have obtained.

11-4 THE NULL HYPOTHESIS

As we have seen, the concept of the null hypothesis plays a crucial role in the testing of hypotheses. Students frequently are puzzled by the fact that we set up a hypothesis that is directly counter to what we hope to show. For example, if we hope to demonstrate the research hypothesis that college students do not come from a population with a mean self-confidence score of 100, we immediately set up the null hypothesis that they do. Or, if we hope to demonstrate the validity of a research hypothesis that the means (μ_1 and μ_2) of the populations from which two samples are drawn are different, we state the null hypothesis that the population means are equal (or, equivalently, $\mu_1 - \mu_2 = 0$). (The phrase "null hypothesis" is most easily seen in this second example, in which it refers to the hypothesis that the difference between the two population means is zero, or *null*.) There are several reasons that we use the null hypothesis. The philosophical argument, used by Fisher when he first introduced the concept, is that we can never prove something to be true, but we can prove something to be false. Observing 3000 people with one head does not prove the statement "Everyone has only one head." However, finding one person with two heads does disprove the statement beyond any shadow of a doubt. While one might argue with Fisher's basic position—and many people have—the null hypothesis retains its dominant place in statistics.

A second and more practical reason for employing the null hypothesis is that it provides us with a starting point for any statistical test. Consider the case in which you wish to show that the mean self-confidence score of college students is greater than 100. Suppose further that you were granted the privilege of proving the truth of some hypothesis. What hypothesis are you going to test? Shall you test the hypothesis that $\mu = 101$, or maybe the hypothesis that $\mu = 112$, or how about $\mu = 113$? The point is that you do not have a *specific* alternative (research) hypothesis in mind, and without one you cannot construct the sampling distribution that you need. However, if you start off by assuming H_0: $\mu = 100$, you can immediately set about obtaining the sampling distribution for $\mu = 100$, and then, with luck, reject that hypothesis and conclude that the mean score of college students is greater than 100, which is what you wanted to show in the first place.

11-5   TEST STATISTICS AND THEIR SAMPLING DISTRIBUTIONS

Sample statistics
Statistics calculated from a sample and used primarily to describe the sample (e.g., $\bar{X}$).

Test statistics
The results of a statistical test (e.g., t).

We have been discussing the sampling distribution of the mean, but that entire discussion would have been essentially the same had we dealt instead with the median, the variance, the range, or any other statistic you care to consider. (Technically, the shape of these distributions would be different, but we are deliberately ignoring such issues in this chapter.) The statistics just mentioned usually are referred to as **sample statistics** because they are used to describe a sample. There is a whole different class of statistics called **test statistics**, however, which are associated with specific statistical procedures and which have their own sampling distributions. They are statistics such as t, F, χ^2, and so on, which you *may* have run across in the past. If you are not familiar with them, don't worry—we will consider them separately in later chapters. This is not the place to go into a detailed explanation of any of them. (I put this chapter where I did because I didn't want anyone to think that he or she was supposed to worry about technical issues.) This chapter is the place, however, to point out that the sampling distributions for test statistics are obtained and used in essentially the same way as the sampling distribution of the mean.

As an illustration, consider the sampling distribution of the statistic t, which will be discussed in the next three chapters. For those who have never heard of the t test, it is sufficient to point out that it is often used, among other things, to answer the question of whether two samples were drawn from populations with the same means. Let μ_1 and μ_2 represent the means of the populations from which the two samples were drawn. The null hypothesis is the hypothesis that the two population means are equal—in other words H_0: $\mu_1 = \mu_2$ (or $\mu_1 - \mu_2 = 0$). If you were extremely patient, you could empirically obtain the sampling distribution of t when H_0 is true by drawing an infinite number of pairs of samples, all from one population, calculating t for each pair of samples (by methods discussed later), and plotting the resulting values of t. In this case H_0 must be true because the samples came from the same population. The resulting distribution is the sampling distribution of t when H_0 is true. If we now had two samples that produced a particular value of t, we would test the null hypothesis by comparing our sample t to the sampling distribution of t. We would reject the null hypothesis if our t did not look like the kinds of t values that the sampling distribution tells us to expect when the null hypothesis is true.

The preceding paragraph could be rewritten substituting chi-square, F, or any other test statistic in place of t, with only minor changes dealing with how the statistic is calculated. Thus we see that all sampling distributions could be obtained in basically the same way (calculate and plot an infinite number of statistics by sampling from a known population). Once this fact is understood, the remainder of the book is largely the elaboration of methods for the calculation of the desired statistic and the description of characteristics of the appropriate sampling distribution.

11-6   USING THE NORMAL DISTRIBUTION TO TEST HYPOTHESES

Much of the discussion so far has dealt with statistical procedures that you do not yet know how to use. This was done deliberately to emphasize the point that the logic and the calculations behind a test are two separate issues. However, we now can use what we already know about the normal distribution to test some simple hypotheses. In the process we can deal with a number of fundamental issues, which are more easily seen by use of a concrete example.

One of the important uses of the normal distribution is the testing of hypotheses. It can be used to test hypotheses either about individual observations or about sample statistics such as the mean. In this chapter we will deal with individual observations, leaving the question of testing sample statistics until later chapters. Note, however, that in the general case we test hypotheses about sample statistics such as the mean rather than about individual observations. However, I am starting with an example of an individual observation because the explanation is somewhat clearer. Because we are dealing with only single observations, the sampling distribution invoked here will be the distribution of individual scores (rather than the distribution of means). The basic logic is the same, and we are using an example of individual scores only because it simplifies the explanation and is something with which you have already had experience.

To take a simple example, assume that we know that the mean rate of finger tapping of normal healthy adults is 100 taps in 20 seconds, with a standard deviation of 20, and that tapping speeds are normally distributed in the population. Assume further that we know that the tapping rate is slower among people with certain neurological problems. (In fact, tapping speeds are an important diagnostic indicator of neurological damage, although the difference in rates between left and right hands is more important than the absolute rate.) Finally suppose that an individual has just been sent to us who taps at a rate of 70 taps in 20 seconds. Is his score sufficiently below the mean for us to assume that he did not come from a population of neurologically healthy people? This situation is diagrammed in Figure 11-2, in which the arrow indicates the location of our piece of data (the person's score).

The logic of the solution to this problem is the same as the logic of hypothesis testing in general. We will begin by assuming that the individual's

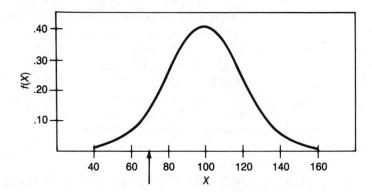

FIGURE 11-2
**Location of a Person's Score
on a Distribution of Scores of
Neurologically Healthy People**

score does come from the population of healthy scores. This is the null hypothesis (H_0). If H_0 is true, we automatically know the mean and standard deviation of the population from which he was supposedly drawn (100 and 20, respectively). With this information we are in a position to calculate the probability that a score *as low as* his would be obtained from this population. If the probability is very low, we can reject H_0 and conclude that he did not come from the healthy population. On the other hand if the probability is not particularly low, then the data represent a reasonable result under H_0, and we would have no reason to doubt its validity, and thus no reason to doubt that the person is healthy. Keep in mind that we are not interested in the probability of a score *equal to* 70 (which, because the distribution is continuous, would be infinitely small) but rather with the probability that the score would be as low as (i.e., less than or equal to) 70.

The individual had a score of 70. What we want to know is the probability of obtaining a score *at least as low as* 70 if H_0 is true. This is something we already know how to find—it is the area below 70 in Figure 11-2. All we have to do is convert the 70 to a z score and then refer z to Appendix D, Table 9.

$$z = \frac{X - \mu}{\sigma} = \frac{70 - 100}{20} = \frac{-30}{20} = -1.5$$

From Appendix D, Table 9, we can see that the probability of a z score of -1.5 or below is .0668. (This is shown in the table opposite $z = 1.50$ and under the column headed "Smaller Portion.")

Decision making

A procedure for making logical decisions on the basis of sample data.

At this point we have to become involved in the **decision-making** aspects of hypothesis testing. We must decide if an event with a probability of .0668 is sufficiently unlikely to cause us to reject H_0. Here we will fall back on arbitrary conventions that have been established over the years. The rationale for these conventions will become clearer as we go along, but for the time being keep in mind that they are merely conventions. One convention calls for rejecting H_0 if the probability under H_0 is less than or equal to .05 ($p \leq .05$), while another convention—more conservative with respect to the probability of rejecting H_0—calls for rejecting H_0 when the probability under H_0 is less than or equal to

Rejection level (Significance level)
The probability with which we are willing to reject H_0 when it is in fact correct.

Rejection region
The set of outcomes of an experiment that will lead to rejection of H_0.

.01. These values of .05 and .01 are often referred to as the **rejection level**, or **significance level**, of the test. Whenever the probability obtained under H_0 is less than or equal to our predetermined significance level, we will reject H_0. Another way of stating this is to say that any outcome whose probability under H_0 is less than or equal to the significance level falls in the **rejection region**, since such an outcome leads us to reject H_0. For the purpose of setting a standard level of rejection for this book we will use the .05 level of significance, keeping in mind that some people would consider this level to be too lenient. When we come to Chapter 15 it will be more apparent why this particular level was chosen over the alternatives.† For our particular example we have obtained a probability value of .0668, which is obviously greater than .05. Because we have specified that we will not reject H_0 unless the probability of the data under H_0 is less than .05, we must conclude that we have no reason to decide that the person did not come from a population of healthy people. More specifically, we conclude that a finger-tapping rate of 70 could reasonably have come from a population of scores with a mean equal to 100 and standard deviation equal to 20. It is very important to note that we have not shown that this person is healthy, but only that we have insufficient reason to believe that he is not. It may be that he is just acquiring the disease and therefore is not quite as different from normal as is usual for his condition. Or maybe he has the disease at an advanced stage but just happens to be an unusually fast tapper. This is an example of the fact that we can never say that we have proved the null hypothesis. We can conclude only that this person does not tap sufficiently slowly for his illness, if any, to be statistically detectable.

The theory of significance testing as just outlined was popularized originally by R. A. Fisher in the first third of the 20th century. The theory was expanded and cast in more of a decision framework by Jerzy Neyman and Egon Pearson between 1928 and 1938—often against the loud and abusive objections of Fisher. Current statistical practice now most closely follows the Neyman–Pearson approach, which places more emphasis than did Fisher's on the fact

Alternative hypothesis (H_1)
The hypothesis that is adopted when H_0 is rejected. Usually the same as the research hypothesis.

that we also have an **alternative hypothesis (H_1)** that is contradictory to the null hypothesis (H_0). Thus if the null hypothesis is

$$H_0: \mu = 100$$

†The particular view of hypothesis testing described here is the classical one that a null hypothesis is rejected if its probability is less than the predefined significance level and not rejected if its probability is greater than the significance level. Currently a substantial body of opinion holds that such cut-and-dried rules are inappropriate and that more attention should be paid to the probability value itself. In other words the classical approach (using a .05 rejection level) would declare $p = .051$ and $p = .150$ to be (equally) "nonsignificant" and $p = .048$ and $p = .00003$ to be (equally) "significant." The alternative view would think of $p = .051$ as "nearly significant" or "marginally significant" ("marginal significance" often refers to $.10 \geqslant p \geqslant .05$) and would think of $p = .0003$ as "very significant." While this view has much to recommend it, it will not be wholeheartedly adopted here. However, most computer programs do print out exact probability levels, and those values, when interpreted judiciously, can be useful. The difficulty comes in defining what is meant by "interpreted judiciously."

then the alternative hypothesis could be

$$H_1: \mu \neq 100$$

or $$H_1: \mu < 100$$

or $$H_1: \mu > 100$$

We will have more to say about these alternative hypotheses shortly.

11-7   TYPE I AND TYPE II ERRORS

Whenever we reach a decision with a statistical test, there is always a chance that our decision was the wrong one. While this is true of almost all decisions, statistical or otherwise, the statistician has one point in her favor that other decision makers normally lack. She not only makes a decision by some rational process, but she can also specify the probability of that decision's being in error. In everyday life we make a decision with only the subjective feeling that we probably made the right choice. (I had an excellent student who went around with the feeling that whatever his choice, it was probably the wrong one.) The statistician on the other hand can state quite precisely the probability that she erroneously rejected H_0 in favor of the alternative hypothesis (H_1) when in fact H_0 was true. This ability to specify the probability of error follows directly from the logic of hypothesis testing.

Consider the previous finger-tapping example, this time ignoring the score obtained from the person. The situation is diagrammed in Figure 11-3, in which the distribution is the distribution of scores from healthy subjects and the shaded portion represents the lowest 5% of the distribution. The actual score that cuts off the lowest 5% is called the **critical value**. Critical values are those values of X (the variable) that describe the boundary, or boundaries, of the rejection region(s). For this particular example the critical value is 67.

If we have a decision rule that says to reject H_0 whenever an outcome falls in the lower 5% of the distribution, we will reject H_0 whenever an individual's score falls in the shaded area, that is, whenever a score as low as his has a

Critical value
The value of a test statistic at or beyond which we will reject H_0.

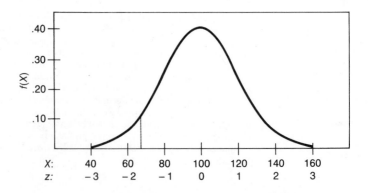

probability of .05 or less of coming from the population of healthy scores. Yet by the very nature of our procedure 5% of the scores from perfectly healthy people will themselves fall in the shaded portion. Thus if we actually have sampled a person who is healthy, we stand a 5% chance of his score being in the shaded tail of the distribution, causing us to erroneously reject the null hypothesis. This kind of error (rejecting H_0 when in fact it is true) is called a **Type I error**, and its probability is designated as **α (alpha)**, the size of the rejection region. In the future whenever we represent a probability by α, we will be referring to the probability of a Type I error.

You might feel that a 5% chance of making an error is too great a risk to take, and suggest that we make our criterion much more stringent—for example by rejecting only the lowest 1% of the distribution. This is a perfectly legitimate procedure, but realize that the more stringent you make your criterion, the more likely you are to make another kind of error—failing to reject H_0 when it is in fact false and H_1 is true. This type of error is called a **Type II error**, and its probability is symbolzied by **β (beta)**.

The major difficulty in terms of Type II errors stems from the fact that if H_0 is false, we almost never know what the true distribution (the distribution under H_1) would look like for the population from which our data came. We know only the distribution of scores under H_0. Put in the present context, this is to say that we know the distribution of scores from healthy people but not from nonhealthy people. It may be that people suffering from some neurological disease tap, on average, considerably more slowly than healthy people, or it may be that they tap, on average, only a little more slowly. This situation is illustrated in Figure 11-4, in which the distribution labeled H_0 represents the distribution of scores from healthy subjects (the set of observations expected under the null hypothesis), and the distribution label H_1 represents our hypothetical distribution of nonhealthy scores (the distribution under H_1). Remember that the curve H_1 is only hypothetical. We really do not know the location of the nonhealthy distribution, other than that it is lower (slower speeds) than the distribution H_0. (I have arbitrarily drawn it with a mean of 80 and a standard deviation of 20.)

The darkly shaded portion in the top half of Figure 11-4 represents the rejection region. Any observation falling in that area (i.e., to the left of about 67) would lead to rejection of the null hypothesis. If the null hypothesis is true, we know that our observation will fall in this area, and we will thus make a Type I error, 5% of the time.

The lightly shaded portion in the bottom half of Figure 11-4 represents the probability (β) of a Type II error. This is a situation in which a person was actually drawn from the nonhealthy population but his score was not sufficiently low to cause us to reject H_0.

In the particular situation illustrated in Figure 11-4 we can in fact calculate β by using the normal distribution to calculate the probability of obtaining a score *greater than* 67 (the critical value) if $\mu = 80$ and $\sigma = 20$. The actual calculation is not important for your understanding of β, and because this chapter was designed specifically to avoid calculation, I will simply state that

Type I error
The error of rejecting H_0 when it is true.

α (Alpha)
The probability of a Type I error.

Type II error
The error of not rejecting H_0 when it is false.

β (Beta)
The probability of a Type II error.

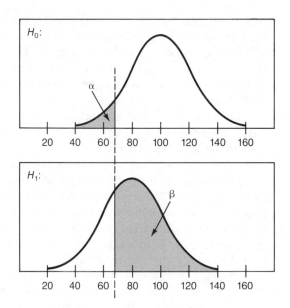

FIGURE 11-4

Areas Corresponding to α and β for Tapping-Speed Example

this probability (i.e., the area labeled β) is .74. Thus for this example 74% of the time when we have a person who is actually nonhealthy (i.e., H_1 is actually true), we will make a Type II error by failing to reject H_0 when it is false—as medical diagnosticians we leave a lot to be desired.

From Figure 11-4 you can see that if we were to reduce the level of α (the probability of a Type I error) from .05 to .01 by moving the rejection region to the left, it would reduce the probability of Type I errors, but it would increase the probability of Type II errors. Setting α at .01 would mean that $\beta = .908$. Thus there is obviously room for debate over what level of significance to use. The decision rests primarily on your opinion concerning the relative importance of Type I and Type II errors for the type of study that you are conducting. If it is important to avoid Type I errors (such as telling someone that he has a disease when he does not), then you would set a stringent (i.e., small) level of α. If on the other hand you want to avoid Type II errors (telling someone to go home and take an aspirin when in fact he needs immediate treatment), then you might set a fairly high level of α. (Setting α at .20 in this example would reduce β to .44.) Unfortunately in practice most people choose an arbitrary level of α, such as .05 or .01, and simply ignore β. In some cases this is probably all that you can do. In other cases, however, there is much more to be done, as we will see in Chapter 15.

I should stress again that Figure 11-4 is hypothetical. I could draw that figure only because I arbitrarily decided that speeds of nonhealthy people were normally distributed with a mean of 80 and a standard deviation of 20. In most everyday situations we do not know the mean and variance of that distribution and can make only educated guesses, thus providing only crude estimates of β. In practice, we can select a value of μ under H_1 that represents the *minimum* difference we would like to be able to detect, since larger differences will have even smaller βs. We will return to this problem in Chapter 15.

From this discussion of Type I and Type II errors we can summarize the decision-making process with a simple table. Table 11-1 presents the four possible outcomes of an experiment. The cells of this table should be self-explanatory. Notice that the cell in the upper right, however, contains a concept **(power)** that we have not yet discussed. The power of a test is the probability of rejecting H_0 when it is actually false. Because the probability of *failing* to reject a false H_0 is β, then power must equal $1 - \beta$. We will have considerably more to say about power in Chapter 15.

Power

The probability of correctly rejecting a false H_0.

TABLE 11-1
Possible Outcomes of the Decision-Making Process

Decision	True State of the World	
	H_0 True	H_0 False
Reject H_0	Type I Error $p = \alpha$	Correct Decision $p = 1 - \beta$ = Power
Fail to Reject H_0	Correct Decision $p = 1 - \alpha$	Type II Error $p = \beta$

11-8 ONE- AND TWO-TAILED TESTS

The preceding discussion brings us to a consideration of one- and two-tailed tests. In our example we knew that nonhealthy subjects tapped more slowly than healthy individuals, and therefore we decided to reject H_0 only if a subject tapped too slowly. However, suppose that our subject had tapped 180 times in 20 seconds. Although this is an exceedingly unlikely event to observe from a healthy subject, it did not fall in the rejection region, which consisted solely of low rates. As a result we find ourselves in the position of not rejecting H_0 in the face of a piece of data that is very unlikely, but not in the direction expected.

The question then arises as to how we can protect ourselves against this type of situation (if protection is thought necessary). The answer is to specify before we run the experiment that we are going to reject a given percentage (say 5%) of the *extreme* outcomes—both those that are extremely high and those that are extremely low. But if we reject the lowest 5% and the highest 5%, then we would in fact reject H_0 a total of 10% of the time when it is actually true—that is, $\alpha = .10$. We rarely are willing to work with α as high as .10 and prefer to see it set no higher than .05. The only way to accomplish this is to reject the lowest 2.5% and the highest 2.5%, making a total of 5%.

The situation in which we reject H_0 for only the lowest (or for only the highest) tapping speeds is referred to as a **one-tailed** or a **directional** test, since we make a prediction of the direction in which the individual will differ from the mean and our rejection region is located in only one tail of the distribution. When we reject extremes in either tail, we have what is called a **two-tailed** or **nondirectional** test. It is important to keep in mind, however, that while we gain something with a two-tailed test (the ability to reject the null hypothesis for extreme scores in either direction), we also lose something. A score that would

**One-tailed test
(Directional test)**

A test that rejects extreme outcomes in only one specified tail of the distribution.

**Two-tailed test
(Nondirectional test)**

A test that rejects extreme outcomes in either tail of the distribution.

fall in the rejection region of a one-tailed test may not fall in the rejection region of the corresponding two-tailed test, because now we reject only 2.5% in each tail.

In the finger-tapping example the decision between a one- and a two-tailed test might seem reasonably clear cut. We know that people with a given disease tap more slowly, and therefore we care only about rejecting H_0 for slow scores— high scores have no diagnostic importance. (Maybe the person is one of those annoying, fidgety types who spends his time tapping on everything in sight and therefore taps rapidly because he has had an unusual amount of practice.) In many other situations, however, we do not know which tail of the distribution is important (or if both are), and we need to guard against extremes in either tail. This situation might arise when we are considering a campaign to persuade children to brush their teeth more often. We might find that the campaign led to an increase in the desired behavior. On the other hand we might find that kids hate to be told to brush their teeth and therefore brush even less frequently just to spite us. In either case we would want to reject H_0.

In general, two-tailed tests are far more common than one-tailed tests. There are several reasons for this. First of all the investigator may have no idea what the data will look like and therefore has to be prepared for any eventuality. Although this situation is rare, it does occur in some exploratory work.

Another common reason for preferring two-tailed tests is that the investigator is reasonably sure that the data will come out one way, but wishes to cover himself in the event that he is wrong. This type of situation arises more often than you might think. (Carefully formed hypotheses have an annoying habit of being phrased in the wrong direction, for reasons that seem so obvious after the event.) A frequent question that arises when the data may come out the other way around is "Why not plan to run a one-tailed test and then, if the data come out the other way, just change your test to a two-tailed test?" This kind of question arises from people who have no intention of being devious, but just do not understand the logic of what they are doing. If you start an experiment with the extreme 5% of the left-hand tail as your rejection region and then turn around and reject any outcome that happens to fall in the extreme 2.5% of the right-hand tail, then you are really working at the 7.5% level. In this situation you will reject 5% of the outcomes in one direction (assuming that the data fell in the desired tail), and you are willing also to reject 2.5% of the outcomes in the other direction (when the data are in the unexpected direction). There is no denying that 5% + 2.5% = 7.5%. To put this another way, would you be willing to flip a coin for an ice cream cone when I have called "heads" but have also reserved the right to switch to "tails" after I saw how the coin landed? Or, would you think it fair of me to shout "2 out of 3" when the first coin came up in your favor? You would object to both of these strategies. This is the reason the choice between a one- and a two-tailed test is made before the data are collected. It is also one of the reasons that two-tailed tests are usually chosen.

Although the preceding discussion argues in favor of two-tailed tests and although in this book we generally will confine ourselves to such procedures, there are no hard and fast rules. The final decision depends upon what you already know about the relative severity of different kinds of errors. It is important to keep in mind that with respect to a given tail of a distribution the difference between a one- and a two-tailed test is that the latter just uses a different cutoff. A two-tailed test at $\alpha = .05$ is more liberal than a one-tailed test at $\alpha = .01$.†

If you have a sound grasp of the logic of testing hypotheses by use of sampling distributions, the remainder of the course is relatively simple. For any new statistic to be encountered, only two basic questions need to be asked:

1. How and with which assumptions is it calculated?

2. What does its sampling distribution look like under H_0?

If you know the answers to these two questions, your test is accomplished by calculating the test statistic for the data at hand and comparing the statistic to the sampling distribution. Because the relevant sampling distributions are tabled at the back of the book, all you really need to know is which test is appropriate for a particular situation and how to calculate its test statistic.

11-9 A FINAL WORKED EXAMPLE

A number of years ago the mean on the Verbal section of the Graduate Record Exam (GRE) was 489 with a standard deviation of 126. The statistics were based on all students taking the exam in that year, the vast majority of whom were native speakers of English. Suppose that in that year we had an application from an individual with a Chinese name who had a particularly low score (e.g., 220). If this individual were a native speaker of English, that score is sufficiently low for us to question his suitability for graduate school unless the rest of the documentation is considerably better. However, if that student is not a native speaker of English I would probably disregard the low score entirely on the grounds that it is a poor reflection of his abilities.

We have two possible choices, namely, the individual is or is not a native speaker of English. If he is a native speaker, we know the mean and standard

---

†One of the reviewers of this book phrased the case for two-tailed tests even more strongly. "It is my (minority) belief that what an investigator *expects to be true* has absolutely no bearing *whatsoever* on the issue of one- versus two-tailed tests. Nature couldn't care less what psychologists' theories predict, and will often show patterns/trends in the opposite direction. Since our goal is to know the truth (not to prove we are astute at predicting), our tests must always allow for testing *both* directions. I say *always* do two-tailed tests, and if you are worried about β, jack the sample size up a bit to offset the loss in power" (Bradley, D., personal communication, 1983). I am personally inclined toward his point of view. Nature is notoriously fickle—or else we are notoriously inept at prediction. On the other hand, a second reviewer (Rodgers, personal communication, 1986) takes exception to this position. While acknowledging that Bradley's point is well considered, Rodgers argues, "To generate a theory about how the world works that implies an expected direction of an effect, but then to hedge one's bet by putting some (up to $\frac{1}{2}$) of the rejection region in the tail other than that predicted by the theory, strikes me as both scientifically dumb and slightly unethical.... Theory generation and theory testing are much closer to the proper goal of science than truth searching, and running one-tailed tests is quite consistent with those goals." Obviously, there is room for disagreement on this issue.

deviation of the population of observations from which his score was sampled. They are 489 and 126, respectively. If he is not a native speaker we have no idea what the mean and standard deviation are for the population from which his score was sampled. We will set up the null hypothesis that this individual is a native speaker, or, more precisely, H_0: $\mu = 489$. We will identify H_1 with the hypothesis that the individual is not a native speaker.

We need to choose between a one-tailed and a two-tailed test. In this particular case we will choose a one-tailed test on the grounds that the GRE is given in English, and it is difficult to imagine that a population of nonnative speakers would have a mean higher than the mean of native speakers of English on a test that is given in English. (*Note*: This does not mean that non-English speakers may not, singly or as a population, outscore English speakers on a fairly administered test. It just means that they are unlikely to do so, especially as a population, when both groups take the test in English.) Because we have chosen a one-tailed test, we have set up the alternative hypothesis as H_1: $\mu < 489$.

Before we can apply our statistical procedures to the data at hand, we must make one additional decision. We have to decide on a level of significance for our test. In this case I have chosen to run the test at the 5% level, in part because I am using $\alpha = .05$ as a standard for this book, but also because I am more worried about a Type II error than I am about a Type I error. If I make a Type I error and erroneously conclude that the student is not a native speaker when in fact he is, it is very likely that the rest of his credentials will exclude him from further consideration anyway. However, if I make a Type II error and do not identify him as a nonnative speaker, I am doing him a real injustice.

Next we need to calculate the probability of a student receiving a score *at least as low as* 220 when H_0: $\mu = 489$ is true. We first calculate the z score corresponding to a raw score of 220.

$$z = \frac{(X - \mu)}{\sigma} = \frac{(220 - 489)}{126} = \frac{-269}{126} = -2.13$$

We then go to the tables of z to calculate the probability that we would obtain a z value less than or equal to -2.13. From Table 9, Appendix D, we find that this probability $= .017$. Because this probability is less than the 5% significance level we chose to operate with, we will reject the null hypothesis on the grounds that it is too unlikely that we would obtain a score as low as 220 if we had sampled an observation from a population of native speakers of English who had taken the GRE. Instead we will conclude that we have an observation from an individual who is not a native speaker of English.

It is important to note that in rejecting the null hypothesis we could have made a Type I error. We know that if we do sample speakers of English, 1.7% of them will score this low. It is possible that our applicant was a native speaker who just did poorly. All that we are saying is that such an event is sufficiently unlikely that we will place our bets with the alternative hypothesis.

11-10 SUMMARY

The purpose of this chapter has been to examine the general theory of hypothesis testing without becoming involved in the specific calculations required to actually carry out a test. We first considered the concept of the sampling distribution of a statistic, which is the distribution that the statistic in question would have if it were computed repeatedly from an infinite number of samples under certain specified conditions. The sampling distribution basically tells us what kinds of values are reasonable to expect for the statistic if the conditions under which the distribution was derived are met. We then examined the null hypothesis and the role it plays in hypothesis testing. We saw that we can test any null hypothesis by asking what the sampling distribution of the relevant statistic would look like if the null hypothesis were true and by then comparing our particular statistic to that distribution. We next saw how a simple hypothesis actually could be tested using what we already know about the normal distribution. Finally we considered Type I and Type II errors and one- and two-tailed tests. Some of the important terms in the chapter are:

□ **Sampling error**
□ **Hypothesis testing**
□ **Sampling distributions**
□ **Sampling distribution of the mean**
□ **Research hypothesis**
□ **Null hypothesis (H_0)**
□ **Sample statistics**
□ **Test statistics**
□ **Rejection level (significance level)**
□ **Rejection region**

□ **Alternative hypothesis (H_1)**
□ **Critical value**
□ **Type I error**
□ **α (Alpha)**
□ **Type II error**
□ **β (Beta)**
□ **Power**
□ **One-tailed test (directional test)**
□ **Two-tailed test (nondirectional test)**

11-11 EXERCISES

11-1 Suppose I told you that last night's NHL hockey game resulted in a score of 26–13. You would probably decide that I had misread the paper and was discussing something other than a hockey score. In effect you have just tested and rejected a null hypothesis.
(a) What was the null hypothesis?
(b) Outline the hypothesis-testing procedure that you have just applied.

11-2 For the past year I found that I spend about $2.00 for lunch, give or take a quarter or so.
(a) Draw a rough sketch of this distribution of daily expenditures.
(b) If, without looking at the bill, I paid for my lunch

with a $5.00 bill and received $2.75 in change, should I worry that I was overcharged?
(c) Explain the logic involved in answering Exercise 11-2(b).

11-3 What would be a Type I error in Exercise 11-2?

11-4 What would be a Type II error in Exercise 11-2?

11-5 Describe what we mean by the rejection region and the critical value using the example in Exercise 11-2.

11-6 Why might I want to adopt a one-tailed test in Exercise 11-2, and which tail should I choose? What would happen if I chose the wrong tail?

11-7 A recently admitted class of graduate students at a large state university has a mean Graduate Record Exam Verbal score of 650 with a standard deviation of 50. (The scores are reasonably normally distributed.) One of the students, who just happens to have a mother on the Board of Trustees, was admitted with a GRE score of 490. Should the local newspaper editor, who loves scandals, write a scathing editorial?

11–8 Why is such a small standard deviation reasonable in Exercise 11-7?

11–9 Why might (or might not) the GRE scores be normally distributed for the restricted sample (admitted students) in Exercise 11-7?

11–10 Imagine that you have just invented a statistical test called the Mode Test for testing whether the mode of a population is some value (e.g., 100). The statistic (M) is calculated as

$$M = \frac{\text{Sample mode}}{\text{Sample range}}$$

Describe how you could obtain the sampling distribution of M. (*Note*: This is a purely fictitious statistic.)

11–11 In Exercise 11-10 what would we call M, in the terminology given in this chapter?

11–12 Describe a situation in daily life in which we routinely test hypotheses without realizing it.

11–13 In Exercise 11-7 what would be the alternative hypothesis (H_1)?

11–14 Define "sampling error."

11–15 What is the difference between a "distribution" and a "sampling distribution"?

11–16 How would decreasing α affect the probabilities given in Table 11-1?

11–17 Give two examples of research hypotheses and state the corresponding null hypotheses.

11–18 For the distributions in Figure 11-4, I said that the probability of a Type II error (β) is .74. Show how this probability was obtained.

11–19 Rerun the calculations in Exercise 11-18 if $\alpha = .01$.

11–20 In the example in Section 11-9, how would the test have differed if we had chosen to run a two-tailed test instead?

HYPOTHESIS TESTS APPLIED TO MEANS— ONE SAMPLE

In Chapter 11 we considered the general logic of hypothesis testing and ignored the specific calculations involved. In this chapter we begin to look at the calculational procedures required for testing some simple hypotheses. In particular we will be concentrating on testing a null hypothesis about the value of a population mean. We will end by testing a null hypothesis about a correlation coefficient.

We will begin with an example referred to in the last chapter. There we considered the case in which we know that Total Behavior Problem scores on the Youth Self Report form are nearly normally distributed with a mean of 50 and a standard deviation of 10. In Chapter 11 we dealt with that example in only a general way. Here we will start over and deal with it much more precisely.

Because there is evidence in the psychological literature that stress in a child's life may lead to subsequent behavior problems, it might be expected that a sample of children who have been subjected to an unusual amount of stress would show an unusually high level of behavior problems. On the other hand, we might expect that such children would feel that they have enough going on in their lives without complicating matters further, in which case they might show an unusually low number of behavior problems. That last possibility does not seem terribly likely, but it is worth guarding against. As a result we are therefore interested in examining a (two-tailed) **experimental hypothesis** that the number of behavior problems among stressed children is different from the number of behavior problems among children in general. We don't test the experimental hypothesis directly, however. Instead we will test the null hypothesis (H_0) that the scores of stressed children came from a population of scores with the same mean as the population of scores of normal children. More specifically, we want

Experimental hypothesis
Another name for the research hypothesis.

to decide between

$$H_0: \mu = 50 \quad \text{and} \quad H_1: \mu \neq 50$$

I have chosen the two-tailed alternative (H_1) because I want to reject H_0 if $\mu < 50$ *or* if $\mu > 50$.

To investigate this problem I have drawn a sample of five children, each of whom is under a high level of stress of one kind or another. I asked the children to complete the Youth Self Report form and obtained the following scores

$$48 \quad 62 \quad 53 \quad 66 \quad 51$$

This sample of five observations has a mean of 56.0 and a standard deviation of 7.65. Thus the five children have an average score that is six points above the mean of the population of normal children. But because this result is based on a sample of only five children, it is quite conceivable that the deviation from 50 could be due to chance (or, phrased differently, due to sampling error). Before we can draw any conclusions, however, we will have to know what values we reasonably could expect sample means to have if we really sampled from a population of normal children.

12-1   SAMPLING DISTRIBUTION OF THE MEAN

Sampling distribution of the mean
The distribution of sample means over repeated sampling from one population.

Central limit theorem
The theorem that specifies the nature of the sampling distribution of the mean.

As you will recall from the previous chapter, the sampling distribution of a statistic is the distribution of values we would expect to obtain for that statistic if we drew an infinite number of samples from the population in question and calculated the statistic on each sample. Because we are concerned here with sample *means*, we need to know something about the **sampling distribution of the mean**. Fortunately all of the important information about the sampling distribution of the mean can be summed up in one very important theorem: the **Central Limit Theorem**. The Central Limit Theorem is a factual statement about the distribution of means. It states:

> Given a population with mean μ and variance σ^2, the sampling distribution of the mean (the distribution of sample means) will have a mean equal to μ (i.e., $\mu_{\bar{X}} = \mu$) and a variance ($\sigma_{\bar{X}}^2$) equal to σ^2/N (and standard deviation [$\sigma_{\bar{X}}$] equal to $\sigma/\sqrt{N}$). The distribution will approach the normal distribution as N, the *sample size*, increases.

This theorem is one of the most important theorems in statistics, because it **not** only tells us what the mean and variance of the sampling distribution of the sample mean must be for any given sample size but also states that as N increases, the shape of this sampling distribution approaches normal, *whatever* the shape of the parent population. The importance of these facts will become clear shortly.

The rate at which the sampling distribution of the mean approaches normal is a function of the shape of the parent population. If the population is itself normal, the sampling distribution of the mean will be normal regardless of N. If the population is symmetric but nonnormal, the sampling distribution of the mean will be nearly normal even for quite small sample sizes, especially if the population is unimodal. If the population is markedly skewed, we may require sample sizes of 30 or more before the means closely approximate a normal distribution.

To illustrate the Central Limit Theorem we will leave the behavior problem example for a moment and consider a more general example. Suppose that we take an infinitely large population of random numbers evenly distributed between 0 and 100. This population will have what is called a **rectangular distribution**—every value between 0 and 100 being equally likely. The distribution of this population is shown in Figure 12-1. In this case the mean (μ) is 50, the standard deviation (σ) is 28.87, and the variance (σ^2) is 833.33.

Rectangular distribution
A distribution in which all outcomes are equally likely.

Now suppose that we drew with replacement 5000 samples of size 5 ($N = 5$) from this population and plotted the resulting sample means. Such sampling can be easily accomplished with the aid of a computer, and in fact the results of just such a procedure are presented in Figure 12-2(a). From Figure 12-2(a) it is apparent that the means, although not exactly normally distributed, are at least peaked in the center and trail off toward the extremes. If you were to go to the effort of calculating the mean and variance of this distribution, you would find that they are extremely close to $\mu = 50$ and $\sigma_{\bar{X}}^2 = \sigma^2/N = 833.33/5 = 166.67$.

Now suppose that we repeated the entire procedure—only this time drawing 5000 samples, each with 30 observations. Again I have actually done this using a computer, and the results are plotted in Figure 12-2(b). Here you see that, just as the Central Limit Theorem predicted, the distribution is approximately normal, the mean (μ) is again 50, and the variance has been reduced to $833.33/30 = 27.78$.

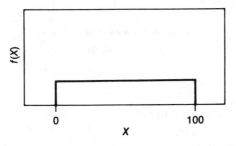

FIGURE 12-1
Rectangular Distribution with
$\mu = 50$, $\sigma = 28.87$

12-2 TESTING HYPOTHESIS ABOUT MEANS—σ KNOWN

From the Central Limit Theorem we know all the important characteristics of the sampling distribution of the mean. (We know its shape, its mean, and its standard deviation.) On the basis of this information we are in a position to

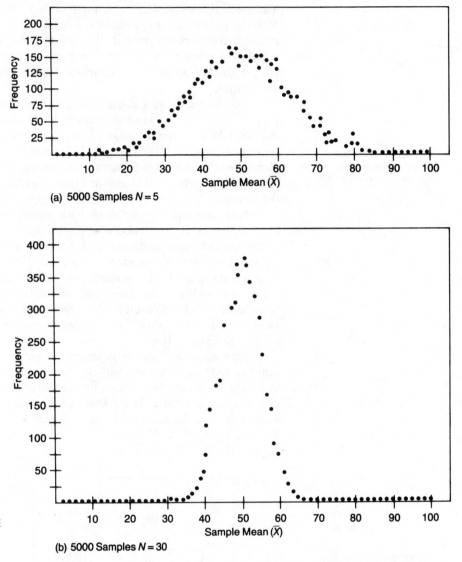

begin testing hypotheses about means. For the sake of continuity it might be
well to go back to something we discussed with respect to the normal
distribution. In Chapter 11 we saw that we could test a hypothesis about the
population from which a single score (in that case a finger-tapping score) was
drawn by calculating

$$z = \frac{X - \mu}{\sigma}$$

and then obtaining the probability of a value of z as low as the one obtained by
use of the tables of the standard normal distribution. Thus we ran a one-tailed

test on the hypothesis that the tapping rate (70) of a single individual was drawn at random from a normally distributed population of healthy tapping rates with a mean of 100 and a standard deviation of 20. We did this by calculating

$$z = \frac{X - \mu}{\sigma} = \frac{70 - 100}{20} = \frac{-30}{20} = -1.5$$

and then using Appendix D, Table 9, to find the area below $z = -1.5$. This value is .0668. Thus approximately 7% of the time we would expect a score as low as this if we were sampling from a healthy population. Because this probability was greater than our selected significance level of $\alpha = .05$, we would not reject the null hypothesis. The tapping rate for the person we examined was not an unusual rate for healthy individuals. Although in this example we were testing a hypothesis about a single observation, exactly the same logic applies to testing hypotheses about sample means.

In most situations in which we test a hypothesis about a population mean we don't have any knowledge about the variance of that population. (This is the main reason that we have t tests, which are the main focus of this chapter.) However, in a limited number of situations we do know σ for some reason, and a discussion of testing a hypothesis when σ is known provides a good transition from what we already know about the normal distribution to what we want to know about t tests. The example of behavior problems is a useful example for this purpose because we do know both the mean and the standard deviation for the population of Total Behavior Problem scores ($\mu = 50$ and $\sigma = 10$). We also know that a random sample of children under stress had a mean score of 56.0, and we want to test the null hypothesis that these five children are a random sample from a population of normal children (i.e., normal with respect to their general level of behavior problems). In other words we want to test $H_0: \mu = 50$ against the alternative $H_1: \mu \neq 50$.

Because we know the mean and standard deviation of the population of general behavior problem scores, we can use the Central Limit Theorem to obtain the sampling distribution when the null hypothesis is true. The Central Limit Theorem states that if we obtain the sampling distribution of the mean from this population, it will have a mean of 50, a variance of $\sigma^2/N = 10^2/5 = 100/5 = 20$, and a standard deviation (usually referred to as the **standard error**)† of $\sigma/\sqrt{N} = 4.47$. This distribution is diagrammed in Figure 12-3. The arrow in Figure 12-3 represents the location of the sample mean.

Because we know that the sampling distribution is normally distributed with a mean of 50 and a standard error of 4.47, we can find areas under the distribution by referring to tables of the standard normal distribution. Thus, for

Standard error
The standard deviation of a sampling distribution.

---

†The standard deviation of any sampling distribution is normally referred to as the *standard error* of that distribution. Thus the standard deviation of means is called the standard error of the mean (symbolized by $\sigma_{\bar{X}}$), whereas the standard deviation of differences between means, which will be discussed in Chapter 14, is called the standard error of differences between means and is symbolized $\sigma_{\bar{X}_1 - \bar{X}_2}$. Minor changes in terminology such as calling a standard deviation a standard error are not really designed to confuse students. They just have that effect.

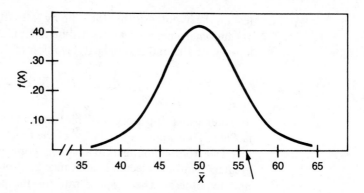

===== **FIGURE 12-3** =====
**Sampling Distribution of the
Mean for Samples of $N = 5$
Drawn from a Population with
$\mu = 50$ and $\sigma = 10$**

example, because two standard errors is $2(4.47) = 8.94$, the area to the right of $\bar{X} = 58.94$ is simply the area under the normal distribution greater than two standard deviations above the mean.

For our particular situation we first need to know the probability of a sample mean greater than or equal to 56, and thus we need to find the area above $\bar{X} = 56$. We can calculate this in the same way we did with individual observations, with only a minor change in the formula for z.

$$z = \frac{X - \mu}{\sigma} \qquad \text{becomes} \qquad z = \frac{\bar{X} - \mu}{\sigma_{\bar{X}}}$$

which can also be written as

$$\frac{\bar{X} - \mu}{\frac{\sigma}{\sqrt{N}}}$$

For our data this becomes

$$\frac{56 - 50}{4.47} = \frac{6}{4.47} = 1.34$$

You will note that the equation for z used here is of the same form as our earlier formula for z. The only differences are that X has been replaced by $\bar{X}$ and σ has been replaced by $\sigma_{\bar{X}}$. These differences occur because we now are dealing with a distribution of means, and thus the data points are now means, and the standard deviation in question is now the standard error of the mean (the standard deviation of means). The formula for z continues to represent (1) a point on a distribution, minus (2) the mean of that distribution, all divided by (3) the standard deviation of the distribution. Now rather than being concerned specifically with the distribution of $\bar{X}$, we have re-expressed the sample mean in terms of z scores and can now answer the question with regard to the standard normal distribution.

From Appendix D, Table 9, we find that the probability of a z as large as 1.34 is .0901. Because we want a two-tailed test of H_0, we need to double the probability to obtain the probability of a deviation as large as 1.34 standard errors *in either direction* from the mean. This is $2(.0901) = .1802$. Thus with a two-tailed test (that stressed children have a mean behavior problem score that is different *in either direction* from that of normal children) at the .05 level of significance we would not reject H_0, because the obtained probability is greater than .05. We would conclude that we have no evidence that stressed children show more or fewer behavior problems than other children.

The test of one sample mean against a known population mean, which we have just performed, is based on the assumption that sample means are normally distributed, or at least that the distribution is sufficiently normal that we will be only negligibly in error when we refer to the tables of the standard normal distribution. Many textbooks will state that we assume that we are sampling from a normal population (i.e., that behavior problem scores themselves are normally distributed), but this is not strictly necessary in practical terms. All that it is necessary to assume is that the sampling distribution of the mean (Figure 12-3) is normal. This assumption can be satisfied in two ways—if either (1) the population from which we sample is normal or (2) the sample size is sufficiently large to produce at least approximate normality by way of the Central Limit Theorem. This is one of the great benefits of the Central Limit Theorem: it allows us to test hypotheses even if the parent population is not normal, provided only that N is sufficiently large.

12-3   TESTING A SAMPLE MEAN WHEN σ IS UNKNOWN (THE ONE-SAMPLE t TEST)

The previous example was chosen deliberately from among a fairly limited number of situations in which the population standard deviation (σ) is known. In the general case, however, we rarely know the value of σ and usually will have to estimate it by way of the *sample* standard deviation (s). When we replace σ with s in the formula, however, the nature of the test changes. We can no longer declare the answer to be a z score and evaluate it with reference to tables of z. Instead we will denote the answer as t and evaluate it with respect to tables of t, which are somewhat different. The reasoning behind the switch from z to t is really rather simple, although most introductory texts tend to ignore it. The basic problem that requires this change to t is related to the sampling distribution of the sample variance.

THE SAMPLING DISTRIBUTION OF s^2

Because the t test uses s^2 as an estimate of σ^2, it is important that we first look at the sampling distribution of s^2. This sampling distribution gives us some insight into the problems we are going to encounter. We saw in Chapter 6 that s^2 is an *unbiased* estimate of σ^2, meaning that with repeated sampling the average value of s^2 will equal σ^2. Although an unbiased estimator is a nice thing, it isn't everything. The problem is that the shape of the sampling distribution of s^2 is

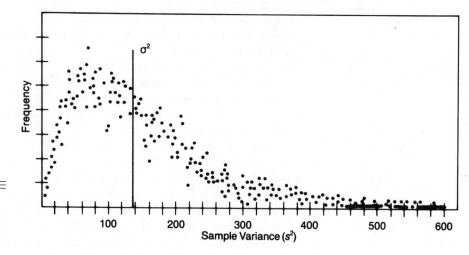

FIGURE 12-4
Sampling Distribution of s^2 from a Normally Distributed Population with $\mu = 50$, $\sigma^2 = 138.89$, and $N = 5$

quite positively skewed, especially for small samples. (In fact it resembles the chi-square distribution, to be discussed in Chapter 19.) An example of a computer-generated sampling distribution of s^2 (where $\sigma^2 = 138.89$) is shown in Figure 12-4. Because of the skewness of this distribution, an individual value of s^2 is more likely to underestimate σ^2 than to overestimate it, and especially so for small samples. (s^2 remains unbiased because when it overestimates σ^2 it does so to such an extent as to balance off the more numerous, but less drastic, underestimates.) As a result of this skewness the resulting value of t is likely to be larger than the value of z that we would have obtained had σ been known, because any one sample variance (s^2) has a better than 50:50 chance of underestimating the population variance (σ^2).

THE t STATISTIC

We will take the formula that we have just developed for z

$$ z = \frac{\bar{X} - \mu}{\sigma_{\bar{X}}} = \frac{\bar{X} - \mu}{\dfrac{\sigma}{\sqrt{N}}} = \frac{\bar{X} - \mu}{\sqrt{\dfrac{\sigma^2}{N}}} $$

and substitute s^2 to give

$$ t = \frac{\bar{X} - \mu}{s_{\bar{X}}} = \frac{\bar{X} - \mu}{\dfrac{s}{\sqrt{N}}} = \frac{\bar{X} - \mu}{\sqrt{\dfrac{s^2}{N}}} $$

Because we know that for any particular sample s^2 is more likely than not to be smaller than the appropriate value of σ^2, we can see that the t formula is more likely than not to produce a larger answer than we would have obtained if we had solved for t using σ^2 itself. As a result it would not really be fair to treat the answer as a z score and use the table of z. To do so would give us too many "significant" results—that is, we would make more than 5% Type I errors when testing at significance level $\alpha = .05$. (For example, when we were calculating z, we rejected H_0 at the .05 level of significance whenever z fell outside the limits of ± 1.96. If we create a situation in which H_0 is true, repeatedly draw samples of $N = 6$, use s^2 in place of σ^2, and calculate t, we will obtain a value of ± 1.96 or greater more than 10% of the time.)

The solution to this problem was supplied by William Gossett, who worked for the Guinness Brewing Company and wrote under the pseudonym of Student. Gossett showed that using s^2 in place of σ^2 would lead to a particular sampling distribution, now generally known as **Student's t distribution**. As a result of Gossett's work all that we have to do is stick in our s^2, denote the answer as t, and evaluate t with respect to its own distribution, much as we evaluated z with respect to the normal distribution. The t distribution is tabled in Appendix D, Table 5, and examples of the actual distribution of t for various sample sizes are shown graphically in Figure 12-5.

As you can see from Figure 12-5, the distribution of t varies as a function of the **degrees of freedom (df)**, which for the moment we will define as one less than the number of observations in the sample. Because the skewness of the sampling distribution of s^2 disappears as the number of degrees of freedom increases, the tendency for s to underestimate σ will also disappear. Thus for an infinitely large number of degrees of freedom t will become normally distributed and equivalent to z.

Although some textbooks advocate using t when $N < 30$ and pretending that $t = z$ for $N > 30$, that approach will not be used here. There is nothing to be gained by using z as an approximation when the exact distribution (i.e., t) is given in the same set of tables.

Student's t distribution
The sampling distribution of the t statistic.

Degrees of freedom (df)
The number of independent pieces of information remaining after estimating a parameter.

DEGREES OF FREEDOM

I have mentioned that the t distribution is a function of the degrees of freedom. For the one-sample case, $df = N - 1$; the one degree of freedom has been lost because we used the sample mean in calculating s^2. To be more precise, we

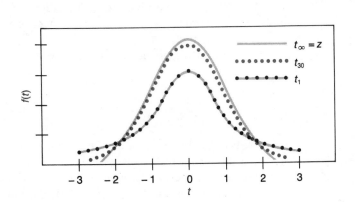

FIGURE 12-5
t Distribution for 1, 30, and ∞
Degrees of Freedom

obtained the variance (s^2) by calculating the deviations of the observations from their own mean ($X - \bar{X}$), rather than from the population mean ($X - \mu$). Because the sum of the deviations about the mean ($\Sigma(X - \bar{X})$) always is equal to 0, only $N - 1$ of the deviations are free to vary (the Nth is determined if the sum of the deviations is to be zero). As an illustration of this point consider the case of five scores whose mean is 10. Four of these scores can be anything you want (e.g., 18, 18, 16, 2), but the fifth score cannot be chosen freely. It must be -4 if the mean is going to be 10. In other words there are only four free numbers in that set of five scores, once the mean is determined, and therefore we have four degrees of freedom. This is the reason the formula for s^2 (defined in Chapter 6) used $N - 1$ in the denominator. Because s^2 is based on $N - 1$ df, we have $N - 1$ degrees of freedom for t.

EXAMPLE OF THE USE OF t: HIGH-SCHOOL COMPETENCY TEST SCORES

At this point a simple example would help illustrate the use of the t test. High schools and state boards of education recently have put considerably greater emphasis on having students achieve a minimal level of competency before they can receive a diploma. In an attempt to defend the expenditure of money over the past year on tutorials and other forms of remedial education, the superintendent of a large school district has collected scores from 20 of this year's seniors on a standardized competency exam. Last year's mean score across the entire school system (the population of interest) was 76.0. This year the mean ($\bar{X}$) for the sample of 20 students was 79.3 with a standard deviation of 6.4. Can these data be taken as evidence that the mean competency score improved, or does it represent a chance result to be commonly expected from a population with $\mu = 76.0$ (which was last year's mean for the population of students' scores)? To put this problem in the language of hypothesis testing,

$$H_0: \mu = 76$$

$$H_1: \mu \neq 76$$

We will use a two-tailed test (since tutoring could have been misfocused and drawn attention away from more productive endeavors) and will work at the 5% level of significance.

From the previous discussion we have

$$t = \frac{\bar{X} - \mu}{s_{\bar{X}}} = \frac{\bar{X} - \mu}{\frac{s}{\sqrt{N}}}$$

Notice that the numerator of the formula for t represents the distance between the sample mean and the population mean given by H_0 and the denominator represents an estimate of the standard deviation of the distribution of sample means. This is the same thing that we had with z, except that the sample variance (or standard deviation) has been substituted for the population variance (or standard deviation).

For our data we have

$$t = \frac{\bar{X} - \mu}{\dfrac{s}{\sqrt{N}}} = \frac{79.3 - 76}{\dfrac{6.40}{\sqrt{20}}}$$

$$= \frac{3.3}{1.43} = 2.31$$

A t value of 2.31 in and of itself is not particularly meaningful unless we can evaluate it against the sampling distribution of t. For this purpose the critical values of t are presented in Appendix D, Table 5, a portion of which is shown in Table 12-1. This table differs in form from the table of the normal distribution (z) because instead of giving the area above and below each specific value of t, which would require too much space, the table instead gives those values of t that cut off particular critical areas—for example, the .05 and .01 levels of significance. Also, in contrast to z, a different t distribution is defined for each possible number of degrees of freedom. We want to work at the two-tailed .05 level. The critical value generally is denoted t_α or, in this case, $t_{.05}$.

In order to use the t tables we must enter the table with the appropriate degrees of freedom. Because we have 20 observations in our data, we have $N - 1 = 20 - 1 = 19\ df$ for this example, and because we want $t_{.05}$, Appendix D, Table 5, or Table 12-1, tells us that the critical value of $t_{.05}(19)$ is ± 2.093.

TABLE 12-1
Abbreviated Version of Appendix D, Table 5, Percentage Points of the t Distribution

			Level of Significance for One-Tailed Test						
	.25	.20	.15	.10	.05	.025	.01	.005	.0005
			Level of Significance for Two-Tailed Test						
df	.50	.40	.30	.20	.10	.05	.02	.01	.001
1	1.000	1.376	1.963	3.078	6.314	12.706	31.821	63.657	636.62
2	0.816	1.061	1.386	1.886	2.920	4.303	6.965	9.925	31.599
3	0.765	0.978	1.250	1.638	2.353	3.182	4.541	5.841	12.924
4	0.741	0.941	1.190	1.533	2.132	2.776	3.747	4.604	8.610
5	0.727	0.920	1.156	1.476	2.015	2.571	3.365	4.032	6.869
6	0.718	0.906	1.134	1.440	1.943	2.447	3.143	3.707	5.959
7	0.711	0.896	1.119	1.415	1.895	2.365	2.998	3.499	5.408
8	0.706	0.889	1.108	1.397	1.860	2.306	2.896	3.355	5.041
9	0.703	0.883	1.100	1.383	1.833	2.262	2.821	3.250	4.781
10	0.700	0.879	1.093	1.372	1.812	2.228	2.764	3.169	4.587
⋮	⋮	⋮	⋮	⋮	⋮	⋮	⋮	⋮	⋮
19	0.688	0.861	1.066	1.328	1.729	2.093	2.539	2.861	3.883
20	0.687	0.860	1.064	1.325	1.725	2.086	2.528	2.845	3.850
21	0.686	0.859	1.063	1.323	1.721	2.080	2.518	2.831	3.819
22	0.686	0.858	1.061	1.321	1.717	2.074	2.508	2.819	3.792
23	0.685	0.858	1.060	1.319	1.714	2.069	2.500	2.807	3.768
24	0.685	0.857	1.059	1.318	1.711	2.064	2.492	2.797	3.745

(The number shown in parentheses after $t_{.05}$ is the degrees of freedom.) This means that if H_0 is true, only 5% of the time would a t computed on a sample of 20 cases lie outside of ± 2.093. Because the value we computed (2.31) was greater than 2.093, we will reject H_0. We will conclude that a sample mean of 79.3 would be unlikely to occur if in fact we had sampled from a population for which $\mu = 76$. The practical result of rejecting H_0 is that we can conclude that mean performance on the competency exam did improve over the past year. Whether this improvement should be credited to the increase in expenditures or to other unknown causes is still an open question, since our test deals only with whether the means have changed and not with the cause of that change. To rule out the possibility that this year's senior class is just smarter than last year's or the possibility that this year's exam is easier, a **control group** that was not given any special treatment would be needed. Whatever the cause, however, this year's seniors did do reliably (significantly) better than last year's.

Control group
A group that does not receive the experimental treatment.

12-4 FACTORS AFFECTING THE MAGNITUDE OF t OR THE DECISION ABOUT H_0

A number of factors affect the magnitude of the t statistic and/or the likelihood of rejecting H_0. They are:

1. the actual obtained difference $(\bar{X} - \mu)$
2. the magnitude of the sample variance (s^2)
3. the sample size (N)
4. the significance level (α)
5. whether the test is a one- or a two-tailed test

It should be obvious that the obtained difference between $\bar{X}$ and μ is important. This follows directly from the fact that the larger the numerator, the larger the t value. But it is also important to keep in mind that the value of $\bar{X}$ is in large part a function of the mean of the population from which the sample was drawn. If this mean is denoted μ_1 and the mean given by the null hypothesis is denoted μ_0, then the likelihood of obtaining a significant result will increase as $\mu_1 - \mu_0$ increases.

When you look at the formula for t, it should be apparent that as s^2 decreases or N increases, the denominator itself will decrease and the resulting value of t will increase. Because variability introduced by the experimental setting itself (caused, for example, by ambiguous instructions, poorly recorded data, distracting testing conditions, and so on) is superimposed on top of whatever variability there is among subjects, we try to reduce s by controlling as many sources of variability as possible. We also make use of the fact that increasing N decreases $s_{\bar{X}}$ by obtaining as many subjects as possible.

Finally, it should be evident that the likelihood of rejecting H_0 will depend upon the size of the rejection region, which in turn depends upon α and upon the location of that region (whether a one-tailed or two-tailed test is used). The role all of these factors play in hypothesis testing will be explored further in Chapter 15.

12-5 A SECOND EXAMPLE—THE MOON ILLUSION

It may be useful to consider a second example, this one taken from a classic paper by Kaufman and Rock (1962) on the moon illusion. Kaufman and Rock concluded that the moon illusion (the commonly observed fact that the moon near the horizon appears larger than the moon at its zenith [highest point overhead]) could be explained on the basis of the greater apparent distance of the moon when it is at the horizon. As part of a very complete series of experiments the authors initially sought to estimate the moon illusion by asking subjects to adjust a variable "moon" appearing to be on the horizon so as to match the size of a standard "moon" appearing at its zenith, or vice versa. (In these measurements they did not use the actual moon, but an artificial one created with special apparatus.) One of the first questions we might ask is whether there really is a moon illusion—that is, whether a larger setting is required to match a horizon moon than a zenith moon. The following data for 10 subjects are taken from Kaufman and Rock's paper and represent the ratio of the diameter of the variable and standard moons. A ratio of 1.00 would indicate no illusion, whereas a ratio other than 1.00 would represent an illusion. (For example, a ratio of 1.5 would mean that the horizon moon appeared to have a diameter 1.5 times the diameter of the zenith moon.) Evidence in support of an illusion would require that we reject $H_0: \mu = 1.00$ in favor of $H_1: \mu \neq 1.00$.

Obtained Ratio: 1.73 1.06 2.03 1.40 0.95 1.13 1.41 1.73 1.63 1.56

For these data $N = 10$, $\bar{X} = 1.463$, and $s = 0.341$. A t test on $H_0: \mu = 1.00$ is given by

$$t = \frac{\bar{X} - \mu}{s_{\bar{X}}} = \frac{\bar{X} - \mu}{\dfrac{s}{\sqrt{N}}} = \frac{1.463 - 1.000}{\dfrac{0.341}{\sqrt{10}}} = \frac{0.463}{0.108} = 4.29$$

From Appendix D, Table 5, we see that with $10 - 1 = 9 \, df$ for a two-tailed test at $\alpha = .05$, the critical value of $t_{.05}(9) = \pm 2.262$. The obtained value of t (often denoted t_{obt}) was 4.29. Because $4.29 > 2.626$, we can reject H_0 at $\alpha = .05$ and conclude that the true mean ratio under these conditions is not equal to 1.00. In fact it is greater than 1.00, which is what we would expect on the basis of our experience. (It is always comforting to see science confirm what we have all known since childhood, but the results also mean that Kaufman and Rock's experimental apparatus performs as it should.)

t_{obt}
The obtained (calculated) value of t.

12-6 CONFIDENCE LIMITS ON THE MEAN

Point estimate
A specific value taken as the estimate of a parameter.

Interval estimates
A range of values estimated to include the parameter.

Confidence interval
Confidence limits
A range of values that has a specified probability of bracketing the parameter. The end points of the interval are the confidence limits.

The previous example of the moon illusion offers an excellent example of a case in which we are particularly interested in estimating the true value of μ—in this case the true ratio of the perceived size of the horizon moon to the perceived size of the zenith moon. The sample mean ($\bar{X}$), as you already know, is an unbiased estimate of μ. When we have one specific estimate of a parameter, we call it a **point estimate**. However, there are also **interval estimates**, which are an attempt to set limits that have a high probability of including the true (population) value of the mean (the mean, μ, of a whole population of observations). What we want, then, are **confidence limits** on μ. These limits enclose what is called a **confidence interval**. In Chapter 7 we saw how to set what were called "probable limits" on an observation. A similar line of reasoning will apply here.

If we want to set limits on μ, given the data at hand, what we really want to do is to ask how large or small μ could be without causing us to reject H_0 if we ran a t test on the obtained sample mean. In other words if μ is quite small, we would have been unlikely to obtain the sample data. The same would be true if μ is quite large. But there are a whole range of values for μ for which we would expect data such as those we obtained. We want to calculate those values of μ.

An easy way to see what we are doing is to start with the formula for t.

$$t = \frac{\bar{X} - \mu}{s_{\bar{X}}} = \frac{\bar{X} - \mu}{\dfrac{s}{\sqrt{N}}}$$

Because we have collected the data, we already know $\bar{X}$, s, and $\sqrt{N}$. We also know that the critical two-tailed value for t at $\alpha = .05$ is $t_{.05}(9) = \pm 2.262$. What we are going to do is to substitute these values in the formula for t and solve for μ.

$$t = \frac{\bar{X} - \mu}{\dfrac{s}{\sqrt{N}}}$$

$$\pm 2.262 = \frac{1.463 - \mu}{\dfrac{0.341}{\sqrt{10}}} = \frac{1.463 - \mu}{0.108}$$

Rearranging to solve for μ, we have

$$\mu = \pm 2.262(0.108) + 1.463 = \pm 0.244 + 1.463$$

Using the $+0.244$ and -0.244 separately to obtain the upper and lower limits for μ, we have

$$\mu_{\text{upper}} = +0.244 + 1.463 = 1.707$$

$$\mu_{\text{lower}} = -0.244 + 1.463 = 1.219$$

and thus we can write the 95% confidence limits as 1.219 and 1.707 and the confidence interval as

$$CI_{.95} = 1.219 \leqslant \mu \leqslant 1.707$$

or, to write a general expression,

$$CI_{.95} = \bar{X} \pm t_{.05}s_{\bar{X}} = \bar{X} \pm t_{.05}\frac{s}{\sqrt{N}}$$

We have a 95% confidence interval because we used the two-tailed critical value of t at $\alpha = .05$. For the 99% limits we would take $t_{.01} = \pm 3.250$. Then the 99% confidence interval is

$$CI_{.99} = \bar{X} \pm t_{.01}(s_{\bar{X}}) = 1.463 \pm 3.250(.108) = 1.112 \leqslant \mu \leqslant 1.814$$

We now can say that the probability is .95 that the interval 1.219–1.707 includes the true mean ratio for the moon illusion, while the probability is .99 that the interval 1.112–1.814 includes μ.† You will note that neither interval includes the value of 1.00, which represents no illusion. We already knew this for the 95% confidence interval because we had rejected that null hypothesis when we ran the t test.

A graphic demonstration of confidence limits is shown in Figure 12-6. To generate this figure I drew 25 samples of $N = 4$ from a population with a mean (μ) of 5.0. For every sample a 95% confidence limit on μ was calculated and plotted. For example, the limits produced from the first sample were approximately 4.46 and 5.72, whereas for the second sample the limits were 4.83 and 5.80. Because in this case we know that the value of μ equals 5, I have drawn a vertical line at that point. Notice that the limits for samples 12 and 14 do not include $\mu = 5$. We would expect that the confidence limits would encompass μ 95 times out of 100. Therefore two misses out of 25 seems reasonable. Notice also that the confidence intervals vary in width. This variability can be explained by the fact that the width of an interval is a function of the standard deviation of the sample, and some samples have larger standard deviations than others.

A word is in order about the interpretation of confidence limits. Statements of the form $p(1.219 < \mu < 1.707) = .95$ are not to be interpreted in the

†Many statisticians would object to this statement as written. They would argue that *before* the experiment is run and the calculations are made, an interval of the form

$$\bar{X} \pm t_{.05}(s_{\bar{X}})$$

has a probability of .95 of encompassing μ. However, once the data are in, an interval such as 1.219–1.707 either includes the value of μ (probability = 1.00) or it doesn't (probability = 0). Put slightly differently,

$$\bar{X} \pm t_{.05}(s_{\bar{X}})$$

is a *random variable*, but the specific interval 1.219–1.707 is not a random variable and therefore does not have a probability associated with it. However, as mentioned in Chapter 8, there are different ways of defining what we mean by a probability. In *subjective* probability terms it is perfectly reasonable to say that my subjective probability is .95 that if you were to tell me the true value of μ it would be found to lie between 1.219 and 1.707.

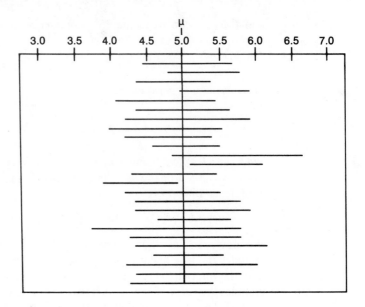

═══ **FIGURE 12-6** ═══
**Confidence Intervals Computed
on 25 Samples from a
Population with $\mu = 5.00$**

usual way. The parameter μ is not a variable. It does not jump around from experiment to experiment. Rather μ is a constant, and the *interval* is what varies from experiment to experiment. Thus we can think of the parameter as a stake and the experimenter, in computing confidence limits, as tossing rings at it. Ninety-five percent of the time a ring of specified width will encircle the parameter, and 5% of the time it will miss. A confidence statement is a statement of the probability that the ring has been on target and *not* a statement of the probability that the target (parameter) landed in the ring.

12-7 USING MINITAB TO RUN ONE-SAMPLE t TESTS

When you have large amounts of data, it is often much more convenient to use a program such as Minitab to compute t values. Table 12-2 is an illustration of the use of Minitab to obtain a one-sample t test and confidence limits for the moon illusion data. Notice that Minitab's results agree, within rounding error, with those that we obtained by hand. Notice also that Minitab computes the exact probability of a Type I error (the **p level**), rather than comparing t to a tabled value. Thus although we concluded that the probability of a Type I error was *less than* .05, Minitab reveals that the actual probability is .0020.† Most computer programs operate in this way.

p level
The *exact* probability that data as extreme as the data we obtained will occur if H_0 is true.

†We could have approximated this probability roughly by use of Appendix D, Table 5. For 9 df a t of 3.169 would have had a *two-tailed* probability of .01, and a value of $t = 4.587$ would have had a *two-tailed* probability of .001. Because the obtained t falls between these two values, its probability is somewhere between .01 and .001.

TABLE 12-2
Minitab for One-Sample *t*
Tests and Confidence Limits

```
MTB > SET THE FOLLOWING DATA IN COLUMN C1
DATA> 1.73 1.06 2.03 1.40 0.95 1.13 1.41 1.73 1.63 1.56
DATA> END
MTB > TTEST AGAINST MU = 1.00 FOR DATA IN COLUMN C1

TEST OF MU = 1.000 VS MU N.E. 1.000

              N      MEAN    STDEV   SE MEAN       T    P VALUE
C1           10     1.465    0.342    0.108     4.30     0.0020

MTB > TINTERVAL FOR 95 PERCENT CONFIDENCE INTERVAL FOR DATA IN COLUMN C1

              N      MEAN    STDEV   SE MEAN    95.0 PERCENT C.I.
C1           10     1.465    0.342    0.108    ( 1.220,  1.710)

MTB > TINTERVAL FOR 99 PERCENT CONFIDENCE INTERVAL FOR DATA IN COLUMN C1

              N      MEAN    STDEV   SE MEAN    99.0 PERCENT C.I.
C1           10     1.465    0.342    0.108    ( 1.114,  1.816)

MTB > STOP
```

12-8 TESTING THE SIGNIFICANCE OF A CORRELATION COEFFICIENT

We've just seen that simply because the sample statistic $\bar{X}$ is not exactly equal to a hypothesized population mean (μ_0) does not imply that it was drawn from a population with some different population mean (μ_1). Similarly, just because a set of sample data produces a correlation coefficient that is different from 0 does not necessarily mean that there is really a non-zero relationship between those two variables in the population. (In fact, small samples [e.g., $N = 5$] can produce chance correlations of ± 0.50 or larger with some regularity.) What we need is a significance test for correlations.

If we let ρ (rho) represent the correlation coefficient between X and Y when we measure the entire population of people or objects, then we can test whether ρ is different from 0. If $\rho = 0$, then X and Y are not linearly related, and knowing X tells us nothing about the corresponding value of Y. If ρ is not 0, then there is some linear relationship between X and Y. The sample correlation coefficient (r) is an estimate of ρ and, as such, can be used to test the null hypothesis that $\rho = 0$. Furthermore when $\rho = 0$, the sampling distribution of r is normal. An estimate of the standard error of the sampling distribution of r is given by

$$s_r = \sqrt{\frac{1 - r^2}{N - 2}}$$

When we were dealing with *means* we defined

$$t = \frac{\bar{X} - \mu}{s_{\bar{X}}}$$

Here we have the difference between a statistic ($\bar{X}$) and its corresponding parameter (μ), divided by the standard error of the statistic ($s_{\bar{X}}$). We are going to follow a parallel process to produce a test on the correlation coefficient. Thus to test $H_0: \rho = 0$ we have

$$t = \frac{r - \rho}{s_r}$$

where again we have the difference between a statistic (r) and the corresponding parameter (ρ), divided by the standard error of the statistic (s_r). In computational terms this test becomes

$$t = \frac{r - \rho}{s_r} = \frac{r - 0}{\sqrt{\dfrac{1 - r^2}{N - 2}}} = \frac{r\sqrt{N - 2}}{\sqrt{1 - r^2}}$$

where r = the sample correlation coefficient

N = the number of pairs of observations

t = Student's t with $N - 2$ df

If we take the example of the speed and accuracy in the Matching Familiar Figures Test from Chapter 9, we find that $r = -0.722$ and $N = 57$. Thus

$$t = \frac{-.722\sqrt{55}}{\sqrt{1 - .521}} = \frac{-.722\sqrt{55}}{\sqrt{.479}} = -7.737$$

From Appendix D, Table 5, we find that for 55 df the critical value for t at the two-tailed 5% level, $t_{.05}(55)$, is (by interpolation) 2.01. Because the obtained value of $t(-7.737)$ clearly exceeds the critical value (± 2.01), we will reject $H_0: \rho = 0$ and conclude that a significant relationship exists between the two variables.

12-9 A FINAL WORKED EXAMPLE

In this section we will return to the t test on means and work through an example of a t test on a null hypothesis about a single population mean (μ). Consider the following example.

A psychologist hypothesizes that with changes in diet and patterns of exercise and other differences between life in the 1980s and life in the 1950s, women should be healthier and even taller. He knows that in the 1950s the mean height of American women was 64 inches, but the tables don't give the standard deviation. To test his hypothesis he sampled 16 women from local medical records and recorded their heights. Would these data lead our experimenter to reject the hypothesis that women, on average, are taller than they were 30 years ago?

First we need to set up the null hypothesis. The psychologist wants to test the hypothesis that women's average height is different from what it was in the 1950s, so he will set up the null hypothesis that it is the same. Thus we have $H_0: \mu = 64$. Next we need to decide on a one-tailed or a two-tailed test and a significance level. For reasons that were given earlier, we will use a two-tailed test and set $\alpha = .05$.

From the data we will first calculate the mean and standard deviation, and then we will calculate t.

Data: 63 65 64 66 67 61 60 66 63 65 68 67 68 63 62 66

$$\bar{X} = \frac{\Sigma X}{N} = \frac{1034}{16} = 64.625$$

$$s^2 = \frac{\Sigma X^2 - \frac{(\Sigma X)^2}{N}}{N-1} = \frac{66,912 - \frac{1034^2}{16}}{15} = \frac{66,912 - 66,822.25}{15} = 5.9833$$

$$s = \sqrt{s^2} = \sqrt{5.9833} = 2.446$$

We are now in a position to solve for t.

$$t = \frac{\bar{X} - \mu}{s/\sqrt{N}} = \frac{64.625 - 64}{2.446/\sqrt{16}} = \frac{0.625}{0.612} = 1.02$$

From Table 5 in Appendix D we find that for $N - 1 = 16 - 1 = 15$ degrees of freedom at $\alpha = .05$, the two-tailed critical value of t is 2.131. Thus we would reject H_0 if our value of t had exceeded ± 2.131. Because t_{obt} was less than the critical value, we cannot reject the null hypothesis. Thus we have insufficient reason to conclude that women are, on average, taller than they were 30 years ago.

12-10 SUMMARY

In this chapter we began by considering the sampling distribution of the mean and how the information it gives is useful in testing hypotheses. We then saw how we could combine what we know about z and what we know about the sampling distribution of the mean to produce a test of a null hypothesis concerning μ. Next we saw how we could go beyond z to make use of a t test when the population standard deviation is not known and must be estimated by the sample standard deviation. We considered the factors that influence the magnitude of t in a particular experiment. Next we considered the construction of confidence limits on the value of a population mean. Finally we examined a t test on the significance of a correlation coefficient. Some of the most important terms in this chapter are:

- Experimental hypothesis
- Sampling distribution of the mean
- Central Limit Theorem
- Rectangular distribution
- Standard error
- Student's t distribution

- Degrees of freedom (df)
- Control group
- Point estimate
- Interval estimates
- Confidence interval (confidence limits)
- p level

12-11 EXERCISES

12–1 Using Appendix D, Table 8 (or any other source of more or less random numbers), plot the distribution of the first 100 least significant (right-most) digits.

12–2 Repeat Exercise 12-1, except calculate and plot the means for 25 samples of five least significant digits. (Group the means into appropriate intervals.)

12–3 Compare the means and standard deviations for the distribution of digits in Exercise 12-1 and the sampling distribution of the mean in Exercise 12-2. Do these answers agree with what the Central Limit Theorem would lead you to expect?

12–4 In what way would the result in Exercise 12-2 differ if you had drawn more samples of size 5?

12–5 In 1979 the 238 students from North Dakota who took the verbal portion of the SAT exam had a mean of 525. The standard deviation was not reported.

(a) Is this result consistent with the idea that the SAT has a mean of 500 and a standard deviation of 100?

(b) Would you have rejected H_0 had you been looking for evidence that SAT scores in general have been declining over the years from a mean of 500?

12–6 Why do the data in Exercise 12-5 not really speak to the issue of whether American education in general is in a terrible state?

12–7 In 1979 the 2345 students from Arizona who took the math portion of the SAT had a mean of 524. Is this consistent with the notion of a population mean of 500 if we assume that $\sigma = 100$?

12–8 Why does the answer to Exercise 12-7 differ substantially from the answer to Exercise 12-5 even though the means are virtually the same?

12–9 It is commonly assumed that Graduate Record Exams produce scores with a mean of 500. In October 1981 the mean verbal score of 5701 college seniors and nonenrolled college graduates in the biological sciences

was 503 with a standard deviation of 104. Is our common belief about the mean of the GRE justified, at least for the biological sciences?

12–10 What are the null hypothesis (H_0) and the alternative hypothesis (H_1) in Exercise 12-9?

12–11 Would it have made sense to run a one-tailed test for Exercise 12-9?

12–12 If you had rejected the null hypothesis in Exercise 12-9, would that be an important finding? Why or why not?

12–13 In a large corporation the mean salary for all males with 3 to 5 years of experience is $27,000. Salaries (expressed in thousands) for a random sample of 10 women also having 3 to 5 years of experience were

   23   26   30   20   18   25   29   21   14   35

Is there evidence of different salary practices for males and females?

12–14 Although most of the salaries in Exercise 12-13 were less than $27,000, you could not reject H_0. Why might that be?

12–15 Compute 95% confidence limits on μ for the data in Exercise 12-5.

12–16 Compute 95% confidence limits on μ for the data in Exercise 12-9.

12–17 How did your approach to Exercise 12-15 and 12-16 differ?

12–18 For the IQ data on females in Appendix C, Data Set, test the null hypothesis that $\mu_{female} = 100$.

12–19 In Exercise 12-18 you probably solved for t instead of z. Why was that necessary?

12–20 Describe the procedures that you would go through to reproduce the results in Figure 12-4.

12–21 Use a t test to test $H_0: \rho = 0$ for the answers to Exercises 9-2 and 9-3.

13

HYPOTHESIS TESTS APPLIED TO MEANS— TWO RELATED SAMPLES

**Related samples
(Repeated measures)
(Matched samples)**
An experimental design in which the same subject is observed under more than one treatment.

In Chapter 12 we considered the situation in which we had one sample mean ($\bar{X}$) and wished to test to see if it was reasonable to believe that such a sample mean would have occurred if we had been sampling from a population with some specified mean (often denoted μ_0). Another way of phrasing this is to say that we were testing to determine if the mean of the population from which we sampled (call it μ_1) was equal to some particular value given by the null hypothesis (μ_0).

In this chapter we are going to move away from the case in which we have one sample of data and wish to perform a test on its mean. Instead we are going to consider the case in which we have two **related samples** (the same analysis applies to what are variously called **repeated measures, matched samples,** correlated samples, paired samples, or dependent samples) and wish to perform a test on the difference between their two means. As you will see, this test is very similar to the test discussed in the previous chapter.

13-1 RELATED SAMPLES

In many, but certainly not all, situations in which we will use the *t* test discussed in this chapter we will have two sets of data from the same subjects. For example, we might ask each of 20 people to rate their level of anxiety before and after donating blood. Or we might record ratings of level of disability made using two different rating systems for each of 20 handicapped individuals in an attempt to see whether one rating system leads to generally lower assessments than the other. In both examples we would have 20 sets of numbers, two numbers for each person, and would expect these two sets of numbers (variables) to be correlated. We need to take this correlation into account in planning our *t* test. To take the anxiety example, people differ widely in level of anxiety. Some seem to be anxious all the time no matter what happens, and others just take things as they come and don't worry about anything. Thus there should be a relationship between an individual's anxiety level before donating blood and the anxiety level after donating blood. In other words if we know what a person's anxiety score was before donation, we can make a reasonable guess what it was after donation. Similarly, some people are severely handicapped, whereas others are only mildly handicapped. If we know that a particular person received a high assessment using one system, it is likely that person also received a relatively high assessment using another system. The relationship between data sets doesn't have to be perfect—in fact it probably never will be. The fact that we can make better-than-chance predictions is sufficient to classify two sets of data as related or matched. (To put this another way, we have related or matched samples when the two variables [e.g., the two sets of anxiety scores] are significantly correlated.)

In the two preceding examples I have chosen situations in which each person in the study contributed two scores. Although this is the most common way of obtaining related samples, it is not the only way. For example, a study of marital relationships might involve asking husbands and wives to rate their satisfaction with their marriage, with the goal of testing to see whether wives are, on average, more or less satisfied than husbands. Here each individual would contribute only one score, but the couple as a unit would contribute a pair of scores. And it is very probable that if the husband is very dissatisfied with the marriage, his wife isn't likely to be in a state of marital bliss—and vice versa.

There are many examples of experimental designs involving related samples. However, they all have one thing in common, and that is the fact that knowing one member of a pair of scores tells you something—maybe not much, but something—about the other member. Whenever this is the case we say that the samples are related. This chapter deals with t tests on the difference between the means of two related samples.

13-2 STUDENT'S t APPLIED TO DIFFERENCE SCORES

As an example of the analysis of related samples we will consider an intervention study designed to promote certain social skills among high school freshmen (a group that gives us ample room for improvement). Before we begin the program we take the group of 15 subjects to a shopping mall, to dinner at the local branch of Hamburger Heaven, and to a movie. We also take a set of judges who count the number of socially inappropriate behaviors exhibited by each subject (e.g., running five abreast through the mall, yelling at passing cars, smearing catsup on the salt shaker, putting out cigarettes in coffee cups, making comments behind necking couples in the movie, and all of those other unlovable behaviors that each of us engaged in when we were that age). After a two-week intervention program, during which we try to instill in our subjects a whole array of adult social skills that we think that they should adopt (and omitting all of the adult social behaviors that we don't wish to nurture), we take the same subjects shopping, eating, and movie-watching again, and let the same judges again count socially inappropriate behaviors.

The data from this hypothetical study are presented in Table 13-1, in

	Before (X_1)	After (X_2)	Difference (D)
	18	12	6
	5	4	1
	19	17	2
	13	11	2
	12	8	4
	17	12	5
	26	27	−1
	3	3	0
	1	3	−2
	20	14	6
	15	12	3
	18	14	4
	10	11	−1
	8	10	−2
	15	9	6
Mean	13.333	11.133	2.200
s	6.914	5.998	2.933

TABLE 13-1
Data and Difference Scores on Number of Socially Inappropriate Behaviors

which the first set of scores is designated X_1 and the second set is designated X_2. The null hypothesis that we want to test is the hypothesis that the mean (μ_1) of the population of scores from which the first set of data was drawn is equal to the mean (μ_2) of the population from which the second set of data was drawn. In other words, we want to test $H_0: \mu_1 = \mu_2$ (or, equivalently, $H_0: \mu_1 - \mu_2 = 0$). Note that we have no interest in the values of μ_1 and μ_2, only whether they are equal. Note also that we will be testing this null hypothesis using data from related samples.

DIFFERENCE SCORES

Difference scores
The set of scores representing the difference between the subject's performance on two occasions.

Although it would seem most obvious to view the data as representing two samples of scores, one set obtained before the training program and one after, it is also possible, and very profitable, to transform the data into one set of scores—the set of differences between X_1 and X_2 for each subject. These differences are called **difference scores** and are shown in the third column of Table 13-1. They can be thought of as the degree of improvement between one measurement session and the next—presumably as a result of our intervention. If in fact the intervention program had *no* effect (i.e., if H_0 is true), the average score would not change from session to session. By chance some subjects would happen to have a higher score on X_2 than on X_1, and some would have a lower score, but *on the average* there would be no difference.

If we now think of our data as being the column of difference scores, the null hypothesis becomes the hypothesis that the mean of a population of difference scores (denoted μ_D) equals 0. Because it can be shown that

$\mu_D = \mu_1 - \mu_2$, then we can write $H_0: \mu_D = \mu_1 - \mu_2 = 0$. But now we can see that we are testing a hypothesis using *one* sample of data (the sample of difference scores), and we already know how to do that from Chapter 12.

THE *t* STATISTIC

We are now at precisely the same place we were in the last chapter when we had a sample of data and a null hypothesis ($\mu = 0$). The only difference is that in this case the data are difference scores, and the mean and standard deviation are based on the differences. Recall that t was defined as the difference between a sample mean and a population mean, divided by the standard error of the mean. Then we have

$$t = \frac{\bar{D} - 0}{s_{\bar{D}}} = \frac{\bar{D} - 0}{\dfrac{s_D}{\sqrt{N}}}$$

where $\bar{D}$ and $s_{\bar{D}}$ are the mean and standard deviation of the difference scores and N is the number of difference scores (i.e., the number of *pairs*, *not* the number of raw scores). For our data

$$t = \frac{\bar{D} - 0}{\dfrac{s_D}{\sqrt{N}}} = \frac{2.20 - 0}{\dfrac{2.933}{\sqrt{15}}} = \frac{2.20}{0.757} = 2.91$$

DEGREES OF FREEDOM

The degrees of freedom for the matched-sample case are exactly the same as they were for the one-sample case. Because we are working with the difference scores, N will be equal to the number of differences (or the number of *pairs* of observations, or the number of *independent* observations—all of which amount to the same thing). Due to the fact that the variance of these difference scores (s_D^2) is used as an estimate of the variance of a population of difference scores (σ_D^2) and because this sample variance is obtained using the sample mean ($\bar{D}$), we will lose one *df* to the mean and have $N - 1\ df$. In other words, df = number of *pairs* minus 1.

We have 15 difference scores in this example, so we will have 14 degrees of freedom. From Appendix D, Table 5, we find that for a two-tailed test at the .05 level of significance, $t_{.05}(14) = \pm 2.145$. Our obtained value of t (2.91) exceeds 2.145, and thus we will reject H_0 and conclude that the difference scores were not sampled from a population of difference scores where $\mu_D = 0$. In practical terms this means that the subjects showed fewer socially undesirable behaviors after the intervention program than before it. Although we would like to think that this means that the program was successful, it may just mean that the students finally noticed that someone was recording their behavior, that we happened to make our second observations on a day when everyone was too tired to do much of anything, or something else we have not even thought of. The fact remains, however, that for whatever reason, the scores were sufficiently lower on the second occasion to allow us to reject $H_0: \mu_D = \mu_1 - \mu_2 = 0$.

13-3   A SECOND EXAMPLE—THE MOON ILLUSION

As a second example we will return to the work by Kaufman and Rock (1962) on the moon illusion. An important hypothesis about the source of the moon illusion was put forth by Holway and Boring (1940), who suggested that the illusion was due to the fact that when the moon was on the horizon, the observer looked straight at it with eyes level, whereas when it was at its zenith, the observer had to elevate his eyes as well as his head to see it. Holway and Boring proposed that this difference in the elevation of the eyes was the cause of the illusion. To test this hypothesis Kaufman and Rock (1962) devised an apparatus that allowed them to present two artificial moons (one at the horizon and one at the zenith) and to control whether or not the subjects elevated their eyes to see the zenith moon. In one case the subject was forced to put his head in such a position as to be able to see the zenith moon with eyes level. In the other case the subject was forced to see the zenith moon with eyes raised. (The horizon moon was always viewed with eyes level.) In both cases the dependent variable was the ratio of the perceived size of the horizon moon to the perceived size of the zenith moon (a ratio of 1.00 would represent no illusion). If Holway and Boring were correct, there should be a greater illusion (larger ratio) in the eyes-elevated condition than in the eyes-level condition, although the "moon" was always perceived to be in the same place, the zenith. The actual data for this experiment are given in Table 13-2.

In this example we want to test the *null* hypothesis that the means are equal under the two viewing conditions. Because we are dealing with related observations (each subject served under both conditions), we will work with the difference scores and test $H_0: \mu_D = 0$. Using a two-tailed test at $\alpha = .05$, the alternative hypothesis is $H_1: \mu_D \neq 0$.

From the formula for a t test on related samples we have

$$t = \frac{\bar{D} - \mu_D}{s_{\bar{D}}} = \frac{\bar{D} - 0}{\dfrac{s_D}{\sqrt{N}}} = \frac{0.019 - 0}{\dfrac{0.137}{\sqrt{10}}} = \frac{0.019}{0.043} = 0.44$$

From Appendix D, Table 5, we find that $t_{.05}(9) = \pm 2.262$. Because $t_{obt} = 0.44$ is less than 2.262, we will fail to reject H_0 and will decide that we have no evidence to suggest that the illusion is affected by the elevation of the eyes.† (In fact these

---

†*Note*: A glance at Appendix D, Table 5, will reveal that any t less than 1.96 (the critical value for z) will never be significant at $\alpha = .05$, regardless of the number of degrees of freedom. Moreover, unless you have at least 50 degrees of freedom, t values less than 2.00 will not be significant, thus often making it unnecessary for you to even bother looking at the table of t.

===== **TABLE 13-2** =====
Magnitude of Moon Illusion When Zenith Moon Is Viewed with Eyes Level and with Eyes Elevated

Subject	Eyes Elevated	Eyes Level	Difference (D)
1	1.65	1.73	−0.08
2	1.00	1.06	−0.06
3	2.03	2.03	0.00
4	1.25	1.40	−0.15
5	1.05	0.95	0.10
6	1.02	1.13	−0.11
7	1.67	1.41	0.26
8	1.86	1.73	0.13
9	1.56	1.63	−0.07
10	1.73	1.56	0.17

$$\bar{D} = 0.019$$
$$s_D = 0.137$$
$$s_{\bar{D}} = 0.043$$

data also include a second test of Holway and Boring's hypothesis, since Holway and Boring would have predicted that there would not be an illusion if subjects viewed the zenith moon with eyes level. In fact the data reveal a considerable illusion under this condition. A test of the significance of the illusion level can be obtained by the methods discussed in Chapter 12, and the illusion is in fact significant.)

===== **13-4   ADVANTAGES AND DISADVANTAGES OF USING RELATED SAMPLES**

In the next chapter we are going to be considering experimental designs in which we use two independent groups of subjects rather than testing the same subjects twice (or some other method of having related samples of data). In many cases independent samples will be useful, but before considering that topic, it is important to understand the strengths and weaknesses of related samples.

Probably the most important advantage of designing an experiment around related samples is that such a procedure allows us to avoid problems associated with variability from subject to subject. For example in Table 13-1 note that some subjects (e.g., subjects #8 and #9) engage in almost no undesirable behaviors. On the other hand subjects #7 and #10 are candidates for some unpleasant action on the part of people around them. The advantage of related-samples designs is that these differences between subjects do not enter into the data we analyze—the difference scores. A change from 26 to 24 is treated exactly the same as a change from 6 to 4. In not allowing variability from subject to subject in overall general level of obnoxious behavior to influence the data by producing a large sample variance, related-samples designs have a considerable advantage over independent samples in terms of power—the ability to reject a false null hypothesis.

A second advantage of related samples over two independent samples is the fact that related samples allow us to control for extraneous variables. Had we measured one group of subjects before they received our intervention and a different group after, there may have been any number of differences between the groups that had nothing to do with our intervention but that would influence the results. That was not a problem in our study because we used the same subjects for both measurement sessions.

A third advantage of related-measures designs is that they require fewer subjects than do independent-sample designs for the same degree of power. This is a substantial advantage, as anyone who has ever tried to recruit subjects can tell you. It is usually much easier to get 20 people to do something twice than to get 40 people to do it once.

Order effect
The effect on performance attributable to the order in which treatments were administered.

Carry-over effect
The effect of previous trials (conditions) on a subject's performance on subsequent trials.

The primary disadvantage of related-measures designs concerns the fact that there may be either an **order effect** or a **carry-over effect** from one session to the next, or the first measurement may influence the treatment itself through processes such as sensitization. For example, if we plan to give a test of knowledge of current events, followed by a crash course in current events, and then follow that with a retest using the same test, it is reasonable to conclude that subjects will be more familiar with the items the second time around and may even have looked up answers during the interval between the two administrations. Similarly in drug studies the effects of the first drug may not have worn off by the next test session. A common problem with related-measures designs arises when a pretest "tips off" subjects as to the purpose of the intervention. For example, a pretest on attitudes toward breastfeeding might make you a wee bit suspicious when some stranger sits down beside you the next day and just happens to launch into a speech on the virtues of breastfeeding. Whenever you have concerns that your study could be contaminated by carry-over effects or that treatment effects might be influenced by pretreatment measures, a related-measures design is not recommended. There are techniques for controlling, though not eliminating, order and carry-over effects. However, we will not discuss them here.

13-5   USING MINITAB FOR *t* TESTS ON RELATED SAMPLES

To use Minitab with related samples we first have to read in the data on the two observations for each subject and then use Minitab to compute a column of difference scores. We then apply the TTEST procedure to these differences. Minitab also can be used to compute confidence limits on μ_D, which is accomplished in the way that we discussed in Chapter 12. (See Table 13-3 for the program and the results of the moon illusion example. Notice that I have used the commands LET and NAME. Their meanings should be apparent. After a variable is named, it can be referred to either by its column number [e.g., C1] or by its name [e.g., 'ELEV']. The name is always enclosed in single quotes.) For these data the confidence interval includes $\mu_D = 0$, which is in line with the fact that the *t* test failed to reject $H_0: \mu_D = 0$.

TABLE 13-3
The Use of Minitab for *t* Tests on Related Samples

```
MTB > SET THE FOLLOWING "ELEVATED" DATA IN COLUMN C1
DATA> 1.65 1.00 2.03 1.25 1.05 1.02 1.67 1.86 1.56 1.73
DATA> END
MTB > NAME C1 'ELEV'
MTB > SET THE FOLLOWING "LEVEL" DATA IN COLUMN C2
DATA> 1.73 1.06 2.03 1.40 0.95 1.13 1.41 1.73 1.63 1.56
DATA> END
MTB > NAME C2 'LEVEL'
MTB > LET C3 = 'LEVEL' - 'ELEV'
MTB > NAME C3 'DIFF'
MTB > TTEST AGAINST MU = 0 FOR DIFFERENCES IN C3

TEST OF MU = 0.0000 VS MU N.E. 0.0000

            N      MEAN    STDEV   SE MEAN        T    P VALUE
DIFF       10    -0.0190   0.1371   0.0434     -0.44       0.67

MTB > TINTERVAL AT 95 PERCENT CONFIDENCE LEVEL FOR DIFFERENCES IN C3

            N      MEAN    STDEV   SE MEAN   95.0 PERCENT C.I.
DIFF       10    -0.0190   0.1371   0.0434    -0.1171, 0.0791)

MTB > TINTERVAL AT 99 PERCENT CONFIDENCE LEVEL FOR DIFFERENCES IN C3

            N      MEAN    STDEV   SE MEAN   99.0 PERCENT C.I.
DIFF       10    -0.0190   0.1371   0.0434  ( -0.1600,  0.1220)

MTB > STOP
```

13-6   SUMMARY

In this chapter we have considered the analysis of data involving two related samples. We saw that the data easily can be reduced to one set of difference scores and that the standard one-sample *t* test can be applied to those difference scores to test the null hypothesis that the mean of the differences does not deviate from 0 more than would be predicted by chance. We then examined the strengths and weaknesses of experimental designs using related-measures designs. Finally we saw how to use Minitab to perform *t* tests for related samples and to compute confidence limits on μ_D. Some of the most important terms in this chapter are:

□ **Related samples (repeated measures) (matched samples)**

□ **Difference scores**

□ **Order effect**

□ **Carry-over effect**

13-7 EXERCISES

13–1 For six months we worked with a group of 15 severely retarded individuals in an attempt to train self-care skills through imitation. For a second six-month period we used physically guided practice with the same individuals. For each six-month session we have ratings on the level of required assistance (high = bad) for each person. The data for each individual follow:

Subject	1	2	3	4	5	6	7	8	9
Imitation	14	11	19	8	4	9	12	5	14
Physical Guidance	10	13	15	5	3	6	7	9	16

Subject	10	11	12	13	14	15
Imitation	17	18	0	2	8	6
Physical Guidance	10	13	1	2	3	6

Have we found that the level of assistance the subjects require has been reduced in the second six-month period?

13–2 Does the study described in Exercise 13-1 give us a clear answer concerning the relative quality of the two approaches? If not, why not?

13–3 How could we improve the study described in Exercise 13-1?

13–4 Construct 95% confidence limits on the true mean difference between the treatments described in Exercise 13-1 using techniques developed in Chapter 12.

13–5 As part of a study to reduce smoking, a national organization ran an advertising campaign to convince people to quit smoking. To evaluate the effectiveness of their campaign they had 15 subjects record the average number of cigarettes smoked per day in the week before and the week after exposure to the ad. The data follow:

Subject	1	2	3	4	5	6	7	8	9
Before	45	16	20	33	30	19	33	25	26
After	43	20	17	30	25	19	34	28	23

Subject	10	11	12	13	14	15
Before	40	28	36	15	26	32
After	41	26	40	16	23	34

Run the appropriate t test.

13–6 Assume that the data in Exercise 13-5 had come out differently. The new data are given next.

Subject	1	2	3	4	5	6	7	8	9
Before	45	16	20	33	30	19	33	25	26
After	59	35	30	40	20	10	20	20	36

Subject	10	11	12	13	14	15
Before	40	28	36	15	26	32
After	46	10	25	8	35	46

Run the appropriate t test.

13–7 Compare the conclusions a careful experimenter would draw from Exercises 13-5 and 13-6.

13–8 Give an example of an experiment in which using related samples would be ill advised because of carry-over effects.

13–9 Using the data for the first 20 subjects in Appendix C, Data Set, test the hypothesis that English grades are generally higher than the overall GPA.

13–10 Assume that the mean and standard deviations of the difference scores in Exercise 13-5 would remain the same if we added more subjects. How many subjects would we need to obtain a significant t? (We will return to this general problem in Chapter 15.)

13–11 Modify the data in Exercise 13-5 by shifting around the entries in row 2 so that occasionally high "Before" scores are paired with low "After" scores. Run a t test on the modified data and notice the effect on t.

13–12 Putting together the answer to Exercise 13-11 and what you know about correlation, how would you expect the degree of correlation between two variables (sets of data) to affect the magnitude of the t test between them?

13–13 In Section 13-4 I explained that by removing subject-to-subject variability from the data, related-samples designs prevent this variability from influencing the data on which the t test is run. This increases our ability to reject a false null hypothesis. Explain in your own words why this is so.

13–14 Give an example of a carry-over effect.

14

HYPOTHESIS TESTS APPLIED TO MEANS— TWO INDEPENDENT SAMPLES

In Chapter 13 we consider a study in which we obtained a set of measures of socially undesirable behavior before and after an intervention program. In that example the *same* subjects were observed both before and after the intervention. While that may have been the best way to evaluate the effects of that intervention program, in a great many experiments it is either impossible or undesirable to obtain data using repeated measurement of the same subjects. For example, if we wanted to determine if males were more socially inept than females, it would be clearly impossible to test the same people as males and then as females. Instead we would need a sample of males and a second, *independent*, sample of females.

One of the most common uses of the t test involves testing the difference between the means of two independent groups. We might wish to compare the mean number of trials needed to reach criterion in a simple visual discrimination task for two groups of rats—one raised under normal conditions and one raised under conditions of sensory deprivation. Or in a memory study we might wish to compare the mean levels of retention of a group of college students asked to recall active declarative sentences and a group asked to recall passive negative sentences. As a final example we might place subjects in a situation in which another person needed help. We could compare the latency of helping behavior when subjects were tested alone and when they were tested in groups.

In conducting any experiment with two independent groups we would most likely find that the two sample means differed by some amount. The important question, however, is whether this difference is sufficiently large to justify the conclusion that the two samples were drawn from different populations—for example, using the example of helping behavior, is the mean of the population of latencies from singly-tested subjects different from the mean of the population of latencies from group-tested subjects? Before we consider a specific example, however, we will need to examine the sampling distribution of differences between means and the t test that results from it.

14-1 DISTRIBUTION OF DIFFERENCES BETWEEN MEANS

Sampling distribution of differences between means
The distribution of the differences between means over repeated sampling from the same population(s).

When we are interested in testing for a difference between the mean of one population (μ_1) and the mean of a second population (μ_2), we will be testing a null hypothesis of the form $H_0: \mu_1 - \mu_2 = 0$ or, equivalently, $\mu_1 = \mu_2$. Because the test of this null hypothesis involves the difference between independent sample means, it is important that we digress for a moment and examine the **sampling distribution of differences between means**. Suppose that we have two populations labeled X_1 and X_2 with means μ_1 and μ_2 and variances σ_1^2 and σ_2^2. We now draw pairs of samples of size N_1 from population X_1 and of size N_2 from population X_2, and record the means and the differences between the means for each pair of samples. Because we are sampling independently from each population, the sample means will be independent. (Means are paired only in the trivial and presumably irrelevant sense of being drawn at the same time.) Because we are only supposing, we might as well go all the way and suppose that we repeated this procedure an infinite number of times. The results are presented schematically in Figure 14-1. In the lower portion of this figure the first two columns represent the sampling distributions of $\bar{X}_1$ and $\bar{X}_2$, and the third column represents the sampling distribution of mean differences ($\bar{X}_1 - \bar{X}_2$). It is this third column in which we are most interested, because we are concerned with testing differences between means. The mean of this distribution can be shown to equal $\mu_1 - \mu_2$. The variance of this distribution of differences is given by what is commonly called the **Variance Sum Law**, a limited form of which states:

Variance Sum Law
The rule giving the variance of a sum (or difference) of two or more variables.

> The variance of a sum or difference of two *independent* variables is equal to the sum of their variances.†

We know from the Central Limit Theorem that the variance of the distribution of $\bar{X}_1$ is σ_1^2/N_1 and the variance of the distribution of $\bar{X}_2$ is σ_2^2/N_2. Because the variables (sample means) are independent, the variance of the difference of these two variables is the sum of their variances. Thus

$$\sigma_{\bar{X}_1 - \bar{X}_2}^2 = \sigma_{\bar{X}_1}^2 + \sigma_{\bar{X}_2}^2 = \frac{\sigma_1^2}{N_1} + \frac{\sigma_2^2}{N_2}$$

†The complete form of the law omits the restriction that the variables must be independent, and states that the variance of their sum or difference is

$$\sigma_{X_1 \pm X_2}^2 = \sigma_1^2 + \sigma_2^2 \pm 2\rho\sigma_1\sigma_2$$

where the notation $\pm$ is interpreted as $+$ when we are speaking of their sum and as $-$ when we are speaking of their difference. The term ρ (rho) in this equation is the correlation in the *population* between the two variables and is equal to 0 when the variables are independent. (The fact that $\rho \neq 0$ when the variables are not independent was what forced us to treat the related sample case separately.)

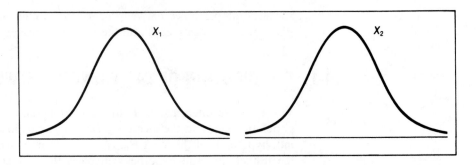

	Sample 1	Sample 2	Mean Difference
	$\bar{X}_{11}$	$\bar{X}_{21}$	$\bar{X}_{11} - \bar{X}_{21}$
	$\bar{X}_{12}$	$\bar{X}_{22}$	$\bar{X}_{12} - \bar{X}_{22}$
	$\bar{X}_{13}$	$\bar{X}_{23}$	$\bar{X}_{13} - \bar{X}_{23}$
	$\vdots$	$\vdots$	$\vdots$
	$\bar{X}_{1\infty}$	$\bar{X}_{2\infty}$	$\bar{X}_{1\infty} - \bar{X}_{2\infty}$
Mean	μ_1	μ_2	$\mu_1 - \mu_2$
Variance	$\dfrac{\sigma_1^2}{N_1}$	$\dfrac{\sigma_2^2}{N_2}$	$\dfrac{\sigma_1^2}{N_1} + \dfrac{\sigma_2^2}{N_2}$
S.D.	$\dfrac{\sigma_1}{\sqrt{N_1}}$	$\dfrac{\sigma_2}{\sqrt{N_2}}$	$\sqrt{\dfrac{\sigma_1^2}{N_1} + \dfrac{\sigma_2^2}{N_2}}$

FIGURE 14-1
Hypothetical Set of Means and
Differences between Means
When Sampling from Two
Populations

Having found the mean and variance of a set of differences between means, we know most of what we need to know. The general form of the sampling distribution of mean differences is presented in Figure 14-2.

The final point to be made about this distribution concerns its shape. An important theorem in statistics states that the sum or difference of two independent normally distributed variables is itself normally distributed. Because Figure 14-2 represents the difference between two sampling distributions of means and because we know that the sampling distribution of means is at least approximately normal for reasonable sample sizes, then the distribution in Figure 14-2 must itself be at least approximately normal.

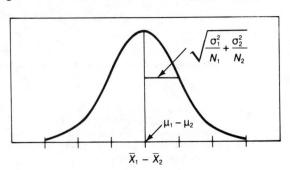

FIGURE 14-2
Sampling Distribution of
Differences between Means

THE t STATISTIC

Given the information we now have about the sampling distribution of mean differences, we can proceed to develop the appropriate test procedure. Assume *for the moment* that knowledge of the population variances (σ_i^2) is not a problem. We have earlier defined z as a statistic (a point on the distribution) minus the mean of the distribution, divided by the standard error of the distribution. Our statistic in the present case is ($\bar{X}_1 - \bar{X}_2$), the observed difference between the sample means. The mean of the sampling distribution is ($\mu_1 - \mu_2$), and, as we saw, the **standard error of differences between means**† is

Standard error of differences between means
The standard deviation of the sampling distribution of differences between means.

$$\sigma_{\bar{X}_1 - \bar{X}_2} = \sqrt{\frac{\sigma_1^2}{N_1} + \frac{\sigma_2^2}{N_2}}$$

Thus we can write

$$z = \frac{(\bar{X}_1 - \bar{X}_2) - (\mu_1 - \mu_2)}{\sigma_{\bar{X}_1 - \bar{X}_2}}$$

$$= \frac{(\bar{X}_1 - \bar{X}_2) - (\mu_1 - \mu_2)}{\sqrt{\frac{\sigma_1^2}{N_1} + \frac{\sigma_2^2}{N_2}}}$$

The critical value for $\alpha = .05$ is $z = \pm 1.96$, as it was for the one-sample tests discussed in Chapter 12.

The preceding formula is not particularly useful, except for the purpose of showing the origin of the appropriate t test, because we rarely know the necessary population variances. (Such knowledge is so rare that it isn't even worth imagining cases in which we would have it, although a few do exist.) However, just as we did in the one-sample case, we can circumvent this problem by using the sample variances as estimates of the population variances. This, for the same reasons discussed earlier for the one-sample t, means that the result will be distributed as t rather than z.

$$t = \frac{(\bar{X}_1 - \bar{X}_2) - (\mu_1 - \mu_2)}{s_{\bar{X}_1 - \bar{X}_2}}$$

$$= \frac{(\bar{X}_1 - \bar{X}_2) - (\mu_1 - \mu_2)}{\sqrt{\frac{s_1^2}{N_1} + \frac{s_2^2}{N_2}}}$$

Because the null hypothesis is generally the hypothesis that $\mu_1 - \mu_2 = 0$, we will

†Remember that the standard deviation of any sampling distribution is called the standard error of that distribution.

usually drop that term from the equation and write

$$t = \frac{\bar{X}_1 - \bar{X}_2}{s_{\bar{X}_1 - \bar{X}_2}}$$

$$= \frac{\bar{X}_1 - \bar{X}_2}{\sqrt{\dfrac{s_1^2}{N_1} + \dfrac{s_2^2}{N_2}}}$$

POOLING VARIANCES

Although the equation for t that we have just developed is quite appropriate when the sample sizes are equal, it requires some modification for unequal sample sizes. This modification is designed to provide a better estimate of the population variance. One of the assumptions required in the use of t for two independent samples is that $\sigma_1^2 = \sigma_2^2$ (i.e., that the samples come from populations with equal variances), regardless of the truth or falsity of H_0. Such an assumption is often a reasonable one and is called the assumption of **homogeneity of variance**. We often begin an experiment with two groups of subjects who are equivalent and then do something to one (or both) group(s) that will raise or lower the subjects' scores. In such a case it often makes sense to assume that the variances will remain unaffected. (You should recall that adding or subtracting a constant to a set of scores has no effect on its variance.) Because the population variances are assumed to be equal, this common variance can be represented by the symbol σ^2, without a subscript.

Homogeneity of variance
The situation in which two or more populations have equal variances.

In our data we have two estimates of σ^2, namely s_1^2 and s_2^2. It seems appropriate to obtain some sort of an average of s_1^2 and s_2^2 on the grounds that this average should be a better estimate of σ^2 than either of the two separate estimates. We do not want to take the simple arithmetic mean, however, because doing so would give equal weight to the two estimates, even if one were based on considerably more observations. What we want is a **weighted average**, in which the sample variances are weighted by their degrees of freedom ($N_i - 1$). If we call this new estimate s_p^2, then

Weighted average
A mean of the form:
$(a_1X_1 + a_2X_2)/(a_1 + a_2)$ where a_1 and a_2 are weighting factors, and $X_1 + X_2$ are the values to be averaged.

$$s_p^2 = \frac{(N_1 - 1)s_1^2 + (N_2 - 1)s_2^2}{N_1 + N_2 - 2}$$

The numerator represents the sum of the variances, each weighted by their degrees of freedom, and the denominator represents the sum of the weights or, equivalently, the degrees of freedom for s_p^2.

The weighted average of the two sample variances is usually referred to as a **pooled variance** estimate (a rather inelegant name, but reasonably descriptive). Having defined our pooled estimate (s_p^2), we now can write

Pooled variance
A weighted average of the separate sample variances.

$$t = \frac{\bar{X}_1 - \bar{X}_2}{s_{\bar{X}_1 - \bar{X}_2}} = \frac{\bar{X}_1 - \bar{X}_2}{\sqrt{\dfrac{s_p^2}{N_1} + \dfrac{s_p^2}{N_2}}} = \frac{\bar{X}_1 - \bar{X}_2}{\sqrt{s_p^2\left(\dfrac{1}{N_1} + \dfrac{1}{N_2}\right)}}$$

Notice that both this formula for t and the one that we used in the previous section involve dividing the difference between the sample means by an estimate of the standard error of the difference between means. The only difference concerns the way in which this standard error is estimated. When example sizes are equal, it makes absolutely no difference whether or not you pool variances; the resulting t will be the same. However, when the sample sizes are unequal, pooling can make quite a difference.

DEGREES OF FREEDOM FOR t

You will note that two sample variances (s_1^2 and s_2^2) have gone into calculating t. Each of these variances is based upon squared deviations about their corresponding sample means, and therefore each sample variance has $N_i - 1$ df. Across the two samples, therefore, we will have $(N_1 - 1) + (N_2 - 1) = N_1 + N_2 - 2\,df$. Thus the t for two independent samples will be based on $N_1 + N_2 - 2$ degrees of freedom.

EXAMPLE: RECALL OF ACTIVE AND PASSIVE SENTENCES

To illustrate the use of t as a test of the difference between two independent means, we will consider first a hypothetical example from the field of verbal learning. Let us suppose that an investigator has had a fight with a journal editor who insists upon using the passive voice in the third person ("It was found that...") rather than the active voice in the first person ("I found that..."). (Journal editors can be as stuffy as other people and, as bureaucrats learned long ago, elaborate sentence structures make even meaningless prose look more impressive.) Our investigator wants to show that subjects exhibit greater recall for active declarative sentences ("Joe rang the bell") than for passive negative sentences ("The bell was not rung by Amy"). The experimenter obtained 35 subjects and assigned them at random to two groups. By chance the first group (Group A) had 15 subjects and the second (Group P) had 20. Group A was read 25 active declarative sentences and was given a recall test after each sentence. Group P heard and recalled passive negative forms of the sentences used for Group A. The dependent variable was the number of sentences correctly recalled by each subject, and the data are presented in Table 14-1.

Before we consider any statistical test, and ideally even before the data are collected, we must specify several features of the test. First we must specify the null and alternative hypotheses:

$$H_0: \mu_1 = \mu_2$$

$$H_1: \mu_1 \neq \mu_2$$

The alternative hypothesis is bidirectional (we will reject H_0 if $\mu_1 < \mu_2$ or if $\mu_1 > \mu_2$), and thus we are using a two-tailed test. For the sake of consistency with other examples in this book, we will let $\alpha = .05$. It is important to keep in mind, however, that there is nothing particularly sacred about these two

	Group A	Group P
	17	13
	17	18
	21	17
	18	13
	22	14
	18	13
	16	18
	15	19
	18	16
	20	14
	21	13
	16	15
	15	14
	16	16
	20	15
		15
		13
		17
		17
		15
Mean	18.00	15.25
Variance	5.286	3.671

TABLE 14-1
Recall of Active Declarative and Passive Negative Sentences

decisions.† Given the null hypothesis as stated, we now can calculate t.

$$t = \frac{\bar{X}_1 - \bar{X}_2}{s_{\bar{X}_1 - \bar{X}_2}}$$

$$= \frac{\bar{X}_1 - \bar{X}_2}{\sqrt{\dfrac{s_1^2}{N_1} + \dfrac{s_2^2}{N_2}}}$$

Because we are testing $H_0: \mu_1 - \mu_2 = 0$, the $\mu_1 - \mu_2$ term has been dropped from the equation. When we pool the variances, we obtain

$$s_p^2 = \frac{(N_1 - 1)s_1^2 + (N_2 - 1)s_2^2}{N_1 + N_2 - 2}$$

$$= \frac{14(5.286) + 19(3.671)}{15 + 20 - 2} = \frac{74.004 + 69.749}{33} = 4.356$$

Note that the pooled variance is somewhat closer in value to s_2^2 than s_1^2 because

---

†If we had a good reason for testing the hypothesis that μ_1 was five points higher than μ_2, for example, we could set $H_0: \mu_1 - \mu_2 = 5$, although this type of situation is rare. Similarly we could set α at .01 or .001 or even .10, although this last value is higher than most people would accept.

of the greater weight given s_2^2 in the formula. Then

$$t = \frac{(18.00 - 15.25)}{\sqrt{\dfrac{4.356}{15} + \dfrac{4.356}{20}}}$$

$$= \frac{2.75}{\sqrt{0.5082}} = \frac{2.75}{0.713} = 3.86$$

For this example we have $N_1 - 1 = 14\,df$ for Group A and $N_2 - 1 = 19\,df$ for Group P, making a total of $N_1 - 1 + N_2 - 1 = 33\,df$. From the sampling distribution of t in Appendix D, Table 5, $t_{.05}(33) = \pm 2.04$ (with linear interpolation). Because the value of t_{obt} far exceeds t_α, we will reject H_0 (at $\alpha = .05$) and conclude that there is a difference between the means of the populations from which our observations were drawn. In other words we will conclude (statistically) that $\mu_1 \neq \mu_2$ and (practically) that $\mu_1 > \mu_2$. In terms of the experimental variables, active declarative sentences are recalled better than passive negative sentences.†

14-2 HETEROGENEITY OF VARIANCE

Heterogeneity of variance
A situation in which samples are drawn from populations having different variances.

As we have seen, one of the assumptions behind the t test for two independent samples is the assumption of homogeneity of variance ($\sigma_1^2 = \sigma_2^2$). When this assumption does not hold (i.e., when $\sigma_1^2 \neq \sigma_2^2$), we have what is called **heterogeneity of variance**. Considerable work has been done examining the practical effect of heterogeneity of variance on the t test. As a result of this work we can come to some general conclusions about the analysis of data that is appropriate with heterogeneous variances.

The first point to keep in mind is that our homogeneity assumption refers to the population variances and not to sample variances—we would rarely expect the sample variances to be exactly equal even if the population variances were. On the basis of sampling studies that have been conducted, the general rule of thumb is that if one sample variance is no more than four‡ times the other *and* if the sample sizes are equal or approximately equal, you may go ahead and compute t as you would normally. Heterogeneity of variance is not likely to have a serious effect on your results under these conditions. On the other hand if one sample variance is more than four times the other or if the variances are quite unequal and the sample sizes are also quite unequal, then an alternative procedure may be necessary. This procedure is easy to apply,

Confounded
Two variables are said to be confounded when they are varied simultaneously and their effects cannot be separated.

†Because active declarative sentences are generally shorter than passive negative sentences, our interpretation of the results could be open to question. Unless our sentences were equated for length, we have no defense against the argument that we have shown merely that shorter sentences are remembered better than longer ones. We have **confounded** the variables of syntax and sentence length.

‡The use of the number four here is probably conservative. Some people would argue for using the standard approach when variances are considerably more different than this.

however. Simply compute t using the *separate* variance estimates (i.e., do not pool). You then go to the t tables using the *smaller* of $N_1 - 1$ and $N_2 - 1$ as the degrees of freedom (rather than $N_1 + N_2 - 2$). This is a conservative test, meaning that if H_0 is true you are less likely to commit a Type I error than the nominal value of α would suggest. As an example of this procedure, suppose that we have the following data:

$$\bar{X}_1 = 111.53 \qquad \bar{X}_2 = 108.38$$

$$s_1^2 = 19.65 \qquad s_2^2 = 3.06$$

$$N_1 = 10 \qquad N_2 = 18$$

Then

$$t = \frac{\bar{X}_1 - \bar{X}_2}{\sqrt{\dfrac{s_1^2}{N_1} + \dfrac{s_2^2}{N_2}}} = \frac{111.53 - 108.38}{\sqrt{\dfrac{19.65}{10} + \dfrac{3.06}{18}}}$$

$$= \frac{3.15}{1.461} = 2.16$$

Because the variances were very unequal (one was over six times the other), we did not pool them. The values of $N_1 - 1$ and $N_2 - 1$ are 9 and 17, respectively, and we will evaluate t by going to Appendix D, Table 5, with 9 df (the smaller of 9 and 17). Here we find that $t_{.05}(9) = \pm 2.262$, which is larger than the obtained value. Thus we will not reject H_0.†

There are more accurate (less conservative) solutions to the problem of heterogeneity of variance, which rely on calculating an adjusted degrees of freedom lying between the smaller of $N_1 - 1$ and $N_2 - 1$ on the one hand and $N_1 + N_2 - 2$ on the other. As you will see, many computer programs, including Minitab, make such an adjustment. For most purposes the conservative approach suggested here is sufficient. (A more complete discussion of the problem of heterogeneity of variance can be found in Howell, 1987.)

14-3 NON-NORMALITY OF DISTRIBUTIONS

We saw earlier that another assumption required for the correct use of the t test is the assumption that the population(s) from which the data are sampled is (are) normally distributed—or at least that the sampling distribution of differences between means is normal. In general, as long as the distributions of sample data are roughly mound-shaped (high in the center and tapering off on either side), the test is likely to be valid. This is especially true for large samples (N_1 and N_2 greater than 30), because then the Central Limit Theorem almost guarantees the near-normality of the sampling distribution of differences between means.

---

†Note that if we had not had a problem with heterogeneity of variance, we would have used $N_1 + N_2 - 2 = 26\ df$, and the difference would have been significant.

14-4 A SECOND EXAMPLE WITH TWO INDEPENDENT SAMPLES

In Chapter 11 we briefly considered a study by Doob and Gross (1968) investigating the effects of status on horn-honking behavior. In their study the driver of either a low- or high-status car remained stopped when a traffic light turned green, and the experimenter observed the behavior of the driver of the following car. One of their measures was the number of seconds that elapsed between the time the light turned green and the time the driver of the following car honked the horn. The data shown in Table 14-2 have been created to have essentially the same means and standard deviations as those reported by Doob and Gross, although their study involved larger sample sizes.

TABLE 14-2
Latency (in Seconds) of Horn Honking as a Function of Status

Low-Status Group ($N = 15$)					High-Status Group ($N = 20$)				
1.68	6.42	8.58	6.85	10.59	9.10	7.83	11.22	5.29	13.20
3.26	9.44	4.84	4.98	12.31	11.79	3.87	7.41	8.40	14.05
9.01	6.13	7.86	6.71	8.14	4.44	8.11	9.81	11.79	6.84
					12.64	8.68	10.66	9.95	9.53

$\bar{X}_1 = 7.12$ $s_{X_1} = 2.77$ $s_{X_1}^2 = 7.67$ $\bar{X}_2 = 9.23$ $s_{X_2} = 2.82$ $s_{X_2}^2 = 7.95$

Doob and Gross were interested in testing the null hypothesis that the latency to respond to a stopped low-status car is equal to the latency to respond to a stopped high-status car (i.e., $H_0: \mu_1 = \mu_2$). They chose a two-tailed alternative hypothesis ($H_1: \mu_1 \neq \mu_2$) and set $\alpha = .05$. Visual inspection of the data suggests that the sample variances are nearly equal ($s_1^2 = 7.67$, $s_2^2 = 7.95$) and that the data are at least unimodal and symmetric, so a t test seems appropriate. Because we have unequal sample sizes, we will pool the sample variances. The pooled variance is given by

$$s_p^2 = \frac{(N_1 - 1)s_1^2 + (N_2 - 1)s_2^2}{N_1 + N_2 - 2}$$

$$= \frac{14(7.67) + 19(7.95)}{15 + 20 - 2} = \frac{107.38 + 151.05}{33} = \frac{258.43}{33}$$

$$= 7.83$$

Then t, using the pooled variances, is

$$t = \frac{\bar{X}_1 - \bar{X}_2}{\sqrt{\dfrac{s_p^2}{N_1} + \dfrac{s_p^2}{N_2}}}$$

$$= \frac{7.12 - 9.23}{\sqrt{\dfrac{7.83}{15} + \dfrac{7.83}{20}}}$$

$$= \frac{-2.11}{\sqrt{0.9135}} = \frac{-2.11}{0.9558}$$

$$= -2.21$$

From Appendix D, Table 5, with $\alpha = .05$ and $df = 33$ we have $t_{.05}(33) = \pm 2.04$. Because $t_{obt} = -2.21$ lies in the rejection region, we will reject H_0 and conclude that $\mu_1 \neq \mu_2$. In practical terms this means that we will conclude that a driver is quicker to blow his or her horn when a low-status car is blocking the intersection than when the car is of high status.

14-5 CONFIDENCE LIMITS ON $\mu_1 - \mu_2$

In addition to testing a null hypothesis about population means (i.e., testing $H_0: \mu_1 - \mu_2 = 0$), it is sometimes useful to set confidence limits on the difference between μ_1 and μ_2. The logic for setting these confidence limits is exactly the same as it was for the one-sample case in Chapter 12. The calculations are exactly the same except that we use the *difference* between the means and the standard error of *differences* between means in place of the mean and the standard error of the mean. Thus for the 95% confidence limits on $\mu_1 - \mu_2$ we have

$$CI_{.95} = (\bar{X}_1 - \bar{X}_2) \pm t_{.05} s_{\bar{X}_1 - \bar{X}_2}$$

For the horn-honking example we have

$$CI_{.95} = (7.12 - 9.23) \pm 2.04 \left(\sqrt{\frac{7.83}{15} + \frac{7.83}{20}} \right)$$

$$= -2.11 \pm 2.04(0.9558) = -2.11 \pm 1.95$$

$$-4.06 \leqslant (\mu_1 - \mu_2) \leqslant -0.16$$

The probability is .95 that an interval such as -4.06 to -0.16 encloses the true difference in latency of honking for low- and high-status cars.

14-6 USE OF MINITAB FOR ANALYSIS OF TWO INDEPENDENT SAMPLE MEANS

Table 14-3 illustrates the use of Minitab to analyze the results of the horn-honking experiment. A RETRIEVE command was used to call up the data (of Table 14-2) that had been saved previously with a Minitab SAVE command. Near the top of the table you will see the stem-and-leaf and boxplot displays for the data for each group separately. (*Note*: Minitab chose different scales for the two stem-and-leaf displays and for the two boxplots. From these displays we can

TABLE 14-3
Minitab Analysis of Horn-Honking Data

```
MTB > RETRIEVE 'TRAFFIC MIN'
MTB > STEM AND LEAF FOR 'LOW'

Stem-and-leaf of LOW       N  = 15
Leaf Unit = 0.10

      1     1 6
      1     2
      2     3 2
      4     4 89
      4     5
     (4)    6 1478
      7     7 8
      6     8 15
      4     9 04
      2    10 5
      1    11
      1    12 3

MTB > STEM AND LEAF FOR 'HIGH'
Stem-and-leaf of HIGH      N  = 20
Leaf Unit = 0.10

      1     3 8
      2     4 4
      3     5 2
      4     6 8
      6     7 48
      9     8 146
     (4)    9 1589
      7    10 6
      6    11 277
      3    12 6
      2    13 2
      1    14 0

MTB > BOXPLOT FOR 'LOW'
```

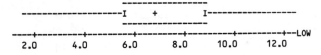

```
                              --------------------
          --------------------I     +      I------------------
                              --------------------
        ----+---------+---------+---------+---------+---------+--LOW
          2.0       4.0       6.0       8.0      10.0      12.0

MTB > BOXPLOT FOR 'HIGH'
```

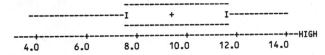

```
                            --------------------
          ------------------I     +      I------------
                            --------------------
        ----+---------+---------+---------+---------+---------+--HIGH
          4.0       6.0       8.0      10.0      12.0      14.0

MTB > POOLED TEST FOR 'LOW' VS 'HIGH'

TWOSAMPLE T FOR LOW VS HIGH
          N     MEAN    STDEV   SE MEAN
LOW      15     7.12     2.77    0.716
HIGH     20     9.23     2.82    0.631

95 PCT CI FOR MU LOW - MU HIGH: (-4.057, -0.1641)
TTEST MU LOW = MU HIGH (VS NE): T=-2.21 P=0.034 DF=33.0
MTB > TWOSAMPLE T TEST FOR 'LOW' AND 'HIGH'

TWOSAMPLE T FOR LOW VS HIGH
          N     MEAN    STDEV   SE MEAN
LOW      15     7.12     2.77    0.716
HIGH     20     9.23     2.82    0.631

95 PCT CI FOR MU LOW - MU HIGH: (-4.059, -0.1616)
TTEST MU LOW = MU HIGH (VS NE): T=-2.21 P=0.035 DF=30.6

MTB > STOP
```

see that the data are symmetrically distributed with no outliers. The pooled t test is shown in the lower portion of the table along with the 95% confidence limits on $\mu_1 - \mu_2$. You can see that these results agree with the ones we obtained earlier. Also included in Table 14-3 for illustrative purposes is a t test using the separate variance estimates (rather than pooling). This procedure leads to essentially the same results, although you can see that, as suggested earlier, the degrees of freedom have been adjusted slightly due to the small differences in the sample variances.

14-7 A FINAL WORKED EXAMPLE

The following data are based on a study by Eysenck (1974), which, among other things, compared the level of recall of older and younger subjects. Eysenck wanted to test the hypothesis that when subjects were required to process verbal information (lists of words), older subjects did less processing and therefore recalled fewer words. (In this study he also showed that there were no differences in recall between the two age groups when in-depth processing was not required.) The following data have been constructed to have the same means and standard deviations as two of the conditions in Eysenck's study, and refer to groups who were told to memorize the words so that they could be recalled later. The dependent variable is the number of items correctly recalled.

| | Age | |
	Younger (18–30)	Older (55–65)
	21	10
	19	19
	17	14
	15	5
	22	10
	16	11
	22	14
	22	15
	18	11
	21	11
ΣX	193	120
ΣX^2	3789	1566
N	10	10

First we need to specify the null hypothesis, the significance level, and whether we will use a one- or two-tailed test. We want to test the null hypothesis that the two age groups recall the same amount of information, so we have $H_0: \mu_1 = \mu_2$. We will set alpha at $\alpha = .05$, in line with what we have used elsewhere in the book. Finally, we will choose to use a two-tailed test because it is reasonably possible for either group to show superior recall.

Next we need to calculate the means and variances.

$$\bar{X}_1 = 193/10 = 19.3 \qquad \bar{X}_2 = 120/10 = 12.0$$

$$s_X^2 = \frac{3789 - \dfrac{193^2}{10}}{9} \qquad s_Y^2 = \frac{1566 - \dfrac{120^2}{10}}{9}$$

$$= 7.122 \qquad\qquad = 14.000$$

With equal sample sizes we do not need to bother pooling the variances, because the resulting t would be the same in either event. However, for the sake of an example I will do so here.

$$s_p^2 = \frac{(N_1 - 1)(s_1^2) + (N_2 - 1)(s_2^2)}{N_1 + N_2 - 2} = \frac{9(7.122) + 9(14.000)}{18} = 10.561$$

Finally, we can calculate t using the pooled variance estimate.

$$t = \frac{(\bar{X}_1 - \bar{X}_2)}{\sqrt{\dfrac{s_p^2}{N_1} + \dfrac{s_p^2}{N_2}}} = \frac{19.3 - 12.0}{\sqrt{\dfrac{10.561}{10} + \dfrac{10.561}{10}}} = \frac{7.300}{\sqrt{2.112}} = 5.02$$

For this example we have $N_1 + N_2 - 2 = 18$ degrees of freedom. From Appendix D, Table 5, we find $t_{.05} = 2.101$. Because $5.02 > 2.101$ we will reject H_0 and conclude that the two population means are not equal. From the data it is apparent that younger subjects recalled more words than older subjects. This is not to say that older subjects are not as smart as younger subjects, but only that for some reason they did not perform as well on this task. (It could well be that older subjects are not willing to process information to the same extent that younger subjects are, possibly because they are not really interested in the experiment.)

14-8 SUMMARY

In this chapter we have considered the use of the t test for testing the null hypothesis that two population means are equal. This test is based on sample means from two independent samples and is probably the most common form of the t test. We also considered the assumptions underlying the use of t, procedures to be applied when the assumption of homogeneity of variance is not met, and confidence limits for mean differences. Some of the most important terms in this chapter are:

□ **Sampling distribution of differences between means**

□ **Variance Sum Law**

□ **Standard error of differences between means**

□ **Homogeneity of variance**

□ **Weighted average**

□ **Pooled variance**

□ **Heterogeneity of variance**

□ **Confounded**

14-9 EXERCISES

14–1 Suppose that we redesigned the study described in Exercise 13-1 to have different subjects serve under the Imitation and Physical Guidance conditions. We obtained the following data:

Imitation	14	11	19	8	4	9	12	5
	14	17	18	0	2	8	6	
Physical Guidance	10	14	5	8	1	10	13	14
	0	1	4	2	3	4	14	

What would you conclude?

14–2 What is the most obvious problem with the data in Exercise 14-1 in terms of finding a significant difference?

14–3 Why was the experimental design that was used in Exercise 13-1 able to produce a statistically significant difference when there wasn't one for Exercise 14-1?

14–4 We randomly assigned nine children to each of two groups and asked them to brush their teeth with toothpaste X or toothpaste Y. We counted the number of cavities per child at the end of 6 months. The data follow:

Toothpaste X	3	3	2	2	3	4	3	1	0
Toothpaste Y	1	3	2	1	0	3	1	0	2

Run the appropriate *t* test.

14–5 What is the role of random assignment in Exercise 14-4?

14–6 In a comparison of different programs advocated by two organizations concerned with weight loss, 20 subjects were enrolled in Program A and 20 in Program B. The amount of weight lost in the next 6 months is shown for those subjects who completed the program.

Program A	25	21	18	20	22	30		
Program B	15	17	9	12	11	19	14	18
	16	10	5	13				

Run the appropriate *t* test after considering the group variances.

14–7 The following data represent alternative data that might have been obtained in the study described in Exercise 14-6.

Program A	25	21	8	20	12	30		
Program B	15	17	9	12	11	19	14	18
	16	10	15	13				

Calculate and evaluate *t* after considering the two sample variances.

14–8 In Exercise 14-7 the means are not the only important statistics. What else might be considered more important?

14–9 Much has been made of the concept of *experimenter bias*, which refers to the fact that for even the most conscientious experimenters there seems to be a tendency for the data to come out in the desired direction. Suppose that we use students as experimenters. All of the experimenters are told that subjects will be given caffeine before the experiment, but half of the experimenters are told that we expect caffeine to lead to good performance and half are told that we expect it to lead to poor performance. The dependent variable is the number of simple arithmetic problems the subjects can solve in 2 minutes. The obtained data are as follows:

Expect Good Performance	19	15	22	13	18	15
	20	25	22			
Expect Poor Performance	14	18	17	12	21	21
	24	14				

What would you conclude?

14–10 Calculate 95% confidence limits on $\mu_1 - \mu_2$ for the data in Exercise 14-9.

14–11 Calculate 95% confidence limits on $\mu_1 - \mu_2$ for the data in Exercise 14-7.

14–12 Using the data in Appendix C, Data Set, use a *t* test to compare ADDSC scores of males and females.

14–13 Using the data in Appendix C, Data Set, compare grade point average for those having ADDSC scores of 65 or less with those having ADDSC scores of 66 or more.

14–14 What does the answer to Exercise 14-13 tell you about the predictive utility of the ADDSC score?

14–15 An experimenter working in the area of decision making asked 12 children to solve as many problems as they could in 10 minutes. One group was told that this was a test of their innate problem-solving ability and a second group was told that this was just a time-filling task. Compute and interpret the appropriate *t* test. The dependent variable is the number of problems solved. The data are as follows:

Innate Ability	4	5	8	3	7
Time-Filling Activity	11	6	9	7	9

14–16 A second experimenter repeated the experiment described in Exercise 14-15 and obtained exactly the same results. However, she felt that it would be more appropriate to record the data in terms of minutes per problem (for example, 4 problems in 10 minutes = 10/4 = 2.50 minutes per problem). Thus her data were

Innate Ability	2.50	2.00	1.25	3.33	1.43
Time-Filling Activity	0.91	1.67	1.11	1.43	1.11

Analyze and interpret these data with the appropriate t test.

14–17 Given the definition of a weighted average on p. 192, show what the pooled variance estimate (s_p^2) would be if the two sample sizes were equal. (*Hint*: Replace $N_1 + N_2$ with N.)

14–18 With respect to the previous exercise, what would happen if $s_1^2 = s_2^2$, regardless of N_i?

14–19 What does a comparison of Exercises 14-15 and 14-16 show you?

15
POWER

Most applied statistical work as it is actually carried out in analyzing experimental results is concerned primarily with minimizing (or at least controlling) the probability of a Type I error (α). When it comes to designing experiments, people generally tend to ignore the fact that there is a probability (β) of another kind of error, labeled a Type II error. Whereas Type I errors deal with the problem of *finding* a difference that is *not* there, Type II errors concern the equally serious problem of *not finding* a difference that *is* there. When we consider the substantial cost in time and money that goes into a typical experiment, it is remarkably shortsighted of experimenters not to recognize the fact that they may, from the start, have a very small chance of finding the effect for which they are looking, even if such an effect actually exists in the population—and even if it is a nontrivial effect that is worth finding.

There are good reasons why investigators historically have tended to avoid concerning themselves with Type II errors. Until recently many textbooks ignored the problem altogether, and those books that did discuss the material discussed it in ways that were not easily understood by the book's intended audience. In the past 20 years, however, Jacob Cohen, a psychologist, has discussed the problem clearly and lucidly in several publications. Cohen (1977) presents a thorough and rigorous treatment of the material. In Welkowitz, Ewen, and Cohen (1982) the material is treated in a slightly simpler way through the use of an approximation technique, which is the approach adopted in this chapter. If you become interested in pursuing this topic, you should have no difficulty with either of the sources just mentioned, or for that matter with any of the many excellent papers Cohen has published on a wide variety of topics.

Speaking in terms of Type II errors is a negative way of approaching the problem, since it keeps reminding us that we might make a mistake. The more positive approach is to speak in terms of **power**, which is defined as the probability of *correctly* rejecting a *false* H_0. Put another way, power equals $1 - \beta$. When we say that the power of a particular experimental design is .65, we

Power
The probability of correctly rejecting a false H_0.

mean that if the null hypothesis is false to the degree expected by the experimenter, the probability is .65 that the results of this experiment will lead us to reject H_0. A more powerful experiment is one that has a greater probability of rejecting a false H_0 than does a less powerful experiment.

This chapter will take the approach of Welkowitz, Ewen, and Cohen (1982) and work with an approximation to the true power of a test. This approximation is an excellent one, especially in light of the fact that we do not really care whether power equals .85 or .83, but rather if it is in the .80s or in the .30s. For purposes of explaining the basic material we will assume for the moment that we are interested in using a t test for testing one sample mean against a specified population mean, although the approach immediately generalizes to the testing of other hypotheses.

15-1 THE BASIC CONCEPT

To review briefly what we already covered in Chapter 11, consider the two distributions in Figure 15-1. The distribution to the left (labeled H_0) represents the sampling distribution of the mean when the null hypothesis is true and the population mean equals μ_0. The heavily shaded right-hand tail of this distribution represents α, the probability of a Type I error, assuming that we are using a one-tailed test. (Otherwise it represents $\alpha/2$.) This area contains the values of a sample mean that would result in significant values of t.

The second distribution (H_1) represents the sampling distribution of the mean when H_0 is false and when the true mean is μ_1. It is readily apparent that even when H_0 is false many of the sample means (and therefore the corresponding values of t) will nonetheless fall to the left of the critical value, causing us to fail to reject a false H_0, thereby committing a Type II error. The probability of this error is indicated by the lightly shaded area in Figure 15-1 and is labeled β.

Lastly, when H_0 is false and the test statistic falls to the right of the critical value, we will correctly reject a false H_0. The probability of doing this is what we mean by power and is shown in the unshaded area of the H_1 distribution.

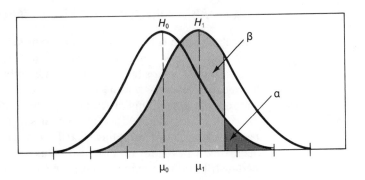

FIGURE 15-1
**Sampling Distribution of $\bar{X}$
under H_0 and H_1**

15-2   FACTORS AFFECTING THE POWER OF A TEST

As you might expect, power is a function of several variables:

1. the probability of a Type I error (α)
2. the true difference between the null and alternative hypotheses ($\mu_0 - \mu_1$)
3. the sample size (N) and σ^2
4. the particular test to be employed

We will discuss this last relationship only with respect to the relative power of independent versus related (matched) samples. In general, when the assumptions behind a particular test are met, the procedures presented in this book (with the possible exception of those discussed in Chapter 20) can be shown to have more power to answer the question at hand than other tests that are available.

POWER AS A FUNCTION OF α

With the aid of Figure 15-1 it is easy to see why we say that power is a function of α. If we are willing to increase α, the cutoff point moves to the left, thus simultaneously decreasing β and increasing power. Unfortunately this is accompanied by a corresponding rise in the probability of a Type I error.

POWER AS A FUNCTION OF $(\mu_0 - \mu_1)$

The fact that power is a function of the nature of the true alternative hypothesis (more precisely, $(\mu_0 - \mu_1)$) is illustrated by comparing Figures 15-1 and 15-2. In Figure 15-2 the distance between μ_0 and μ_1 has been increased, and this has resulted in a substantial increase in power. This is not particularly surprising, since all we are saying is that the chances of finding a difference depend on how large the difference is. (It is easier to distinguish between oranges and apples than between oranges and tangerines.)

POWER AS A FUNCTION OF THE SAMPLE SIZE (N) AND σ^2

The relationship between power and sample size (and between power and σ^2) is only a little subtler. Because we are interested in means or differences between means, we are interested, directly or indirectly, in the sampling distribution of the mean. We know that $\sigma_{\bar{X}}^2 = \sigma^2/N$. From this equation we can see that the variance of the sampling distribution of the mean decreases as either N increases or σ^2 decreases. Figure 15-3, in comparison with Figure 15-2, illustrates what happens to the two sampling distributions (H_0 and H_1) as we increase N or decrease σ^2. In Figure 15-3 we see that as $\sigma_{\bar{X}}^2$ decreases, the overlap between the two distributions is reduced, with a resulting increase in power.

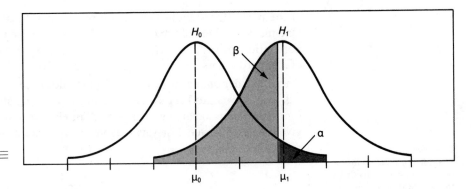

FIGURE 15-2
Effect on Power of Increasing Distance Between μ_0 and μ_1

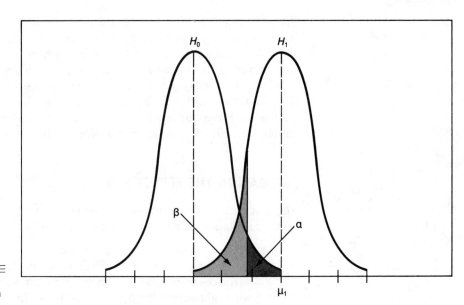

FIGURE 15-3
Effect on Power of a Decrease in Standard Error of the Mean

If an experimenter is going to be concerned with the power of a test, then she is most likely going to be interested in those variables governing power that can be manipulated easily. Because N is more easily manipulated than either σ^2 or $(\mu_0 - \mu_1)$ and because tampering with α produces undesirable side effects (increasing the probability of a Type I error), discussions of power are generally concerned with the effects of varying sample size.

15-3 EFFECT SIZE

As we have seen in Figures 15-1 through 15-3, power depends upon the degree of overlap between the sampling distributions under H_0 and H_1. Furthermore, this overlap is a function of *both* the distance between μ_0 and μ_1 (the population mean if H_0 is true and the population mean if H_1 is true) and the standard error of the mean (the standard deviation of either of these sampling distributions). One measure, then, of the degree to which H_0 is false would be the difference in population means under H_0 and H_1 ($\mu_1 - \mu_0$) expressed in terms of the number of standard errors (i.e., $(\mu_1 - \mu_0)/\sigma_{\bar{X}}$). The problem with this measure, however, is that the denominator ($\sigma_{\bar{X}} = \sigma/\sqrt{N}$) includes the sample size. In practice we will usually wish to keep N separate from ($\mu_1 - \mu_0$) and σ so that we can solve for the power associated with a given N or else for that value of N required for a given level of power. For this reason we will take as our distance measure, or **effect size,**

Effect size
The difference between two population means divided by the standard deviation of either population.

$$\gamma = \frac{\mu_1 - \mu_0}{\sigma}$$

Gamma (γ)
The symbol for effect size.

We will ignore the sign of γ **(gamma)**. Gamma is a measure of the degree to which μ_1 and μ_0 differ in terms of the standard deviation of the parent population. As an example, if we expect a group of children who have suffered from malnutrition to have a mean IQ that is 8 points below normal (where $\sigma = 16$), we are talking about an effect size of one-half of a standard deviation (i.e., the malnourished group will be below average by $8/16 = 1/2$ a standard deviation). From our equation we see that γ is estimated independently of N, simply by estimating μ_1, μ_0, and σ. We will incorporate N at a later date.

ESTIMATING THE EFFECT SIZE

The first task becomes that of estimating γ, because it will form the basis for future calculations. This can be done in one of three ways.

1. *Prior research.* We often can obtain at least a rough approximation of γ by looking at past data. Thus we could look at sample means and variances from other studies and make an informed guess at the values we might expect for $\mu_1 - \mu_0$ and for σ. In practice this task is not as difficult as it might seem, especially when you realize that even a rough approximation is far better than no approximation at all.

2. *Personal assessment of what difference is important.* In many cases an investigator is able to say, "I am interested in detecting a difference of at least 10 points between μ_1 and μ_0." The investigator essentially is saying that differences less than this have no important or useful meaning, whereas greater differences do. Here we are given the value of $\mu_1 - \mu_0$ directly, without any necessary knowledge of the particular values of μ_1 and μ_0. All that remains is to estimate σ from other data. As an example, the investigator might say that he is interested in finding a study guide that will raise scores on the College Board Examination (SAT) by 40 points above normal. We already know that the standard deviation for this test is approximately 100. Thus $\gamma = 40/100 = 0.40$. If, instead of saying that he wanted to raise scores by 40 points, the experimenter said that he wanted to raise them by 4/10 of a standard deviation, he would

have been giving us γ directly. In some cases this type of statement is possible.

3. *The use of special conventions.* When we encounter a situation in which there is no way that we can estimate the required parameters, we can fall back on a set of conventions proposed by Cohen (1977). Cohen has defined three values of γ. For a justification of these levels the reader is referred to Cohen's work. Cohen's rule of thumb is

Effect Size	γ
Small	.20
Medium	.50
Large	.80

Thus when all else fails, the experimenter simply can decide whether he is after a small, medium, or large effect, and set γ accordingly. It must be emphasized, however, that this solution should be chosen only when the other alternatives are not feasible.

You might think it is peculiar to be asked to define the difference you are looking for before the experiment is conducted. Many people would respond by claiming that if they knew how the experiment would come out, they wouldn't have needed to run it in the first place. Although many experimenters behave in this way, if you consider this excuse carefully, you will start to question its validity. Do we really not know, at least vaguely, what will happen in our experiments, and if not, why are we running them? And even if we have no idea what to expect, we should at least consider what is the minimum effect that we would be interested in detecting. While there is an occasional legitimate "I-wonder-what-would-happen-if" experiment, "I don't know" usually translates to "I haven't thought that far ahead."

COMBINING THE EFFECT SIZE AND *N*

In discussing the effect size (γ), a decision was made to split the sample size from the effect size to make it easier to deal with N separately. The final thing we will need is a method for combining the effect size with the sample size to determine the power of an experiment for a given N and effect size. For this we will use the symbol δ **(delta)**

$$\delta = \gamma[f(N)]$$

Delta (δ)
A value used in referring to power tables that combines gamma and the sample size.

where the particular function of N, $f(N)$, will be defined differently for each individual test. In this equation the notation $f(N)$, read "f of N," is used as a general way of stating that δ depends not only on γ but also in some unspecified way on N as well. For example, we will see that in the one-sample t test we will compute δ by replacing $f(N)$ with $\sqrt{N}$, whereas in the two-sample t test we will replace $f(N)$ with $\sqrt{N/2}$. The nice thing about this system is that it will allow us to use the same table of δ for power calculations for all of the statistical procedures to be considered. How we will actually use δ is illustrated in the next section.

It is probably worth restating why we have gone to all of this work to define γ without regard to N and have then put N back in when it comes to defining δ. When you are planning an experiment, $(\mu_1 - \mu_0)$ and σ, and therefore γ, are more or less fixed. But the choice of N is up to you. We want to be able to compute power, by way of δ, for a given γ when N is 20, for example, and then when N is 50. We don't want to have to repeat a set of laborious calculations every time we change our N. By defining γ independently of N and then having a simple formula to put the two together, we save ourselves a lot of work.

15-4   POWER CALCULATIONS FOR THE ONE-SAMPLE t TEST

As the first example we will examine the calculation of power for the one-sample t test. In the previous section we saw that δ is based on γ and some function of N. For the one-sample t that function will be $\sqrt{N}$, and δ will then be defined as

$$\delta = \gamma\sqrt{N}$$

A small amount of algebra will show that δ is now the difference between μ_1 and μ_0 divided by the standard error of the mean (recall that γ equals $\mu_1 - \mu_0$ divided by the standard deviation).

$$\delta = \gamma\sqrt{N} = \frac{\mu_1 - \mu_0}{\sigma}\sqrt{N} = \frac{\mu_1 - \mu_0}{\left(\dfrac{\sigma}{\sqrt{N}}\right)} = \frac{\mu_1 - \mu_0}{\sigma_{\bar{X}}}$$

As an example assume that a clinical psychologist wants to test the hypothesis that individuals who seek treatment for psychological problems have a higher IQ than normal. She wants to use the IQs of 25 randomly selected clients drawn from a wide variety of clinical settings and is interested in finding the power of detecting a difference of 5 points between the mean of the general population and the mean of the population from which her sample of clients is drawn. Thus $\mu_1 = 105$, $\mu_0 = 100$, and $\sigma = 15$—the last two parameters being the mean and standard deviation of most IQ tests when administered to the general population.

$$\gamma = \frac{105 - 100}{15} = 0.33$$

Then

$$\delta = \gamma\sqrt{N}$$
$$= 0.33\sqrt{25} = 0.33(5) = 1.65$$

	Alpha for Two-Tailed Test			
δ	.10	.05	.02	.01
1.00	0.26	0.17	0.09	0.06
1.10	0.29	0.20	0.11	0.07
1.20	0.33	0.22	0.13	0.08
1.30	0.37	0.26	0.15	0.10
1.40	0.40	0.29	0.18	0.12
1.50	0.44	0.32	0.20	0.14
1.60	0.48	0.36	0.23	0.17
1.70	0.52	0.40	0.27	0.19
1.80	0.56	0.44	0.30	0.22
1.90	0.60	0.48	0.34	0.25
⋮	⋮	⋮	⋮	⋮

Although the experimenter expects the sample mean to be above the mean of the general population, she plans to use a two-tailed test at $\alpha = .05$ to protect against unexpected events. Given δ, we immediately can determine the power of the test from the table of power in Appendix D, Table 4. A portion of this table is reproduced in Table 15-1. To use Appendix D, Table 4, we simply go down the left-hand margin until we come to $\delta = 1.65$ and then read across to the column headed .05. The table does not have an entry for $\delta = 1.65$, but it does have entries for $\delta = 1.60$ and $\delta = 1.70$. For $\alpha = .05$ this means that power is between 0.36 and 0.40. By linear interpolation we will say that power is equal to 0.38. This means that if H_0 really is false and μ_1 is 105, only 3% of the time will the clinician obtain data that will produce a significant value of t when testing the difference between her *sample* mean and that specified by H_0. This is a rather discouraging result, because it means that if the true mean is really 105, $100\% - 38\% = 62\%$ of the time the study as designed will *not* obtain a significant result.

Because the experimenter was intelligent enough to examine the question of power before she began her experiment, she still has the chance to make changes that will lead to an increase in power. She could, for example, set α at .10, thus increasing power to approximately 0.50, but this is probably unsatisfactory. (Journal editors, for example, generally hate to see α set at any value greater than .05.) Alternatively the experimenter could make use of the fact that power increases as N increases.

ESTIMATING REQUIRED SAMPLE SIZE

It is fine to say that a smart experimenter can increase power by increasing N, but how large an N is needed? The answer to that question depends simply on the level of power that is desired. Suppose that you wished to modify the previous example to have power equal to 0.80. The first thing you need to do is read the table in Appendix D, Table 4, backward to find out what value for δ is associated with the specified degree of power. From the table we see that for power equal to 0.80, δ must equal 2.80. Thus we have δ and can simply solve for N by a minor algebraic manipulation.

$$\delta = \gamma\sqrt{N}$$

$$N = \left(\frac{\delta}{\gamma}\right)^2$$

$$= \left(\frac{2.80}{0.33}\right)^2 = 8.40^2 = 70.56$$

Because clients generally come in whole lots, we will round off to 71. Thus if the experimenter wants to have an 80% chance of rejecting H_0 when $\gamma = 0.33$ (i.e., when $\mu_1 = 105$, or 95), she will have to obtain the IQs for 71 randomly selected clients. Although she may feel that this is a larger number of clients than she can easily test, there is no alternative other than to settle for a lower level of power.

You might wonder why we selected power equal to 0.80 in the previous example. Remember that with this degree of power we still run a 20% chance of making a Type II error. The answer lies in the question of practicality. Suppose for example that the experimenter had wanted power to equal 0.95. A few simple calculations will show that this would require a sample of N equal to 119, and for power equal to 0.99 she would need approximately 167 subjects. These may well be unreasonable sample sizes for a particular experimental situation or for the resources of the experimenter. While increases in power are generally bought by increases in N, at high levels of power the cost can be very high. In addition it is a case of diminishing returns because δ increases as a function of the square root of N. If you are taking data from data tapes supplied by the Bureau of the Census, that is one thing. It is quite a different matter when you are studying identical twins reared apart.

15-5 POWER CALCULATIONS FOR DIFFERENCES BETWEEN TWO INDEPENDENT MEANS

The treatment of power in the situation in which we wish to test the difference between two independent means is very similar to our treatment of the case in which we had only one mean. In the previous section we obtained γ by taking the difference between μ under H_1 (i.e., μ_1) and μ under H_0 (i.e., μ_0) and dividing by σ. In the present case we will do something similar, although this time we are going to be working with differences between means. Thus we want the difference between the two population means $(\mu_1 - \mu_2)$ under H_1 minus the difference $(\mu_1 - \mu_2)$ under H_0, again divided by σ. (You will recall that we assume $\sigma_1^2 = \sigma_2^2 = \sigma^2$.) But $(\mu_1 - \mu_2)$ under H_0 is zero in all usual applications, so we can drop that term from the formula. Thus

$$\gamma = \frac{(\mu_1 - \mu_2) - 0}{\sigma} = \frac{\mu_1 - \mu_2}{\sigma}$$

The numerator refers to the difference between population means to be expected under H_1 and the denominator represents the common standard deviation of both populations.

EQUAL SAMPLE SIZES

For the sake of an example, assume that we wish to test the difference in amount of hoarding behavior between normal rats and rats who were deprived during infancy. A somewhat similar experiment conducted by Hunt (1941) would suggest that the mean number of pellets hoarded by the deprived group would be approximately 35 and for the nondeprived group would be approximately 15. In addition Hunt's data would suggest a value of 17 for σ. Thus, at least as a rough approximation, we expect $\mu_1 = 35$, $\mu_2 = 15$, and $\sigma = 17$. Then

$$\gamma = \frac{\mu_1 - \mu_2}{\sigma} = \frac{20}{17} = 1.18$$

We are saying that we expect a difference of 1.18 standard deviations between the two means.

First we will investigate the power of an experiment with 10 observations in each of two groups. We will define δ in the two-sample case as

$$\delta = \gamma \sqrt{\frac{N}{2}}$$

where N equals the number of cases *in any one sample* (there are $2N$ cases in all). Thus

$$\delta = \gamma \sqrt{\frac{N}{2}} = (1.18) \sqrt{\frac{10}{2}}$$

$$= 1.18 \sqrt{5} = 1.18(2.236) = 2.63$$

From Appendix D, Table 4, we see by interpolation that for $\delta = 2.63$ with a two-tailed test at $\alpha = .05$, power equals 0.75. Thus if we actually ran this experiment with 10 subjects in each group and if the estimate of δ is correct, then we have a 75% chance of actually rejecting H_0. This is a high degree of power for so few subjects, but of course we are dealing with a fairly large effect.

We next wish to turn the question around and ask how many subjects would be needed for power equal to 0.90. (It is reasonable here to try to boost power to 0.90 [reduce β to .10] because we already know that as few as 10 subjects per group would give us power equal to 0.75 with the effect size that we have.) From the table we see that this would require δ equal to 3.25.

$$\delta = \gamma \sqrt{\frac{N}{2}}$$

Squaring for easier rearrangements of terms, we have

$$\delta^2 = \frac{\gamma^2 N}{2}$$

Then $\quad N = \dfrac{2\delta^2}{\gamma^2} = \dfrac{2(3.25)^2}{1.18^2} = \dfrac{2(10.5625)}{1.3924} = 15.17$

Because N refers to the number of subjects per sample, we would need 15 subjects per sample for a total of 30 subjects if power is to be 0.90. That is slightly on the large side for a typical study using laboratory rats—which must be bought, housed, and fed at considerable expense. Whether it is worth the expense depends upon the importance of the research.

UNEQUAL SAMPLE SIZES

In the previous section we dealt with the case in which the two samples are of equal size. However, we also run experiments in which the two sample sizes are unequal because of the nature of the experiment. This obviously presents difficulties when we try to solve for δ, because we need one value for N to insert in our formula. What value can we use?

Harmonic mean
The number of elements to be averaged divided by the sum of the reciprocals of the elements.

The simplest solution is to let N be the **harmonic mean** of the two sample sizes. In general the harmonic mean of k numbers $(X_1, X_2, \ldots, X_k)$ is defined as

$$\bar{X}_h = \frac{k}{\Sigma \dfrac{1}{X_i}}$$

For example, for the numbers 8, 12, and 13 the harmonic mean is

$$\bar{X}_h = \frac{3}{1/8 + 1/12 + 1/13} = 10.52$$

For the case of two sample sizes (N_1 and N_2) the formula reduces to

$$\bar{N}_h = \frac{2}{\dfrac{1}{N_1} + \dfrac{1}{N_2}}$$

Multiplying top and bottom by $N_1 N_2$ yields a simpler formula:

$$\bar{N}_h = \frac{2N_1 N_2}{N_1 + N_2}$$

We then can use $\bar{N}_h$ in place of N in calculating δ. Notice that the harmonic mean deals with terms of the form $1/N$. Because the standard error of the mean also varies as a function of $1/N$, we use the harmonic mean rather than the usual arithmetic mean in calculating δ.

An interesting finding arises from playing with different values of N in the previous formula. For a fixed total number of subjects we will have the greatest degree of power when the subjects are divided equally between the two groups. When you have unequal sample sizes and can add more subjects to the study, add them in such a way as to balance the groups.

15-6   POWER CALCULATIONS FOR THE t TEST FOR RELATED SAMPLES

When we move to the situation in which we want to test the difference between two matched samples, the problem becomes somewhat more difficult, and an additional parameter must be considered. For this reason the analysis of power for this case is frequently impractical. However, the general solution to the problem illustrates an important principle of experimental design and thus justifies close examination of the related-sample case. (This section is not written with the expectation that everyone will run out and make power calculations for a related-sample experiment—most experienced experimenters don't do it either. The important thing is not the arithmetic, but the conclusions that follow.)

We are going to define γ as

$$\gamma = \frac{\mu_1 - \mu_2}{\sigma_D}$$

where $\mu_1 - \mu_2$ represents the expected mean difference (the expected mean of the difference scores). The problem arises from the fact that σ_D is not the standard deviation of the populations of X_1 and X_2, but rather the standard deviation of difference scores drawn from these populations. Although we might be able to make an intelligent guess at σ_1 or σ_2, we probably have no idea about σ_D.

If we are willing to make the assumption that the two sets of scores have the same population standard deviations ($\sigma_1 = \sigma_2 = \sigma$), then it is easy to show that

$$\sigma_D = \sigma\sqrt{2(1 - \rho)}$$

where ρ is the correlation in the population between X_1 and X_2 and can take on values between $+1$ and -1, being positive for almost all situations in which we would likely want a related-sample t. In this formula, σ is the standard deviation of the population of scores for X_1 or X_2 (because $\sigma_1 = \sigma_2 = \sigma$).

Assuming for the moment that we can estimate ρ, from here on the procedure is the same as for the case of the one-sample t. We define

$$\gamma = \frac{\mu_1 - \mu_2}{\sigma_D} = \frac{\mu_1 - \mu_2}{\sigma\sqrt{2(1 - \rho)}}$$

and
$$\delta = \gamma\sqrt{N}$$

We then refer the value of δ to the tables.

As an example, assume that we want to see if cognitive performance of young children is better in the morning than at night. Consequently we want to administer a commonly used standardized achievement test to a sample of 20 children just before their bedtime, send them to bed, and readminister the test the next morning. (We will ignore the problem of practice effects and the question of whether this study might better be designed with two groups of children, one-half of whom are tested in the morning first and one-half tested at night first.) Suppose that we want to evaluate the power for finding a difference between means as great as three points. Information on most standardized tests is available in many textbooks. From such a source we might find that the standard deviation of test scores is 10. The correlation between scores on two administrations of the test is nothing but the short-term reliability of the test, and a reasonable value for the reliability is 0.92. Thus

$$\sigma_D = \sigma\sqrt{2(1 - \rho)}$$

$$= 10\sqrt{2(1 - 0.92)} = 10\sqrt{2(0.08)} = 4.0$$

$$\gamma = \frac{\mu_1 - \mu_2}{\sigma_D}$$

$$= \frac{3}{4.0} = 0.75$$

$$\delta = \gamma\sqrt{N}$$

$$= 0.75\sqrt{20} = 3.35$$

Power $= 0.92$ for $\alpha = .05$.

Suppose, on the other hand, that we had used a less reliable test for which $\rho = 0.50$. We will assume that σ remains unchanged. Then

$$\sigma_D = 10\sqrt{2(1 - 0.50)}$$

$$= 10\sqrt{2(0.50)} = 10\sqrt{1} = 10$$

$$\gamma = \frac{\mu_1 - \mu_2}{\sigma_D}$$

$$= \frac{3}{10} = 0.30$$

$$\delta = 0.30\sqrt{20}$$

$$= 1.34$$

Power $= 0.27$ for $\alpha = .05$.

Here you see that as ρ drops, so does power. When $\rho = 0$, the two samples are (linearly) independent, and thus the related-sample case has been reduced to the independent-sample case except for the difference in the degrees of freedom, which would be obscured by the approximation used to generate Appendix D, Table 4. The very important point to be made here (and the reason behind all of these calculations) is that for all practical purposes the minimum power for the related-sample case occurs when $\rho = 0$ and we have independent samples. Thus for all situations in which we are even remotely likely to use related samples (i.e., when we expect a positive correlation between X_1 and X_2), the related-sample design is more powerful than the corresponding independent-groups design. This illustrates one of the main advantages of designs that use related samples.

15-7 POWER CONSIDERATIONS IN TERMS OF SAMPLE SIZE

The present discussion of power illustrates that reasonably large sample sizes are almost a necessity if you are to run experiments that have a good chance of rejecting H_0 when it is in fact false—especially if the effect is small. As an illustration, a few minutes of calculation will show that if we want to have power equal to 0.80 and if we accept Cohen's definitions for small, medium, and large effects, our samples must be quite large. Table 15-2 presents the total Ns required (at power = 0.80, $\alpha = .05$) for small, medium, and large effects for the tests we have been discussing. These figures indicate that power (at least a substantial amount of it) is a very expensive commodity—especially for small effects. While it could be argued that this is a good thing, since otherwise the literature would contain many more trivial results than it already does, that will come as little comfort to most experimenters. The general rule is to look for big effects, to use large samples, or to employ sensitive experimental designs such as those involving use of repeated measures, which reduce experimental error and thus make small differences translate into large effect sizes.

TABLE 15-2
Total Sample Sizes Required for Power = 0.80, $\alpha = .05$, Two-Tailed

Effect Size	γ	One-sample t	Two-sample t
Small	0.20	196	784
Medium	0.50	32	126
Large	0.80	13	49

15-8 SUMMARY

In this chapter we have considered those factors that contribute to the power of a test. We have seen that the most easily manipulated factor is the sample size, and we have considered ways of calculating the power for a given sample size and, conversely, the sample size needed for a specified level of power. Finally we considered the unwelcome conclusion that high levels of power often may require more subjects than we can reasonably expect. Some of the most important terms in this chapter are:

- □ **Power**
- □ **Effect size**
- □ **Gamma** (γ)
- □ **Delta** (δ)
- □ **Harmonic mean**

15-9 EXERCISES

15–1 Over the past 10 years a small New England college has been able to hold its mean SAT score (and, by inference, the mean of the population from which it draws its students) at 520 with a standard deviation of 80. A major competitor would like to demonstrate that standards have slipped and that the college is now really drawing from a population of students with a mean of 500. They plan to run a t test on the mean SAT scores of next fall's entering class.

(a) What is the effect size in question?

(b) What is the value of δ if the size of next fall's class is 100?

(c) What is the power of the test?

15–2 Diagram the situation described in Exercise 15-1 along the lines of Figure 15-1.

15–3 In Exercise 15-1 what sample sizes would be needed to raise power to 0.70, 0.80, and 0.90, respectively?

15–4 Unbeknownst to the competition, the first college referred to in Exercise 15-1 has started a major campaign to increase the quality of its new students. The college is hoping to show a 30-point gain in the mean SAT score for next year. If 100 students enroll next fall, what is the power of a t test used to test the significance of any increase?

15–5 Diagram the situation described in Exercise 15-4 along the lines of Figure 15-1.

15–6 A physiological psychology laboratory has been studying avoidance behavior in rabbits for several years and has published numerous papers on the topic. It is clear from this research that the mean response latency for a particular task is 5.8 seconds with a standard deviation of 2 seconds (based on many hundreds of rabbits). Now the investigators wish to create lesions in certain areas in the amygdala and demonstrate poorer avoidance conditioning in those animals. They expect latencies to decrease by about 1 second (i.e., the rabbits will repeat the punished response sooner), and they plan to run a one-sample t test (with $H_0: \mu_0 = 5.8$).

(a) How many subjects do they need to have at least a 50:50 chance of success?

(b) How many subjects do they need to have at least an 80:20 chance of success?

15–7 Suppose that the laboratory referred to in Exercise 15-6 decided not to run one group and compare it against $\mu_0 = 5.8$ but to run two groups (one with and one without lesions). They still expect the same degree of difference, however.

(a) How many subjects do they now need (overall) if they are to have power equal to 0.60?

(b) How many subjects do they now need (overall) if they are to have power equal to 0.90?

15–8 As it turns out, a research assistant has just finished running the experiment described in Exercise 15-7 without having carried out any power calculations. He tried to run 20 subjects in each group, but he accidentally tipped over a rack of cages and had to void 5 subjects in the experimental group. What is the power of this experiment?

15–9 I have just conducted a study comparing cognitive development of low-birthweight (premature) and normal babies at one year of age. Using a scale I devised, I found that the sample means of the two groups were 25 and 30, respectively, with a pooled standard deviation of 8. There were 20 subjects in each group. *If we assume* that the true means and standard deviations have been estimated exactly, what was the *a priori* probability (the probability before the experiment was conducted) that this study would in fact find a significant difference?

15–10 We will modify Exercise 15-9 to have means of 25 and 28, with a pooled standard deviation of 8 and sample sizes of 20 and 20.

(a) What is the *a priori* power of this experiment?

(b) Run the t test on the data.

(c) What, if anything, does the answer to Exercise 15-10(a) have to say about the answer to 15-10(b)?

15-11 Two graduate students recently have completed their dissertations. Each used a t test for two independent groups. One found a barely significant t using 10 subjects per group. The other found a barely significant t using 45 subjects per group. Which result impresses you the most?

15-12 Draw a diagram (analogous to Figure 15-1) to defend your answer to Exercise 15-11.

15-13 Make up a simple two-group example to demonstrate that for a total of 30 subjects power increases as the sample sizes become more nearly equal.

15-14 A poor beleaguered Ph.D. candidate has the impression that he must find significant results if he wants to successfully defend his dissertation. He wants to show a difference in social awareness, as measured by his own scale, between a normal group and a group of ex-delinquents. He has a problem, however. He has data to suggest that the normal group has a true mean equal to 38, and he has 50 of those subjects. He has access either to 100 college students who have been classed as delinquent in the past or to 25 high school dropouts with a history of delinquency. He suspects that the scores of the college group come from a population with a mean of approximately 35, whereas the scores of the dropout group come from a population with a mean of approximately 30. If he can use only one of these groups, which should he use?

15-15 Generate a table analogous to Table 15-2 for power equal to 0.80, with α equal to .01, two-tailed.

15-16 Generate a table analogous to Table 15-2 for power equal to 0.60, with α equal to .05, two-tailed.

15-17 Assume that we want to test a null hypothesis about a single mean at $\alpha = .05$, one-tailed. Further assume that all necessary assumptions are met. Is there ever a case in which we are more likely to reject a true H_0 than we are to reject H_0 if it is false? (In other words, can power ever be less than α?)

15-18 If $\sigma = 15$, $N = 25$, and we are testing $H_0: \mu = 100$ versus $H_1: \mu > 100$, what value of the mean under H_1 would result in power being equal to the probability of a Type II error? (*Hint*: This is most easily solved by sketching the two distributions. Which areas are you trying to equate?)

ONE-WAY ANALYSIS OF VARIANCE

Analysis of variance (ANOVA)
A statistical technique for testing for differences in the means of several groups.

The **analysis of variance (ANOVA)** currently enjoys the status of being probably the most used (some would say abused) statistical technique in psychological research. The popularity and usefulness of this technique can be attributed to two facts. First of all the analysis of variance, like t, deals with differences between sample means, but unlike t, it has no restriction on the number of means. Instead of asking merely whether two means differ, we can ask whether 3, 4, 5, or k means differ. Second, the analysis of variance allows us to deal with two or more independent variables simultaneously, asking not only about the individual effects of each variable separately but also about the interacting effects of two or more variables.

This chapter will be concerned with the underlying logic of the analysis of variance (which is really quite simple) and the analysis of the results of experiments employing only one independent variable. In addition we will deal with a few related topics, which are most easily understood in the context of a one-variable analysis (**one-way ANOVA**). Subsequent chapters will deal with the analysis of experiments involving two or more variables and with designs in which repeated measurements are made on each subject.

One-way ANOVA
An analysis of variance where the groups are defined on only one independent variable.

16-1 A HYPOTHETICAL SAMPLING STUDY

Probably the easiest way to understand the analysis of variance is by way of a hypothetical example. We want to investigate helping behavior directed toward people of different ages. To do this we take subjects who are 20, 40, or 60 years old, load them down with packages and a crying child, have them board a subway at rush hour, and record the length of time before someone offers them a seat. Our experimental hypothesis is that older subjects are offered a seat sooner than younger subjects.

Because this is a hypothetical study, we will go all the way and assume that we are able to obtain unlimited sample sizes. In other words assume that we took all 20-year-old people in the United States and measured the length of time before each was offered a seat. The results of this part of the experiment would consist of a huge number of data points, the distribution of which is represented in Figure 16-1(a). This distribution actually represents the population of scores for all 20-year-olds and will have a mean and variance designated μ_1 and σ_1^2, respectively. Assume that this distribution is more or less normally distributed.

Now suppose that we started all over again, this time using all 40-year-olds in the country. Again we would have a whole population of data points, which would be distributed as in Figure 16-1(b). This distribution would also be more or less normal, and we will designate its mean and variance as μ_2 and σ_2^2, for the moment saying nothing about the relationship between μ_1 and μ_2 or between σ_1^2 and σ_2^2.

Finally, assume that we repeat the procedure yet a third time using all the 60-year-old people in the country. These data are plotted in Figure 16-1(c). They are also roughly normally distributed and have a mean (μ_3) and a variance (σ_3^2).

At this point our work is done and we can state with absolute certainty the relationship between μ_1, μ_2, and μ_3. The word *certainty* is appropriate in the last sentence because, since we have measured entire populations, we have *calculated* μ_1, μ_2, and μ_3, and do not have to estimate them. We merely have to look at the means to see if they are different.

As was noted in the chapters on t tests, it is obvious that we cannot conduct experiments by measuring whole populations of interest. In the real world we have to be content with samples of data based on more reasonable numbers of subjects. The main question remains the same ("How do the population means differ, if at all?"), but now we will be required to answer the question using estimates of the μ_j, rather than using the true values of the μ_j themselves. Keeping in mind this hypothetical experiment, let us examine the problem in more detail and then impose two assumptions for the purpose of simplification.

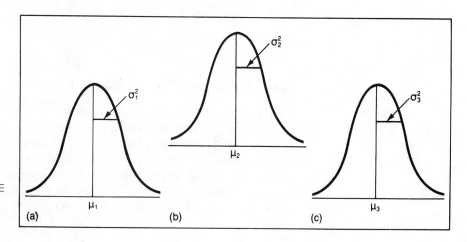

FIGURE 16-1
Results of Hypothetical
Experiment on Time to Obtain
a Seat on a Subway

(a)   (b)   (c)

THE NULL HYPOTHESIS

Because we want to know whether the mean time to be offered a seat is the same for all three ages, it follows that the null hypothesis can be written as

$$H_0: \mu_1 = \mu_2 = \mu_3 = \mu$$

where the symbol μ without a subscript represents the common value of the three population means. The null hypothesis could be false for several different reasons, for example, because $\mu_1 = \mu_2$ but μ_3 is different, but we will for the moment consider only the case in which it is either completely true or it is false, whatever the reason.

THE POPULATION

One of the difficulties students frequently encounter concerns the meaning of the word *population*. As mentioned in Chapter 1, a population is a collection of *numbers*, not a collection of rats or people or anything else. Thus strictly speaking we are not trying to say that a population of people of a given age is the same as a population of people of a different age, but rather that a population of *scores* obtained under one condition has a mean greater than or less than a population of scores obtained under another condition. This may appear to be a rather trivial point, but it isn't. Obviously there are major differences between 20- and 60-year-old people, and there is no doubt that they represent different populations of *people*. However, it is not obvious that the scores on "time to be offered a seat" are from different populations of *scores*. In this context one useful approach is to think of 20-, 40-, and 60-year-old people running around with numbers (latency scores) taped to their noses. We do not care which population of human beings the people were drawn from, but only whether God, when applying the numbers, sampled those numbers from one shopping bag (population) or from two or three different ones.

THE ASSUMPTION OF NORMALITY

For reasons dealing with our final test of significance, we will make the assumption that time to obtain a seat is normally distributed around μ_j for each population. This is no more than the assumption that the observations in Figures 16-1(a–c) are normally distributed. As with t, this assumption deals primarily with the sampling distribution of the mean rather than the distribution of observations. Moreover, even substantial departures from normality may, under certain conditions, have remarkably little influence on the final result.

THE ASSUMPTION OF HOMOGENEITY OF VARIANCE

A second major assumption will be the assumption that each population of scores has the same variance, specifically

$$\sigma_1^2 = \sigma_2^2 = \sigma_3^2 = \sigma_e^2$$

Here we will use the notation σ_e^2 to indicate the common value held by the three variances. The subscript e is an abbreviation for *error*, since this variance is error variance—that is, variance *within* a particular population and thus unrelated to any group (age) differences.† As you will see later, under certain conditions this assumption too can be relaxed without doing too much damage to the final result.

You should note that the assumptions of normality and homogeneity of variance are not new. They are the same assumptions that we made with the t test for two independent samples, except that here we are extending them to more populations.

16-2   THE LOGIC OF THE ANALYSIS OF VARIANCE

Consider for a moment the effect of our two major assumptions—normality and homogeneity of variance. By making these assumptions we have said that the three populations from which the scores of the 20-, 40-, and 60-year-old subjects were sampled have the same shape and the same dispersion. As a result, the only way left for them to differ is in terms of their means. (In fact if the null hypothesis is true, $\mu_1 = \mu_2 = \mu_3$ and, because the populations are identical, nothing will be lost by acting as if we have sampled from one population.)

Suppose that due to limited resources we are able to obtain only nine scores for each age group. The variance of the nine scores for the 20-year-old group (Group 1) is an estimate of the population variance of the scores of all potential 20-year-old subjects. We can indicate this by writing $s_1^2 \doteq \sigma_1^2$, where the $\doteq$ is read "estimates," or "is estimated by," depending on the context. Similarly $s_2^2 \doteq \sigma_2^2$ and $s_3^2 \doteq \sigma_3^2$. Because we have assumed $\sigma_1^2 = \sigma_2^2 = \sigma_3^2 = \sigma_e^2$, then s_1^2, s_2^2, and s_3^2 are all estimates of σ_e^2, the common population variance. For the sake of obtaining the best possible estimate of σ_e^2, we will pool these three estimates by taking their mean (assuming that $n_1 = n_2 = n_3$):

$$\frac{s_1^2 + s_2^2 + s_3^2}{3} = \bar{s}_j^2 \doteq \sigma_e^2$$

This pooling of variances is exactly equivalent to what we did when we pooled variances in the t test (although here we have more than two variances). This average value of the three sample variances ($\bar{s}_j^2$) is one estimate of the population

---

†In terms of the discussion in Chapter 10 this is error variance in the sense that it is variability that cannot be predicted from group membership since people in the same group (population) obviously don't differ on the grouping variable.

MS_{within} (MS_{error})
Variability among subjects in the same treatment group.

variance (σ_e^2) and is what we will later refer to as MS_{within} or MS_{error} (read "mean square within" or "mean square error"). It is important to note that this estimate does *not* depend on the truth or falsity of H_0, because s_j^2 is calculated on each sample separately.

    Now let us assume that H_0 is true. If this is the case, then the three samples of nine cases can be thought of as three independent samples from the same population, and we have another possible estimate of σ_e^2. You should recall that the Central Limit Theorem stated that the variance of means drawn from the same population equals the variance of the population divided by the sample size. Under H_0 the sample means have been drawn from the same population (or identical populations, which amounts to the same thing) and therefore

$$s_{\bar{X}}^2 \doteq \frac{\sigma_e^2}{n}$$

where n is the size of each sample. We can reverse the usual order of things and, instead of estimating the variance of means from the variance of the population, we can estimate the variance of the population(s) from the variance of the sample means ($s_{\bar{X}}^2$). If we clear fractions we have

$$ns_{\bar{X}}^2 \doteq \sigma_e^2$$

$MS_{between\,groups}$ (MS_{group})
Variability among treatment means

This term is known as $MS_{between\,groups}$ or, more simply, as MS_{group}.

    These few steps can be illustrated rather easily. This has been done for three equal-sized groups in Figure 16-2. This figure emphasizes that the average of the sample variances is MS_{error} and the variance of the sample means, *multiplied by the sample size, is MS_{group}.*

    We now have two estimates of the population variance (σ_e^2). One of these estimates (MS_{error}) is independent of the truth or falsity of H_0. The other (MS_{group}) is an estimate of σ_e^2 *only as long as H_0 is true* (only as long as the conditions of the Central Limit Theorem are met, namely that the means are drawn from one population). Otherwise MS_{group} would estimate the variability of group means in addition to σ_e^2. If the two estimates (MS_{error} and MS_{group}) agree, we will have support for the truth of H_0, and if they disagree, we will have support for the falsity of H_0. But before we consider ways of defining what we mean by "agreement," I can illustrate the logic just described by way of two very simple examples that have been deliberately constructed to represent more or less ideal results under the conditions H_0 true and H_0 false. Never in practice will data be as neat and tidy as these.

═══ **FIGURE 16-2** ═══
Illustration of Meaning of MS_{error} and MS_{group} When Sample Sizes Are Equal

$$s_1^2 \leftarrow \text{Sample } 1 \rightarrow \bar{X}_1$$
$$s_2^2 \leftarrow \text{Sample } 2 \rightarrow \bar{X}_2$$
$$s_3^2 \leftarrow \text{Sample } 3 \rightarrow \bar{X}_3$$

Variance of $\bar{X}_i = s_{\bar{X}}^2$

$$\text{Average} = s_j^2$$
$$= MS_{error}$$

$$n(s_{\bar{X}}^2) = MS_{group}$$

EXAMPLE—THE CASE OF A TRUE H_0

As we saw earlier, when H_0 is true, $\mu_1 = \mu_2 = \mu_3$, and any samples drawn from these three populations can be thought of as coming from just one population. In the first example three samples of $n = 9$ have been chosen to resemble data that might be drawn from the same normally distributed population with a mean of 5 and a variance of 10. For example these data might represent the number of information-seeking comments uttered by nine subjects in each of three groups prior to the onset of a socialization-training experiment. Because the experiment has not yet begun, we hope not to find group differences. The data are presented in Table 16-1 for the $k = 3$ groups. From this table we can see that the average variance within each group is 9.250, a respectable estimate of $\sigma_e^2 = 10$. The variance of the group means is 1.000, and because we know H_0 to be true,

$$s_{\bar{X}}^2 \doteq \frac{\sigma_e^2}{n}$$

$$\sigma_e^2 = ns_{\bar{X}}^2 = 9(1) = 9$$

This value is also reasonably in agreement with σ_e^2 and with our other estimate based upon the variability within treatments. Because these two estimates agree, we would conclude that we have no reason to doubt the truth of H_0. Put another way, the three samples do not vary more than we would expect if H_0 were true.

TABLE 16-1

Representative Data for the Case in Which H_0: True

Group 1	Group 2	Group 3
3	1	5
6	4	2
9	7	8
6	4	8
3	1	2
12	10	8
6	4	5
3	1	2
9	7	8
$\bar{X}_j = $ 6.3333	4.3333	5.3333
$s_j^2 = $ 10.0000	10.0000	7.750

Grand Mean $(GM) = 5.3333$

$$s_{\bar{X}}^2 = \frac{\Sigma(\bar{X}_j - GM)^2}{k - 1} = 1.000$$

$$\bar{s}_j^2 = \frac{10.00 + 10.00 + 7.75}{3} = 9.250$$

$$MS_{error} = \bar{s}_j^2 = 9.25$$

$$MS_{group} = ns_{\bar{X}}^2 = 9(1) = 9$$

EXAMPLE—THE CASE OF A FALSE H_0

Next we consider an example in which we know H_0 to be false because I made it false. The data in Table 16-2 have been obtained by adding or subtracting constants to or from the data in Table 16-1. These data might represent the number of information-seeking comments uttered by people in three different groups at the end of our socialization-training session. We now have data that might have been produced by sampling from three normally distributed populations, all with variance equal to 10. However, Group 1 scores might have come from a population with μ equal to 8, whereas scores for Groups 2 and 3 might have come from a population with μ equal to 4. This represents a substantial departure from H_0.

From Table 16-2 you will note that the variance within each treatment remains unchanged, since adding or subtracting a constant has no effect on the variance within groups. This illustrates the earlier statement that the variance within groups (MS_{error}) is independent of the null hypothesis. The variance among the group means, however, has increased substantially, reflecting the differences among the population means. In this case the estimate of σ_e^2 based on sample means is $ns_{\bar{X}}^2 = 9(6.333) = 57$, a value that is way out of line with the estimate of 9.25 given by the variance within groups (MS_{error}). The most logical conclusion would be that $ns_{\bar{X}}^2$ is not merely estimating population variance (σ_e^2) but is estimating σ_e^2 *plus* the variance of the population means themselves. In other words the scores differ not only because of random error; they also differ because we have been successful in teaching our subjects to ask information-

TABLE 16-2
Representative Data for the Case in Which H_0: False

Group 1	Group 2	Group 3
5	0	5
8	3	2
11	6	8
8	3	8
5	0	2
14	9	8
8	3	5
5	0	2
11	6	8

$\bar{X}_j =$ 8.3333   3.3333   5.3333
$s_j^2 =$ 10.0000   10.0000   7.750

Grand Mean $(GM) = 5.6667$

$$s_{\bar{X}}^2 = \frac{\Sigma(\bar{X}_j - GM)^2}{k - 1} = 6.333$$

$$\bar{s}_j^2 = \frac{10.00 + 10.00 + 7.75}{3} = 9.250$$

$MS_{error} = \bar{s}_j^2 = 9.25$
$MS_{group} = ns_{\bar{X}}^2 = 9(6.333) = 57$

seeking questions. In fact we know this to be the case because the data have been deliberately manufactured for this purpose.

SUMMARY OF THE LOGIC OF THE ANALYSIS OF VARIANCE

From the preceding discussion we can state the logic of the analysis of variance very concisely. To test H_0 we calculate two estimates of the population variance; one (MS_{error}) is independent of the truth or falsity of H_0, while the other (MS_{group}) is dependent upon H_0. If the two agree, we have no reason to reject H_0. If they disagree, we conclude that underlying differences in treatment means must have contributed to the second estimate, inflating it and causing it to differ from the first. We therefore reject H_0. This illustrates how an analysis of *variance* allows us to draw inferences about *means*.

16-3 CALCULATIONS FOR THE ANALYSIS OF VARIANCE

The calculations for the analysis of variance are actually quite simple and straightforward. The formulae appear to be different from the kinds of formulae you saw for t tests, but this difference is really a function of the fact that here we are going to emphasize the use of totals and sums of squares instead of means and variances.

SUMS OF SQUARES

In the analysis of variance most of our computations deal with sums of squares, which, in this context, are merely the sum of squared deviations about the mean $\Sigma(X - \bar{X})^2$, or some multiple of that. The advantage of sums of squares and the reason that we begin by calculating them is that they can be added and subtracted, whereas mean squares usually cannot be. In Chapter 6 we saw that we could write $\Sigma(X - \bar{X})^2$ as $\Sigma X^2 - (\Sigma X)^2/N$ and use that formula for computational purposes. We will do exactly the same thing here except that to avoid a proliferation of summation signs we will replace ΣX with G (for **Grand Total**) and have $\Sigma X^2 - G^2/N$. We will calculate the sums of squares using either this formula or a variation of it.

Grand total (G)
The sum of all of the observations.

TOTALS

Although we have been speaking of group means, we actually will carry out our calculations in terms of group totals. This distinction is one of convenience rather than substance, since totals are linearly related to means. If two groups of the same size have different totals, they obviously have different means.

THE CALCULATIONS

For the sake of consistency we will apply the analysis of variance to the data in Table 16-2. These data and the resulting computations, which are discussed in detail on page 229, are presented in Table 16-3.

In section (a) of Table 16-3 you see the observations, the individual groups totals (T_j), and the grand total $(G = \Sigma X)$. The use of the notation T_j to represent the total of the jth group will be followed throughout the discussion of the analysis of variance. Although it would be more correct to speak of the jth

TABLE 16-3
Calculations of Analysis of Variance for Data in Table 16-2

(a) Data

Group 1	Group 2	Group 3	
5	0	5	
8	3	2	
11	6	8	
8	3	8	
5	0	2	
14	9	8	
8	3	5	
5	0	2	
11	6	8	
$T_j = 75$	30	48	$G = 153$

(b) Calculations

$$SS_{total} = \Sigma X^2 - \frac{G^2}{N}$$

$$= (5^2 + 8^2 + \cdots + 2^2 + 8^2) - \frac{153^2}{27}$$

$$= 1203 - 867 = 336$$

$$SS_{group} = \frac{\Sigma T_j^2}{n} - \frac{G^2}{N}$$

$$= \frac{(75^2 + 30^2 + 48^2)}{9} - \frac{153^2}{27}$$

$$= \frac{8829}{9} - 867$$

$$= 981 - 867 = 114$$

$$SS_{error} = SS_{total} - SS_{group}$$

$$= 336 - 114 = 222$$

(c) Summary Table

Source	df	SS	MS	F
Groups	2	114	57.00	6.162
Error	24	222	9.25	
Total	26	336		

treatment total as $\Sigma_i X_{ij}$, such a notational system can become exceedingly awkward. In later analyses in which there is more than one independent variable, T_j can be extended to T_{row_i} and T_{column_j} without confusion and without any loss of clarity.

Section (b) of Table 16-3 contains the calculations required to perform a one-way analysis of variance. Some elaboration is required at this point.

SS_{total}
The sum of squares of all scores regardless of group membership.

SS_{total}   The SS_{total} (read "sum of squares total") represents the sum of squares of all the observations, regardless of which treatment produced them. It is the sum of all the squared observations, minus the grand total squared divided by N:

$$SS_{total} = \Sigma X^2 - \frac{G^2}{N}$$

SS_{group}
The sum of squares of group totals divided by the number of scores per group.

SS_{group}   The SS_{group} term is a measure of differences due to groups (in effect, differences between group means) and is directly related to the variability of the group totals. To calculate SS_{group} we simply square and sum each of the group totals, divide by the number of observations on which each total is based (in this case n), and subtract G^2/N. To gain a better appreciation of exactly what SS_{group} represents, the formula for it could be written somewhat differently (where k represents the number of groups):

$$SS_{group} = \frac{\Sigma T_j^2}{n} - \frac{G^2}{N}$$

$$= \frac{\Sigma T_j^2}{n} - \frac{(\Sigma T_j)^2}{nk} = \frac{\Sigma T_j - \dfrac{(\Sigma T_j)^2}{k}}{n} = \frac{\Sigma(T_j - \bar{T})^2}{n}$$

From this equation we can see that SS_{group} represents the sum of squared deviations of the treatment totals about the mean of the totals ($\bar{T}$), divided by n. The n in this case is exactly the same divisor that we discussed in connection with the Central Limit Theorem. (It appears in the denominator rather than in the numerator simply because we are working with totals rather than means.) Its purpose is eventually to produce an estimate of σ_e^2. In all of the sums of squares discussed in the analysis of variance, the same general principle applies.

General Rule for the Calculation of Any Sum of Squares   In conjunction with this discussion of SS_{group} it is now possible to lay down a general rule for the calculation of any sum of squares (SS), other than those we will calculate by subtraction:

For any SS except SS_{error}, square the relevant totals, divide by the number of observations on which each total is based, sum the results, and subtract G^2/N.

This rule will allow you to calculate the SS for any example in this book, no matter how complex the experimental design. In the one-way analysis of variance the "relevant totals" just referred to are the totals for the various groups. When we come to the two-way analysis of variance in the next chapter, we will just generalize this rule to allow for different dimensions along which groups are formed. (The rule also applies to the calculation of SS_{total}, but there the relevant totals become the individual observations, and the divisor is therefore 1, which is usually not shown.)

SS_{error}
The sum of the sums of squares within each group.

SS_{error}   In practice SS_{error} is usually obtained by subtraction. Because it can be shown easily that

$$SS_{total} = SS_{group} + SS_{error}$$

then it must also be true that

$$SS_{error} = SS_{total} - SS_{group}$$

This is the procedure presented in Table 16-3. An alternative method of calculation is available, however. As you will recall from earlier discussions, we seek a term that is not influenced by differences among treatments, and therefore a term that represents the variability within each of the three treatments separately. To this end we could calculate a sum of squares within Treatment 1—SS_{error_1}, and a similar term for the SS within each of the other treatments:

$$SS_{error_1} = 5^2 + 8^2 + \cdots + 11^2 - \frac{75^2}{9} = 705 - 625 = 80$$

$$SS_{error_2} = 0^2 + 3^2 + \cdots + 6^2 - \frac{30^2}{9} = 180 - 100 = 80$$

$$SS_{error_3} = 5^2 + 2^2 + \cdots + 8^2 - \frac{48^2}{9} = 318 - 256 = 62$$

$$SS_{error} = 222$$

When we sum these individual terms, we obtain 222, which agrees exactly with the answer we obtained in Table 16-3. This simply goes to show that SS_{error} is a measure of the variability within each group.

THE SUMMARY TABLE

Part (c) of Table 16-3 is the summary table for the analysis of variance. It is called a summary table for the rather obvious reason that it summarizes a series of calculations, making it possible to tell at a glance what the data have to offer.

Sources of Variation   The first column of the summary table contains the sources of variation—the word "variation" being synonymous with the phrase "sum of squares." As you can see from the table, there are three sources of variation: the total variation, the variation due to groups (variation between group means), and the variation due to error (variation within 'groups). These sources reflect the fact that we have partitioned the total sum of squares into two portions, one portion representing variability between the several groups and the other representing variability within the individual groups.

Degrees of Freedom   The degrees of freedom column represents the allocation of the total number of degrees of freedom between the two sources of variation. The calculation of df is probably the easiest part of our task. The total degrees of freedom (df_{total}) are always $N - 1$, where N is the total number of observations. The degrees of freedom between groups (df_{group}) always equal $k - 1$, where k is the number of groups. The degrees of freedom for error (df_{error}) are most easily thought of as what is left over, although they can be calculated more directly as the sum of the degrees of freedom within each treatment. In our example $df_{total} = 27 - 1 = 26$. Of these 26 df, 2 are associated with differences between groups and the remaining 24 are associated with variability within the groups.

Rather than learning a set of equations for calculating degrees of freedom (a most unsatisfactory undertaking), it is important to understand the rationale underlying the allocation of df. SS_{total} is the sum of N squared deviations around one point—the grand mean. The fact that we have taken deviations around this one (estimated) point has cost us 1 df, thus leaving us with $N - 1$ df. SS_{group} is the sum of deviations of the k group means around one point (again the grand mean), and again we have lost 1 df in estimating this point, leaving us with $k - 1$ df. SS_{error} represents k sets of n deviations about one point (the group mean), losing us 1 df for each group and leaving $k(n - 1) = N - k$ df.

To repeat this in a slightly different form, the total variability is based on N scores and therefore has $N - 1$ df. The variability of treatment means is based on k scores (means or totals) and therefore has $k - 1$ df. The variability within any one treatment is based on n scores and thus has $n - 1$ df, but because we sum k of these within-treatment terms, we will have k times $n - 1 = k(n - 1)$ df.

Sums of Squares   There is little to be said about the column labeled SS. It simply contains the sums of squares obtained in section (b) of the table.

Mean Squares   The column of mean squares contains the two estimates of σ_e^2. These values are obtained by dividing the sums of squares by their corresponding df. Thus $114/2 = 57$ and $222/24 = 9.25$. We typically do not calculate a MS_{total}, because we have no use for it. If we were to do so, however, this term would represent the variance of all N observations.

While it is true that mean squares are variances, it is important to keep in mind what these terms are variances of. Thus MS_{error} is the (average) variance of the observations within each treatment. However, MS_{group} is not the variance of group means or totals, but rather the variance of those means (or totals) corrected by n to produce an estimate of the population variance (σ_e^2)—in other words it is an estimate of σ_e^2 based on the variance of group means.

The F Statistic   The last column, headed F, is the most important one in terms of testing the null hypothesis. F is obtained by dividing MS_{group} by MS_{error}. As I said earlier, MS_{error} is an estimate of the population variance (σ_e^2). MS_{group} is also

---

df_{total}
Degrees of freedom associated with $SS_{total} = N - 1$.

df_{group}
Degrees of freedom associated with $SS_{group} = k - 1$.

df_{error}
Degrees of freedom associated with $SS_{error} = k(n - 1)$.

an estimate of population variance (σ_e^2) *if* H_0 is true, but not if it is false. If H_0 is true, then both MS_{error} and MS_{group} are estimating the same thing, and as such they should be approximately equal. If this is the case, the ratio of one to the other will be approximately 1, give or take a fair amount for sampling error. Thus all we have to do is compute the ratio and determine whether or not it is close enough to 1 to indicate support for the null hypothesis.

An alternative way of looking at F is to denote the variance of the *population means* (μ_1, μ_2, μ_3) as σ_τ^2. (Remember that we have denoted the variance of the populations themselves as σ_e^2.) Then if we use a ($\hat{}$) to represent an estimate of the corresponding parameter

$$MS_{error} = \hat{\sigma}_e^2 \quad \text{and} \quad MS_{group} = \hat{\sigma}_e^2 + n\hat{\sigma}_\tau^2$$

If H_0 is true, $\mu_1 = \mu_2 = \mu_3$ and σ_τ^2 will be zero, leaving

$$F = \frac{\hat{\sigma}_e^2}{\hat{\sigma}_e^2} \approx 1$$

If H_0 is false, however, σ_τ^2 will not be zero and

$$F = \frac{\hat{\sigma}_e^2 + n\hat{\sigma}_\tau^2}{\hat{\sigma}_e^2} > 1$$

The question remains, however, as to how large a departure from 1.0 we need to have for our obtained value of F before we decide that there are differences among the populations means and thus reject H_0. The answer to this lies in the fact that if H_0 is true, the ratio

$$\frac{MS_{group}}{MS_{error}}$$

is distributed as the F distribution tabled in **Appendix D, Table 2**, on df_{group} and df_{error} degrees of freedom. (A portion of Appendix D, Table 2, is shown in Table 16-4.) Because the shape of the F distribution, and thus areas under it, depend on the degrees of freedom for the two mean squares, this table looks somewhat different from other tables you have seen. In this case we select the column corresponding to the degrees of freedom for the mean square in the numerator of F (i.e., $k-1$) and the row corresponding to the degrees of freedom for the mean square in the denominator (i.e., $k(n-1)$). The intersection of this row and column gives us the critical value of F at the level of α shown at the top of the table.

To use Appendix D, Table 2, we first have to find the particular table corresponding to our level of α. Because in this book we are routinely setting α equal to .05, we begin with that table. Because we have 2 df for the numerator (MS_{group}) and 24 df for the denominator (MS_{error}), we move down the second column until we come to the row labeled 24. The intersection of this row and column contains the entry 3.40. This is the critical value of F. We would expect to exceed an F of 3.40 only 5% of the time if H_0 were true. Because our obtained $F = 6.162$ exceeds $F_{.05} = 3.40$, we will reject H_0 and conclude that the groups

TABLE 16-4   Abbreviated Version of Appendix D, Table 2, Critical Values of the F Distribution   Alpha = .05.

					Degrees of Freedom for Numerator						
	1	2	3	4	5	6	7	8	9	10	15
1	161.4	199.5	215.8	224.8	230.0	233.8	236.5	238.6	240.1	242.1	...
2	18.51	19.00	19.16	19.25	19.30	19.33	19.35	19.37	19.38	19.40	...
3	10.13	9.55	9.28	9.12	9.01	8.94	8.89	8.85	8.81	8.79	...
4	7.71	6.94	6.59	6.39	6.26	6.16	6.09	6.04	6.00	5.96	...
5	6.61	5.79	5.41	5.19	5.05	4.95	4.88	4.82	4.77	4.74	...
6	5.99	5.14	4.76	4.53	4.39	4.28	4.21	4.15	4.10	4.06	...
7	5.59	4.74	4.35	4.12	3.97	3.87	3.79	3.73	3.68	3.64	...
8	5.32	4.46	4.07	3.84	3.69	3.58	3.50	3.44	3.39	3.35	...
9	5.12	4.26	3.86	3.63	3.48	3.37	3.29	3.23	3.18	3.14	...
10	4.96	4.10	3.71	3.48	3.33	3.22	3.14	3.07	3.02	2.98	...
11	4.84	3.98	3.59	3.36	3.20	3.09	3.01	2.95	2.90	2.85	...
12	4.75	3.89	3.49	3.26	3.11	3.00	2.91	2.85	2.80	2.75	...
13	4.67	3.81	3.41	3.18	3.03	2.92	2.83	2.77	2.71	2.67	...
14	4.60	3.74	3.34	3.11	2.96	2.85	2.76	2.70	2.65	2.60	...
15	4.54	3.68	3.29	3.06	2.90	2.79	2.71	2.64	2.59	2.54	...
16	4.49	3.63	3.24	3.01	2.85	2.74	2.66	2.59	2.54	2.49	...
17	4.45	3.59	3.20	2.96	2.81	2.70	2.61	2.55	2.49	2.45	...
18	4.41	3.55	3.16	2.93	2.77	2.66	2.58	2.51	2.46	2.41	...
19	4.38	3.52	3.13	2.90	2.74	2.63	2.54	2.48	2.42	2.38	...
20	4.35	3.49	3.10	2.87	2.71	2.60	2.51	2.45	2.39	2.35	...
22	4.30	3.44	3.05	2.82	2.66	2.55	2.46	2.40	2.34	2.30	...
24	4.26	3.40	3.01	2.78	2.62	2.51	2.42	2.36	2.30	2.25	...
26	4.23	3.37	2.98	2.74	2.59	2.47	2.39	2.32	2.27	2.22	...
28	4.20	3.34	2.95	2.71	2.56	2.45	2.36	2.29	2.24	2.19	...
30	4.17	3.32	2.92	2.69	2.53	2.42	2.33	2.27	2.21	2.16	...
40	4.08	3.23	2.84	2.61	2.45	2.34	2.25	2.18	2.12	2.08	...
50	4.03	3.18	2.79	2.56	2.40	2.29	2.20	2.13	2.07	2.03	...
60	4.00	3.15	2.76	2.53	2.37	2.25	2.17	2.10	2.04	1.99	...
120	3.92	3.07	2.68	2.45	2.29	2.18	2.09	2.02	1.96	1.91	...
200	3.89	3.04	2.65	2.42	2.26	2.14	2.06	1.98	1.93	1.88	...
500	3.86	3.01	2.62	2.39	2.23	2.12	2.03	1.96	1.90	1.85	...
1000	3.85	3.01	2.61	2.38	2.22	2.11	2.02	1.95	1.89	1.84	...

Degrees of Freedom for Denominator (left axis label)

were sampled from populations with different means. (Had we chosen to work at α equal to .01, you should be able to find from Appendix D, Table 2, that $F_{.01}(2,24) = 5.61$ and conclude that we would still reject H_0.)

16-4   UNEQUAL SAMPLE SIZES

Most experiments are designed originally with the idea of having the same number of observations in each treatment. Frequently, however, things do not work out that way. Animals occasionally die during an experiment from causes having nothing to do with the treatment. Subjects are remarkably unreliable, and many fail to arrive for testing or are eliminated for failure to follow instructions. There is even a report in the literature in which an experimental animal was eliminated from the study for repeatedly biting the experimenter (Sgro and Weinstock, 1963). Moreover in studies conducted on intact groups, such as school classes, groups are nearly always unequal in size for reasons that may have nothing to do with the experiment.

If the sample sizes are not equal, the analysis discussed earlier is not appropriate without modification. For the case of one independent variable, however, this modification is relatively minor.

For the case of equal sample sizes we have defined

$$SS_{group} = \frac{\Sigma T_j^2}{n} - \frac{G^2}{N}$$

where n is the number of observations in each group. We were able to divide each of the T_j^2 (and therefore ΣT_j^2) by n, because n was common to all treatments. If the sample sizes differ, however, and we define n_j as the number of subjects in the jth treatment ($\Sigma n_j = N$), we can rewrite the equation as

$$SS_{group} = \Sigma \frac{T_j^2}{n_j} - \frac{G^2}{N}$$

which, when all n_i are equal, reduces to the original form.

AN ADDITIONAL EXAMPLE— ADAPTATION TO MATERNAL ROLES

An additional example of a one-way analysis of variance will also illustrate the treatment of unequal sample sizes. In a study of the development of low-birthweight (LBW) infants (Nurcombe, Howell, Rauh, Teti, Ruoff, and Brennan, 1985), mothers were interviewed when the infants were 6 months old. There were three groups in the experiment—a LBW Experimental group, a LBW Control group, and a Full-term group. The LBW Experimental group was part of an intervention program, and we hoped to show that these mothers would adapt to their new role as well as mothers of full-term infants. On the other hand we expected that mothers of low-birthweight infants who did not receive the intervention program would have some trouble adapting. (Being the parent of a low-birthweight baby is not an easy task, especially for the first few months.)

The actual data from this study are presented in part (a) of Table 16-5. In part (b) of the table are the calculations for the analysis of variance, and in part (c) is the summary table. Notice that the calculations are carried out just as they would be for the case of equal sample sizes except that for SS_{group} each value of T_j^2 is divided by the corresponding sample size as we go along.

From the summary table we see that the obtained F value is 5.53 and that it is based on 2 and 90 degrees of freedom. From Appendix D, Table 2, we see by interpolation that

$$F_{.05}(2,90) = 3.11$$

TABLE 16-5

Adaptation to Maternal Role in Three Groups of Mothers (Low Scores are Associated with Better Adaptation)

(a) Data

Group 1 LBW Experimental			Group 2 LBW Control			Group 3 Full-term		
24	10	16	21	17	13	12	12	12
13	11	15	19	18	25	25	17	20
29	13	12	10	18	16	14	18	14
12	19	16	24	13	18	16	18	14
14	11	12	17	21	11	13	18	12
11	11	12	25	27	16	10	15	20
12	27	22	16	29	11	13	13	12
13	13	16	26	14	21	11	15	17
13	13	17	19	17	13	20	13	15
13	14					23	13	11
						16	10	13
						20	12	11
						11		

$\Sigma X = 434$	495	549	$G = 1478$
$n = 29$	27	37	$N = 93$
$\bar{X} = 14.97$	18.33	14.84	

(b) Calculations

$$SS_{total} = \Sigma X^2 - \frac{G^2}{N}$$

$$= 24^2 + 10^2 + \cdots + 11^2 + 11^2 - \frac{1478^2}{93}$$

$$= 25{,}562 - 23{,}489.075$$

$$= 2072.925$$

$$SS_{group} = \Sigma \frac{T_j^2}{n_j} - \frac{G^2}{N}$$

$$= \frac{434^2}{29} + \frac{495^2}{27} + \frac{549^2}{37} - \frac{1478^2}{93}$$

$$= 23{,}716.007 - 23{,}489.075$$

$$= 226.932$$

$$SS_{error} = SS_{total} - SS_{group}$$

$$= 2072.925 - 226.932$$

$$= 1845.993$$

(c) Summary Table

Source	df	SS	MS	F
Groups	2	226.932	113.466	5.53
Error	90	1845.993	20.511	
Total	92	2072.925		

(i.e., 90 is halfway between 60 and 120 *df*, so we will take as our critical value the value halfway between 3.15 and 3.07). Because 5.53 > 3.11, we will reject H_0 and conclude that not all of the scores for each group were drawn from populations with equal means. In fact it looks as if the first and third groups are about equal, whereas the second group has a higher mean (poorer adaptation). However, the *F* tells us only that we can reject $H_0 \colon \mu_1 = \mu_2 = \mu_3$. It does *not* tell us which groups are different from which other groups. To draw those kinds of conclusions we will need to use special techniques known as multiple comparison procedures.

16-5   MULTIPLE COMPARISON PROCEDURES

Multiple comparison techniques
Techniques for making comparisons between two or more individual means subsequent to an ANOVA.

When we run an analysis of variance and obtain a significant *F* value, what we have shown is simply that the overall null hypothesis is false. We do not know, however, which of a number of possible alternative hypotheses (e.g., $H_1 \colon \mu_1 \neq \mu_2 \neq \mu_3$; $H_2 \colon \mu_1 \neq \mu_2 = \mu_3$) is true. **Multiple comparison techniques** allow us to investigate hypotheses involving means of individual groups or sets of groups. Thus, for example, we might be interested in whether Group 1 is different from Group 2 or whether the combination of Groups 1 and 2 is different from Group 3.

One of the major problems with making comparisons among groups is that unrestricted use of these comparisons can lead to an excessively high probability of a Type I error. For example, if we have ten groups where the complete null hypothesis is true ($H_0 \colon \mu_1 = \mu_2 = \mu_3 = \cdots = \mu_{10}$), *t* tests between all pairs of means will lead to making at least one Type I error about 60% of the time. In other words the experimenter who thinks she is working at the $\alpha = .05$ level of significance is actually working at $\alpha = .60$. While it is nice to find significant differences, it is not nice to find ones that are not really there. Psychologists have enough trouble explaining all the real differences we find without having to worry about spurious differences as well.

In an attempt to control the likelihood of Type I errors, statisticians have developed a large number of procedures for comparing individual means. (For a discussion of many of these techniques see Howell, 1987.) Fortunately one of the best techniques is also one of the simplest, and it is applicable to most of the multiple comparison problems you are likely to encounter. This procedure is often referred to as the **protected *t*** or Fisher's **least significant difference test**, and we will consider it first.

Protected *t*
(Least significant difference test)
A technique in which we run *t* tests between pairs of means only if the analysis of variance was significant.

The procedures for using a protected *t* are really very simple. *The first requirement for a protected t is that the overall F for an analysis of variance must be significant.* If the *F* was not significant, no comparisons between pairs of means are allowed. You simply declare that there are no group differences and stop right there. On the other hand if the overall *F* is significant, you then can proceed to make any (or all) pairwise comparisons between individual means by use of a modified *t* test. The modification is simply to replace the pooled variance estimate (s_p^2) in the standard *t* formula by MS_{error} from the overall analysis of variance. This is not as strange a thing to do as it might appear. Because MS_{error} is defined as the average of the variances within each group, if there were only two groups in the experiment, the MS_{error} from the analysis of variance would be the same as the s_p^2 from the two-sample t test. In comparing among several groups we use MS_{error} instead of s^2 because it is based on variability within all the groups rather than within just the two groups we are comparing at the moment. As such it is presumably a better estimate of σ_e^2.† Along with the use of this error term comes the advantage that the resulting t will have df_{error} degrees of freedom rather than just the $n_1 + n_2 - 2$ degrees of freedom it otherwise would have had.

When we replace s_p^2 with MS_{error}, the formula for t becomes

$$t = \frac{\bar{X}_i - \bar{X}_j}{\sqrt{\dfrac{MS_{error}}{n_i} + \dfrac{MS_{error}}{n_j}}} = \frac{\bar{X}_i - \bar{X}_j}{\sqrt{MS_{error}\left(\dfrac{1}{n_i} + \dfrac{1}{n_j}\right)}}$$

To illustrate the use of the protected t we can take the data on maternal adaptation from the previous example. In that case we did find a significant overall F, which allows us to look further in our analysis. Given the nature of that study, there are two questions we would be interested in asking:

1. Are there differences between mothers in the LBW Control group and mothers in the Full-term group?

2. Are there differences between mothers in the LBW Control and Experimental groups?

The first question asks whether mothers of low-birthweight infants have more difficulty adapting than do mothers of full-term infants. The second question asks whether the intervention program makes a difference in adaptation. Note that it makes little sense to compare the LBW Experimental group with the Full-term group because if we did find a difference we could not tell whether it was due to intervention effects or to birthweight effects. In this comparison intervention and birthweight are *confounded*.

The results on maternal adaptation are presented in Table 16-6, in which the obtained values of t are -2.77 and 3.04 for the two comparisons. We will use a two-tailed test at $\alpha = .05$, and we have 90 degrees of freedom for our error

---

†If we let SS_j represent the sum of squares within group$_j$ (i.e., $SS_j = \Sigma(X_{ij} - \bar{X}_j)^2$), then

$$s_p^2 = \frac{(n_1 - 1)s_1^2 + (n_2 - 1)s_2^2}{n_1 + n_2 - 2} = \frac{SS_1 + SS_2}{df_1 + df_2}$$

Furthermore

$$MS_{error} = \frac{(n_1 - 1)s_1^2 + (n_2 - 1)s_2^2 + \cdots + (n_k - 1)s_k^2}{n_1 + n_2 + \cdots + n_k - k} = \frac{SS_1 + SS_2 + \cdots + SS_k}{df_1 + df_2 + \cdots + df_k}$$

Thus with two groups

$$s_p^2 = MS_{error}$$

	Group 1 LBW Experimental	Group 2 LBW Control	Group 3 Full-term
$\bar{X}_j =$	14.97	18.33	14.84
$n_j =$	29	27	37
$MS_{error} =$	20.511		
$df_{error} =$	90		

(a) μ_1 Versus μ_2

$$t = \frac{\bar{X}_1 - \bar{X}_2}{\sqrt{MS_{error}\left(\dfrac{1}{n_1} + \dfrac{1}{n_2}\right)}}$$

$$= \frac{14.97 - 18.33}{\sqrt{20.511\left(\dfrac{1}{29} + \dfrac{1}{27}\right)}}$$

$$= \frac{-3.36}{\sqrt{1.467}} = \frac{-3.36}{1.21} = -2.77$$

(b) μ_2 Versus μ_3

$$t = \frac{\bar{X}_2 - \bar{X}_3}{\sqrt{MS_{error}\left(\dfrac{1}{n_2} + \dfrac{1}{n_3}\right)}}$$

$$= \frac{18.33 - 14.84}{\sqrt{20.511\left(\dfrac{1}{27} + \dfrac{1}{37}\right)}}$$

$$= \frac{3.49}{\sqrt{1.314}} = \frac{3.49}{1.15} = 3.04$$

term. From Appendix D, Table 5, we find that $t_{.05}(90) = \pm 1.98$. Thus for both comparisons we can reject the null hypothesis, because both values of t_{obt} are greater than ± 1.98. We will therefore conclude that there is a difference in adaptation between mothers of low-birthweight and full-term infants, with the full-term mothers showing better adaptation. We will also conclude that the intervention program is effective.

You might well ask why we call this particular multiple comparison procedure a "protected t." Or, you may have heard somewhere that it is a bad idea to run all sorts of t tests between pairs of means. This is a good place to address both these concerns at the same time.

One of the primary considerations in running a set of multiple comparisons is to hold down the probability of making *at least* one Type I error. In other words, if we ran an analysis of variance and then three comparisons, we want to ensure that the probability is low that we haven't made a Type I error

Familywise error rate
Probability that a family of
comparisons contains at least
one Type I error.

anywhere, either in the original overall F or in any of the three comparisons. The probability of making such an error is called the **familywise error rate** because it deals with the probability that the *family* of comparisons contains *at least one* Type I error. For familywise error rates, making ten Type I errors is no worse than making one. In each case you have made an error. (Put differently, making only one is no better than making ten.) If we just ran t tests between all pairs of means, the familywise error rate might become unacceptably high. We need to impose some conditions to prevent this from happening. This is what a protected t test does by the simple expedient of requiring that no tests may be run unless the overall F from the analysis of variance is significant. To see why this simple step works, consider the following examples.

Suppose that we have only two means and *the null hypothesis is true*. The probability of making a Type I error would be the probability that the original F was significant by chance, which is .05. If that F was significant we have already made our Type I error, and even if we went on and ran a t test, we couldn't make the situation worse. If the F was not significant, we cannot run the protected t and so do not increase the error rate.† Thus with two means the familywise error rate is .05.

Now suppose that we have three means. First assume that the complete null hypothesis is true—that is, suppose that $\mu_1 = \mu_2 = \mu_3$. First we run the overall F. The probability of finding a significant difference (which would be a Type I error because H_0 is true) is .05, and that represents our first Type I error out of the "at least one" that the familywise error rate allows us. If the F is not significant we stop right there and have no further chances of making a Type I error. In other words, when the complete null hypothesis is true, the probability of making *at least one* Type I error is limited by our rule to .05, which is what we want. Next suppose that the complete null hypothesis is false but that one mean is different from the other two (e.g., $\mu_1 = \mu_2 \neq \mu_3$). Then, because the complete null hypothesis is not true, it is impossible to make a Type I error with our F test. If we have a significant F, which we would hope to be the case, we can go on and test, for example, each pair of means—Group 1 versus Group 2, Group 1 versus Group 3, and Group 2 versus Group 3. But there is only one of those tests for which the null hypothesis is true, and therefore there is only one chance of making a Type I error. Thus here again the probability of at least one Type I error is only .05. Finally, suppose that all means are different from each other. Here we have no possibility of making a Type I error, because there is no true null hypothesis to erroneously declare false. From examination of these possibilities we can conclude that with three means the familywise error rate is at most .05.

A similar line of reasoning applies to the case of four means. However, in this case it is possible that there is more than one true null hypothesis. For example, Groups 1 and 2 could be equal and Groups 3 and 4 could be equal. Or,

---

†With only two means the t and the analysis of variance are equivalent tests, but that is not important here. The point is that if there is a Type I error on the F we already have at least one error, and if F is not significant we can't test further.

Groups 1, 2, and 3 could be equal, but different from Group 4. In this case the maximum possible familywise error rate will be greater than .05, but it is still reasonable, especially if you do not plan to run all possible comparisons. Having a familywise error rate that could go as high as .10 or .15 is not as good as having one of .05. But it is not the end of the world. Simply by demanding a significant overall F before running multiple comparisons (which is where the protection comes from) is surprisingly effective in controlling familywise error rates, at least when we have only a few groups. This is the reason I have stressed the protected t in this chapter. It does a good job of controlling the familywise error rate if you have a relatively small number of groups, while at the same time being a test that you can easily apply and that has a reasonable degree of power.

THE SCHEFFÉ TEST

Scheffé test
A relatively conservative multiple comparison procedure.

Not everyone likes the protected t test, and people have requested that I include a second multiple comparison test procedure for those who would prefer more stringent control over familywise error rates. I have chosen what is called the **Scheffé test** because it is easy to use and because it is popular with people who prefer stringent control. My presentation of it will be slightly different from that of other books, but it is algebraically equivalent and builds nicely on what you have already learned about computing the protected t.

First of all, with the Scheffé test we drop the requirement that the overall F from the analysis of variance be significant. We can run multiple comparisons with Scheffé's test regardless of whether or not the overall F is significant.

Next, you run any and all comparisons that you wish among pairs of means exactly as you did with the protected t. In other words you apply exactly the same formula. The only difference is that when you have calculated your t, you square it and treat it as a legitimate value of F. When we compare two groups, t^2 and F will be identical.)

Finally, you compare that F to the critical values of F in the F table in Appendix D, Table 2. But here is where the difference comes in. In the ordinary course of events it would not make any difference if you compared your t to $t_{.05}$ on $k(n - 1)$ degrees of freedom or compared your F to $F_{.05}$ on 1 and $k(n - 1)$ degrees of freedom. The result would be the same. But we are not going to compare our F to the critical value of F on 1 and $k(n - 1)\, df$. Instead we are going to compare our F to $(k - 1)$ *times* the F on $(k - 1)$ and $k(n - 1)\, df$. In other words, we are doing everything we did with the protected t (except requiring the overall F to be significant), but now we are changing the critical value to make the test more conservative.

A worked example using Scheffé's test appears near the end of this chapter. An important point to keep in mind, however, is that by holding down the familywise error rate, Scheffé has also made his test much more conservative. By that I mean that he has made it harder to reject a true null hypothesis by making it harder to reject *any* null hypothesis—even false ones.

16-6 VIOLATIONS OF ASSUMPTIONS

As we have seen, the analysis of variance is based upon the assumptions of normality and homogeneity of variance. In practice, however, the analysis of variance is a very robust statistical procedure, and the assumptions can frequently be violated with relatively minor effects.

In general, if the populations can be assumed to be either symmetric or at least similar in shape (e.g., all negatively skewed) and if the largest variance is no more than four or five times the smallest, the analysis of variance is most likely to be valid. (Some argue that it would be valid for even greater differences between the variances.) It is important to note, however, that heterogeneity of variance and unequal sample sizes do not mix. If you have reason to anticipate unequal variances, make every effort to keep your sample sizes as equal as possible. This is particularly true when you plan to run a series of multiple comparisons.

For those situations in which the assumptions underlying the analysis of variance are seriously violated, there are alternative procedures for handling the analysis. Some of these procedures involve transforming the data (e.g., converting X to $\sqrt{X}$) and then performing standard statistical tests on the transformed data. Other procedures involve using quite different tests, and they are discussed at some length in Chapter 20.

16-7 MAGNITUDE OF EFFECT

Magnitude of effect
A measure of the degree to which variability among observations can be attributed to treatments.

Eta squared (η^2)
A measure of the magnitude of effect.

Simply because we obtain a significant difference among our treatment means does not mean that the differences are large or important. There are many real differences that are trivial. No statistical procedure can tell us whether a difference, no matter how large, is of any practical importance to the rest of the world. However, there are procedures that give us some help in this direction.

One of the simplest measures of the **magnitude of effect** is called **eta squared (η^2)**. While eta squared is a biased measure (in the sense that it tends to overestimate the value we would obtain if we were able to measure whole populations of scores), its calculation is so simple and it is so useful as a first approximation that it is worth discussing. In any analysis of variance, SS_{total} tells us how much overall variability there is in the data. Some of that variability is due to the fact that different groups of subjects are treated differently and therefore have different scores, and some of it is just due to random error—differences among people who are treated alike. The differences of importance are the differences among scores that can be attributed to our treatment, or group effects, and they are measured by SS_{group}. If we form the ratio

$$\eta^2 = \frac{SS_{group}}{SS_{total}}$$

we can say what percentage of the variability among observations can be attributed to group effects.† For our maternal adaptation data

$$\eta^2 = \frac{226.932}{2072.925} = .11$$

Thus we can conclude that 11% of the variability in adaptation scores can be attributed to group membership. Although that might at first seem like a small percentage, if you stop to think about the high level of variability among mothers you have known, explaining even 10% of it is a noteworthy accomplishment.

Although η^2 is a quick and easy measure to calculate, and can be estimated in your head when reading research reports, it is a biased statistic. It will tend to overestimate the true value in the population. A much less biased estimate is afforded by another statistic called **omega squared (ω^2)**. For the analysis of variance discussed in this chapter we can define

Omega squared (ω^2)
Another measure of the magnitude of effect.

$$\omega^2 = \frac{SS_{group} - (k-1)MS_{error}}{SS_{total} + MS_{error}}$$

where k represents the number of groups. For our example

$$\omega^2 = \frac{226.932 - (3-1)(20.511)}{2072.925 + 20.511} = \frac{185.910}{2093.436} = 0.089$$

This value is somewhat lower than the value we obtained for η^2. However, it still suggests that we are accounting for approximately 9% of the variability.

16-8 THE USE OF MINITAB FOR A ONE-WAY ANALYSIS OF VARIANCE

An illustration of how Minitab can be used to run a one-way analysis of variance is presented in Table 16-7 for the maternal adaptation data. Histograms for each of the three groups show that the data are at least unimodal and do not contain serious outliers, although there are too few data points to say much about normality. The analysis of variance summary table appears after the histograms and agrees within rounding error with the analysis in Table 16-5. Finally you see the confidence limits on μ_j for each group. These limits reflect the results we obtained with our multiple comparison procedures.

16-9 A FINAL WORKED EXAMPLE

The following example illustrates a one-way analysis of variance with unequal sample sizes. It also illustrates the use of Scheffé's test.

---

†If you created a variable (X) by entering 1 for all subjects in Group 1 and a 2 for all subjects in Group 2, and if you let Y be the dependent variable, then the squared correlation coefficient (r^2) between X and Y would be equivalent to η^2.

TABLE 16-7
Minitab Analysis of Maternal Adaptation Data

```
MTB > RETRIEVE 'MATERN.MIN'
MTB > HISTOGRAM OF C1-C3 WITH LOWER END = 10 AND INTERVAL = 2

Histogram of C1   N = 29

Midpoint   Count
   10.00      1    *
   12.00      9    *********
   14.00      9    *********
   16.00      4    ****
   18.00      1    *
   20.00      1    *
   22.00      1    *
   24.00      1    *
   26.00      0
   28.00      1    *
   30.00      1    *


Histogram of C2   N = 27

Midpoint   Count
   10.00      1    *
   12.00      2    **
   14.00      4    ****
   16.00      3    ***
   18.00      6    ******
   20.00      2    **
   22.00      3    ***
   24.00      1    *
   26.00      3    ***
   28.00      1    *
   30.00      1    *


Histogram of C3   N = 37

Midpoint   Count
   10.00      2    **
   12.00     10    **********
   14.00      9    *********
   16.00      5    *****
   18.00      5    *****
   20.00      4    ****
   22.00      0
   24.00      1    *
   26.00      1    *

MTB > AOVONEWAY ON THE DATA IN COLUMNS C1-C3

ANALYSIS OF VARIANCE
SOURCE    DF       SS       MS        F
FACTOR     2    226.9    113.5     5.53
ERROR     90   1846.0     20.5
TOTAL     92   2072.9
                                  INDIVIDUAL 95 PCT CI'S FOR MEAN
                                  BASED ON POOLED STDEV
LEVEL      N     MEAN    STDEV   ----+---------+---------+---------+--
C1        29   14.966    4.844   (--------*-------)
C2        27   18.333    5.166                   (--------*------)
C3        37   14.838    3.708   (------*------)
                                 ----+---------+---------+---------+--
POOLED STDEV =     4.529         14.0      16.0      18.0      20.0

MTB > STOP
```

The nucleus accumbens is a forebrain structure that has been shown to be involved in locomotor activity in rats. Administration of low doses of tetrahydrocannabinol (THC, the major active ingredient in marijuana) is known to increase locomotor activity, whereas high doses are known to lead to a decrease in activity. In an attempt to examine whether THC is acting within the nucleus accumbens to produce its effects on activity, Conti and Musty (1984) bilaterally injected either a placebo or 0.1, 0.5, 1, or 2 micrograms (μg) of THC directly into the nucleus accumbens of rats. The investigators recorded the change in the activity level of the animals after injection. It was expected that activity would increase more with smaller injections than with larger ones. The data in Table 16-8 represent the amount of change (decrease) in each animal.

First we will set up the null hypothesis. The null hypothesis is the hypothesis that all of these samples were drawn from populations with the same mean. In other words, $H_0: \mu_1 = \mu_2 = \mu_3 = \mu_4 = \mu_5$. For consistency we will test this null hypothesis with a significance level of $\alpha = .05$.

Next we will run the overall analysis of variance, starting with the calculation of the sums of squares.

$$SS_{total} = \Sigma X^2 - \frac{G^2}{N} = (30^2 + 27^2 + \cdots + 53^2) - \frac{2160^2}{47}$$

$$= 113,556 - 99,268.085 = 14,287.91$$

$$SS_{groups} = \frac{\Sigma T_j^2}{n_j} - \frac{G^2}{N} = \frac{340^2}{10} + \frac{508^2}{10} + \frac{543^2}{9} + \frac{388^2}{8} + \frac{381^2}{10} - \frac{2160^2}{47}$$

$$= 103,461.50 - 99,268.085 = 4193.41$$

$$SS_{error} = SS_{total} - SS_{groups} = 14,287.91 - 4193.41 = 10,094.50$$

We can now put these terms in a summary table.

Source	df	SS	MS	F
Groups	4	4,193.41	1048.35	4.36
Error	42	10,094.50	240.35	
Total	46	14,287.91		

TABLE 16-8

Data from the Study by Conti and Musty (1984)

			Group			
	Placebo	0.1 μg	0.5 μg	1 μg	2 μg	
	30	60	71	33	36	
	27	42	50	78	27	
	52	48	38	71	60	
	38	52	59	58	51	
	20	28	65	35	29	
	26	93	58	35	34	
	8	32	74	46	24	
	41	46	67	32	17	
	49	63	61		50	
	49	44			53	
Total	340	508	543	388	381	2160 = G
Mean	34.00	50.80	60.33	48.50	38.10	45.96
n	10	10	9	8	10	47

Finally, we compare $F = 4.36$ to the critical value from Appendix D, Table 2. We have $4\,df$ for Groups and $42\,df$ for Error. The critical value from the appendix is 2.61, if we round off to 40 degrees of freedom for the denominator. Because our obtained value exceeds 2.61, we will reject the null hypothesis and conclude that there are differences in activity levels among the five drug groups, presumably reflecting differences due to the dosage of THC administered.

The experimental hypothesis had predicted that the low-dose groups would show greater increases in activity than the high-dose groups. Therefore we might wish to compare the $0.5\,\mu g$ group with the $2\,\mu g$ group. It would also be interesting to compare the $2\,\mu g$ group with the placebo group to see if those groups were different. We will make both these comparisons using the Scheffé test. As discussed in the text, we will perform this test by first running t tests between the groups just as we did with the protected t.

Comparison of Groups 3 and 5 ($0.5\,\mu g$ versus $2\,\mu g$)

$$t = \frac{\bar{X}_3 - \bar{X}_5}{\sqrt{MS_{error}\left(\dfrac{1}{n_3} + \dfrac{1}{n_5}\right)}}$$

$$= \frac{60.33 - 38.10}{\sqrt{240.35\left(\dfrac{1}{9} + \dfrac{1}{10}\right)}}$$

$$= \frac{22.23}{\sqrt{240.35(0.2111)}} = \frac{22.23}{\sqrt{50.74}} = \frac{22.23}{7.12} = 3.12$$

$$F = t^2 = 3.12^2 = 9.73$$

Comparison of Groups 1 and 5 (placebo versus $2\,\mu g$)

$$t = \frac{\bar{X}_1 - \bar{X}_5}{\sqrt{MS_{error}\left(\dfrac{1}{n_1} + \dfrac{1}{n_5}\right)}}$$

$$= \frac{34.00 - 38.10}{\sqrt{240.35\left(\dfrac{1}{10} + \dfrac{1}{10}\right)}}$$

$$= \frac{-4.10}{\sqrt{240.35(0.20)}} = \frac{-4.10}{\sqrt{48.07}} = \frac{-4.10}{6.93} = 0.59$$

$$F = t^2 = 0.59^2 = 0.35$$

Notice that for both t tests I have squared the resulting value to obtain an F. These two values of F can be referred to the tables of F in Appendix D, Table 2. To do this we first need the critical value of F on 4 and 42 degrees of freedom. This value (if we round the denominator degrees of freedom to 40) is 2.61. We next multiply this critical value of F by $k - 1 = 4$ to obtain 10.44. Any value of F that exceeds this value will be declared significant. Because our two F values are 9.73 and 0.35, we will not reject the null hypothesis in either case.

You might wonder why we did not reject the null hypothesis for either of these comparisons, although we would have rejected it for the comparison of Groups 3 and 5 had we been using a protected t. The major reason is that Scheffé's test is a more conservative test. In the first place it does a better job than does the protected t of keeping the familywise error rate, in this case, to $\alpha = .05$. But beyond that it is still a very conservative test. That is why I prefer the protected t when we have only a few groups. I would rather let the familywise error rate slip up too much than find myself with such a conservative test that I have difficulty finding any differences to be significant. However, there are many people who would disagree with me.

16-10   SUMMARY

The analysis of variance is one of our most powerful statistical tools. In this chapter we began by examining the logic behind the analysis and then turned to the calculations. After considering the calculations for the case of equal sample sizes, we took up the problem of unequal sample sizes and saw that for the one-way analysis of variance we need to make only minor changes in the formulae. We then considered the problem of isolating group differences by means of multiple comparison procedures. After discussing the effects of violating the assumptions behind the test, we considered the problem of estimating the magnitude of experimental effects. Some of the most important terms in the chapter are:

- **Analysis of variance (ANOVA)**
- **One-way ANOVA**
- MS_{within} (MS_{error})
- $MS_{between\,groups}$ (MS_{group})
- **Grand total (G)**
- SS_{total}
- SS_{group}
- SS_{error}
- df_{total}
- df_{group}

- df_{error}
- **Multiple comparison techniques**
- **Protected t (least significant difference test)**
- **Familywise error rate**
- **Scheffé test**
- **Magnitude of effect**
- **Eta squared (η^2)**
- **Omega squared (ω^2)**

16-11 EXERCISES

16–1 To investigate maternal behavior of laboratory rats we separated the rat pup from the mother and recorded the time (in seconds) required for the mother to retrieve the pup. We ran the study with 5-, 20-, and 35-day-old pups because we were interested in whether retrieval time varies with age of pup. The data are given below, where there are six pups per group.

5 Days Old	15	10	25	15	20	18
20 Days Old	30	15	20	25	23	20
35 Days Old	40	35	50	43	45	40

Run a one-way analysis of variance with $\alpha = .05$.

16-2 Use a protected t with the data in Exercise 16-1 to evaluate the difference between 5- and 20-day-old pups and the difference between 20- and 35-day-old pups.

16-3 Assume that you have just collected data to answer the question of whether the person paying a restaurant bill (Host) orders a less expensive meal than his or her partner (Guest). To avoid confusing the issue you chose to look at only same-sex pairs and to record the price of the meal for only one person in each pair. Subjects are assigned to groups on the basis of whether or not the subject eventually picked up the tab. The dependent variable is the cost of the entrée.

Host	9.50	8.75	10.25	9.00	9.25
Guest	10.75	9.50	8.50	10.50	12.25

(a) Run the analysis of variance on these two groups.

(b) Run an independent t test on the same data, square the t, and compare the results. (*Note*: This relationship between F and t holds only when we have two groups.)

(c) Why was it necessary to ensure that we had data on only one member of each pair? (Answer with respect to what you know about t.)

16-4 It might be predicted that consumer buying behavior would vary with the location of the product in the store, even if the product in question has a high degree of brand loyalty. We therefore look at the purchases of well-known and unknown brands of cigarettes when they are in their usual place behind the counter and when they are prominently displayed next to the cash register. The dependent variable is the number of packs of each brand sold per day. (For the time being we will ignore the fact that this design might better be analyzed by techniques to be discussed in Chapter 17.)

Known Brand/ Usual Location	15	23	18	16	25	29	17
Known Brand/ Prominent Location	24	14	15	19	30	26	18
Unknown Brand/ Usual Location	10	5	8	12	13	6	10

Unknown Brand/ Prominent Location	15	13	10	17	18	11	15

(a) Run a one-way analysis of variance.

(b) Now run a one-way analysis of variance on Groups 1 and 3 combined versus Groups 2 and 4 combined. What question does this test ask?

16-5 Refer to Exercise 16-1. Assume that for reasons beyond our control the data for the last pup in the 5-day-old group could not be used, nor could the data for the last two pups in the 35-day-old group. Rerun the analysis of variance using the remaining data.

16-6 Refer to Exercise 16-3. Suppose that we collected two additional data points for the Host group. The data now look like the following:

Host	9.50	8.75	10.25	9.00	9.25	11.75	9.00
Guest	10.75	9.50	8.50	10.50	12.25		

(a) Rerun the analysis of variance.

(b) Run an independent t without pooling the variance.

(c) Run an independent t after pooling the variance.

(d) Which of these values of t corresponds (after squaring) to the F in part (a)?

16-7 Calculate η^2 and ω^2 for the data in Exercise 16-3.

16-8 Some words in a prose passage are particularly important for the meaning of the passage, whereas other words are of no real importance. If it is hypothesized that good readers read primarily the important words, then if these words were capitalized, and the other words were not, it might be expected that the passage would be read more rapidly. We define three groups that read the same passage. For Group 1 no words are capitalized. For Group 2 a random set of words is capitalized. For Group 3 the important words are capitalized. The dependent variable is the time to read the passage (in seconds).

	n	**Mean**	**Standard Deviation**
Group 1	10	30.2	6.21
Group 2	10	38.3	7.55
Group 3	10	25.6	5.75

(a) Run the analysis and draw whatever conclusions seem warranted.

(b) Point out at least one major failing in the design of this experiment as it relates to the hypothesis that good readers look for important words.

(c) What does rejection of H_0 mean in this case?

16–9 What would we conclude if we had the same means and standard deviations in Exercise 16-8 but if the ns had each been 5 instead of 10?

16–10 Use protected t tests for the data in Exercise 16-8 to clarify the meaning of the significant F.

16–11 The data in Exercise 16-9 also produced a significant F. Do you have more or less faith in the effect? Why?

16–12 Using the data in Appendix C, Data Set, compare the grades in English (ENGG) for the three different levels of English (ENGL).

16–13 Why should you feel a bit uncomfortable about the answer to Exercise 16-12?

16–14 When the numerator for F has one degree of freedom, the F is equal to the square of the t for the corresponding t test. We saw this in Exercises 16-3 and 16-6. Now go back to the Minitab printout in Table 10-4. Calculate the F from the analysis of variance table and show that it is the square of a t test on r.

16–15 For the data in Appendix C, Data Set, form three groups. Group 1 has ADDSC scores of 40 or below, Group 2 has ADDSC scores between 41 and 59, and Group 3 has ADDSC scores of 60 or above. Run an analysis of variance on the GPA scores for these three groups. (*Hint*: If you are using Minitab the RECODE and CHOOSE commands will make life easier.)

16–16 Compute η^2 and ω^2 from the results in Exercise 16-15.

16–17 Darley and Latané (1968) recorded the speed with which subjects summoned help for a person in trouble. Subjects thought that they were either alone with the person (Group 1, $n = 13$), that one other person was there (Group 2, $n = 26$), or that four other people were there (Group 3, $n = 13$). The dependent variable was speed ($= 1/\text{time} \times 100$). The mean speed scores for the three groups were .87, .72, and .51, respectively. The MS_{error} was 0.053. Reconstruct the analysis of variance. (*Hint*: Compute group totals first.) What would you conclude?

16–18 Using the data in Exercise 16-1, calculate SS_{error} directly rather than by subtraction and show that this is the same answer you found in that exercise.

16–19 Use Scheffé's test for the data in Exercise 16-1 and compare your answer to the answer to Exercise 16-2.

16–20 Use Scheffé's test for the data in Exercise 16-8. What would you conclude? How does this compare to the answer for 16-10?

17

FACTORIAL ANALYSIS OF VARIANCE

In Chapter 16 we dealt with a one-way analysis of variance, which is an experimental design having only one independent variable. In this chapter we are going to extend the analysis of variance to cover experimental designs involving two or more independent variables. For purposes of simplicity we will consider only experiments involving two independent variables, although the extension to more complex designs is quite simple (see Howell, 1987).

Consider a simple study in which we collect data on a dependent variable labeled Self-Confidence from three different groups of teenagers. Students in Group A participate primarily in athletic activities; students in Group S participate primarily in social activities; and students in Group U participate in no activities (they are uninvolved). This is a simple one-way design because we have only one independent variable (Group). Now suppose that we expand the design by collecting data from high school sophomores and seniors. This study would now contain two independent variables, designated Activity (with three **levels**: Athletic, Social, and Uninvolved) and Class (with two levels: Sophomore and Senior). In this context the independent variables are often referred to as **factors**, so we could speak of an Activity factor and a Class factor. The experiment I have just described has what is called a **two-way factorial design**.

If we wanted to expand this experiment even further, we could classify subjects additionally as male and female. We then would have what is called a *three-way factorial design*, with Activity, Class, and Sex as factors.

When we have an experimental design in which every level of every variable is paired with every level of every other variable, we have what is called a **factorial design**. In other words a factorial design is one in which we include all *combinations* of the levels of the independent variables. An example of a factorial design is shown in Table 17-1. In this chapter we will restrict ourselves to factorial designs in which the different treatment combinations are given to separate groups of subjects. When the research plan calls for the same subject to

Levels
The different values of an independent variable.

Factors
Another word for independent variables in the analysis of variance.

Two-way factorial design
An experimental design involving two variables in which every level of one variable is paired with every level of the other variable.

Factorial design
An experimental design in which every level of each variable is paired with every level of each other variable.

249

	Activity		
	Athletic	**Social**	**Uninvolved**
Sophomore Class	Athletic Sophomores	Social Sophomores	Uninvolved Sophomores
Senior Class	Athletic Seniors	Social Seniors	Uninvolved Seniors

be included under more than one treatment or combination of treatments, we will speak of *repeated-measures designs*. The discussion of simple repeated-measures designs will be covered in Chapter 18. Thus if we measured people when they were sophomores and measured those *same* people again when they were seniors, we would have a repeated-measures design and would not be able to use the analysis described in this chapter.

Factorial designs have several very important advantages over one-way designs. First of all they allow greater generalizability of the results. Consider the study involving Activity and Class. If we were to run an experiment using only the three Activity conditions, we would most likely use only one Class, and thus our results would apply only to that Class. When we use a factorial design with the three Activity conditions and two Classes, our results on Activity are averaged across the Classes, quite possibly resulting in a much broader interpretation of the data. At the same time we retain the ability to examine the data for each individual Class if we so desire.

Interaction

A situation in a factorial design in which the effects of one independent variable depend upon the level of another independent variable.

The second important feature of factorial designs is that they allow us to look at the **interaction** of variables. An interaction is present when the effect of one variable depends upon the particular level of another variable. If, for example, there were substantial differences in Self-Confidence for the different Activity levels when we looked at Sophomores, but no differences when we looked at Seniors, then the effect of Activity would depend on the Class the students are in. Thus we would say that Activity and Class interact. If on the other hand whatever differences there are among Activity groups are the same for Sophomores and Seniors, then the effect of Activity is independent of Class and there is no interaction.

A third advantage of a factorial design is its economy in terms of subjects. Because we will be averaging the effects of one variable across all levels of the other variable, a two-variable factorial will require fewer subjects than two one-ways (one on Activity and one on Class) for the same degree of power. Each subject is exposed to one level of each of two independent variables simultaneously—so we obtain information on two effects for the price of one. Essentially we are getting something for nothing, which is always nice.

As mentioned earlier, factorial designs are labeled by the number of variables involved. A factorial design with two independent variables or factors is called a two-way factorial, and one with three factors is called a three-way factorial. An alternative method of labeling designs is in terms of the number of levels of each variable. Our Self-Confidence study had two levels of the Class condition and three levels of Activity. As such, it might be referred to as a **2 × 3 factorial design**, where the first number refers to the number of rows and the second to the number of columns in the design shown in Table 17-1. A study with three variables, two of them having three levels and one having four levels, might be called a 3 × 3 × 4 factorial. The terms *two-way* and *2 × 3* are both common ways of designating designs.

In what follows we will concern ourselves primarily with the two-way analysis. Higher-order analyses are simply extensions of the two-way, and many of the issues we will discuss are most simply explained in terms of two variables.

2 × 3 Factorial design
A factorial design with one variable having two levels and the other having three levels.

17-1 NOTATION

In this chapter the notation will be kept as simple as possible so as not to add unnecessary confusion. The terms that commonly are used are illustrated in Table 17-2. The first thing to note is that names of factors are generally designated by the first letter (capitalized) of the factor name, and the individual levels of each factor are indicated by that capital letter with the appropriate subscript (e.g., for Class, Sophomores are denoted C_1 and Seniors are denoted C_2). The number of levels of the factor will be denoted by a lowercase letter corresponding to that factor. Thus Activity (A) has $a = 3$ levels, whereas Class (C) has $c = 2$ levels. Any specific combination of one level of one factor and one level of another (e.g., Social Seniors) is called a **cell**, and the number of observations per cell will be denoted by n. The total number of observations is $N = acn$, because there are $a \times c$ cells, each with n observations.

Cell
The combination of a particular row and column—the set of observations obtained under identical treatment conditions.

The subscripts i and j are used as general (nonspecific) notations for the level of rows and columns. Thus $cell_{ij}$ is the cell in the ith row and the jth column. $Cell_{23}$, for example, would be the Uninvolved Seniors. (Refer to Table 17-1.) The totals for the individual levels of Activity will be denoted T_{A_j}, whereas Class totals will be denoted T_{C_i}. Here again the subscripts A and C refer to the variable names, and T stands for "total." Cell totals are denoted as T_{ij}, and the Grand Total (the total of all N scores) is shown as either G or ΣX. Needless subscripts serve only as a source of confusion, and wherever possible they will be omitted. The notation described here will be used throughout the discussion of the analysis of variance, and it is important that you thoroughly understand it

TABLE 17-2
Factorial Design Showing Definitions of Terms

Class	Activity			
	A_1	A_2	A_2	
C_1	T_{11}	T_{12}	T_{13}	T_{C_1}
C_2	T_{21}	T_{22}	T_{23}	T_{C_2}
	T_{A_1}	T_{A_2}	T_{A_3}	$G = \Sigma X$

before proceeding. The advantage of this system is that it easily generalizes to other examples. Thus if we had a Drug × Sex factorial, it should be clear that T_{D_1} and T_{S_2} refer to the total of the first level of the Drug variable and to the second level of the Sex variable, respectively.

17-2   AN EXAMPLE—STUDENT SELF-CONFIDENCE

As an example we will take the 2 × 3 design that we have been discussing. The data and the analysis are shown in Table 17-3. The cell means are shown just for your information. The dependent variable is a Self-Confidence rating for each student. The rating scale runs from 0 to 25, with higher scores representing greater Self-Confidence. There are five observations per cell. Before we consider any calculations, look at the row and column means. These means give us a general idea of what to expect from the analysis. From the means you can see that Seniors (C_2) tend to show more Self-Confidence than Sophomores (C_1), regardless of Activity level, and that the Uninvolved students seem to have the lowest Self-Confidence. Moreover, the pattern of results across the cells for the three Activities seems to depend upon Class, since for Sophomores the Social group is approximately equal to the Uninvolved group, whereas for Seniors the Athletic and Social groups are nearly equal. Whether these conclusions suggested by the means are real or not is what the analysis of variance is designed to tell us.

Partition
To divide the total sum of squares into its constituent parts.

In the one-way analysis of variance we **partitioned** (split up) the total sum of squares (SS_{total}) into differences between groups (SS_{group}) and differences within the same group (SS_{error}). In the two-way we will do the same thing except that we do not have a single "group" term. What we do have is six cells, representing six different groups of subjects. But the cells are composed of people in different Activity groups, in different Classes, and in different Activity × Class combinations. What we are going to do with the two-way is to first partition SS_{total} into variability within cells (SS_{error}) and variability between the cell totals (SS_{cells}). We then will partition SS_{cells} into differences due to Classes (SS_C), differences due to Activity (SS_A), and the interaction of Class and Activity (SS_{CA}). This can be shown diagrammatically as follows:

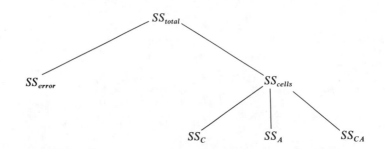

≡≡ **TABLE 17-3** ≡≡
Data and Calculations for 2 × 3 Factorial Design

(a) Data

Class	A_1 (Athletic)	A_2 (Social)	A_3 (Uninvolved)	Class Totals T_{C_j}
		Activity		
C_1 (Sophomores)	9 14 11 6 15 $\overline{55}$	10 6 8 7 12 $\overline{43}$	7 12 7 6 8 $\overline{40}$	138
C_2 (Seniors)	17 12 14 18 11 $\overline{72}$	15 18 16 13 15 $\overline{77}$	10 8 4 2 7 $\overline{31}$	180
Activity Totals (T_{A_i})	127	120	71	318 = G

(b) Cell Means

Class	A_1	A_2	A_3	Class Means
		Activity		
C_1	11.0	8.6	8.0	9.2
C_2	14.4	15.4	6.2	12.0
Activity Means	12.7	12.0	7.1	

(c) Calculations

$$SS_{total} = \Sigma X^2 - \frac{G^2}{N}$$

$$= 9^2 + 14^2 + \cdots + 2^2 + 7^2 - \frac{318^2}{30}$$

$$= 3900 - 3370.8 = 529.2$$

$$SS_{cells} = \frac{\Sigma T_{ij}^2}{n} - \frac{G^2}{N}$$

$$= \frac{55^2 + \cdots + 31^2}{5} - \frac{318^2}{30}$$

$$= 3709.6 - 3370.8 = 338.8$$

$$SS_{error} = SS_{total} - SS_{cells}$$

$$= 529.2 - 338.8 = 190.4$$

$$SS_C = \frac{\Sigma T_{C_i}^2}{na} - \frac{G^2}{N}$$

$$= \frac{138^2 + 180^2}{5(3)} - \frac{318^2}{30}$$

$$= 3429.6 - 3370.8 = 58.8$$

TABLE 17-3
(c) Calculations
(continued)

$$SS_A = \frac{\Sigma T_{A_j}^2}{nc} - \frac{G^2}{N}$$

$$= \frac{127^2 + 120^2 + 71^2}{5(2)} - \frac{318^2}{30}$$

$$= 3557.0 - 3370.8 = 186.2$$

$$SS_{CA} = SS_{cells} - SS_C - SS_A$$

$$= 338.8 - 58.8 - 186.2 = 93.8$$

(d) Summary Table

Source	df	SS	MS	F
Class	1	58.8	58.8	7.41*
Activity	2	186.2	93.1	11.74*
C × A	2	93.8	46.9	5.91*
Error	24	190.4	7.93	
Total	29	529.2		

*$p < .05$

The calculations for the sums of squares appear in part (c) of Table 17-3. Many of these calculations should be familiar, because they resemble the procedures used with a one-way. For example, SS_{total} is computed in exactly the same way that it was computed in Chapter 16, and in exactly the same way in which it is always computed. We sum all of the squared observations and subtract the Grand Total squared divided by N, that is, G^2/N.

The sum of squares for cells (SS_{cells}) is nothing but the SS_{group} we would obtain if this were a one-way analysis of variance with six groups (i.e., ignoring the factorial nature of the design). In other words we simply sum the squared cell totals, divide by the number of observations on which each cell total is based (n), and then subtract G^2/N.

The sum of squares for error is also obtained in the same way that it was in the one-way, if you consider SS_{cells} as a kind of SS_{group}. We simply subtract SS_{cells} from SS_{total}, and SS_{error} is what is left over. This makes sense because if SS_{total} is composed of both differences between the cell totals (SS_{cells}) and differences within the cells (SS_{error}), then subtracting SS_{cells} from SS_{total} leaves only differences within the cells.

SS_C is obtained just as it would be if this were a one-way and Activity were not a variable. In other words we simply compute the sum of squares on the Class totals. The same thing can be said for Activity, except that here you ignore the Class variable.

You will note that ΣT_C^2 is divided by na and ΣT_A^2 is divided by nc. If you try to remember these denominators as formulae, you will only succeed in accumulating unnecessary, and easily forgotten, information. The denominators represent the number of scores per total, and nothing more. Each class total is based on $na = (6)(3) = 18$ scores and each activity on $nb = (6)(2) = 12$ scores.

The SS_{cells} is a measure of how much the cell totals (and thus the cell means) differ. Two cell totals may differ for any of three reasons. They may differ because they come from different levels of Class; they may also differ because they come from different levels of Activity; and they may differ because of an interaction between Class and Activity. We know how much difference there is among the six cells (SS_{cells}). SS_C tells us how much of this difference can be attributed to differences in Class, and SS_A tells us how much can be attributed to differences in Activity. Whatever cannot be attributed to C or A must be attributable to the interaction of C and A (i.e., SS_{CA}). Thus to obtain SS_{CA} we simply subtract SS_C and SS_A from SS_{cells}. What is left over is SS_{CA}. In our example

$$SS_{CA} = SS_{cells} - SS_C - SS_A$$
$$93.8 = 338.8 - 58.8 - 186.2$$

The summary table for the analysis of variance is shown in part (d) of Table 17-3. The source column and the sum-of-squares column should be self-explanatory. The degrees-of-freedom column should also be familiar from what you know about the one-way. The $df_{total} = N - 1$, as they always do. The degrees of freedom for the effects of Class and Activity are just $c - 1$ and $a - 1$, as they would be in separate one-way analyses. The degrees of freedom for the interaction is the only really new term. We *always* compute $df_{interaction}$ as the product of the degrees of freedom for each component of the interaction. Thus $df_{CA} = df_C \times df_A = 1 \times 2 = 2$. Finally, the degrees of freedom for error are most easily obtained by subtraction. Thus $df_{error} = df_{total} - df_C - df_A - df_{CA}$. Alternatively, because MS_{error} is the average of the CA cell variances and because each cell variance has $n - 1$ df, MS_{error} has $ca(n - 1)$ degrees of freedom. These rules for degrees of freedom apply to any factorial analysis of variance, no matter how complex.

Just as with the one-way analysis of variance, the mean squares are obtained by dividing the sums of squares by the corresponding degrees of freedom. This is the same procedure we will use in any analysis.

Finally, to calculate F, we divide each mean square by MS_{error}. Thus for Class, $F_C = MS_C/MS_{error}$; for Activity, $F_A = MS_A/MS_{error}$; and for $C \times A$, $F_{CA} = MS_{CA}/MS_{error}$. Each of these Fs is based on the number of degrees of freedom for the term in question and the df_{error}. Thus the F for Class is on 1 and 24 df, whereas the Fs for Activity and the interaction are on 2 and 24 df. From Appendix D, Table 2, we find that the critical values of F are $F_{.05}(1,24) = 4.26$ and $F_{.05}(2,24) = 3.40$.

INTERPRETATION

From part (d) of Table 17-3 we see that all three Fs exceed their appropriate critical values and thus lead to rejection of the corresponding null hypotheses. Thus we can conclude that, averaged across (ignoring) Activity, Seniors have a

Main effect
The effect of one independent variable averaged across the levels of the other independent variables.

higher level of Self-Confidence than do Sophomores. We can also conclude that averaged across Class, Self-Confidence varies with Activity. Overall there appear to be higher levels of Self-Confidence for the Athletic and Social groups than for the Uninvolved group. These two effects are called **main effects** because each is concerned with the effect of *one* variable at a time, ignoring the other variable. However, we also have a significant interaction in this analysis, which may cast doubt on the meaning of one or both main effects. It may not be very useful to know that there is a main effect of Activity, for example, if the interaction is telling you that the Activity effect is not the same for each Class. The best way to interpret an interaction is to plot the means of one variable separately for each level of the other variable. You can see such a plot in Figure 17-1, in which the Activity means have been plotted separately for each Class. Here we can see the interaction in that the pattern of the Activity means for one Class is quite different from the pattern of the Activity means for the other Class. In such a case conclusions with respect to either main effect are probably not advisable.

17-3   INTERACTIONS

Students often have difficulty understanding what it means to say that two variables interact. I have said previously that a significant interaction means that the effect of one variable depends upon the level of the other variable. You saw this graphically in Figure 17-1. It may make the situation clearer to consider several plots of cell means that represent the presence or absence of an interaction. In Figure 17-2 the top three plots represent the case in which there is no interaction. You will note that in all three cases the lines are parallel, even though they may go up and down. Another way of saying this is to say that the difference between B_1 and B_2 (the effect of B) at A_1 is the same as at A_2 and at A_3. In the bottom set of three plots the lines are clearly not parallel. In the first, one line is flat and the other line rises. In the second, the lines actually cross. In the third, the lines don't cross, but they move in opposite directions. In every case

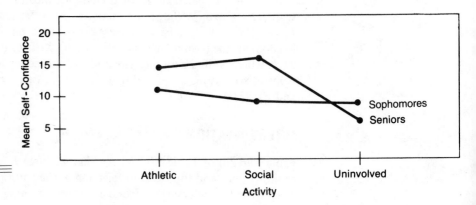

FIGURE 17-1
Plot of Class × Activity
Interaction

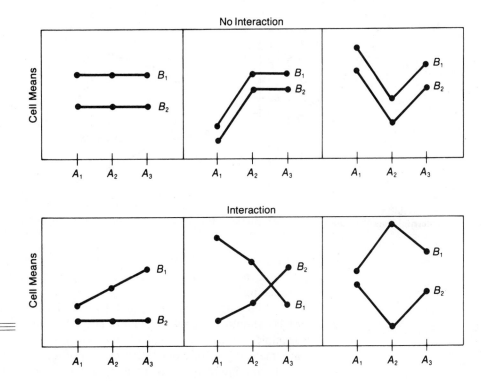

the effect of *B* is *not* the same at the different levels of *A*. Whenever the lines are (significantly) nonparallel, we say that we have an interaction.

One of the major benefits of factorial designs is the fact that they allow us to examine the interaction of variables. Indeed in many cases the interaction term may well be of greater interest than the main effects (the effects of variables taken individually). Consider, for example, a study in which we endeavor to change opinions concerning some issue. It might be reasonable to assume that if we took subjects who have no particular opinion on the issue, the more extreme our communication (within limits), the more the shift in the direction of the communication. On the other hand if subjects are strongly opposed to the position we advocate, stronger and stronger communications might well result in more and more of a shift *away* from our position. Data from such a hypothetical study are illustrated in the left half of Figure 17-3.

In this experiment it is obviously of very little interest to ask if there are differences between the two groups. Of course there are. We selected our groups on that basis initially, and our theory certainly would not predict that they will come closer together. At the same time we probably have very little interest in the main effect of the Strength-of-Communication variable. Because we expect that one set of scores will increase and the other will decrease, it is probably not of any interest how these diverging curves average out in the end. It is the interaction term that is of primary interest. We have predicted that the two groups will behave in different ways to different levels of the Communication

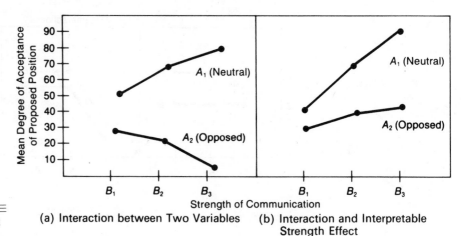

FIGURE 17-3
Hypothetical Data Illustrating
Interactions

(a) Interaction between Two Variables   (b) Interaction and Interpretable
Strength Effect

variable, and that is precisely what a significant interaction would tell us is happening.

Many people will argue that if you find a significant interaction, the main effects should be ignored. Some readers may see either of the two previous examples as an illustration of this principle. However, it is not reasonable automatically to rule out interpretation of main effects in the presence of *any* significant interaction. As an illustration of the problem, consider the data plotted in the right half of Figure 17-3 as representing alternative data we might have obtained from the communication experiment. These data are purely hypothetical, but they illustrate the point nicely.

Here we see that the two variables interact, since one curve has a much steeper slope than the other. However, both groups rise to some extent as the strength of the communication increases, and if this effect is significant, it may be worth knowing about. With a significant effect for Strength we would have data to suggest that if you cannot select your audience, you should make your message strong rather than weak (at least within the limits established by this study). For both groups a strong message will have more effect than a weak one, although the effect is not as noticeable for the Opposed group.

The important point in this discussion is that when an interaction is significant, the experimenter should look even more carefully than usual at the data before making any statements about the main effects. These statements may be justified or they may not, depending on the nature of the data.

17-4 SIMPLE EFFECTS

Simple effect
The effect of one independent
variable at one level of
another independent variable.

A very important technique for analyzing data that contain significant interactions is the examination and testing of what are called **simple effects**. A simple effect is defined as the effect of one variable at *one* level of the other variable. In our example the effect of the Communication variable for the Neutral group would be a simple effect. The effect of the Communication variable for the Opposed group would be another simple effect. A third simple effect might be the difference between Groups for the weakest level of the Communication variable.

The calculations associated with simple effects are very easy to carry out. As an illustration consider the earlier data on Self-Confidence. The overall difference between Sophomores and Seniors is a main effect, but the difference between Sophomores and Seniors *for only those people involved in Social Activities* is a simple effect. From our data the Social–Sophomore combination had a mean of 8.6, whereas the Social–Senior combination had a mean of 15.4. To compute the sum of squares for this simple effect we merely pretend that we have data only for people involved in Social Activities and we compute SS_{class} for just those data. The general formula for the simple effect of A at the first level of B (B_1) would be

$$SS_{A \text{ at } B_1} = \frac{\Sigma T^2_{A \text{ at } B_1}}{n} - \frac{(\Sigma T_{B_1})^2}{na}$$

For the case of the simple effect of Class at Social we have

$$SS_{Class \text{ at } Social} = \frac{43^2 + 77^2}{5} - \frac{120^2}{10} = 115.6$$

This is a sum of squares just like the sum of squares for a main effect. Because it is based on two totals it will have $2 - 1 = 1$ *df*. Therefore

$$MS_{Class \text{ at } Social} = \frac{115.6}{1} = 115.6$$

Using the error term from the original analysis

$$F = \frac{MS_{Class \text{ at } Social}}{MS_{error}} = \frac{115.6}{7.93} = 14.58$$

Because $F_{.05}(1,24) = 4.26$, we will reject H_0 and conclude that there are differences in Self-Confidence between Sophomores and Seniors involved in Social Activities. In other words the difference between the means 8.6 and 15.4 is significant.

As a second example we might wish to be sure that there is an Activity effect for the data on Sophomores. (A significant main effect for Activity would not guarantee this, because the main effect might be attributable to a large Activity effect for Seniors that would cause the *overall* Activity means to differ even if there were no differences for Sophomores. Such a result would most likely produce a significant interaction.) To obtain this simple effect we have

$$SS_{Activity \text{ at } Sophomore} = \frac{55^2 + 43^2 + 40^2}{5} - \frac{138^2}{15}$$

$$= 25.2$$

With three activities we have $3 - 1 = 2\ df$. Thus

$$MS_{Activity\ at\ Sophomore} = \frac{25.2}{2}$$

$$= 12.6$$

and

$$F = \frac{12.6}{7.93} = 1.59$$

Because $F_{.05}(2,24) = 3.40$, we cannot reject H_0. We will have to conclude that our data are consistent with the hypothesis that when you look only at Sophomores, Self-Confidence is the same for people involved in these different activities.

17-5 UNEQUAL SAMPLE SIZES

When we were dealing with a one-way analysis of variance, unequal sample sizes did not present a serious problem—we simply adjusted our formula accordingly. That is definitely not the case with factorial designs. Whenever we have a factorial design with unequal cell sizes, the calculations become considerably more difficult and the interpretation can be very unclear. The best solution is not to have unequal n's in the first place. Unfortunately the world is not always cooperative, and unequal n's are often the result. An extensive discussion of this problem is contained in Howell (1987).†

17-6 MAGNITUDE OF EFFECT

The methods for estimating the magnitude of effect for variables in a factorial design are simple extensions of the methods used with a one-way design. The most easily computed measure is again eta squared (η^2), although it is still a biased estimate of the value that we would obtain if we obtained observations on whole populations. For each effect (main effects or interactions) in the factorial design we compute η^2 by dividing the sum of squares for that effect by SS_{total}. For our example

$$\eta_C^2 = \frac{SS_C}{SS_{total}} = \frac{58.8}{529.2} = 0.11$$

$$\eta_A^2 = \frac{SS_A}{SS_{total}} = \frac{186.2}{529.2} = 0.35$$

---

†If you fall back on using computer programs to handle data with unequal n's—and you probably will—I recommend the BMDP series. If you use the SPSS package, be sure that you request Option 9 for the ANOVA program. The default option tests silly null hypotheses. At present Minitab does not readily handle unequal n's with factorial designs.

$$\eta^2_{CA} = \frac{SS_{CA}}{SS_{total}} = \frac{93.8}{529.2} = 0.18$$

$$\eta^2_{error} = \frac{SS_{error}}{SS_{total}} = \frac{190.4}{529.2} = 0.36$$

Thus within this experiment differences due to Class account for 11% of the variability, differences due to Activity account for 35%, and the interaction of these two variables accounts for 18%. Thirty-six percent of the variability is error variance and thus cannot be accounted for by either the main effects or the interaction.

As with the one-way analysis, η^2 is handy for making rough estimates of the contribution of variables. But a considerably less biased estimate is given by ω^2. The calculations, though somewhat more cumbersome, are straightforward.

$$\omega^2_C = \frac{SS_C - (c-1)MS_{error}}{SS_{total} + MS_{error}}$$

$$= \frac{58.8 - (1)7.93}{529.2 + 7.93} = 0.09$$

$$\omega^2_A = \frac{SS_A - (a-1)MS_{error}}{SS_{total} + MS_{error}}$$

$$= \frac{186.2 - (2)7.93}{529.2 + 7.93} = 0.32$$

$$\omega^2_{CA} = \frac{SS_{CA} - (c-1)(a-1)MS_{error}}{SS_{total} + MS_{error}}$$

$$= \frac{93.8 - (1)(2)7.93}{529.2 + 7.93} = 0.15$$

You will note that these values are slightly smaller than the values for η^2, although their interpretation is basically the same.

17-7   A SECOND EXAMPLE— MATERNAL ADAPTATION REVISITED

In Chapter 16 we considered an example of actual data on maternal adaptation for mothers of LBW (Experimental and Control) and Full-term infants (Nurcombe et al., 1985). We saw there that mothers in the Experimental (Intervention) and Full-term groups adapted better than those in the LBW Control group. A more complete analysis of those data might involve breaking down the groups by Maternal Education (High School or Less versus More Than High School). The authors of that study thought that the mothers with less education might benefit more from the Experimental program than would more

(a) Data

		Group 1	Group 2	Group 3	
		LBW Experimental	LBW Control	Full-term	Education Totals
High School Education or Less		14	25	18	
		20	19	14	
		22	21	18	
		13	20	20	
		13	20	12	
		18	14	14	
		13	25	17	
		14	18	17	
		127	162	130	419
More Than High School Education		11	18	16	
		11	16	20	
		16	13	12	
		12	21	14	
		12	17	18	
		13	10	20	
		17	16	12	
		13	21	13	
		105	132	125	362
Group Totals		232	294	255	781 = G

(b) Calculations

$$SS_{total} = \Sigma X^2 - \frac{G^2}{N}$$

$$= 14^2 + \cdots + 13^2 - \frac{781^2}{48}$$

$$= 13,363 - 12,707.52 = 655.48$$

$$SS_{cells} = \frac{\Sigma T_{ij}^2}{n} - \frac{G^2}{N}$$

$$= \frac{127^2 + \cdots + 125^2}{8} - \frac{781^2}{48}$$

$$= 12,918.375 - 12,707.52 = 210.86$$

$$SS_{error} = SS_{total} - SS_{cells}$$

$$= 655.48 - 210.86 = 444.62$$

$$SS_{educ} = \frac{\Sigma T_E^2}{ng} - \frac{G^2}{N}$$

$$= \frac{419^2 + 362^2}{(8)(3)} - \frac{781^2}{48}$$

$$= 12,775.21 - 12,707.52 = 67.69$$

TABLE 17-4
(b) Calculations
    (continued)

$$SS_{group} = \frac{\Sigma T_G^2}{ne} - \frac{G^2}{N} = \frac{232^2 + 294^2 + 255^2}{(8)(2)} - \frac{781^2}{48} = 122.79$$

$$SS_{EG} = SS_{cells} - SS_{educ} - SS_{group} = 210.86 - 67.69 - 122.79 = 20.38$$

(c) Summary Table

Source	df	SS	MS	F
Education	1	67.69	67.69	6.39*
Group	2	122.79	61.40	5.80*
E × G	2	20.38	10.19	<1
Error	42	444.62	10.59	
Total	47	655.48		

*$p < .05$

highly educated mothers. If this were true, the LBW Control versus LBW Experimental differences would be larger for the Low Education group than for the High Education group, giving us a significant interaction. The data and calculations for this analysis are presented in Table 17-4. These data are a subset of the real data, from which only the first eight observations in each cell have been selected. (The results agree with the results on the full data set.) You will note that there is both a Group effect and an Education effect (as indicated by the asterisks (*) following the F value), but that there is no interaction. (When F is less than 1, we normally report "$F < 1$" rather than give the actual value.) The lack of an interaction means that Group differences do not depend upon Education level, which runs counter to our experimental hypothesis. We would conclude from this analysis that both the amount of Education and the presence or absence of the intervention program had an effect on maternal adaptation. However, differences in adaptation observed among the groups did not depend upon the level of education.

17-8 USING MINITAB FOR FACTORIAL ANALYSIS OF VARIANCE

The printout from a Minitab analysis of the data in the previous example is shown in Table 17-5. The first two columns of data (C_1 and C_2) contain information on Education level (coded 1 or 2) and Group (coded 1, 2, or 3), and the third column (C_3) contains the dependent variable. Notice that Minitab does not print the F values, but they are easily obtained by dividing the mean squares by the error term. You will also see that the cell means and the row and column means are presented. This is very helpful for interpreting the interaction effect, if any, and the cell means can be used to make a plot of the results. Finally, notice that Minitab produces confidence limits on the three Group means and on the two Education means.

===== **TABLE 17-5** =====
Minitab Analysis of Data in
Table 17-4

```
MTB > RETRIEVE 'TWOWA.MIN'
MTB > PRINT C1-C3
 ROW   EDUC   GROUP   ADAPT

   1     1      1       14
   2     1      1       20
   3     1      1       22
   4     1      1       13
   5     1      1       13
   6     1      1       18
   7     1      1       13
   8     1      1       14
   9     1      2       25
  10     1      2       19
  11     1      2       21
  12     1      2       20
  13     1      2       20
  14     1      2       14
  15     1      2       25
  16     1      2       18
  17     1      3       18
  18     1      3       14
  19     1      3       18
  20     1      3       20
  21     1      3       12
  22     1      3       14
  23     1      3       17
  24     1      3       17
  25     2      1       11
  26     2      1       11
  27     2      1       16
  28     2      1       12
  29     2      1       12
  30     2      1       13
  31     2      1       17
  32     2      1       13
  33     2      2       18
  34     2      2       16
  35     2      2       13
  36     2      2       21
  37     2      2       17
  38     2      2       10
  39     2      2       16
  40     2      2       21
  41     2      3       16
  42     2      3       20
  43     2      3       12
  44     2      3       14
  45     2      3       18
  46     2      3       20
  47     2      3       12
  48     2      3       13
MTB > TWOWAY ANOVA ON 'ADAPT' BY 'GROUP' AND 'EDUC'
     ANALYSIS OF VARIANCE   ADAPT

        SOURCE        DF      SS       MS
        GROUP          2    122.8     61.4
        EDUC           1     67.7     67.7
        INTERACTION    2     20.4     10.2
        ERROR         42    444.6     10.6
        TOTAL         47    655.5

MTB > STOP
```

17-9　A FINAL WORKED EXAMPLE

In Chapter 14 I referred to a study of recall of verbal material by Eysenck (1974).
At that time we considered only part of the overall study. In this section we will
examine the experiment in its entirety.

Eysenck was interested in looking at recall as a function of (1) Age of Subjects and (2) Level of Processing. He was trying to test the hypothesis that material that was more completely processed by the individual was better recalled. He further hypothesized that older subjects would recall less material overall, but that the major difference would come in conditions that required more processing. In other words, in conditions with minimal processing, differences between younger and older subjects would be small or nonexistent. In conditions that required more processing, age differences would be substantial. If this expectation were to hold, we would have an Age by Condition interaction.

Eysenck varied the depth of processing involved in his tasks by varying the instructions to subjects. In the Counting condition subjects were shown a list of words and asked to count the number of letters in each word. In the Rhyming condition subjects were asked to make up a word that rhymed with each word on the list. The Adjective condition required the subject to think of an adjective that would be appropriate to modify the words on the list. In the Imagery condition subjects were asked to think of an image that the words evoked. Finally, in the Intentional condition subjects were told to memorize the words for later recall. In all conditions subjects were asked to recall the words after they had gone through the list as instructed, but only in the last condition were subjects warned in advance that they would have to recall them. It should be apparent that as we move from the Counting condition up to at least the Imagery condition, subjects are required to process the words more completely.

The study included 50 subjects in the 18-to-30–year age range and 50 subjects in the 55-to-65–year age range. The data in Table 17-6 have been created to have the same means and standard deviations as those reported by Eysenck. The table contains all the calculations for a standard analysis of variance, and we will discuss each of these in turn. Before beginning the analysis, it is important to note that the data themselves are approximately normally distributed with acceptably equal variances. You can tell from the cell and marginal totals that recall appears to increase with greater processing, and younger subjects seem to recall more items than do older subjects. Notice also that the difference between younger and older subjects seems to depend on the task, with greater differences for those tasks that involve deeper processing. We will have more to say about these results after we consider the analysis itself.

From the summary table it is clear that both main effects and the interaction are significant at $p < .05$. Thus younger subjects, overall, recalled more words than did older subjects; tasks that involved greater processing showed better recall than tasks involving less processing; and, most important, the differences between the two age groups were greater in those tasks involving greater processing.

As a final illustration of the calculation of simple effects, we might wish to ask if there are Age differences in that condition that requires the least processing and, for good measure, in that condition that requires the most. Also, for the sake of an example, we can ask if there are significant differences among the Conditions for the older subjects.

TABLE 17-6
Data and Computations for
Example from Eysenck (1974)
(a) Data

			Recall Conditions			
	Counting	Rhyming	Adjective	Imagery	Intentional	T_{A_i}
	9	7	11	12	10	
	8	9	13	11	19	
	6	6	8	16	14	
	8	6	6	11	5	
Old	10	6	14	9	10	
	4	11	11	23	11	
	6	6	13	12	14	
	5	3	13	10	15	
	7	8	10	19	11	
	7	7	11	11	11	
	70	69	110	134	120	503
Age						
	8	10	14	20	21	
	6	7	11	16	19	
	4	8	18	16	17	
	6	10	14	15	15	
Young	7	4	13	18	22	
	6	7	22	16	16	
	5	10	17	20	22	
	7	6	16	22	22	
	9	7	12	14	18	
	7	7	11	19	21	
	65	76	148	176	193	658
T_{C_j}	135	145	258	310	313	1161 = G

(b) Calculations

$$\Sigma X^2 = 16,147 \qquad G^2/N = 1161^2/100 = 13,479.21$$

$$SS_{total} = \Sigma X^2 - G^2/N = 16,147 - 13,479.21 = 2667.79$$

$$SS_{Age} = \frac{\Sigma T_A^2}{nc} - \frac{G^2}{N} = \frac{503^2 + 658^2}{50} - \frac{1161^2}{100}$$

$$= 13,719.46 - 13,479.21 = 240.25$$

$$SS_{Cond} = \frac{\Sigma T_C^2}{na} - \frac{G^2}{N} = \frac{135^2 + 145^2 + 258^2 + 310^2 + 313^2}{20} - \frac{1161^2}{100}$$

$$= 14,994.15 - 13,479.21 = 1514.94$$

$$SS_{cells} = \frac{\Sigma T_{ij}^2}{n} - \frac{G^2}{N} = \frac{70^2 + 69^2 + \cdots + 176^2 + 193^2}{10} - \frac{1161^2}{100}$$

$$= 15,424.70 - 13,479.21 = 1945.49$$

$$SS_{AC} = SS_{cells} - SS_A - SS_C$$

$$= 1945.49 - 240.25 - 1514.94 = 190.30$$

$$SS_{error} = SS_{total} - SS_{cells} = 2667.79 - 1945.49 = 722.30$$

(c) Summary Table

Source	df	SS	MS	F
Age	1	240.25	240.250	29.94*
Condition	4	1514.94	378.735	47.19*
AC	4	190.30	47.575	5.93*
Error	90	722.30	8.026	
Total	99	2667.79		

*$p < .05$

To obtain the simple effects of Age at the Counting and Imagery conditions separately, we need to take the Age totals for each of those conditions. We then run what amounts to a one-way analysis of variance under each of the two conditions, but using the MS_{error} from the overall analysis of variance to compute our Fs. Similarly for the effect of conditions for the older subjects. These calculations follow:

1. Simple effect of Age at Count:

$$SS_{A \text{ at Count}} = \frac{70^2 + 65^2}{10} - \frac{135^2}{20} = 912.50 - 911.25 = 1.25$$

$$MS_{A \text{ at Count}} = \frac{SS_{A \text{ at Count}}}{1} = 1.25$$

$$F = \frac{MS_{A \text{ at Count}}}{MS_{error}} = \frac{1.250}{8.026} < 1$$

2. Simple effect of Age at Imagery:

$$SS_{A \text{ at Imagery}} = \frac{134^2 + 176^2}{10} - \frac{310^2}{20} = 4893.20 - 4805.00 = 88.20$$

$$MS_{A \text{ at Imagery}} = \frac{SS_{A \text{ at Imagery}}}{1} = 88.20$$

$$F = \frac{MS_{A \text{ at Imagery}}}{MS_{error}} = \frac{88.20}{8.026} = 10.99$$

3. Simple effect of Condition at Old:

$$SS_{C \text{ at Old}} = \frac{70^2 + 69^2 + \cdots + 120^2}{10} - \frac{503^2}{50}$$

$$= 5411.70 - 5060.18 = 351.52$$

$$MS_{C \text{ at Old}} = \frac{SS_{C \text{ at Old}}}{4} = \frac{351.52}{4} = 87.88$$

$$F = \frac{MS_{c \text{ at Old}}}{MS_{error}} = \frac{87.88}{8.026} = 10.95$$

From these simple effects we can see that there are no differences in recall between younger and older subjects for the simplest task, but there are differences for a task that involves a great deal of processing. We can also see that for older subjects there are significant differences in recall as a function of the required depth of processing.

17-10 SUMMARY

In this chapter we have extended the discussion of the analysis of variance to include designs involving two independent variables. In the factorial analysis we have assumed that there are still different subjects in the different cells. We considered some of the advantages of factorial designs, especially the fact that they allow us to look at the interaction effects of two variables. We also considered briefly the topic of simple effects (the effect of one variable at *one* level of the other variable), the problems posed by unequal sample sizes, and procedures for estimating the magnitude of experimental effects. Some of the most important terms in this chapter are:

□ Levels   □ 2 × 3 factorial design
□ Factors   □ Cell
□ Two-way factorial design   □ Partition
□ Factorial design   □ Main effect
□ Interaction   □ Simple effect

17-11 EXERCISES

17-1 In a more complete study of restaurant behavior than we had in Chapter 16 (Exercise 16-3) we observe restaurant patrons who sit as same-sex couples. We record the price of the entrée ordered by one person in each pair and categorize subjects on the basis of the subject's sex and whether or not he/she pays the bill. The data follow:

Host		Guest	
Male	Female	Male	Female
8.00	8.25	9.75	8.75
7.00	8.75	10.25	9.00
8.25	9.75	9.50	9.25
9.00	8.00	9.00	8.50
8.25	9.25	10.50	8.75

Run a two-way analysis of variance on these data.

17-2 In a study of mother–infant interaction, mothers are rated by trained observers on the quality of their

interactions with their infants. Mothers were classified on the basis of whether or not this was their first child (primiparous versus multiparous) and on the basis of whether this was a low-birthweight (LBW) infant or a full-term (FT) infant. The data represent a score on a 12-point scale, on which a higher score represents better mother–infant interaction.

Primiparous		Multiparous	
LBW	FT	LBW	FT
6	8	7	9
5	7	8	8
5	7	8	9
4	6	9	9
9	7	8	3
6	2	2	10
2	5	1	9
6	8	9	8
5	7	9	7
5	7	8	10

Run and interpret the appropriate analysis of variance.

17–3 Referring to Exercise 17-2, it seems obvious that the sample sizes do not reflect the relative frequency of these characteristics in the population. Would you expect the mean for all these primiparous mothers to be a good estimate of the population of primiparous mothers? Why?

17–4 Use simple effect procedures to compare low-birthweight and normal-birthweight conditions for multiparous mothers.

17–5 In a study of memory processes, animals were tested on a one-trial avoidance learning task. The animals were presented with a fear-producing stimulus on the *learning* trial as soon as they stepped across a line in the test chamber. The dependent variable was the time it took them to step across the line on the subsequent (*test*) trial. Three groups of animals differed in terms of the area in which electrodes were implanted in their brains (Neutral Site, Area A, or Area B). Each group was further divided and given electrical stimulation either 50, 100, or 150 msec after crossing the line and being presented with the fear-inducing stimulus. If the brain area that was stimulated is involved in memory, stimulation would be expected to interfere with memory consolidation and retard learning of the avoidance response, and the animal should not show any hesitancy in recrossing the line. The data on latency to recross the line are as follows:

	Neutral Site		Stimulation Area Area A			Area B		
50	**100**	**150**	**50**	**100**	**150**	**50**	**100**	**150**
25	30	28	11	31	23	23	18	28
30	25	31	18	20	28	30	24	21
28	27	26	26	22	35	18	9	30
40	35	20	15	23	27	28	16	30
20	23	35	14	19	21	23	13	23

Run the analysis of variance.

17–6 Plot the cell means in Exercise 17-5.

17–7 Use the protected t test to compare the Neutral Site to each of the other sites, ignoring Delay of Stimulation. (*Hint*: Follow the procedures outlined in Chapter 16, but be sure that you take n_i as the number of scores on which $\bar{X}_i$ is based.)

17–8 Use Scheffé's test in place of the protected t in Exercise 17-7.

17–9 Use simple effects to examine the effect of Delay of Stimulation in Area A.

17–10 If you go back to Exercise 16-4, you will see that it really forms a 2×2 factorial. Run the factorial analysis and interpret the results.

17–11 In Exercise 16-4 you ran a test between Groups 1 and 3 combined versus Groups 2 and 4 combined. How does that test compare to testing the main effect of Location in Exercise 17-10? Is there any difference?

17–12 Calculate η^2 and ω^2 for the data in Section 17-9.

17–13 Make up a set of data for a 2×2 design that has two main effects but no interaction.

17–14 Make up a set of data for a 2×2 design that has no main effects but does have an interaction.

17–15 Describe a reasonable experiment in which the primary interest would be in the interaction effect.

17–16 Calculate η^2 and ω^2 for Exercise 17-1.

17–17 Calculate η^2 and ω^2 for Exercise 17-2.

17–18 Make up a diagram like that on page 252 to show the partition of the degrees of freedom.

17–19 Calculate η^2 and ω^2 for the Minitab output in Table 17-5.

17–20 By comparing the formulae for η^2 and ω^2, tell when these two different statistics would be in close agreement and when they would disagree noticeably.

17–21 In the Eysenck (1974) study analyzed in Section 17-9, the real test of Eysenck's hypothesis about changes with age is found in the interaction. Why?

REPEATED-MEASURES DESIGNS

Between-subjects designs
Designs in which different subjects serve under the different treatment levels.

Repeated-measures design
An experimental design in which each subject receives all levels of at least one independent variable.

In the previous two chapters we have been concerned with experimental designs in which there are different subjects in each group or cell. They are called **between-subjects designs** because they involve comparisons between different groups of subjects. However, many experimental designs involve having the same subject serve under more than one treatment condition. For example, we might take a baseline measurement of some behavior (i.e., a measurement before any treatment program begins), take another measurement at the end of a treatment program, and then yet a third measurement at the end of a six-month follow-up period. A design such as this one in which subjects are measured repeatedly is called a **repeated-measures design**. Such designs are the subject of this chapter.

There are a wide variety of repeated-measures designs, depending on whether each subject serves under all levels of all variables or whether some variables involve different groups of subjects while others involve the same subjects. In this chapter we will be concerned only with the simplest case, in which there is one independent variable and each subject serves under all levels of that variable. For the analysis of more complex designs you can refer to Howell (1987) or Winer (1971).

18-1 AN EXAMPLE—
THE TREATMENT OF MIGRAINE HEADACHES

As an example of a simple repeated-measures design we will consider a study of the effectiveness of relaxation techniques in controlling migraine headaches. The data described here are fictitious, but they are in general agreement with data collected by Blanchard et al. (1978), who ran a very similar, though more complex, study.

For our experiment we recruited nine migraine sufferers and asked them to record the frequency and duration of migraine headaches. After four weeks of baseline recording during which no training was given, we had a six-week period of relaxation training. (Each experimental subject participated in the program at a different time, so such things as changes in climate and holiday events [e.g., Christmas] should not systematically influence the data.) For our example we will analyze the data for the last two weeks of baseline and the last three weeks of training. The dependent variable is the duration (hours/week) of headaches in each of those five weeks. The data and the calculations are shown in Table 18-1.

Look first at the data in Table 18-1. You will note that there is a great deal of variability in the data, but much of that variability comes from the fact that some people have more and/or longer-duration headaches than others, which really has very little to do with the intervention program. What we are able to do with a repeated-measures design, but were not able to do with between-subjects designs, is to remove this variability from SS_{total}. This has the effect of removing subject differences from the error term and producing a smaller MS_{error} than we would otherwise have. We do this by calculating a term called $SS_{subjects}$, which measures differences among people in terms of their reported headache durations. The $SS_{subjects}$ term is then subtracted from SS_{total}, along with SS_{weeks}, when we calculate SS_{error}. (In the previous design, in which every score represented a different subject, if we had calculated a $SS_{subjects}$ it would have been the same thing as SS_{total}.)

From Table 18-1 you can see that SS_{total} is calculated in the usual manner. Similarly $SS_{subjects}$ and SS_{weeks} are calculated just as main effects always are (square the relevant totals, sum, divide by the number of observations per total, and subtract G^2/N). Finally the error term is obtained by subtracting $SS_{subjects}$ and SS_{weeks} from SS_{total}.

TABLE 18-1
Analysis of Data on Migraine Headaches
(a) Data

Subject	Baseline Week 1	Baseline Week 2	Training Week 3	Training Week 4	Training Week 5	Subject Totals
1	21	22	8	6	6	63
2	20	19	10	4	9	62
3	7	5	5	4	5	26
4	25	30	13	12	4	84
5	30	33	10	8	6	87
6	19	27	8	7	4	65
7	26	16	5	2	5	54
8	13	4	8	1	5	31
9	26	24	14	8	17	89
Week Totals	187	180	81	52	61	561 = G
Week Means	20.78	20.00	9.00	5.78	6.78	12.47

TABLE 18-1
(b) Calculations
(continued)

$$SS_{total} = \Sigma X^2 - \frac{G^2}{N}$$

$$= 21^2 + 20^2 + \cdots + 5^2 + 17^2 - \frac{561^2}{45}$$

$$= 10{,}483 - 6993.8 = 3489.2$$

$$SS_{subjects} = \frac{\Sigma T_S^2}{w} - \frac{G^2}{N}$$

$$= \frac{63^2 + \cdots + 89^2}{5} - \frac{561^2}{45}$$

$$= 7827.4 - 6993.8 = 833.6$$

$$SS_{weeks} = \frac{\Sigma T_W^2}{n} - \frac{G^2}{N}$$

$$= \frac{187^2 + \cdots + 61^2}{9} - \frac{561^2}{45}$$

$$= 8928.3 - 6993.8 = 1934.5$$

$$SS_{error} = SS_{total} - SS_{subjects} - SS_{weeks}$$

$$= 3489.2 - 833.6 - 1934.5 = 721.1$$

(c) Summary Table

Source	df	SS	MS	F
Subjects	8	833.6		
Weeks	4	1934.5	483.625	21.46*
Error	32	721.1	22.534	
Total	44	3489.2		

*$p < .05$

    The summary table is shown in part (c) of Table 18-1. You will notice that I have computed an F for Weeks, but not for Subjects. The reason for this is that MS_{error} is not an appropriate denominator for an F on subjects, because both numerator and denominator would not necessarily be estimating the same thing even if H_0 were true. Therefore we cannot test the Subjects variable. This is not a great loss, however, because we rarely are concerned with determining whether subjects are different from one another. We only computed $SS_{subjects}$ to allow us to compute an appropriate error term to test Weeks.

    The F value for Weeks is based on 4 and 32 degrees of freedom, and $F_{.05}(4,32) = 2.68$. We can therefore reject $H_0: \mu_1 = \mu_2 = \cdots = \mu_5$ and conclude that the relaxation program led to a reduction in the duration per week of headaches reported by subjects. Examination of the means in Table 18-1 reveals that during the last three weeks of training the amount of time per week involving migraine headaches was about one-third of what it was during baseline.

You may have noticed that no Subjects × Weeks interaction is shown in the summary table. With only one score per cell, the interaction term *is* the error term, and in fact some people prefer to use S × W instead of Error. No matter whether you think of it as Error or as the S × W interaction, this term is still the appropriate denominator for the *F* on Weeks.

18-2 MULTIPLE COMPARISONS

If we should wish to carry the analysis further and make comparisons among means, we can use the protected *t* procedure discussed in Chapter 16. The MS_{error} in this analysis would be the appropriate term to use in the protected *t*. For our data the results are clearcut, and there is little or nothing to be gained by making multiple comparisons. However, it is useful to demonstrate the procedure because it allows us to check on one of our methodological assumptions and also to see how to test means of combined groups.

The first comparison we might wish to make is the comparison of the two means for the Baseline period. We want to be sure that there was no improvement even before treatment began, simply as a result of being in an experimental situation. Because the overall *F* was significant, we can use the protected *t* to make this comparison. For *t* we have

$$t = \frac{\bar{X}_i - \bar{X}_j}{\sqrt{MS_{error}\left(\frac{1}{n_i} + \frac{1}{n_j}\right)}} = \frac{\bar{X}_1 - \bar{X}_2}{\sqrt{MS_{error}\left(\frac{1}{n_1} + \frac{1}{n_2}\right)}}$$

$$= \frac{20.78 - 20.00}{\sqrt{22.53(1/9 + 1/9)}} = \frac{0.78}{\sqrt{5.01}} = \frac{0.78}{2.24} = 0.35$$

This *t* has df_{error} degrees of freedom because MS_{error} was used in place of the pooled variance. A *t* of 0.35 is clearly not significant at $\alpha = .05$. Thus we have no reason to suspect an improvement before the introduction of treatment. Note that we were able to run the protected *t* test *as if* the means were from two independent samples because the error term has been adjusted accordingly.

The most obvious comparison, given the nature of the experiment, is between the Baseline trials and the Training trials. The 18 Baseline observations have a mean of 20.39, and the 27 Training observations have a mean of 7.19. Thus

$$t = \frac{\bar{X}_i - \bar{X}_j}{\sqrt{MS_{error}\left(\frac{1}{n_i} + \frac{1}{n_j}\right)}}$$

$$= \frac{20.39 - 7.19}{\sqrt{22.53(1/18 + 1/27)}} = \frac{13.20}{\sqrt{2.086}} = \frac{13.20}{1.44} = 9.17$$

Again this t has 32 degrees of freedom because it uses MS_{error}. This t is definitely significant at $\alpha = .05$, indicating a difference in the mean duration of headaches between the Baseline and Training phases of the study.

You might wonder how we can apply what *appears* to be a standard independent groups t test when we know that the data are not independent. You will recall that in Chapter 13 we handled dependent observations by forming differences and then taking the standard deviation of the differences. In a footnote in Chapter 14 (page 189) I pointed out that this had been necessary because we could not easily calculate the variances of differences (of *dependent* samples) directly from X_1 and X_2 unless we knew the correlation between X_1 and X_2. However, for a repeated-measures analysis of variance MS_{error} is in fact an estimate of the standard error of the differences, even though we don't use difference scores to calculate it. You can easily demonstrate this to yourself by running a repeated-measures analysis of variance and a t test for two related samples on the same set of data (e.g., use the Baseline data from this experiment) and noticing the similarities among the terms you calculate.

18-3 ASSUMPTIONS INVOLVED IN REPEATED-MEASURES DESIGNS

Repeated-measures designs involve the same assumptions of normality and homogeneity of variance that are required for any analysis of variance. In addition they also require (for most practical purposes) the assumption that the correlations among pairs of levels of the repeated variable are constant. In the case of our example this would mean that we assume that (in the population) the correlation between Week 1 and Week 2 is the same as the correlation between Weeks 2 and 3, and so on. For example, if the correlation between Duration at Week 1 and Duration at Week 2 is 0.50, then the correlation between Duration for any other pair of Weeks should also be about 0.50. This is a rather stringent assumption, and one that probably is violated at least as often as it is met. The test is not seriously affected unless this assumption is quite seriously violated. If it is seriously violated, there are two things you can do to ease the situation. The first thing is to limit the levels of the independent variable to those that have a chance of meeting the assumption. For example, if you are running a learning study in which *everyone* starts out knowing nothing and ends up knowing everything, the correlation between early and late trials will be near zero, whereas the correlations between pairs of intermediate trials probably will be high. In this case do not include the earliest and latest trials in your analysis. They probably wouldn't tell you much anyway.

The second thing you can do is to use a conservative procedure proposed by Greenhouse and Geisser (1959). For our example we had $(w-1)$ and $(w-1) \times (n-1)$ df for our F. Greenhouse and Geisser showed that if you took the same F

but evaluated it on 1 and $1(n-1)\,df$, you would have a conservative test no matter how serious the violation. For a further discussion of this correction and for a less conservative (but more complex) one, see Howell (1987).

18-4   ADVANTAGES AND DISADVANTAGES OF REPEATED-MEASURES DESIGNS

The major advantage of repeated-measures designs has already been discussed. Where there are large individual differences among subjects, these differences lead to large variability in the data. When subjects are measured only once, we cannot separate subject differences from random error, and everything goes into the error term. However, when we measure subjects repeatedly, we can assess subject differences and separate them from error. This produces a more *powerful* experimental design and thus makes it easier to reject H_0.

The disadvantages of repeated-measures designs are similar to the disadvantages we discussed with respect to related sample t tests (which are just a special case of repeated-measures designs). When subjects are used repeatedly, there is always the risk of carry-over effects from one trial to the next. For example, the drug you administer on Trial 1 may not have worn off by Trial 2. Similarly a subject may learn something on early trials that will help her on later trials. In some situations this problem can be reduced by **counter-balancing** the order in which treatments are administered. Thus half the subjects might have Treatment A followed by Treatment B, and the other half might receive Treatment B followed by Treatment A. This counter-balancing will not make carry-over effects disappear, but it may make them affect both treatments equally. Although there are disadvantages associated with repeated-measures designs, in most situations the advantages outweigh the disadvantages, and such designs are popular and are extremely useful in experimental work.

Counter-balancing
An arrangement of treatment conditions designed to balance out practice effects.

18-5   USING MINITAB TO ANALYZE DATA IN A REPEATED-MEASURES DESIGN

Minitab was not designed to analyze repeated-measures designs and normally cannot be used for that purpose. However, it is possible to trick Minitab into analyzing the data in Table 18-1 by pretending that this is a Subjects × Weeks factorial (i.e., ignoring the fact that Weeks is a repeated measure) and then calculating only the F for Weeks. The printout from this analysis is shown in Table 18-2. Notice that the cell means are also the individual observations, because $n = 1$ in all cells. Although it is possible to use such tricks to analyze more complex designs, it isn't really worth the effort. If you really need to analyze complex repeated-measures designs, I suggest you find someone who can show you how to use the BMDP or SAS computer packages.

```
MTB > RETRIEVE 'HEAD.MIN'
MTB > TWOWAY ANOVA ON 'DURATION' BY 'SUBJ' AND 'WEEK'

ANALYSIS OF VARIANCE   DURATION

SOURCE       DF       SS      MS
SUBJ          8     833.6   104.2
WEEK          4    1934.5   483.6
ERROR        32     721.1    22.5
TOTAL        44    3489.2

MTB > STOP
```

18-6 A FINAL WORKED EXAMPLE

As a final example I will adapt an example from Chapter 17 to illustrate the differences and similarities between repeated measures and the more traditional analysis of variance. In Chapter 17 we used the data from Eysenck (1974) on recall as a function of depth of processing. We examined the simple effect of Conditions on older subjects, which really amounts to a one-way analysis of variance using just the older subjects, except that we use MS_{error} from the overall analysis. In this chapter I will use the same set of numbers on older subjects for the sake of continuity. However, I am going to rearrange the data points to look like what we would expect to obtain if everyone served under each of the five recall conditions rather than only one.† I have merely shifted scores up and down in a column so that an individual who was one of the poorer scorers under one condition is also a poor scorer under the other conditions, and similarly for subjects showing good recall. The numbers in each group are still the same. (If you moved these new data back into Chapter 17 you would obtain exactly the same results.) The data follow, with an additional column on the right for the Subject totals:

Subject	Count	Rhyming	Adjective	Imagery	Intent	Subject Total
1	4	3	6	9	5	27
2	5	6	8	12	10	41
3	6	6	10	11	15	48
4	6	8	11	11	11	47
5	7	6	14	11	11	49
6	7	7	11	10	11	46
7	8	7	13	19	14	61
8	8	6	13	16	14	57
9	9	9	13	12	10	53
10	10	11	11	23	19	74
Totals	70	69	110	134	120	503

†We would never cavalierly rearrange real data like this. I did it here only to show the differences and similarities between the two experimental situations.

First we will calculate the SS_{total}:

$$SS_{total} = \Sigma X^2 - \frac{G^2}{N} = 4^2 + 5^2 + \cdots + 19^2 - \frac{503^2}{50}$$

$$= 5847 - 5060.18 = 786.82$$

We now have two main effects to calculate, one based on the Condition totals and one based on the Subject totals:

$$SS_{conditions} = \frac{T_C^2}{n} - \frac{G^2}{N} = \frac{70^2 + 69^2 + \cdots + 120^2}{10} - \frac{503^2}{50}$$

$$= 5411.70 - 5060.18 = 351.52$$

$$SS_{Subjects} = \frac{T_S^2}{c} - \frac{G^2}{N} = \frac{27^2 + 41^2 + \cdots + 74^2}{5} - \frac{503^2}{50}$$

$$= 5339 - 5060.18 = 278.82$$

The error term can now be obtained by subtraction:

$$SS_{error} = SS_{total} - SS_{Conditions} - SS_{Subjects}$$

$$= 786.82 - 351.52 - 278.82 = 156.48$$

This error term is also equivalent to the Conditions × Subjects interaction, as described in the text.

We now set up the Summary Table:

Source	df	SS	MS	F
Subjects	9	278.82		
Conditions	4	351.52	87.88	20.22
Error	36	156.48	4.35	
Total	49	786.82		

To test the F for the Conditions effect we go to the F table with 4 and 36 degrees of freedom. From Appendix D, Table 2, we find, with interpolation, that the critical value of F is 2.65. Because $20.22 > 2.65$, we will reject the null hypothesis and conclude that recall of verbal material varies with the conditions under which that material is learned.

If you go back to the example in Chapter 17 (page 267), you will see that I computed the simple effect of Condition for the older group. That F should differ for two reasons. The first reason is minor and is due to the fact that in Chapter 17 the error term was based on the full set of data and not just the data for the older subjects. That shouldn't really change things very much. The second reason for obtaining a noticeably different F is that in this example I have acted as if the subjects served under *all* conditions rather than just one. This means that any systematic subject differences will be removed from the error term. That is exactly what happened. In the previous analysis MS_{error} was 8.026. Here it is

4.35. This difference has resulted in an F that is approximately twice as large as the former F.

It is important to keep in mind that I have moved the data around slightly to produce subjects who were consistently poor or consistently good. But this is nothing more than you would expect to find if you used the same subjects under all conditions. From a comparison of the F here and the one in Chapter 17, you can see that you generally increase the power of an experiment, and therefore the probability of finding a significant difference, by using a repeated-measures design if it is practical and appropriate.

18-7 SUMMARY

In this chapter we have seen how to handle data in which individual subjects have served under all levels of one or more independent variables. We examined a simple case of a repeated-measures design and saw that such designs remove differences among subjects from the error term. By eliminating individual differences from MS_{error}, repeated-measures designs are generally more powerful than comparable between-subjects designs. Some of the most important terms in this chapter are:

□ **Between-subjects designs**   □ **Counter-balancing**
□ **Repeated-measures designs**

18-8 EXERCISES

18-1 It is at least part of the folklore that repeated experience with the Graduate Record Examination (GRE) leads to better scores, even without any intervening study. We obtained eight subjects and gave them the GRE verbal exam every Saturday morning for three weeks. The data are given in the following table:

Subject	Test Session		
	1	2	3
1	550	570	580
2	440	440	470
3	610	630	610
4	650	670	670
5	400	460	450
6	700	680	710
7	490	510	510
8	580	550	590

Run the appropriate analysis of variance. What, if any-

thing, would you conclude about practice effects on the GRE?

18-2 Use the data from Exercise 18-1 to answer (a) and (b).

(a) Delete the data for the third session and run a (related-sample) t test between sessions 1 and 2.

(b) Now run a repeated-measures analysis of variance on those same two columns and compare this F with the square of the preceding t.

18-3 In an attempt to demonstrate the practical uses of basic learning principles, a psychologist with an interest in behavior modification has collected data on a study designed to teach self-care skills to severely retarded children. He collected data during a baseline phase, at the end of a training phase, and at a follow-up session six months after training ended. The children were scored (blind) by a rater who rated them on a 10-point scale of self-sufficiency. The data are given below. Run and interpret the appropriate analysis.

Baseline	Training	Follow-Up
8	9	7
5	7	5
3	2	3
5	7	2
2	9	5
6	7	9
5	8	6
6	5	7
4	7	3
4	9	5

18–4 Use protected t tests with the data in Exercise 18-3 to help in the interpretation of the results. (*Hint*: As I pointed out, you can calculate the t test *as if* these were independent samples because MS_{error} has been adjusted accordingly—by removing subject differences.)

18–5 Give an example of a situation in which you might profitably use a repeated-measures analysis of variance.

18–6 Using the data on variables V72 to V78 for the first ten States for Exercises 9-10 to 9-15, run a repeated-measures analysis of variance to test the experimental hypothesis that SAT verbal scores changed across time. (*Note*: In this case repeated measurements are made on States rather than on Subjects.)

18–7 What null hypothesis did you test in Exercise 18-6?

18–8 Why did we treat Years in Exercise 18-6 as a repeated measure rather than as a between-subjects measure?

18–9 Use protected t tests with the data in Table 18-1 to compare performance at
(a) the beginning and end of Baseline, and
(b) the beginning and end of Training.
(*Hint*: See the note in Exercise 18-4.)

18–10 Run the repeated-measures analysis of variance and the t test for two related samples on the two baseline weeks in Table 18-1. Note the similarities.

18–11 Shift the data around (within columns) for Exercise 18-3 in such a way as to maximize the correlations between trials. Then rerun the analysis and note the change in F.

19

CHI-SQUARE

In Saint-Exupery's *The Little Prince*† the narrator, remarking that he believes the prince came from an asteroid known as B-612, explains his attention to a detail such as the precise number of the asteroid by commenting

> Grown-ups love figures. When you tell them you have made a new friend, they never ask you any questions about essential matters. They never say to you, "What does his voice sound like? What games does he love best? Does he collect butterflies?" Instead they demand: "How old is he? How many brothers has he? How much does he weigh? How much does his father make?" Only from these figures do they think they have learned anything about him.

In some ways the first eighteen chapters of this book have concentrated on dealing with the kinds of numbers Saint-Exupery's grown-ups like so much. This chapter will be devoted to the analysis of largely nonnumerical data.

In Chapter 1 I drew a distinction between measurement data (sometimes called quantitative data) and categorical data (sometimes called frequency data). When we deal with measurement data, each observation represents a score along some continuum, and the most common statistics are the mean and the standard deviation. When we deal with categorical data, on the other hand, the data consist of the frequencies of observations falling into each of two or more categories ("Does your friend have a gravelly voice or a high-pitched voice?" or "Is he a collector of butterflies, coins, or baseball cards?")

As an example, we could ask 100 subjects to classify a vaguely worded newspaper editorial as to whether it favored or opposed unrestricted dissemination of birth control information (no neutral or undecided response is

†Antoine de Saint-Exupery. Tr. by Katherine Woods. New York: Harcourt Brace Jovanovich, Inc., 1943, pp. 15–16.

allowed). The results might look as follows:

Editorial Viewed As		
In Favor	Opposed	Total
58	42	100

Here the data are the numbers of observations falling into each of the two categories. Given such data, we might be interested in asking whether significantly more people view the editorial as in favor of the issue than view it as opposed or whether the editorial is really neutral and the frequencies just represent a chance deviation from a 50:50 split. (Recall that subjects were forced to choose between *in favor* and *opposed*.)

A differently designed study might collect the same data on the newspaper editorial but might also classify respondents as to their own views on the topic about the dissemination of birth control information. This study might arrive at the following data:

Respondent	Editorial Viewed As		
	In Favor	Opposed	
In Favor	46	24	70
Opposed	12	18	30
	58	42	100

Here we see that people's judgments of the editorial depend on their own point of view, with the majority (46/70) of those in favor of unrestricted dissemination of birth control information viewing the editorial as being on their side and those opposed (18/30) generally seeing the editorial as siding with them. (In other words, respondents' personal opinions and their judgments about the editorial are not independent of one another.)

Although these two examples appear somewhat different in terms of the way the data are arranged and in terms of the experimental questions being asked, the same statistical technique—the **chi-square test**—is applicable to both. However, because the research questions we are asking and the way that we apply the test are different in the two situations, we will deal with them separately.

Chi-square test
A statistical test often used for analyzing categorical data.

19-1 ONE CLASSIFICATION VARIABLE— THE CHI-SQUARE GOODNESS-OF-FIT TEST

The head of the English department at a large state university has been concerned about the quality of teaching by members of her faculty. It so happened that four faculty members were scheduled to teach the freshman composition course in the same time slot during the spring semester. Looking at registration requests, where no attempt had been made to balance class size, she found the following data:

	Instructor				
	Brown	Washington	Karp	Rodriguez	Total
Enrollment	25	40	15	36	116

Does she have any reason to believe that students are more likely to enroll for some sections of the course and to avoid others? Or, put in the framework of a null hypothesis, are these data consistent with the hypothesis that students are equally likely to enroll for each section?

Goodness-of-fit test
A test for comparing observed frequencies with theoretically predicted frequencies.

This example involves one independent variable (Instructor), and the test to be used is called a **goodness-of-fit test** because we are interested in testing how well some hypothetical model (in this case equal probability of enrollment in each section) fits the obtained data. If students do in fact sign up at random, rather than seeking out particular instructors, then we would expect that the probability of enrolling for any one instructor's section would be the same as the probability of enrolling for any other instructor's section. Because there are four instructors, the probability of picking each instructor, if choosing randomly, equals .25. To put it another way, if 116 students enroll at random for the four sections, we would expect $116/4 = 29$ in each section. The question then reduces to "Are the differences between the obtained frequencies (25, 40, 15, and 36) and the expected frequencies (29 per section) small enough to be explained by chance (random sampling error) or are the differences too large for such an explanation?"

THE CHI-SQUARE (χ^2) STATISTIC

We will answer this question using the chi-square (χ^2) statistic, which is defined as

$$\chi^2 = \sum \frac{(O - E)^2}{E}$$

where

$$O = \text{the observed frequency in each category}$$

$$E = \text{the expected frequency in each category}$$

and the summation is taken over all categories.

Examination of this equation will make it clear why it is applicable to the question we want to ask. Notice that in the numerator we are directly measuring how far the observed frequencies deviate from the expected frequencies. The greater the deviations, the larger the value of χ^2. The denominator plays a useful role in terms of keeping the deviations in perspective. If we had expected 5 observations in a given category and obtained 15, that 10-point difference is substantial. On the other hand if we had expected 500 and obtained 510, that 10-point difference would be brushed aside as inconsequential. When we divide by E, we are weighting the size of the squared deviations from the expected frequency by the size of the expected frequency.

To apply the chi-square test to our data, we have the following:

	Instructor				
	Brown	Washington	Karp	Rodriguez	Total
Observed (O)	25	40	15	36	116
Expected (E)	29	29	29	29	116

$$\chi^2 = \sum \frac{(O - E)^2}{E}$$

$$\chi^2 = \frac{(25 - 29)^2}{29} + \frac{(40 - 29)^2}{29} + \frac{(15 - 29)^2}{29} + \frac{(36 - 29)^2}{29}$$

$$= 0.55 + 4.17 + 6.76 + 1.69 = 13.17$$

THE CHI-SQUARE DISTRIBUTION

To test the null hypothesis that the probabilities of enrolling for different sections are equal, we need to evaluate the obtained value of χ^2 against the sampling distribution of chi-square tabled in Appendix D, Table 1. A portion of Appendix D, Table 1, is presented in Table 19-1. The chi-square distribution, like other distributions we have seen, depends upon the degrees of freedom. For the goodness-of-fit test the degrees of freedom are defined as $k - 1$, where k stands for the number of categories. Examples of the chi-square distribution for four different degrees of freedom are shown in Figure 19-1, along with the critical values and shaded rejection region for $\alpha = .05$. You can see that the

TABLE 19-1   Abbreviated Version of Appendix D, Table 1, Upper Percentage Points of the χ^2 Distribution

df	.995	.990	.975	.950	.900	.750	.500	.250	.100	.050	.025	.010	.005
1	0.00	0.00	0.00	0.00	0.02	0.10	0.45	1.32	2.71	3.84	5.02	6.63	7.88
2	0.01	0.02	0.05	0.10	0.21	0.58	1.39	2.77	4.61	5.99	7.38	9.21	10.60
3	0.07	0.11	0.22	0.35	0.58	1.21	2.37	4.11	6.25	7.82	9.35	11.35	12.84
4	0.21	0.30	0.48	0.71	1.06	1.92	3.36	5.39	7.78	9.49	11.14	13.28	14.86
5	0.41	0.55	0.83	1.15	1.61	2.67	4.35	6.63	9.24	11.07	12.83	15.09	16.75
6	0.68	0.87	1.24	1.64	2.20	3.45	5.35	7.84	10.64	12.59	14.45	16.81	18.55
7	0.99	1.24	1.69	2.17	2.83	4.25	6.35	9.04	12.02	14.07	16.01	18.48	20.28
8	1.34	1.65	2.18	2.73	3.49	5.07	7.34	10.22	13.36	15.51	17.54	20.09	21.96
9	1.73	2.09	2.70	3.33	4.17	5.90	8.34	11.39	14.68	16.92	19.02	21.66	23.59
⋮	⋮	⋮	⋮	⋮	⋮	⋮	⋮	⋮	⋮	⋮	⋮	⋮	⋮

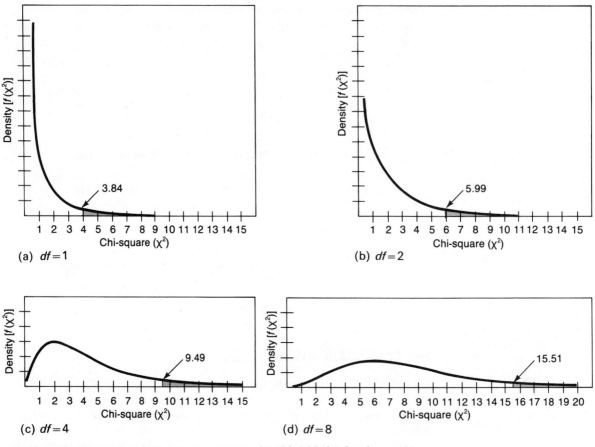

FIGURE 19-1   Chi-square Distribution for *df* = 1, 2, 4, and 8 with Critical Values for α = .05

critical value for a specified level of α (e.g., α = .05) will be larger for larger degrees of freedom. For our example we have four instructors, leaving $4 - 1 = 3\ df$. From Appendix D, Table 1, or Table 19-1 you will see that, at $\alpha = .05$, $\chi^2_{.05}(3) = 7.82$. Thus if H_0 is true, only 5% of the time would we have an obtained value of χ^2 greater than 7.82. Because our obtained value is 13.17, we will reject H_0 and conclude that the four sections of freshman composition are not equally popular.

AN EXAMPLE WITH UNEQUAL EXPECTED FREQUENCIES

In the previous example all the expected frequencies were equal (i.e., 29) because we wanted to see if students enrolled at random for the four sections. Suppose, however, that we wanted to see if enrollment varied by the rank of the instructor. The department has eight full professors, two associate professors, and six assistant professors, all teaching the composition course in the same time slot. If we calculate enrollments by the rank of the instructor, we find the following:

	Rank			
	Assistant	**Associate**	**Full**	**Total**
Observed (*O*)	142	46	210	398
Expected (*E*)	149.25	49.75	199	398

Notice that many more students are enrolled in sections taught by full professors than in sections taught by assistant or associate professors. However, that is what we would expect because there are more full professors than assistant or associate professors. Because 50% of the instructors are full professors, if there were no bias in enrollment (i.e., H_0 is true), we would expect 50% of the 398 ($=199$) students to be enrolled in their sections. Similarly with 6 out of 16 instructors being assistant professors we would expect $6/16 = 37.5\%$ of the students to enroll in their courses ($.375 \times 398 = 149.25$). Finally, we would expect $2/16 = 12.5\%$ to enroll in courses taught by associate professors ($.125 \times 398 = 49.75$). These expected frequencies are shown below the observed frequencies. For these data

$$\chi^2 = \sum \frac{(O - E)^2}{E}$$

$$\chi^2 = \frac{(142 - 149.25)^2}{149.25} + \frac{(46 - 49.75)^2}{49.75} + \frac{(210 - 199)^2}{199}$$

$$= .35 + .28 + .61 = 1.24$$

With three categories we have $3 - 1 = 2\ df$, and $\chi^2_{0.5}(2) = 5.99$. We cannot reject the null hypothesis. We have no reason to doubt that students enroll at the same rate for instructors in the different ranks. *If* enrollment reflects teaching ability, full professors do not appear to be better teachers than assistant or associate professors. However, many other factors (such as course content and grading practices) also influence enrollment. Moreover, imagine how difficult the data would have been to interpret if we had not restricted our example to introductory composition courses taught at the same time of day.

19-2   TWO CLASSIFICATION VARIABLES— CONTINGENCY TABLE ANALYSIS

In the two previous examples we have considered the case in which data are categorized along only one dimension (classification variable). Often, however, data are categorized with respect to two variables and we are interested in asking whether these variables are independent of one another. In other words we want to test whether the distribution of responses for one variable depends upon the level of the other variable. At the beginning of this chapter we very briefly considered an example in which how a subject viewed the message of an editorial about birth control was itself dependent on the subject's own opinion about birth control. Another example of this type of analysis comes from a study by Jackson and Padgett (1982) on a phenomenon known as social loafing. Social loafing refers to the observation that when people work as a team they often do less work than when they work alone. Jackson and Padgett analyzed songs written by the Beatles. (Although we are not going to examine the data in terms of social loafing, it is worth noting that Jackson and Padgett's ultimate conclusion was that after 1967—the year in which relationships within the group began to disintegrate—McCartney and Lennon were guilty of social loafing in that the songs they wrote together were less successful than the songs they wrote separately.) We are going to use the data to answer a related question concerning whether their pre-1967 songs, regardless of authorship, were more or less successful than the ones that came later. For purposes of analysis a song was classed as successful if it was also released as a 45 rpm single. The data on this question can be displayed in what is known as a 2×2 **contingency table**. (It is called a 2×2 table because each variable has two levels.)

Contingency table
A two-dimensional table in which each observation is classified on the basis of two variables simultaneously.

Year Written

Successful	1966 or Before	1967 or Later	
Yes	37	16	53
No	47	62	109
	84	78	162

In this contingency table we see some evidence that the earlier songs were more successful. Of the 84 songs written in 1966 or before, 37 were also issued as singles. However, from 1967 on, only 16 of the 78 songs were classed as successful and released as singles. A statistical test of the null hypothesis that success is independent of the year in which the song was written is given by the same chi-square test that we used to test goodness of fit. The only difference will be the calculation of expected values.

EXPECTED FREQUENCIES FOR CONTINGENCY TABLES

Expected frequency
The expected value for the number of observations in a cell if H_0 is true.

Marginal totals
Totals for the levels of one variable summed across the levels of the other variable.

For a contingency table the **expected frequency** for a given cell is obtained by multiplying together the totals for the row and column in which the cell is located and dividing by the total sample size (N). (These totals are known as **marginal totals**.) If E_{ij} is the expected frequency for the cell in row i and column j, R_i and C_j are corresponding row and column totals, and N is the total number of observations, then

$$E_{ij} = \frac{R_i C_j}{N}$$

For our example, then

$$E_{11} = \frac{(53 \times 84)}{162} = 27.48$$

$$E_{12} = \frac{(53 \times 78)}{162} = 25.52$$

$$E_{21} = \frac{(109 \times 84)}{162} = 56.52$$

$$E_{22} = \frac{(109 \times 78)}{162} = 52.48$$

CALCULATION OF CHI-SQUARE

In Table 19-2 are shown the observed and expected frequencies for each cell. The calculation of χ^2 is straightforward and uses the same formula we used with the goodness-of-fit test.

$$\chi^2 = \sum \frac{(O - E)^2}{E}$$

$$= \frac{(37 - 27.48)^2}{27.48} + \frac{(16 - 25.52)^2}{25.52} + \frac{(47 - 56.52)^2}{56.52} + \frac{(62 - 52.48)^2}{52.48}$$

$$= 3.30 + 3.55 + 1.60 + 1.73 = 10.18$$

TABLE 19-2
Observed and Expected Frequencies for Beatles' Songs

Successful	Observed			Expected		
	1966 or Before	1967 or Later		1966 or Before	1967 or Later	
Yes	37	16	53	27.48	25.52	53
No	47	62	109	56.52	52.48	109
	84	78	162	84	78	162

DEGREES OF FREEDOM

Before we can compare our value of χ^2 to the tabled value in Appendix D, Table 1, we must know the degrees of freedom. For the analysis of contingency tables the degrees of freedom are always given by

$$df = (R - 1)(C - 1)$$

where $R =$ the number of rows

$C =$ the number of columns

For our example we have $R = 2$ and $C = 2$, and we therefore have $(2 - 1) \times (2 - 1) = 1\ df$. It may seem strange to have only 1 df with 4 cells, but you can see that once you know the row and column totals, you only need to know one cell frequency to be able to determine the rest.

EVALUATION OF χ^2

With 1 df the critical value of χ^2 is found in Appendix D, Table 1, to be 3.84. Because our obtained χ^2 (10.18) exceeds the critical value, we will reject the null hypothesis that the variables are independent of each other. In this case whether or not a song was successful (i.e., whether it was released as a single) depends in part upon whether it was written before or after 1967. Before we conclude absolutely that the quality of the Beatles' songs decreased after 1967, however, it is important to rule out a number of other possibilities. For example, it could be that the record industry issued fewer 45s after 1967 or that in that year the Beatles established a policy of promoting LPs at the expense of 45s. Nonetheless the data do show a change in the proportion of songs released as 45s. The only questions concern the interpretation of this result.

19-3 THE SPECIAL CASE OF 2 × 2 TABLES

In this book I have deliberately avoided discussing formulae that apply to special cases when the general formula will accomplish the same thing. It is usually easier to do a tiny bit more work on calculations than it is to remember another formula. However, in the case of a 2 × 2 table there is a formula that allows you to skip the calculation of expected frequencies, and in fact allows you to calculate χ^2 on a calculator without ever writing down intermediate results.

Suppose that we imagine a 2 × 2 table with the cells and marginal totals labeled as follows:

A	B	$A + B$
C	D	$C + D$
$A + C$	$B + D$	N

Then

$$\chi^2 = \frac{N(AD - BC)^2}{(A + B)(C + D)(A + C)(B + D)}$$

Using the McCartney and Lennon data, we have

Successful	1966 or Before	1967 or Later	
Yes	37	16	53
No	47	62	109
	84	78	162

$$\chi^2 = \frac{N(AD - BC)^2}{(A + B)(C + D)(A + C)(B + D)}$$

$$= \frac{162[(37)(62) - (16)(47)]^2}{(53)(109)(84)(78)} = \frac{162(1542)^2}{(53)(109)(84)(78)}$$

$$= 10.18$$

This is exactly the same value of χ^2 we obtained in the previous calculations.

Students often have trouble with this formula because they forget which letter refers to which cell of the table. So do I. But notice what you are doing. You are multiplying cells that are diagonal to each other and then subtracting one product from the other. (It doesn't even matter which you subtract from which, because you are going to square the result anyway.) Next you multiply this squared answer by N and then divide by all the row and column totals. Moreover, if you really become confused and divide when you should have multiplied, or vice versa, you will generally obtain such an outlandish answer that you will know something is wrong.

Correction for Continuity   Many books advocate that for 2×2 tables you apply what is called a correction for continuity (also known as Yates's Correction). This correction simply amounts to reducing the numerator by one-half unit before squaring. The correction was quite common in the past, but it has lost favor as we have learned more about the analysis of contingency tables. As Camilli and Hopkins (1978) point out, such a correction only makes sense if we have what are called "fixed marginal totals." Put differently, we would only use the correction if we found ourselves in a situation where we knew exactly what the row and column totals would be *before* we ran the experiment. Because such situations are so rare, I am not going to cover the correction in more detail. For more extensive coverage see Howell (1987).

19-4   CHI-SQUARE FOR LARGER CONTINGENCY TABLES

The previous example involved two variables (Success and Date), each of which had two levels. This particular design is referred to as a 2×2 contingency analysis and is a special case of more general $R \times C$ designs (where, again, R and C represent the number of rows and columns). As an example of the analysis of a larger contingency table we can analyze data collected by Darley and Latané (1968) on bystander intervention. Darley and Latané asked subjects to participate in a discussion carried on over an intercom system (supposedly to preserve confidentiality). One group of subjects were led to believe that they were speaking with only the discussion leader (later termed the victim); a second group of subjects thought one other person was involved in the discussion; and a third group thought that four other people were involved. In fact the subject was alone in all cases. Partway through the discussion the victim on the other end of the line pretended to have a seizure and began asking for help. He even stated that he was afraid that he might die without help. One of the dependent variables was the number of subjects in each group who tried to obtain help for the victim. The results are hardly encouraging for those of us who like to believe in the kindness of our fellow creatures. For the group of subjects each of whom thought he or she was alone with the victim, 85% tried to obtain help (the other 15% apparently decided to let nature take its course). On the other hand for those subjects who thought that one other person was listening, the response rate dropped to 62%. Worst of all, when the subjects thought there were four other listeners, the response rate was a meager 31%. Although it is conceivable that these differences were due to chance, that doesn't seem very likely. We can use chi-square to test the null hypothesis that helping behavior is independent of the number of bystanders. The data are presented in Table 19-3. The expected frequencies were obtained in the same way they were obtained in the 2×2 case. In other words the expected frequency in the upper-left cell is $(13 \times 31)/52 = 7.75$.

$$\chi^2 = \sum \frac{(O - E)^2}{E}$$

$$= \frac{(11 - 7.75)^2}{7.75} + \frac{(2 - 5.25)^2}{5.25} + \frac{(16 - 15.50)^2}{15.50}$$

$$+ \frac{(10 - 10.50)^2}{10.50} + \frac{(4 - 7.75)^2}{7.75} + \frac{(9 - 5.25)^2}{5.25}$$

$$= 1.36 + 2.01 + 0.02 + 0.02 + 1.81 + 2.68$$

$$= 7.90$$

In this example we have $(3 - 1)(2 - 1) = 2$ df, and the critical value of χ^2 is 5.99. Because the obtained value of χ^2 is greater than the critical value, we will reject H_0. If you expect something unpleasant to happen to you, be sure there are not too many people around—one is about right.

TABLE 19-3
Observed and Expected Frequencies for Helping Behavior as a Function of the Number of Bystanders

		Observed — Sought Assistance		Expected — Sought Assistance		
		Yes	No	Yes	No	
Number of Bystanders	0	11	2	7.75	5.25	13
	1	16	10	15.50	10.50	26
	4	4	9	7.75	5.25	13
		31	21	31	21	52

19-5 THE PROBLEM OF SMALL EXPECTED FREQUENCIES

Chi-square is an important and valid test for examining either goodness of fit or the independence of variables (contingency tables). However, the test is not appropriate when the *expected* frequencies are too small. The chi-square test is based in part on the assumption that if the experiment were repeated an infinite number of times with the same marginal frequencies, the obtained frequencies in any given cell would be normally distributed around the expected frequency. But if the expected frequency is small (e.g., 1.0), there is no way that the observed frequencies could be normally distributed around it. In cases in which the expected frequencies are too small, chi-square may not be a valid statistical test. The problem, however, is how we define "too small." There are almost as many definitions as there are statistics textbooks, and the issue still is being debated in the statistical journals. I will take the admittedly conservative position here that for small contingency tables (9 or fewer cells) all expected frequencies should be at least 5. For larger tables this restriction can be relaxed somewhat. There are people who argue that the test is conservative and produces few Type I errors, even with much smaller expected frequencies, but even they are forced to admit that when the total sample size is very small—as is frequently the case when the expected frequencies are small—the test has remarkably little power to detect false null hypotheses. (See Camilli and Hopkins, 1978, for a more complete discussion of this issue.)

19-6 THE USE OF CHI-SQUARE AS A TEST ON PROPORTIONS

The chi-square test is often used as a test on proportions or differences between two independent proportions. However, this is the same test we have been using all along. We simply change the way we conceive of our proportions (i.e., we change proportions to frequencies). Two simple examples will make the point very easily.

The first example involves a single proportion. A developer wants to build a large office building on what is now a city park. The building will bring in a large number of jobs, but it will also ruin the park, and there is considerable difference of opinion about the project. The developer has hired a well-respected polling agency, which has interviewed a random sample of 40 residents of the area. They found that 60% of those polled favored the project and 40% of those polled were opposed. Is the developer safe in claiming that the majority opinion in the area is on her side, or could these results have occurred by chance if the residents are evenly divided? We will use chi-square to test the null hypothesis that the population is evenly split—that is, that the true value of P (the proportion in the population in favor of the project) is 0.50.

Because 40 people were polled and the proportion in favor was .60, then $.60 \times 40 = 24$ people were in favor and 16 were opposed. If H_0 is true we would have an expected frequency of 20 for each alternative. Thus

	In Favor	Opposed	
Obtained	24	16	40
Expected	20	20	40

Now we can compute

$$\chi^2 = \sum \frac{(O-E)^2}{E} = \frac{(24-20)^2}{20} + \frac{(16-20)^2}{20} = \frac{4^2 + 4^2}{20} = 1.60$$

We have 1 df in this case, and from the tables of χ^2 we find that at $\alpha = .05$ the critical value of $\chi^2 = 3.84$. Thus we cannot reject $H_0: P = .50$. The developer does not have reliable evidence that more than half the population favors the project.

The second example involves testing the difference between two independent proportions and is based on a study of helping behavior by Latané and Dabbs (1975). In this study, experimenters were instructed to walk into elevators and, just after the elevator started, drop a handful of pencils or coins on the floor. The dependent variable was whether or not bystanders helped pick up the pencils, and one of the independent variables was the sex of the bystanders. The study was conducted in three cities (Columbus, Seattle, and Atlanta), but we will concentrate on the data from Columbus, where sex differences were least. We will also ignore any effect of the sex of the experimenter. Basically Latané and Dabbs found that 23% of the female bystanders and 28% of the male bystanders helped pick up the dropped items. (It is interesting that about three-quarters of the bystanders just stood there.) The question of interest is whether the difference between 23% and 28% is statistically significant. In order to answer this question we must know the total sample sizes. In this case there were 1303 female bystanders and 1320 males. (Notice the large sample sizes that are easily obtained in this type of experiment.) Because we know the sample sizes, we can convert the proportions to frequencies easily. Thus

	Sex of Bystander	
	Female	Male
Help	23%	28%
No Help	77%	72%
Number	1303	1320

becomes

	Sex of Bystander		
	Female	Male	
Help	300	370	670
No Help	1003	950	1953
Number	1303	1320	2623

The entry of 300 in the upper-left corner of this table was obtained by taking 23% of 1303. The other entries were obtained in an analogous way.

Because this is a 2×2 table, we can simplify the calculations by using the formula

$$\chi^2 = \frac{N(AD - BC)^2}{(A + B)(C + D)(A + C)(B + D)}$$

$$= \frac{2623[(300)(950) - (370)(1003)]^2}{(670)(1953)(1303)(1320)}$$

$$= \frac{2623(-86,110)^2}{(670)(1953)(1303)(1320)} = 8.64$$

Because the critical value on 1 df at $\alpha = .05$ is 3.84, I will reject H_0 and conclude that the proportions are significantly different. We can conclude that under the conditions of this study males are more willing to help than females.

19-7   NONINDEPENDENT OBSERVATIONS

Aside from questions about small expected frequencies, the chi-square test also is based on the assumption that observations are independent of one another. In practical terms what this means is that subjects must contribute one, *and only one*, observation to the data. If, when Darley and Latané ran the bystander study, they had decided to use each subject two or three times to save recruiting more subjects, a chi-square analysis of the data would not have been appropriate. Fortunately they knew better. This problem has a habit of sneaking into even those analyses carried out by experienced investigators, however. The simplest rule is that N (the total of the row or column totals) *must* be equal to the number of *subjects* (not observations) in the experiment. If it is too large, you are probably using more than one observation from each subject. If it is too small, you have omitted some data (such as counting only how many subjects sought help for the victim and forgetting about counting those who did not seek help).

19-8   MINITAB ANALYSIS OF CONTINGENCY TABLES

Minitab does not have a procedure for running goodness-of-fit tests, but it does have two procedures for analyzing contingency tables, depending upon how the data are presented. The procedure most likely to be useful to you is shown in Table 19-4 and is self-explanatory. The data analyzed there are the data from the first bystander study (see Table 19-3).

```
MTB >   READ THE DATA INTO COLUMNS C1 AND C2
DATA>   11   2
DATA>   16  10
DATA>    4   9
DATA>   END
        3 ROWS READ

MTB >   CHISQ ON THE DATA IN COLUMNS C1 AND C2

EXPECTED COUNTS ARE PRINTED BELOW OBSERVED COUNTS

               C1        C2      TOTAL
        1      11         2        13
              7.75      5.25

        2      16        10        26
             15.50     10.50

        3       4         9        13
              7.75      5.25

  TOTAL        31        21        52

CHISQ =  1.363 + 2.012 +
         0.026 + 0.024 +
         1.815 + 2.679 = 7.908

   DF = 2
```

19-9   A FINAL WORKED EXAMPLE

We will take as our final example a study by Geller, Witmer, and Orebaugh (1976). These authors were studying littering behavior and were interested, among other things, in whether a message about not littering would be effective if placed on the handbills that are often given out in supermarkets advertising the daily specials. To oversimplify a fairly complex study, two of Geller's conditions involved passing out handbills in a supermarket. Under one condition (Control) the handbills contained only a listing of the daily specials. In the other condition (Message), the handbills also included the notation "Please don't litter. Please dispose of this properly." At the end of the day, Geller and his students searched the store for handbills. They recorded the number that were found in Trashcans; the number that were left in shopping carts, on the floor, and various places where they didn't belong (denoted Litter); and the number that could not be found and were apparently Removed from the premises. The data obtained under the two conditions are shown in Table 19-5 and are taken from a larger table reported by Geller et al.

This contingency table can appropriately be analyzed using the chi-square test because we have 1772 independent observations falling into mutually exclusive cells. We will test the null hypothesis that the Location of the fliers at the end of the day is independent of the instructions on the flier, and we will set $\alpha = .05$.

We will calculate the expected frequencies by the same procedure we have used before. Namely, for a contingency table $E = RT \times CT/GT$. Therefore

TABLE 19-5
Data from Study by Geller,
Witmer, and Orebaugh (1976)
(Expected frequencies in
parentheses)

		Location			
		Trashcan	Litter	Removed	
Instructions	Control	41 (61.66)	385 (343.98)	477 (497.36)	903
	Message	80 (59.34)	290 (331.02)	499 (478.64)	869
		121	675	976	1772

the expected number of fliers from the Control group (the fliers without the message) found in the Trashcan, if H_0 were true, would be $E_{11} = (903)(121)/1772 = 61.66$. Similarly, the number of people who received the antilittering Message and Removed their fliers would be expected to be $E_{23} = (869)(976)/1772 = 478.64$. The expected frequencies are shown in parentheses in Table 19-5.

The calculation of χ^2 is based on the same formula we have been using all along:

$$\chi^2 = \sum \frac{(O - E)^2}{E} = \frac{(41 - 61.66)^2}{61.66} + \frac{(385 - 343.98)^2}{343.98} + \cdots + \frac{(499 - 478.64)^2}{478.64}$$

$$= 25.79$$

There are 2 df for Table 19-5, because $(R-1)(C-1)=(2-1)(3-1)=2$. The critical value of $\chi^2 = 5.99$, so we are led to reject H_0 and to conclude that the location in which handbills were left depended on the instructions given. In other words, Instruction and Location are not independent. From the data, it is evident that, when subjects were asked not to litter, a higher percentage of handbills were thrown in the trashcan or taken out of the store, and fewer were left lying in the shopping carts or on the floors and shelves.

19-10 SUMMARY

This chapter was concerned with the use of the chi-square test for the analysis of frequency data. We first considered the test for goodness of fit for the situation in which there is only one variable of classification. We then dealt with the use of chi-square for testing the independence of two variables, which is the way the test is most commonly used. Finally we considered the problem of small expected frequencies and the need for the independence of observations. Some of the most important terms in this chapter are:

□ **Chi-square test**   □ **Expected frequency**
□ **Goodness-of-fit test**   □ **Marginal totals**
□ **Contingency table**

19-11 EXERCISES

19-1 The chairman of a Psychology department suspects that some of his faculty are more popular than others. There are three sections of Introductory Psychology (taught at 10:00 A.M., 11:00 A.M., and 12:00 P.M.) by Professors Anderson, Klansky, and Kamm. The number of students who enroll for each are given below.

Professor Anderson	Professor Klansky	Professor Kamm
25	32	10

Run the appropriate chi-square test and interpret the results.

19-2 From the point of view of designing a valid experiment there is an important difference between Exercise 19-1 and a similar example used in this chapter. The data in Exercise 19-1 will not really answer the question that the chairman wants answered. What is the problem and how could the experiment be improved?

19-3 I have a theory that if you ask subjects to sort one-sentence characteristics of people (e.g., "I eat too fast") into five piles ranging from *not at all like me* to *very much like me*, the percentage of items placed in each pile will be approximately 10%, 20%, 40%, 20%, and 10% for the five piles. I have one of my children sort 50 statements and obtain the following data:

8   10   20   8   4

Do these data support my hypothesis?

19-4 To what population does the answer to Exercise 19-3 generalize?

19-5 In an old study by Clark and Clark (1939), black children were shown black dolls and white dolls and were asked to select one to play with. Out of 252 children, 169 chose the white doll and 83 chose the black doll. What can we conclude about the behavior of these children?

19-6 Following up the study referred to in Exercise 19-5, Hraba and Grant (1970) repeated the Clark and Clark (1939) study. The studies were not exactly equivalent, but the results are interesting. They found that out of 89 black children, 28 chose the white doll and 61 chose the black doll. Run the appropriate chi-square test on their data and interpret the results.

19-7 Combine the data from Exercises 19-5 and 19-6 into a two-way contingency table and run the appropriate test. How does the question that the two-way classification addresses differ from the questions addressed by Exercises 19-5 and 19-6?

19-8 Community Mental Health Centers tend to see a variety of problems, but some centers seem to see more of one kind of problem than others. Out of the last 100 clients seen by each center, a count has been made of those classed as having Social Adjustment Problems, Problems with Living, and Other Problems. The data follow:

	Mental Health Center			
	A	**B**	**C**	
Social Adjustment	50	40	40	130
Problems with Living	26	34	20	80
Other Problems	24	26	40	90
	100	100	100	300

(a) What null hypothesis would the chi-square test on this table actually test?

(b) Run the appropriate analysis.

(c) Interpret the results.

19-9 Use the data in Exercise 19-8 to demonstrate how chi-square varies as a function of sample size.

(a) Cut each cell entry in half and recompute chi-square.

(b) What does this have to say about the role of the sample size in hypothesis testing?

19-10 Howell and Huessy (1985) used a rating scale to classify children as showing or not showing Attention Deficit Disorder (ADD)-like behavior in the second grade. They then classified these same children again in the fourth and fifth grades. At the end of the ninth grade they examined school records and noted which children were enrolled in remedial English. In the following data all children who were ever classified as ADD have been combined into one group (labeled ADD):

Classification	Remedial English	Nonremedial English	
Normal	22	187	209
Add	19	74	93
	41	261	302

Does behavior during elementary school discriminate between those who will later be in Remedial and Nonremedial English during high school?

19-11 In Exercise 19-10 children were classified as those who never showed ADD-like behavior and those who showed ADD behavior at least once in the second, fourth, or fifth grade. If we do not collapse across categories, we obtain the following data:

	Never	Second Grade	Fourth Grade	Second and Fourth Grades
Remedial English	22	2	1	3
Nonremedial English	187	17	11	16

	Fifth Grade	Second and Fifth Grades	Fourth and Fifth Grades	Second, Fourth, and Fifth Grades
Remedial English	2	4	3	4
Nonremedial English	16	7	8	6

(a) Run the chi-square test.

(b) What would you conclude, ignoring the small expected frequencies?

(c) How comfortable do you feel with these small expected frequencies, and how might you handle the problem?

19-12 It would be possible to calculate a one-way chi-square test on the data in row 1 of Exercise 19-11. What hypothesis would you be testing if you did that? How would that hypothesis differ from the one you tested in Exercise 19-11?

19-13 The Post Office is interested in evaluating the speed of mail delivery. They mail letters to Washington, D.C., from a variety of distances, and record the number of days it takes for the mail to arrive. The data follow:

Days to Deliver	Distance 50 miles	150 miles	300 miles	3000 miles
One	5	10	15	5
Two	10	10	5	5
Three or More	15	5	10	10

(a) Run the chi-square test.

(b) Interpret the results.

19-14 In the example of a goodness-of-fit test with unequal expected frequencies, why was it necessary that all instructors teach in the same time slot?

19-15 Suppose that in the study by Latané and Dabbs (1975) referred to on page 292 there were only 100 males and 100 females involved. Compute χ^2 in this case.

19-16 What does the answer to Exercise 19-15 have to say about the effects of sample size on the power of an experiment?

19-17 In a recent survey of 150 students in a large lecture course, 45% thought that the course needed major improvement and 55% thought that it was just fine. Is this difference significant?

19-18 In what way does the answer to Exercise 19-17 miss the point?

20

NONPARAMETRIC AND DISTRIBUTION-FREE STATISTICAL TESTS

Parametric tests
Statistical tests that involve assumptions about, or estimation of, population parameters.

Nonparametric tests (Distribution-free tests)
Statistical tests that do not rely on parameter estimation or precise distribution assumptions.

Most of the statistical procedures we have discussed in the preceding chapters have involved both the estimation of one or more parameters of the distribution of scores in the population(s) from which the data were sampled and assumptions concerning the shape of that distribution. For example the t test makes use of the sample variance (s^2) as an estimate of the population variance (σ^2) and also requires the assumption that the population from which we sampled is normal (or at least that the sampling distribution of the mean is normal). Tests, such as the t test, that involve either assumptions about specific parameters or else their estimation, are referred to as **parametric tests**.

There is a class of tests, however, that does not rely on parameter estimation and/or distribution assumptions. Such tests are usually referred to as **nonparametric tests** or **distribution-free tests**. By and large, if a test is nonparametric it is also distribution-free, and in fact it is the distribution-free nature of the test that is most valuable to us. Although the two names often are used interchangeably, the tests will be referred to here as distribution-free tests.

The argument over the value of distribution-free tests has gone on for many years, and it certainly cannot be resolved in this chapter. Many feel that, for the vast majority of cases, parametric tests are sufficiently robust to make distribution-free tests unnecessary. Others, however, believe just as strongly in the unsuitability of parametric tests and the overwhelming superiority of the distribution-free approach. (Bradley, 1968, is a forceful and articulate spokesman for the latter group.) Regardless of the position you take on this issue, it is important that you be familiar with the most common distribution-free procedures and with their underlying rationale. These tests are too prevalent in the experimental literature simply to be ignored.

The major advantage generally attributed to distribution-free tests is also the most obvious—they do not rely on any very seriously restrictive assumptions concerning the shape of the sampled population(s). This is not to say that distribution-free tests do not make *any* distribution assumptions, but only that the assumptions they do require are far more general than those required for the parametric tests. The exact null hypothesis being tested may depend, for example, on whether or not two populations are symmetric or have a similar shape. None of these tests, however, makes an *a priori* assumption about the specific shape of the distribution; that is, the validity of the test is not affected by whether or not the distribution of the variable in the population is normal. A parametric test, on the other hand, usually includes some type of normality assumption, and if that assumption is false, the conclusions drawn from that test may be inaccurate. Another characteristic of distribution-free tests that often acts as an advantage is the fact that many of them, especially the ones discussed in this chapter, are more sensitive to medians than to means. Thus if the nature of your data is such that you are interested primarily in medians, then the tests presented here may be particularly useful to you.

Those who argue in favor of using parametric tests in every case do not deny that the distribution-free tests are more liberal in the assumptions they require. They argue, however, that the assumptions normally cited as being required of parametric tests are overly restrictive in practice and that the parametric tests are remarkably unaffected by violations of distribution assumptions.

The major disadvantage generally attributed to distribution-free tests is their lower power relative to the corresponding parametric test. In general, when the assumptions of the parametric test are met, the distribution-free test requires more observations than the comparable parametric test for the same level of power. Thus for a given set of data the parametric test is more likely to lead to rejection of a false null hypothesis than is the corresponding distribution-free test. Moreover, even when the distribution assumptions are violated to a moderate degree, the parametric tests are thought to maintain their advantage.

It often is claimed that the distribution-free procedures are particularly useful because of the simplicity of their calculations. However, for an experimenter who has just invested six months in collecting her data, a difference of five minutes in computation time hardly justifies the use of a less desirable test.

There is one other advantage of distribution-free tests. Because many of them rank the raw scores and operate on those ranks, they offer a test of differences in central tendency that are not affected by one or a few very extreme scores (outliers). An extreme score in a set of data actually can make the parametric test *less* powerful, because it inflates the variance, and hence the error term, as well as biasing the mean by shifting it toward the outlier (the latter may increase *or* decrease the mean difference).

This chapter will be concerned with four of the most important distribution-free methods. The first two are analogues of the t test—one for independent samples and one for matched samples. The next two tests are distribution-free analogues of the analysis of variance—the first for k independent groups and the second for k repeated measures. All of these tests are members of a class known as **rank-randomization tests** because they deal with ranked data and take as the distribution of their test statistic, when the null hypothesis is true, the theoretical distribution of randomly distributed ranks. Because these tests convert raw data to ranks, the shape of the underlying distribution of scores in the population becomes of less importance. Thus both

Rank-randomization tests
A class of nonparametric tests based on the theoretical distribution of randomly assigned ranks.

the sets

$$11 \quad 14 \quad 15 \quad 16 \quad 17 \quad 22$$

(data that might have come from a normal distribution)

and

$$11 \quad 12 \quad 13 \quad 30 \quad 31 \quad 32$$

(data that might have come from a bimodal distribution)

reduce to the ranks

$$1 \quad 2 \quad 3 \quad 4 \quad 5 \quad 6$$

20-1 MANN–WHITNEY TEST

Mann–Whitney test
A nonparametric test for comparing the central tendency of two independent samples.

One of the most common and best-known distribution-free tests is the **Mann–Whitney test** for two independent samples. This test often is thought of as the distribution-free analogue of the t test for two independent samples, although it tests a slightly different, and broader, null hypothesis. Its null hypothesis is the hypothesis that the two samples were drawn at random from identical populations (not just populations with the same mean), but it is especially sensitive to population differences in central tendency. Thus rejection of H_0 is generally interpreted to mean that the two distributions had different central tendencies, but it is possible that rejection actually resulted from some other difference between the populations. Notice that when we gain one thing (freedom from assumptions), we pay for it with something else (loss of specificity).

The Mann–Whitney test is a variation on a test originally devised by Wilcoxon and called the Rank-Sum test. Because Wilcoxon also devised another test, to be discussed in the next section, we will refer to this one as the Mann–Whitney test to avoid confusion. Although the test as devised by Mann and Whitney used a slightly different test statistic, the statistic to be used in this chapter (the sum of the ranks of the scores in one of the groups) is often advocated because it is so much easier to calculate. Either test statistic would lead to exactly the same conclusion when applied to the same set of data.

The logical basis of the Mann–Whitney test is particularly easy to understand. Assume that we have two independent treatment groups, with n_1 observations in Group 1 and n_2 observations in Group 2. Further assume that the null hypothesis is *false* to a very substantial degree and that the population from which Group 1 scores have been sampled contains values generally lower than the population from which Group 2 scores were drawn. Then if we were to rank all $n_1 + n_2 = N$ scores from lowest to highest without regard to group membership, we would expect that the lower ranks generally would fall to Group 1 scores and the higher ranks to Group 2 scores. Going one step further, if we were to sum the ranks assigned to each group, the sum of the ranks in Group 1 would be expected to be appreciably smaller than the sum of the ranks in Group 2.

Now consider the case, in which the null hypothesis is *true* and the scores for the two groups were sampled from identical populations. In this situation if we were to rank all N scores without regard to group membership, we would expect some low ranks and some high ranks in each group, and the sum of the ranks assigned to Group 1 would be roughly equal to the sum of the ranks assigned to Group 2. These situations are illustrated in Table 20-1.

Mann and Whitney (and Wilcoxon) based their tests on the logic just described, using the sum of the ranks in one of the groups as the test statistic. If that sum is too small relative to the other sum, we will reject the null hypothesis. More specifically, we will take as our test statistic the sum of the ranks assigned to the *smaller* group, or, if $n_1 = n_2$, the *smaller* of the two sums. Given this value, we can use tables of the Mann–Whitney statistic (W_S) to test the null hypothesis.

To take a specific example, consider the following hypothetical data on the number of recent stressful life events reported by a group of Cardiac patients in a local hospital and a control group of Orthopedic patients in the same hospital. It is well-known that stressful life events (marriage, new job, death of spouse, etc.) are associated with illness, and it is reasonable to expect that many Cardiac patients would have experienced more recent stressful events than Orthopedic patients (who just happened to break an ankle while tearing down a building or a collarbone while skiing). It would appear from the data that this expectation is borne out. Because we have some reason to suspect that Life Stress scores probably are not symmetrically distributed in the population (especially for Cardiac patients if our research hypothesis is true), we will choose to use a distribution-free test. In this case we will use the Mann–Whitney test because we have two independent groups.

	Cardiac Patients						Orthopedic Patients				
Raw Data	32	8	7	29	5	0	1	2	2	3	6
Ranks	11	9	8	10	6	1	2	3.5	3.5	5	7

To apply the Mann–Whitney test we first rank all 11 scores from lowest to highest, assigning tied ranks to tied scores (see the discussion on ranking in

TABLE 20-1
Illustration of Typical Results to Be Expected under H_0 False and H_0 True

	H_0 False											
	Group 1						Group 2					
Raw Data	10	12	17	13	19	20	30	26	25	33	18	27
Ranks (R_i)	1	2	4	3	6	7	11	9	8	12	5	10
ΣR_i			23						55			

	H_0 True											
	Group 1						Group 2					
Raw Data	22	28	32	19	24	33	18	25	29	20	23	34
Ranks (R_i)	4	8	10	2	6	11	1	7	9	3	5	12
ΣR_i			41						37			

Chapter 9). The Orthopedic group is the smaller of the two and if those patients generally have had fewer recent stressful life events, then the sum of the ranks assigned to that group should be relatively low. Letting W_S stand for the sum of the ranks in the smaller group (the Orthopedic group), we find

$$W_S = 2 + 3.5 + 3.5 + 5 + 7 = 21$$

We can evaluate the obtained value of W_S by using a table (Appendix D, Table 7) that gives the *smallest* value of W_S we would expect to obtain by chance if the null hypothesis were true. From Appendix D, Table 7, we find that for $n_1 = 5$ subjects in the smaller group and $n_2 = 6$ subjects in the larger group (n_1 is *always* the number of subjects in the smaller group) the entry for $\alpha = .025$ (one-tailed) is 18. This means that for a difference between groups to be significant at the one-tailed .025 level, or the two-tailed .05 level, W_S must be less than or equal to 18. Because we found W_S to be equal to 21, we cannot reject H_0. (By way of comparison, if we ran a t test on these data, ignoring the fact that one sample variance is almost 50 times the other and that the data suggest that our prediction of the shape of the distribution of Cardiac scores may be correct, t would be 1.52 on 9 *df*, a nonsignificant result.)

The entries in Appendix D, Table 7, are for a one-tailed test and will lead to rejection of the null hypothesis only if the sum of the ranks for the smaller group is sufficiently *small*. It is possible, however, that the larger ranks could be congregated in the smaller group, in which case if H_0 is false, the sum of the ranks would be larger than chance expectation rather than smaller. One rather awkward way around this problem would be to rank the data all over again, this time ranking from high to low. If we did this, then the smaller ranks would now appear in the smaller group and we could proceed as before. We do not have to go through the process of reranking data, however. We can accomplish the same thing by making use of the symmetric properties of the distribution of the rank sum by calculating a statistic called W_S'. The statistic W_S' is the sum of the ranks for the smaller group that we would have found if we had reversed our ranking and ranked from highest to lowest.

$$W_S' = 2\bar{W} - W_S$$

where $2\bar{W} = n_1(n_1 + n_2 + 1)$ and is tabled in Appendix D, Table 7. We then can evaluate W_S' against the tabled value and have a one-tailed test on the *upper* tail of the distribution. For a two-tailed test of H_0 (which is what we normally want) we calculate W_S and W_S', enter the table with whichever is smaller, and double the listed value of α.

To illustrate W_S and W_S', consider the following two sets of data:

Set 1	Group 1				Group 2				
X	2	15	16	19	18	23	25	37	82
Ranks	1	2	3	5	4	6	7	8	9
$W_S = 11$					$W_S' = 29$				

Set 2	Group 1				Group 2				
X	60	40	24	21	23	18	15	14	4
Ranks	9	8	7	5	6	4	3	2	1
$W_S = 29$					$W'_S = 11$				

Notice that the two data sets exhibit the same degree of *extremeness*, in the sense that for the first set four of the five lowest ranks are in Group 1, and in the second set four of the five highest ranks are in Group 1. Moreover, W_S for Set 1 is equal to W'_S for Set 2, and vice versa. Thus if we establish the rule that we will calculate both W_S and W'_S for the *smaller* group and refer the *smaller* of W_S and W'_S to the tables, we will come to the same conclusion with respect to the two data sets.

THE NORMAL APPROXIMATION

Appendix D, Table 7, is suitable for all cases in which n_1 and n_2 are less than or equal to 25. For larger values of n_1 and/or n_2 we can make use of the fact that the distribution of W_S approaches a normal distribution as sample sizes increase. This distribution has

$$\text{Mean} = \frac{n_1(n_1 + n_2 + 1)}{2}$$

and   Standard error $= \sqrt{\dfrac{n_1 n_2 (n_1 + n_2 + 1)}{12}}$

Because the distribution is normal and we know its mean and standard deviation (the standard error), we can calculate z:

$$z = \frac{\text{Statistic} - \text{Mean}}{\text{Standard deviation}}$$

$$= \frac{W_S - \dfrac{n_1(n_1 + n_2 + 1)}{2}}{\sqrt{\dfrac{n_1 n_2 (n_1 + n_2 + 1)}{12}}}$$

and obtain from the tables of the normal distribution an approximation of the true probability of a value of W_S at least as low as the one obtained.

To illustrate the computations for the case in which the larger ranks fall in the smaller groups and to illustrate the use of the normal approximation (although we don't really need to use an approximation for such small sample sizes), consider the data in Table 20-2. These data are hypothetical (but probably reasonable) data on the birthweight (in grams) of children born to mothers who did not seek prenatal care until the third trimester and those born to mothers who received prenatal care starting in the first trimester.

Beginning of Care			
Third Trimester		First Trimester	
Birthweight	Rank	Birthweight	Rank
1680	2	2940	10
4900	17	3380	16
3110	14	3830	18
2760	5	2810	9
1700	3	2800	8
2790	7	3210	15
3050	12	3080	13
2660	4	2950	11
1400	1		
2775	6		

$W_S = \Sigma$ (ranks in Group 2) $= 100$

$W'_S = 2\bar{W} - W_S = 152 - 100 = 52$

$$z = \frac{W_S - \dfrac{n_1(n_1 + n_2 + 1)}{2}}{\sqrt{\dfrac{n_1 n_2(n_1 + n_2 + 1)}{12}}}$$

$$= \frac{100 - \dfrac{8(8 + 10 + 1)}{2}}{\sqrt{\dfrac{8(10)(8 + 10 + 1)}{12}}}$$

$$= \frac{100 - 76}{\sqrt{126.6667}} = 2.13$$

For the data in Table 20-2 the sum of the ranks in the smaller group equals 100. From Appendix D, Table 7 we find $2\bar{W} = 152$, and thus $W'_S = 2\bar{W} - W_S = 52$. Because 52 is smaller than 100, we enter Appendix D, Table 7, with $W'_S = 52$, $n_1 = 8$, and $n_2 = 10$. (n_1 is defined as the smaller sample size.) Because we want a two-tailed test, we will double the tabled value of α. The critical value of W_S (or W'_S) for a two-tailed test at $\alpha = .05$ is 53, meaning that only 5% of the time would we expect a value of W_S or W'_S less than or equal to 53 if H_0 is true. Our obtained value of W'_S is 52, which thus falls in the rejection region, and we will reject H_0. We will conclude that mothers who do not receive prenatal care until the third trimester tend to give birth to smaller babies. This probably does not mean that not having care until the third trimester *causes* smaller babies, but only that variables associated with delayed care (e.g., young mothers, poor nutrition, or poverty) are also associated with lower birthweight.

The use of the normal approximation for evaluating W_S is illustrated in the bottom part of Table 20-2. Here we find that $z = 2.13$. From Appendix D, Table

9, we find that the probability of W_S or W'_S as small as 52 (a z as extreme as ± 2.13) is $2(0.0166) = 0.033$. Because this value is smaller than our traditional cutoff of $\alpha = .05$, we will reject H_0 and again conclude that there is sufficient evidence to say that failing to seek early prenatal care is related to lower birthweight. Note that both the exact solution and the normal approximation lead to the same conclusion with respect to H_0. (With the normal approximation it is not necessary to calculate and use W'_S, because use of W_S will lead to the same value of z except for the reversal of its sign. It would be instructive for you to calculate t for the same set of data.)

THE TREATMENT OF TIES

When the data contain tied scores, any test that relies on ranks is likely to be somewhat distorted. There are several different ways of dealing with ties. You can assign tied ranks to tied scores (as we have been doing), you can flip a coin and assign consecutive ranks to tied scores, or you can assign untied ranks in whatever way will make it hardest to reject H_0. In actual practice most people simply assign tied ranks. Although that may not be the statistically best way to proceed, it is clearly the most common and is the method we will use here.

THE NULL HYPOTHESIS

The Mann–Whitney test evaluates the null hypothesis that the two sets of scores were sampled from identical populations. This is broader than the null hypothesis tested by the corresponding t test, which dealt specifically with means (primarily as a result of the underlying assumptions that ruled out other sources of difference). If the two populations are assumed to have the same shape and dispersion, then the null hypothesis tested by the Mann–Whitney test would actually deal with the central tendency (in this case the medians) of the two populations, and if the populations are also symmetric, the test will be a test of means. In any event the Mann–Whitney test is particularly sensitive to differences in central tendency.

20-2   WILCOXON'S MATCHED-PAIRS SIGNED-RANKS TEST

Wilcoxon is credited with developing the most popular distribution-free test for independent groups, which I have referred to as the Mann–Whitney test because of their work on it. He also developed the most popular test for matched groups (or paired scores). This test is the distribution-free analogue of the t test for related samples, and it tests the null hypothesis that two related (matched) samples were drawn either from identical populations or from symmetric populations with the same mean. More specifically, it tests the null hypothesis that the distribution of difference scores (in the population) is symmetric about zero. This is the same hypothesis tested by the corresponding t test when that test's normality assumption is met.

Wilcoxon's matched-pairs signed-ranks test
A nonparametric test for comparing the central tendency of two matched (related) samples.

The development of the logic behind **Wilcoxon's matched-pairs signed-ranks test** is straightforward and can be illustrated with a simple example. Assume that we want to test the often-stated hypothesis that a long-range program of running will reduce blood pressure. To test this hypothesis we measure the blood pressure of a number of subjects, ask them to engage in a systematic program of running for six weeks, and again test their blood pressure at the end of that period. Our dependent variable will be the change in blood pressure over the six-week interval. If running does reduce blood pressure, we would expect most of the subjects to show a lower reading the second time, and thus a positive pre–post difference. We also would expect that those whose blood pressure actually went up (and thus have a negative pre–post difference) would be only *slightly* higher. On the other hand, if running is worthless as a method of controlling blood pressure, then about one-half of the difference scores will be positive and one-half will be negative, and the positive differences will be about as large as the negative ones. In other words, if H_0 is really true, we would no longer expect most changes to be in the predicted direction with only small changes in the unpredicted direction.

As is illustrated in the following numerical example, in carrying out the Wilcoxon matched-pairs signed-ranks test we first calculate the difference score for each pair of measurements. We then rank all difference scores *without* regard to the sign of the difference, then assign the algebraic sign of the differences to the ranks themselves, and finally sum the positive and negative ranks separately. The test statistic (T) is taken as the smaller of the absolute values (i.e., ignoring the sign) of the two sums, and is evaluated against the tabled entries in Appendix D, Table 6. (It is important to note that in calculating T we attach algebraic signs to the ranks only for convenience. We could just as easily, for example, circle those ranks that went with improvement and underline those that went with deterioration. We are merely trying to differentiate between the two cases.)

Assume that the study previously described produced the following data on systolic blood pressure before and after the six-week training session:

Before	130	170	125	170	130	130	145	160
After	120	163	120	135	143	136	144	120
Difference (B − A)	10	7	5	35	−13	−6	1	40
Rank of Difference	5	4	2	7	6	3	1	8
Signed Rank	5	4	2	7	−6	−3	1	8

$T_+ = \Sigma \text{ (positive ranks)} = 27$

$T_- = \Sigma \text{ (negative ranks)} = -9$

The first two rows contain the subjects' blood pressures as measured before and after a six-week program of running. The third row contains the difference scores, obtained by subtracting the "after" score from the "before." Notice that only two subjects showed a negative change—that is, increased blood pressure. Because these difference scores don't appear to reflect a population distribution that is anywhere near normal, we have chosen to use a distribution-free test. In the fourth row all the difference scores have been ranked without regard to the direction of the change, and in the fifth row the appropriate sign has been appended to the ranks to discriminate those whose blood pressure decreased from those whose blood pressure increased. At the bottom of the table we see the sum of the positive and negative ranks (T_+ and T_-). Because T is defined as the smaller absolute value of T_+ and T_-, $T = 9$.

To evaluate T we refer to Appendix D, Table 6, a portion of which is shown in Table 20-3. This table has a somewhat different format from the other tables we have seen. The easiest way to understand what the entries in the table represent is by way of an analogy. Suppose that to test the fairness of a coin you were going to flip it eight times and reject the null hypothesis, at $\alpha = .05$ (one-tailed), if there were too few heads. Out of eight flips of a coin there is no set of outcomes that has a probability of *exactly* .05 under H_0. The probability of one or fewer heads is .0352, and the probability of two or fewer heads is .1445. Thus if we want to work at $\alpha = .05$, we can either reject for one or fewer heads, in which case the probability of a Type I error is actually .0352 (less than .05), or we can reject for two or fewer heads, in which case the probability of a Type I error is actually .1445 (very much greater than .05). The same kind of problem arises with T because it, like the binomial distribution that gave us the probabilities of heads and tails, is a discrete distribution.

In Appendix D, Table 6, we find that for a one-tailed test at $\alpha = .025$ (or a two-tailed test at $\alpha = .05$) with $n = 8$ the entries are 3(.0195) and 4(.0273). This tells us that if we want to work at a (one-tailed) $\alpha = .025$, we can either reject H_0 for $T \leqslant 3$ (in which case α actually equals .0195) or we can reject for $T \leqslant 4$ (in which case the true value of α is .0273). Because we want a two-tailed test, the probabilities should be doubled to 3(.0390) and 4(.0546). Because we obtained a T value of 9, we would not reject H_0, whichever cutoff we choose. We will

TABLE 20-3
Critical Lower-Tail Values of T and Their Associated Probabilities.
Abbreviated Version of Appendix D, Table 6.

	Nominal Alpha (One-Tailed)							
	.05		**.025**		**.01**		**.005**	
N	**T**	**α**	**T**	**α**	**T**	**α**	**T**	**α**
5	0	.0313						
	1	.0625						
6	2	.0469	0	.0156				
	3	.0781	1	.0313				
7	3	.0391	2	.0234	0	.0078		
	4	.0547	3	.0391	1	.0156		
8	5	.0391	3	.0195	1	.0078	0	.0039
	6	.0547	4	.0273	2	.0117	1	.0078
9	8	.0488	5	.0195	3	.0098	1	.0039
	9	.0645	6	.0273	4	.0137	2	.0059
10	10	.0420	8	.0244	5	.0098	3	.0049
	11	.0527	9	.0322	6	.0137	4	.0068
11	13	.0415	10	.0210	7	.0093	5	.0049
	14	.0508	11	.0269	8	.0122	6	.0068
	⋮		⋮		⋮		⋮	

conclude therefore that we have no reason to doubt that blood pressure is unaffected by a short (six-week) period of daily running. It is going to take a lot more than six weeks to make up for a lifetime of dissipated habits.

TIES

Ties can occur in the data in two different ways. One way would be for a subject to have the same before and after scores, leading to a difference score of zero, which has no sign. In this case we normally eliminate that subject from consideration and reduce the sample size accordingly, although this leads to some bias in the data.

In addition, we could have tied difference scores that lead to tied rankings. If both the tied scores are of the same sign, we can break the ties in any way we wish (or assign tied ranks) without affecting the final outcome. If the scores are of opposite signs, we normally assign tied ranks and proceed as usual.

THE NORMAL APPROXIMATION

When the sample size is larger than 50, which is the limit for Appendix D, Table 6, a normal approximation is available to evaluate T. For larger sample sizes we know that the sampling distribution is approximately normally distributed with

$$\text{Mean} = \frac{n(n + 1)}{4} \quad \text{and} \quad \text{Standard error} = \sqrt{\frac{n(n + 1)(2n + 1)}{24}}$$

Thus we can calculate
$$z = \frac{T - \dfrac{n(n + 1)}{4}}{\sqrt{\dfrac{n(n + 1)(2n + 1)}{24}}}$$

and evaluate z using Appendix D, Table 9. The procedure is directly analogous to that used with the Mann–Whitney test and will not be repeated here.

20-3 KRUSKAL–WALLIS ONE-WAY ANALYSIS OF VARIANCE

Kruskal–Wallis one-way analysis of variance
A nonparametric test analogous to a standard one-way analysis of variance.

The **Kruskal–Wallis one-way analysis of variance** is a direct generalization of the Mann–Whitney test to the case in which we have three or more independent groups. As such it is the distribution-free analogue of the one-way analysis of variance discussed in Chapter 16. It tests the hypothesis that all samples were drawn from identical populations and is particularly sensitive to differences in central tendency.

To perform the Kruskal–Wallis test we simply rank all scores without regard to group membership and then compute the sum of the ranks for each group. The sums are denoted by R_j. If the null hypothesis is true, we would expect the R_js to be more or less equal (aside from differences due to the size of the samples). A measure of the degree to which the R_j differ from one another is provided by

$$H = \frac{12}{N(N+1)} \sum_{j=1}^{k} \frac{R_j^2}{n_j} - 3(N+1)$$

where

$$k = \text{the number of groups}$$

$$n_j = \text{the number of observations in Group}_j$$

$$R_j = \text{the sum of the ranks in Group}_j$$

$$N = \Sigma\, n_j = \text{total sample size}$$

H is then evaluated against the χ^2 distribution on $k - 1$ df.

As an example assume that the data in Table 20-4 represent the number of simple arithmetic problems (out of 85) solved (correctly or incorrectly) in one hour by subjects given a depressant drug, a stimulant drug, or a placebo. Notice that in the Depressant group three of the subjects were too depressed to do much of anything and in the Stimulant group three of the subjects ran up against the limit of 85 available problems. These data are decidedly nonnormal, and we will convert the data to ranks and use the Kruskal–Wallis test. The calculations are shown in the lower part of the table. The obtained value of H is 10.36, which

TABLE 20-4
Kruskal–Wallis Test Applied to Data on Problem Solving

Depressant		Stimulant		Placebo	
Score	Rank	Score	Rank	Score	Rank
55	9	73	15	61	11
0	1.5	85	18	54	8
1	3	51	7	80	16
0	1.5	63	12	47	5
50	6	85	18		
60	10	85	18		
44	4	66	13		
		69	14		
R_j	35		115		40

$$H = \frac{12}{N(N+1)} \sum_{j=1}^{k} \frac{R_j^2}{n_j} - 3(N+1)$$

$$= \frac{12}{19(20)} \left(\frac{35^2}{7} + \frac{115^2}{8} + \frac{40^2}{4} \right) - 3(19+1)$$

$$= \frac{12}{380} (2228.125) - 60 = 70.36 - 60 = 10.36$$

$$\chi^2_{.05}(2) = 5.99$$

can be treated as a χ^2 on $3 - 1 = 2\,df$. The critical value of $\chi^2_{.05}(2)$ is found in Appendix D, Table 1, to be 5.99. Because $10.36 > 5.99$, we can reject H_0 and conclude that the three drugs lead to different rates of performance.

20-4   FRIEDMAN'S RANK TEST FOR *k* CORRELATED SAMPLES

Friedman's rank test for *k* correlated samples
A nonparametric test analogous to a one-way repeated-measures ANOVA.

The last test to be discussed in this chapter is the distribution-free analogue of the one-way repeated-measures analysis of variance, **Friedman's rank test for *k* correlated samples**. This test is closely related to a standard repeated-measures analysis of variance applied to ranks instead of raw scores. It is a test on the null hypothesis that the scores for each treatment were drawn from identical populations, and it is especially sensitive to population differences in central tendency.

Assume that we want to test the hypothesis that the judged quality of a lecture is related to the number of visual aids used. The experimenter obtains 17 people who frequently give lectures to local business groups on a variety of topics. Each lecturer delivers the same lecture to three different, but equivalent, audiences—once with no visual aids, once with a few transparencies to illustrate major points, and once with transparencies and flip charts to illustrate every point to be made. At the end of each lecture the audience is asked to rate the lecture on a 75-point scale, and the mean rating across all members of the audience is taken as the dependent variable. Because the same lecturers serve under all three conditions, we would expect the data to be correlated. Terrible lecturers are terrible no matter how many visual aids they use. Hypothetical data are presented in Table 20-5, in which a higher score represents a more favorable rating. The ranking of the raw scores *within each subject* are shown in parentheses.

If the null hypothesis is true, we would expect the rankings to be randomly distributed within each lecturer. Thus one lecturer might do best with no visual aids, another might do best with many aids, and so on. If this were the case, the sum of the rankings in each condition (column) would be approximately equal. On the other hand if a few visual aids were to lead to the most popular lecture, then most lecturers would have their highest rating under that condition, and the sum of the rankings for the three conditions would be decidedly unequal.

To apply Friedman's test we rank the raw scores for each lecturer separately and then sum the rankings for each condition. We then evaluate the variability of the sums by computing

$$\chi^2_F = \frac{12}{Nk(k + 1)} \sum_{j=1}^{k} R_j^2 - 3N(k + 1)$$

where

$R_j = $ the sum of the ranks for the jth condition

$N = $ the number of subjects (lecturers)

$k = $ the number of conditions

TABLE 20-5		Number of Visual Aids	
Hypothetical Data on Rated Quality of Lectures			
Lecturer	None	Few	Many
1	50(1)	58(3)	54(2)
2	32(2)	37(3)	25(1)
3	60(1)	70(3)	63(2)
4	58(2)	60(3)	55(1)
5	41(1)	66(3)	59(2)
6	36(2)	40(3)	28(1)
7	26(3)	25(2)	20(1)
8	49(1)	60(3)	50(2)
9	72(1)	73(2)	75(3)
10	49(2)	54(3)	42(1)
11	52(2)	57(3)	47(1)
12	36(2)	42(3)	29(1)
13	37(3)	34(2)	31(1)
14	58(3)	50(1)	56(2)
15	39(1)	48(3)	44(2)
16	25(2)	29(3)	18(1)
17	51(1)	63(2)	68(3)
	30	45	27

$$\chi_F^2 = \frac{12}{Nk(k+1)} \sum_{j=1}^{k} R_j^2 - 3N(k+1)$$

$$= \frac{12}{(17)(3)(4)} (30^2 + 45^2 + 27^2) - 3(17)(4)$$

$$= \frac{12}{204} (3654) - 204$$

$$= 214.94 - 204 = 10.94$$

This value of χ_F^2 can be evaluated with respect to the standard χ^2 distribution on $k - 1$ df.

For the data in Table 20-5, $\chi_F^2 = 10.94$ on 2 df. Because $\chi_{.05}^2(2) = 5.99$, we will reject H_0 and conclude that the judged quality of a lecture differs as a function of the degree to which visual aids are included. The data would suggest that some visual aids are helpful, but that too many of them can detract from what the lecturer is saying. (*Note:* The null hypothesis we have just tested says nothing about differences among subjects [lecturers], and in fact subject differences are completely eliminated by the ranking procedure.)

20-5 SUMMARY

This chapter has summarized briefly a set of procedures that require far fewer restrictive assumptions concerning the populations from which our data have been sampled. We first discussed the Mann–Whitney test, which is the distribution-free analogue of the independent sample t test. To perform the test we simply ranked the data and asked if the distribution of ranks resembled the distribution we would expect if the null hypothesis were true. The same general logic applies to the Wilcoxon matched-pairs signed-ranks test, which is the distribution-free test corresponding to the matched-sample t test. We then discussed two distribution-free tests that are analogous to an analysis of variance on independent measures (the Kruskal–Wallis) and repeated measures (the Friedman). Although it is important to be familiar with these four tests simply because they are commonly used, it was argued at the beginning of the chapter that the advantages we gain by limiting our assumptions may not be worth the loss in power that often accompanies the use of distribution-free tests. Whatever one's stand on this question, the general principle remains that the overriding concern in the use and interpretation of any statistical procedure is not statistical sophistication, but common sense. Some of the most important terms in this chapter are:

- **Parametric tests**
- **Nonparametric tests (distribution-free tests)**
- **Rank-randomization tests**
- **Mann–Whitney test**

- **Wilcoxon's matched-pairs signed-ranks test**
- **Kruskal–Wallis one-way analysis of variance**
- **Friedman's rank test for k correlated samples**

20-6 EXERCISES

20–1 McConaughy (1980) has argued that younger children organize stories in terms of simple descriptive ("and then...") models, whereas older children incorporate causal statements and social inferences. Suppose that we asked two groups of children differing in age to summarize a story they just read. We then counted the number of statements in the summary that can be classed as inferences. The data are:

Younger Children	0	1	0	3	2	5	2
Older Children	4	7	6	4	8	7	

(a) Analyze these data using the two-tailed rank-sum test.

(b) What would you conclude?

20–2 Kapp, Frysinger, Gallagher, and Hazelton (1979) have demonstrated that lesions in the amygdala can reduce certain responses commonly associated with fear (e.g., decreases in heart rate). If fear is really reduced, then it should be more difficult to train an avoidance response in lesioned animals because the aversiveness of the stimulus will be reduced. Assume two groups of rabbits:

one group has lesions in the amygdala, and the other is an untreated control group. The following data represent number of trials to learn an avoidance response for each animal.

Group with Lesions	15	14	15	8	7	22
	36	19	14	18	17	

Control Group	9	4	9	10	6	6
	4	5	9			

(a) Analyze the data using the Mann–Whitney test (two-tailed).

(b) What would you conclude?

20–3 Repeat the analysis in Exercise 20-2 using the normal approximation.

20–4 Repeat the analysis in Exercise 20-2 using the appropriate one-tailed test.

20–5 Nurcombe and Fitzhenry-Coor (1979) have argued that training in diagnostic techniques should lead a clinician to generate (and test) more hypotheses in coming to a decision about a case. Suppose that we take ten psychiatric residents who are just beginning their residency and ask them to watch a videotape of an interview and to record their thoughts on the case every few minutes. We then count the number of hypotheses each resident includes in his or her written remarks. The experiment is repeated at the end of the residency with a comparable videotape. The data are:

Subject	1	2	3	4	5	6	7	8	9	10
Before	8	4	2	2	4	8	3	1	3	9
After	7	9	3	6	3	10	6	7	8	7

(a) Analyze the data using Wilcoxon's matched-pairs signed-ranks test.

(b) What would you conclude?

20-6 Referring to Exercise 20-5,

(a) Repeat the analysis using the normal approximation.

(b) How well do the two answers agree? Why don't they agree exactly?

20-7 It has been argued that first-born children tend to be more independent than later-born children. Suppose that we develop a 25-point scale of independence and rate each of 20 first-born children and their second-born siblings using our scale. We do this when both siblings are adults, thus eliminating obvious age effects. The data on independence are as follows (a higher score means that the person is more independent):

Sibling Pair	1	2	3	4	5	6	7
First Born	12	18	13	17	8	15	16
Second Born	10	12	15	13	9	12	13

Sibling Pair	8	9	10	11	12	13	14
First Born	5	8	12	13	5	14	20
Second Born	8	10	8	8	9	8	10

Sibling Pair	15	16	17	18	19	20
First Born	19	17	2	5	15	18
Second Born	14	11	7	7	13	12

(a) Analyze the data using Wilcoxon's matched-pairs signed-ranks test.

(b) What would you conclude?

20-8 Rerun the analysis in Exercise 20-7 using the normal approximation.

20-9 The results in Exercise 20-7 are not quite as clearcut as we might like. Plot the differences as a function of the first-born's score. What does this figure suggest?

20-10 What is the difference between the null hypothesis tested by the Mann–Whitney test and the corresponding t test?

20-11 What is the difference between the null hypothesis tested by Wilcoxon's matched-pairs signed-ranks test and the corresponding t test?

20-12 One of the arguments put forth in favor of distribution-free tests is that they are more appropriate for ordinal scale data. This issue was addressed earlier in the book in a different context. Give a reason why this argument is not a good one.

20-13 Why is rejection of the null hypothesis using a t test a more specific statement than rejection of the null hypothesis using the appropriate distribution-free test?

20-14 Three rival professors teaching English I all claim the honor of having the best students. To settle the issue eight students are randomly drawn from each class and are given the same exam, which is graded by a neutral professor who does not know from which class the students came. The data are:

Professor A	82	71	56	58	63	64	62	53
Professor B	55	88	85	83	71	70	68	72
Professor C	65	54	66	68	72	78	65	73

Run the appropriate test and draw the appropriate conclusions.

20-15 A psychologist operating a group home for delinquent adolescents needs to show that it is successful at reducing delinquency. He samples ten adolescents living at home whom the police have identified as having problems, ten similar adolescents living in foster homes, and ten adolescents living in the group home. As an indicator variable he uses truancy (number of days truant in the past semester), which is readily obtained from school records. On the basis of the following data, draw the appropriate conclusions:

Natural Home	15	18	19	14	5	8	12	13	7
Foster Home	16	14	20	22	19	5	17	18	12
Group Home	10	13	14	11	7	3	4	18	2

20-16 As an alternative method of evaluating a Group Home, suppose that we take 12 adolescents who have been declared delinquent. We take the number of days truant (1) during the month before they are placed in the home, (2) during the month they live in the home, and (3) during the month after they leave the home. The data are:

Adolescent	1	2	3	4	5	6
Before	10	12	12	19	5	13
During	5	8	13	10	10	8
After	8	7	10	12	8	7

Adolescent	7	8	9	10	11	12
Before	20	8	12	10	8	18
During	16	4	14	3	3	16
After	12	5	9	5	3	2

Apply Friedman's test. What do you conclude?

20–17 What advantage does the study described in Exercise 20-16 have over the study described in Exercise 20-15?

20–18 It would be possible to apply Friedman's test to the data in Exercise 20-5. What would we lose if we did?

20–19 For the data in Exercise 20-5 we could say that three out of ten residents used fewer hypotheses the second time and seven used more. We could test this with χ^2. How would this differ from Friedman's test applied to those data?

20–20 The history of statistical hypothesis testing really began with a tea-tasting experiment (Fisher, 1935), so it seems fitting for this book to end with one. The owner of a small tearoom doesn't think that people really can tell the difference between the first cup made with a given tea bag and the second and third cups made with the same bag (that is why it is still a *small* tearoom). He chooses eight different brands of tea bags, makes three cups of tea with each, and then has a group of customers rate each cup on a 20-point scale (without knowing which cup is which). The data are shown here, with higher ratings indicating better tea:

	Cup		
Tea Brands	First	Second	Third
1	8	3	2
2	15	14	4
3	16	17	12
4	7	5	4
5	9	3	6
6	8	9	4
7	10	3	4
8	12	10	2

Using Friedman's test, draw the appropriate conclusions.

21

CHOOSING THE APPROPRIATE ANALYSIS

Most of this book has been concerned with presenting and explaining procedures commonly used to describe and analyze experimental data. It is important for you to know *how* to apply those procedures, but it is equally important for you to know *when* to apply them. One of the greatest difficulties students face when presented with real data is to know which of the many procedures they have learned is applicable to that set of data.

In Chapter 1 I presented a brief discussion of the tree diagram that is found on the inside front cover. That diagram is designed to help you consider the relevant issues involved in selecting a statistical test (the issue of the type of data, the question of relationships versus differences, the number of groups, and whether variables are independent or dependent). The tree diagram is largely self-explanatory, and it is worth your time to go over it and make sure you understand the distinctions that are made. At the same time it is difficult to use something such as that diagram effectively unless you have had practice in doing so. The following examples are designed to give you that practice.

On the next few pages are 20 examples of research studies drawn from the published literature. Each of these studies is an example of an actual study that resulted in data that someone had to analyze. Your task is to identify the appropriate statistical procedure to be used in each case. In some cases there may be several procedures that could all be properly applied, and in other cases there may be room for disagreement over just what procedure would be best. Moreover, in some cases the appropriate procedure may simply be the calculation of one or more descriptive statistics, whereas in others—the majority—some sort of hypothesis testing is called for. In all cases you should assume that the assumptions required by the standard parametric tests are met unless you are told otherwise. For some of the examples I have noted what the experimenter found. This is simply for your interest and is not intended to be part of the question.

In selecting the examples given here I have occasionally simplified the actual experiment in minor ways—usually by omitting either independent or dependent variables. I have tried not to change the nature of the experiment in any important way. Should you be interested in following up any of these studies, they are all listed in the references. If you would like even more practice, the summaries of studies that are found in *Psychological Abstracts* offer excellent examples.

I have supplied my answers to each of these examples in the answer section at the end of the book. As I said, there is occasionally room for disagreement over the appropriate analysis. My approach may in fact differ from that of the original experimenter, who had a better grasp of the data than I can have. If your answer differs from mine, be sure that you understand why I gave the answer that I did and consider whether yours is just a different way of answering the same question, whether it answers an entirely different question, or whether you have failed to take something into account.

21-1 EXERCISES

21–1 Berndt, Schwartz, and Kaiser (1983) were concerned with whether or not ten different psychological scales for the assessment of depression are suitable for use with adolescents and young adults. They specifically wanted to know whether subjects or clients could understand the questions. Using standard readability formulae, they computed readability scores for each of the ten depression inventories. What statistical procedures would they most likely use?

21–2 Harper and Wacher (1983) examined the relationship between scores on the Denver Developmental Screening Test and scores on individually administered intellectual measures for 555 three- to four-year-old children. How would they best assess these relationships?

21–3 Do people pay any attention to the pictures that are included in introductory psychology textbooks? Goldstein, Bailis, and Chance (1983) presented 47 subjects with a large number of pictures and asked them to pick out the ones they recognized. Many of the pictures were taken from the introductory psychology textbook the students were using. The experimenters also presented the same pictures to 56 students who were using a different text. For each subject they recorded the percentage of pictures correctly identified. In addition, they asked subjects in the first group to indicate the degree to which they used textbook pictures in general as study aids. How would you analyze the data on recognition and the data on reported use of pictures?

21–4 Newman, Olson, Hall, and Hornak (1983) presented subjects with a series of target words to learn. Each target was accompanied by a cue word that was either strongly or weakly associated with the target (e.g., Table–Chair or Table–Round). During a recall task subjects were asked to recall the target words and were presented with a different set of cues that were either strongly or weakly associated with the target, or else they were presented with no cue at all. The dependent variable was the number of target words recalled. How would you analyze these data?

21–5 In studying what is called latent spatial learning, Sutherland and Linggard (1982) taught rats to swim to a small underwater (and therefore invisible) platform from a variety of locations in a round pool of water. Some rats had never seen the pool, some previously had been placed directly on the platform in a different location in the pool, and some previously had been placed on the platform in the same location. The dependent variable was the speed with which rats learned to swim to the platform. What is the most likely statistical analysis of these data?

21–6 Lundberg (1983) studied the origins of what is usually called Type A behavior. He administered a questionnaire to 15 children aged 3 to 6 and scored the children with respect to the competitiveness, impatience/anger, and aggressiveness components of Type A behavior. Those above the median were classed as Type A and those below the median were classed as Type B. (This is called a "median split.") He then measured heart rate and blood pressure during an emotional event. How should he analyze these data for each of the dependent variables? (*Note*: There were differences, but only in systolic blood pressure.)

21–7 Supramaniam (1983) investigated proofreading errors committed by good and poor readers on easy and difficult passages. The same subjects proofread both passages. We have not covered the computational procedures for the analysis of these data, but you should be able to describe the type of analysis needed.

21–8 Linn and Hodge (1982) investigated locus of control in hyperactive and control subjects. Locus of control refers to the degree to which people view positive and negative outcomes as being attributable to their own internally controlled behaviors, such as skill or hard work, or to external events, such as luck or task difficulty, over which they have no control. Sixteen hyperactive and 16 control subjects were administered the Nowicki–Strickland Locus of Control Scale and the Peabody Picture Vocabulary Test (a general intelligence test).

How should they deal with the locus of control scores and of what use are the Peabody scores?

21–9 Obrzut, Hansen, and Heath (1982) classified 153 Hispanic children as poor visual processors on the basis of the Matching Familiar Figures Test (MFFT). They then assigned the children to one of three treatment groups. One group received tutoring in visual information processing, another group received small-group instruction with regular classroom materials, and the third group was a control group receiving no special treatment. The dependent variable was the child's score on a second administration of the MFFT. What analysis is appropriate?

21–10 Pliner (1982) was interested in investigating whether familiarity with a flavor leads to greater approval—the "acquired-taste" phenomenon. She had 24 undergraduates taste unfamiliar tropical fruit juices either 0, 5, 10, or 20 times. They were then asked to rate the degree to which they liked the taste of the juice. What statistical procedures are suitable for analyzing these data? What test would she use if she wanted a distribution-free test? (*Note*: She found the effect that she had expected—greater familiarity led to greater approval.)

21–11 Fagerström (1982) studied the effect of using nicotine gum as an adjunct to a standard program for giving up smoking. One group received the standard psychological treatment program normally employed by Fagerström's clinic. A second group received the same program but was also supplied with gum containing nicotine, which they were instructed to chew when they felt the need to smoke. Each group contained 50 subjects, and subjects were classified as abstinent or not at one month and at six months. How should he analyze his data? What problem arises from the fact that there was not a group who were given plain-old-candy-store gum? (*Note*: The experimental [gum] group had abstinence rates of 90% and 64% at one and six months, respectively, and the control group had rates of 60% and 45%.)

21–12 Payne (1982) asked male and female subjects to rank ten common job characteristics (e.g., salary, workload, etc.) for their personal importance to the subject and their perceived importance to a member of the opposite sex. The data were collected from 92 subjects in 1973 and from 145 subjects in 1981. How should she analyze these data?

21–13 Cochran and Urbanczyk (1982) were concerned with the effect of the height of a room on the desired personal space of subjects. They tested 48 subjects in both a high-ceiling (10-ft) and a low-ceiling (7-ft) room. Subjects stood with their backs to a wall while a stranger approached. They were told to say "stop" when the approaching stranger's nearness made them feel uncomfortable. The dependent variable was the distance at which the subject said "stop." What should the experimenters do with their data? What would they do instead if they were unwilling to use a parametric test? (*Note*: The distance was greater with a lower ceiling, which suggests that interpersonal space is not dependent just on horizontal distance.)

21–14 Robinson, Barret, and Skeen (1983) compared scores on a scale of locus of control for 20 unwed adolescent fathers and 20 unwed adolescent nonfathers. How could they analyze these data if they were unwilling to make parametric assumptions? (*Note*: They found no difference.)

21–15 Smith and Plant (1982) studied sex differences in job satisfaction. They first matched pairs of male and female university professors on the basis of four variables known to be related to job satisfaction (i.e., years of service, rank, highest degree, and department). They then used a paper-and-pencil measure of job satisfaction to obtain a score for each subject on five satisfaction areas—work, pay, promotion, supervision, and co-workers. What statistical procedure is appropriate for these data, treating each satisfaction area separately?

21–16 Hosch and Cooper (1982) looked at the role that being a victim rather than just a bystander had on eyewitness identification. In the control condition a confederate of the experimenter entered the experimental room with a subject, completed a few forms, and left. In another condition the confederate did the same thing, but as she was leaving she stole the *experimenter's* calculator. In the third condition the confederate stole the *subject's* watch instead, which the subject had been instructed to leave on the table. There were two dependent variables. The first was whether or not the subject was able to correctly identify the confederate from a set of six photographs, and the second was the subject's subjective rating, on a 9-point scale, of his or her confidence in the identification. The experimenter was most interested in seeing whether being a victim of a theft led to better, and more confident, identification than just observing a theft. How can these data be analyzed? (*Note*: The two theft conditions did not differ and there was *no* relationship between accuracy and confidence.)

21–17 Bradley and Kjungja (1982) experimented with the perception of subjective triangles. When you look at three points that form a triangle, there is a subjective impression of lines connecting those points to form the contours of the triangle. Bradley and Kjungja asked subjects to view the subjective triangle while it was stationary and again while it was rotating in a circle. The subject was instructed to say whether the subjective contours were stronger while the triangle was stationary or while it was rotating. Out of 37 subjects, 35 said that the contours were stronger when the triangle was rotating. How could they test whether this difference was significant—although here a test isn't really needed?

21–18 Brown et al. (1982) investigated drug-induced amnesia as a way of throwing light on organically produced amnesia. They presented subjects with a list of words and then injected the subjects with either lorazepam (which produces amnesia) or saline. After 1.5 hours they asked all subjects to recall the words they had learned. They also asked the same subjects to learn a list after the drug had been injected and to recall it after 1.5 hours. If lorazepam interferes with the storage of material in memory, then only recall of the second list should be affected. If lorazepam interferes with retrieval rather than storage, then recall of both lists should be disrupted. What statistical test would be appropriate for analyzing these data? This is another case in which you do not know how to perform the analysis, but you should be able to describe the design. (*Note*: Recall of the predrug list was unaffected, but the list studied after the administration of the drug was poorly recalled.)

21–19 Hicks and Guista (1982) asked seven subjects who habitually had less than 6.5 hours of sleep per night and nine subjects who habitually had more than 8.5 hours of sleep per night to complete the Stanford Sleepiness Scale (SSS) at 2-hour intervals for 30 days. The SSS is a measure of alertness and simply requires the subject to rate his or her level of alertness by responding with a number between 1 (very alert) and 7 (struggling to stay awake). The authors actually broke the data into seven different times of day, but for purposes of this example assume that the dependent variable is each subject's mean SSS score over the 30-day period. What is the appropriate analysis of these data?

21–20 The right side of a person's face resembles the whole face more than does the left side. Kennedy, Beard, and Carr (1982) asked 91 subjects to view full-face pictures of six different faces. Testing of recall was conducted one week later, when subjects were presented with pictures of 12 faces and were asked to identify the ones they had seen earlier. At testing, subjects were divided into three groups of roughly equal size. One group was presented with full-face photographs, one group only saw the right side of the face in the photograph, and one group only saw the left side. The dependent variable was the number of errors. The authors were not satisfied that the assumptions of parametric tests were met. How could they compare the three groups and how could they compare the two partial-face groups? (*Note*: Contrary to the prediction the left side turned out to be easier to recognize than the right side.)

ARITHMETIC REVIEW

Standard Symbols and Basic Information	**Parentheses**
Addition and Subtraction	**Fractions**
Multiplication and Division	**Algebraic Operations**

The following is intended as a quick refresher of some of the simple arithmetic operations that you learned in high school but probably have not used since. Although some of what follows will seem so obvious that you wonder why it is there, people sometimes forget the most obvious things.

One of the things that students never seem to learn is that it is easy to figure out most of these principles for yourself. For example if you can't remember whether

$$\frac{18.1}{28.6 + 32.7} \quad \text{can be reduced to} \quad \frac{18.1}{28.6} + \frac{18.1}{32.7}$$

(it cannot, but it is one of the foolish things that I can never keep in my head), try it out with very simple numbers. Thus

$$\frac{2}{1 + 4} = \frac{2}{5} = 0.4$$

is obviously not the same as

$$\frac{2}{1} + \frac{2}{4} = 2.5$$

It is often quicker to check on a procedure by using small numbers than by looking it up.

STANDARD SYMBOLS AND BASIC INFORMATION

Numerator	The thing on the top.
Denominator	The thing on the bottom.
a/b	a = Numerator; b = Denominator.
$+, -, \times, \div$ **(or /)**	Symbols for addition, subtraction, multiplication, and division. Called *operators*.

$X = Y$	X equals Y.
$X \approx Y$ or $X \simeq Y$	X approximately equal to Y.
$X \neq Y$	X unequal to Y.
$X < Y$	X less than Y. (*Hint*: The small end points at the smaller number.)
$X \leqslant Y$	X less than or equal to Y.
$X > Y$	X greater than Y.
$X \geqslant Y$	X greater than or equal to Y.
$X < Y < Z$	X less than Y less than Z (i.e., Y is between X and Z).
$X \pm Y$	X plus or minus Y.
$|X|$	Absolute value of X—ignore the sign of X.
$\dfrac{1}{X}$	The reciprocal of X.
X^2	X squared.
X^n	X raised to the nth power.
$\sqrt{X} = X^{1/2}$	Square root of X.

ADDITION AND SUBTRACTION

$8 - 12 = -4$	To subtract a larger number from a smaller one, subtract the smaller from the larger and make the result negative.
$-8 + 12 = 12 - 8 = 4$	The order of operations is not important.

MULTIPLICATION AND DIVISION

$2(3)(6) = 2 \times 3 \times 6$	If no operator appears before a parenthesis, hereafter denoted ( ), multiplication is implied.
$2 \times 3 \times 6 = 2 \times 6 \times 3$	Numbers can be multiplied in any order.
$\dfrac{2 \times 8}{4} = \dfrac{2}{4} \times 8 = 2 \times \dfrac{8}{4} = \dfrac{16}{4} = 4$	Division can take place in any order.
$7 \times 3 + 6 = 21 + 6 = 27$	Multiply or divide *before* you add or subtract the result.
$2 \times 3 = 6;\ (-2)(-3) = 6$ $\dfrac{6}{3} = 2;\ \dfrac{-6}{-3} = 2$	Multiplication or division of numbers with the *same* sign produces a positive answer.
$(-2)3 = -6;\ \dfrac{-6}{3} = -2$	Multiplication or division of numbers with *opposite* signs produces a negative answer.
$(-2)(3)(-6)(-4) = (-6)(24)$ $= -144$	With several numbers having different signs work in pairs to get the correct sign.

PARENTHESES

$2(7-6+3)=2(4)=8$
or $2(7)+2(-6)+2(3)=$
   $14-12+6=8$

When multiplying, either perform the operations inside ( ) before multiplying, or multiply *each* element within the ( ) and then sum.

$2(7-6+3)^2=$
$2(4)^2=2(16)=32$

When the parenthetical term is raised to a power, perform the operations inside the ( ), raise the result to the appropriate power, and then carry out the other operations.

FRACTIONS

$\dfrac{1}{5}=0.20$

To convert to a decimal, divide the numerator by the denominator.

$\dfrac{4}{3}$

The reciprocal of $\frac{3}{4}$. To take the reciprocal of a fraction, stand it on its head.

$3\times\dfrac{6}{5}=\dfrac{3\times6}{5}=\dfrac{18}{5}=3.6$

To multiply a fraction by a whole number, multiply the numerator by that number.

$\dfrac{3}{5}\times\dfrac{6}{7}\times\dfrac{1}{2}=\dfrac{3\times6\times1}{5\times7\times2}$

To multiply a series of fractions multiply numerators together and multiply denominators together.

$=\dfrac{18}{70}=0.26$

$\dfrac{1}{3}+\dfrac{4}{3}=\dfrac{5}{3}=1.67$

To add fractions with the *same* denominator, add the numerators and divide by the common denominator.

$\dfrac{1}{6}+\dfrac{4}{3}=\dfrac{1}{6}+\dfrac{8}{6}=\dfrac{9}{6}=1.5$

To add fractions with *different* denominators, multiply the numerator and the denominator by a constant to equate the denominators and follow the previous rule.

$\dfrac{8}{13}+\dfrac{12}{25}$

$=\left(\dfrac{25}{25}\times\dfrac{8}{13}\right)+\left(\dfrac{13}{13}\times\dfrac{12}{25}\right)$

This is a more elaborate example of the same rule.

$=\dfrac{200}{325}+\dfrac{156}{325}=\dfrac{356}{325}$

$=1.095$

$\dfrac{8}{1/3}=8\left(\dfrac{3}{1}\right)=24$

To divide by a fraction, multiply by the reciprocal of that fraction.

ALGEBRAIC OPERATIONS

Most algebraic operations boil down to moving things from one side of the equation to the other. Mathematically the rule is that whatever you do to one side of the equation you must do to the other side.

Solve the following equation for X:

$$3 + X = 8$$

We want X on one side and the answer on the other. All we have to do is to subtract 3 from both sides to get

$$3 + X - 3 = 8 - 3$$

$$X = 5$$

If the equation had been

$$X - 3 = 8$$

We would have added 3 to both sides:

$$X - 3 + 3 = 8 + 3$$

$$X = 11$$

For equations involving multiplication or division we follow the same principle.

$$2X = 21$$

Dividing both sides by 2 we have

$$\frac{2X}{2} = \frac{21}{2}$$

$$X = 10.5$$

and

$$\frac{X}{7} = 13$$

$$\frac{7X}{7} = 7(13)$$

$$X = 91$$

Personally I prefer to think of things in a different, but perfectly equivalent, way. When you want to get rid of something that has been added (or subtracted) to (or from) one side of the equation, move it to the other side and reverse the sign.

$$3 + X = 12 \qquad \text{or} \qquad X - 7 = 19$$

$$X = 12 - 3 \qquad\qquad X = 19 + 7$$

When the thing you want to get rid of is in the numerator, move it to the other side and put it in the denominator.

$$7.6X = 12$$

$$X = \frac{12}{7.6}$$

When the thing you want to get rid of is in the denominator, move it to the numerator on the other side and multiply.

$$\frac{X}{8.9} = 14.6$$

$$X = 14.6(8.9)$$

Notice that with more complex expressions you must multiply (or divide) everything on the other side of the equation. Thus

$$7.6X = 12 + 8$$

$$X = \frac{12 + 8}{7.6}$$

For complex equations, just work one step at a time.

$$7.6(X + 8) = \frac{14}{7} - 5$$

First get rid of the 7.6:

$$X + 8 = \frac{14/7 - 5}{7.6}$$

Now get rid of the 8:

$$X = \frac{14/7 - 5}{7.6} - 8$$

Now clean up the messy fraction:

$$X = \frac{2 - 5}{7.6} - 8 = \frac{-3}{7.6} - 8 = -0.395 - 8 = -8.395$$

SYMBOLS AND NOTATION

GREEK LETTER SYMBOLS

α	Level of significance—probability of a Type I error (alpha)
β	Probability of a Type II error (beta)
γ	Effect size (gamma)
δ	Noncentrality parameter (delta)
η^2	Eta squared
μ	Population mean (mu)
$\mu_{\bar{x}}$	Mean of the sampling distribution of the mean
ρ	Population correlation coefficient (rho)
σ	Population standard deviation (sigma)
σ^2	Population variance
Σ	Summation notation (sigma—upper case)
ϕ	Phi coefficient
χ^2	Chi-square
χ_F^2	Friedman's chi-square
ω^2	Omega squared

ENGLISH LETTER SYMBOLS

a	Intercept; Number of levels of variable A in analysis of variance
b	Slope (also called regression coefficient)
CI	Confidence interval
cov_{XY}	Covariance of X and Y
df	Degrees of freedom
E	Expected frequency; Expected value
F	F statistic
G	Grand total—total of all the scores
GM	Grand mean
H	Kruskal–Wallis statistic
$H_0; H_1$	Null hypothesis; Alternative hypothesis

MS	Mean square
MS_{error}	Mean square error
n, n_i, N_i	Number of cases in a sample
$N(0, 1)$	Read "normally distributed with $\mu = 0$, $\sigma^2 = 1$"
O	Observed frequency
p	General symbol for probability
r, r_{XY}	Pearson's correlation coefficient
r_{pb}	Point-biserial correlation coefficient
r_S	Spearman's rank-order correlation coefficient
R	Multiple correlation coefficient
RLL	Real lower limit
s^2, s_X^2	Sample variance
s_p^2	Pooled variance
s, s_X	Sample standard deviation
s_D	Standard deviation of difference scores
$s_{\bar{D}}$	Standard error of the mean of difference scores
$s_{\bar{X}}, s_{\bar{X}_1 - \bar{X}_2}$	Standard error of the mean; Standard error of differences between means
$s_{Y - \hat{Y}}$	Standard error of estimate
SP_{XY}	Sum of products of X and Y
SS_A	Sum of squares for variable A
SS_{AB}	Interaction sum of squares
SS_{error}	Error sum of squares
SS_Y	Sum of squares for variable Y
$SS_{\hat{Y}}$	Sum of squares of predicted values of Y
$SS_{Y - \hat{Y}}$	Error sum of squares $= SS_{error}$
t	Student's t statistic
$t_{.05}$	Critical value of t
T	Wilcoxon's matched-pairs signed-ranks statistic
T_j	Total for group j
T_{A_i}	Total for the ith level of variable A
W_S, W_S'	Mann–Whitney statistic
$\bar{X}, \bar{X}_i$	Sample mean
$\bar{X}_h$	Harmonic mean
$\hat{Y}, \hat{Y}_i$	Predicted value of Y
z	Normal deviate (also called standard score)

DATA SET

Howell and Huessy (1985) reported on a study of 386 children who had, and had not, exhibited during childhood symptoms of attention deficit disorder (ADD)—previously known as hyperkinesis or minimal brain dysfunction. In 1965 teachers of all second-grade school children in a number of schools in northwestern Vermont had been asked to complete a questionnaire for each of their students dealing with behaviors commonly associated with ADD. Questionnaires on these same children were again completed when they were in the fourth and fifth grades and, for purposes of this data set only, those three scores were averaged to produce a score labeled ADDSC. The higher the score, the more ADD-like behaviors the child exhibited. At the end of ninth grade and again at the end of twelfth grade, information on the performances of these children was obtained from school records. Some of these variables are presented in the accompanying table for a sample of 88 of these students. These data offer the opportunity to examine questions about whether later behavior can be predicted from earlier behavior and to examine academically related variables and their interrelationships. The data are referred to in many of the homework exercises at the end of each chapter. A description of each variable follows:

ADDSC	The average of the three ADD-like behavior scores obtained in elementary school.
SEX	1 = male; 2 = female
REPEAT	1 = repeated at least one grade; 0 = did not repeat a grade
IQ	IQ obtained from a group-administered IQ test
ENGL	Level of English in ninth grade: 1 = remedial; 2 = general; 3 = college prep
ENGG	Grade in English in ninth grade: 4 = A; 3 = B; etc.
GPA	Grade point average in ninth grade
SOCPROB	Social problems in ninth grade: 1 = yes; 0 = no
DROPOUT	1 = dropped out before completing high school; 0 = did not drop out

ADDSC	SEX	REPEAT	IQ	ENGL	ENGG	GPA	SOCPROB	DROPOUT	ADDSC	SEX	REPEAT	IQ	ENGL	ENGG	GPA	SOCPROB	DROPOUT
45	1	0	111	2	3	2.60	0	0	43	1	0	107	1	2	2.00	0	0
50	1	0	102	2	3	2.75	0	0	51	1	0	95	2	2	2.75	0	0
49	1	0	108	2	4	4.00	0	0	70	1	1	97	2	3	2.67	1	1
55	1	0	109	2	2	2.25	0	0	69	1	1	93	2	2	2.00	0	0
39	1	0	118	2	3	3.00	0	0	65	1	1	81	1	2	2.00	0	0
68	1	1	79	2	2	1.67	0	1	63	2	0	89	2	2	1.67	0	0
69	1	1	88	2	2	2.25	1	1	44	2	0	111	2	4	3.00	0	0
56	1	0	102	2	4	3.40	0	0	61	2	1	95	2	1	1.50	0	1
58	1	0	105	3	1	1.33	0	0	40	2	0	106	2	4	3.75	0	0
48	1	0	92	2	4	3.50	0	0	62	2	0	83	3	1	0.67	0	0
34	1	0	131	2	4	3.75	0	0	59	1	0	81	2	2	1.50	0	0
50	2	0	104	1	3	2.67	0	0	47	2	0	115	1	4	4.00	0	0
85	1	0	83	2	3	2.75	1	0	50	2	0	112	2	3	3.00	0	0
49	1	0	84	2	2	2.00	0	0	50	2	0	92	2	3	2.33	0	0
51	1	0	85	2	3	2.75	0	0	65	2	0	85	2	2	1.75	0	0
53	1	0	110	2	2	2.50	0	0	54	2	0	95	3	2	3.00	0	0
36	2	0	121	1	4	3.55	0	0	44	2	0	115	2	4	3.75	0	0
62	2	0	120	2	3	2.75	0	0	66	2	0	91	2	4	2.67	1	1
46	2	0	100	2	4	3.50	0	0	34	2	0	107	1	4	3.50	0	0
50	2	0	94	2	2	2.75	1	1	74	2	0	102	2	0	0.67	0	0
47	2	0	89	1	2	3.00	0	0	57	2	1	86	3	3	2.25	0	0
50	2	0	93	2	4	3.25	0	0	60	2	0	96	1	3	3.00	1	0
44	2	0	128	2	4	3.30	0	0	36	2	0	114	2	3	3.50	0	0
50	2	0	84	2	3	2.75	0	0	50	1	0	105	2	2	1.75	0	0
29	2	0	127	1	4	3.75	0	0	60	1	0	82	2	1	1.00	0	0
49	2	0	106	2	3	2.75	0	0	45	1	0	120	2	3	3.00	0	0
26	1	0	137	2	3	3.00	0	0	55	1	0	88	2	1	1.00	0	1
85	1	1	82	3	2	1.75	1	1	44	1	0	90	1	3	2.50	0	0
53	1	0	106	2	3	2.75	1	0	57	2	0	85	2	3	2.50	0	0
53	1	0	109	2	2	1.33	0	0	33	2	0	106	1	4	3.75	0	0
72	1	0	91	2	2	0.67	0	0	30	2	0	109	1	4	3.50	0	0
35	1	0	111	2	2	2.25	0	0	64	1	0	75	3	2	1.00	1	0
42	1	0	105	2	2	1.75	0	0	49	1	1	91	2	3	2.25	0	0
37	1	0	118	2	4	3.25	0	0	76	1	0	96	2	2	1.00	0	0
46	1	0	103	3	2	1.75	0	0	40	1	0	108	2	3	2.50	0	0
48	1	0	101	1	3	3.00	0	0	48	1	0	86	2	3	2.75	0	0
46	1	0	101	3	3	3.00	0	0	65	1	0	98	2	2	0.75	0	0
49	1	1	95	2	3	3.00	0	0	50	1	0	99	2	2	1.30	0	0
65	1	1	108	2	3	3.25	0	0	70	1	0	95	2	1	1.25	0	0
52	1	0	95	3	3	2.25	1	0	78	1	0	88	3	3	1.50	0	0
75	1	1	98	2	1	1.00	0	1	44	1	0	111	2	2	3.00	0	0
58	1	0	82	2	3	2.50	0	1	48	1	0	103	2	1	2.00	0	0
43	2	0	100	1	3	3.00	0	0	52	1	0	107	2	2	2.00	0	0
60	2	0	100	2	3	2.40	0	0	40	1	0	118	2	2	2.50	0	0

STATISTICAL TABLES

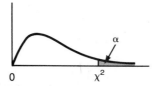

TABLE 1   **Upper Percentage Points of the χ^2 Distribution.** (Source: The entries in this table were computed by the author.)

df	.995	.990	.975	.950	.900	.750	.500	.250	.100	.050	.025	.010	.005
1	0.00	0.00	0.00	0.00	0.02	0.10	0.45	1.32	2.71	3.84	5.02	6.63	7.88
2	0.01	0.02	0.05	0.10	0.21	0.58	1.39	2.77	4.61	5.99	7.38	9.21	10.60
3	0.07	0.11	0.22	0.35	0.58	1.21	2.37	4.11	6.25	7.82	9.35	11.35	12.84
4	0.21	0.30	0.48	0.71	1.06	1.92	3.36	5.39	7.78	9.49	11.14	13.28	14.86
5	0.41	0.55	0.83	1.15	1.61	2.67	4.35	6.63	9.24	11.07	12.83	15.09	16.75
6	0.68	0.87	1.24	1.64	2.20	3.45	5.35	7.84	10.64	12.59	14.45	16.81	18.55
7	0.99	1.24	1.69	2.17	2.83	4.25	6.35	9.04	12.02	14.07	16.01	18.48	20.28
8	1.34	1.65	2.18	2.73	3.49	5.07	7.34	10.22	13.36	15.51	17.54	20.09	21.96
9	1.73	2.09	2.70	3.33	4.17	5.90	8.34	11.39	14.68	16.92	19.02	21.66	23.59
10	2.15	2.56	3.25	3.94	4.87	6.74	9.34	12.55	15.99	18.31	20.48	23.21	25.19
11	2.60	3.05	3.82	4.57	5.58	7.58	10.34	13.70	17.28	19.68	21.92	24.72	26.75
12	3.07	3.57	4.40	5.23	6.30	8.44	11.34	14.85	18.55	21.03	23.34	26.21	28.30
13	3.56	4.11	5.01	5.89	7.04	9.30	12.34	15.98	19.81	22.36	24.74	27.69	29.82
14	4.07	4.66	5.63	6.57	7.79	10.17	13.34	17.12	21.06	23.69	26.12	29.14	31.31
15	4.60	5.23	6.26	7.26	8.55	11.04	14.34	18.25	22.31	25.00	27.49	30.58	32.80
16	5.14	5.81	6.91	7.96	9.31	11.91	15.34	19.37	23.54	26.30	28.85	32.00	34.27
17	5.70	6.41	7.56	8.67	10.09	12.79	16.34	20.49	24.77	27.59	30.19	33.41	35.72
18	6.26	7.01	8.23	9.39	10.86	13.68	17.34	21.60	25.99	28.87	31.53	34.81	37.15
19	6.84	7.63	8.91	10.12	11.65	14.56	18.34	22.72	27.20	30.14	32.85	36.19	38.58
20	7.43	8.26	9.59	10.85	12.44	15.45	19.34	23.83	28.41	31.41	34.17	37.56	40.00
21	8.03	8.90	10.28	11.59	13.24	16.34	20.34	24.93	29.62	32.67	35.48	38.93	41.40
22	8.64	9.54	10.98	12.34	14.04	17.24	21.34	26.04	30.81	33.93	36.78	40.29	42.80
23	9.26	10.19	11.69	13.09	14.85	18.14	22.34	27.14	32.01	35.17	38.08	41.64	44.18
24	9.88	10.86	12.40	13.85	15.66	19.04	23.34	28.24	33.20	36.42	39.37	42.98	45.56
25	10.52	11.52	13.12	14.61	16.47	19.94	24.34	29.34	34.38	37.65	40.65	44.32	46.93
26	11.16	12.20	13.84	15.38	17.29	20.84	25.34	30.43	35.56	38.89	41.92	45.64	48.29
27	11.80	12.88	14.57	16.15	18.11	21.75	26.34	31.53	36.74	40.11	43.20	46.96	49.64
28	12.46	13.56	15.31	16.93	18.94	22.66	27.34	32.62	37.92	41.34	44.46	48.28	50.99
29	13.12	14.26	16.05	17.71	19.77	23.57	28.34	33.71	39.09	42.56	45.72	49.59	52.34
30	13.78	14.95	16.79	18.49	20.60	24.48	29.34	34.80	40.26	43.77	46.98	50.89	53.67
40	20.67	22.14	24.42	26.51	29.06	33.67	39.34	45.61	51.80	55.75	59.34	63.71	66.80
50	27.96	29.68	32.35	34.76	37.69	42.95	49.34	56.33	63.16	67.50	71.42	76.17	79.52
60	35.50	37.46	40.47	43.19	46.46	52.30	59.34	66.98	74.39	79.08	83.30	88.40	91.98
70	43.25	45.42	48.75	51.74	55.33	61.70	69.34	77.57	85.52	90.53	95.03	100.44	104.24
80	51.14	53.52	57.15	60.39	64.28	71.15	79.34	88.13	96.57	101.88	106.63	112.34	116.35
90	59.17	61.74	65.64	69.13	73.29	80.63	89.33	98.65	107.56	113.14	118.14	124.13	128.32
100	67.30	70.05	74.22	77.93	82.36	90.14	99.33	109.14	118.49	124.34	129.56	135.82	140.19

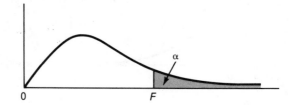

TABLE 2   **Critical Values of the F Distribution**   **Alpha = .05.**   (Source: The entries in this table were computed by the author.)

	Degrees of Freedom for Numerator															
	1	**2**	**3**	**4**	**5**	**6**	**7**	**8**	**9**	**10**	**15**	**20**	**25**	**30**	**40**	**50**
1	161.4	199.5	215.8	224.8	230.0	233.8	236.5	238.6	240.1	242.1	245.2	248.4	248.9	250.5	250.8	252.6
2	18.51	19.00	19.16	19.25	19.30	19.33	19.35	19.37	19.38	19.40	19.43	19.44	19.46	19.47	19.48	19.48
3	10.13	9.55	9.28	9.12	9.01	8.94	8.89	8.85	8.81	8.79	8.70	8.66	8.63	8.62	8.59	8.58
4	7.71	6.94	6.59	6.39	6.26	6.16	6.09	6.04	6.00	5.96	5.86	5.80	5.77	5.75	5.72	5.70
5	6.61	5.79	5.41	5.19	5.05	4.95	4.88	4.82	4.77	4.74	4.62	4.56	4.52	4.50	4.46	4.44
6	5.99	5.14	4.76	4.53	4.39	4.28	4.21	4.15	4.10	4.06	3.94	3.87	3.83	3.81	3.77	3.75
7	5.59	4.74	4.35	4.12	3.97	3.87	3.79	3.73	3.68	3.64	3.51	3.44	3.40	3.38	3.34	3.32
8	5.32	4.46	4.07	3.84	3.69	3.58	3.50	3.44	3.39	3.35	3.22	3.15	3.11	3.08	3.04	3.02
9	5.12	4.26	3.86	3.63	3.48	3.37	3.29	3.23	3.18	3.14	3.01	2.94	2.89	2.86	2.83	2.80
10	4.96	4.10	3.71	3.48	3.33	3.22	3.14	3.07	3.02	2.98	2.85	2.77	2.73	2.70	2.66	2.64
11	4.84	3.98	3.59	3.36	3.20	3.09	3.01	2.95	2.90	2.85	2.72	2.65	2.60	2.57	2.53	2.51
12	4.75	3.89	3.49	3.26	3.11	3.00	2.91	2.85	2.80	2.75	2.62	2.54	2.50	2.47	2.43	2.40
13	4.67	3.81	3.41	3.18	3.03	2.92	2.83	2.77	2.71	2.67	2.53	2.46	2.41	2.38	2.34	2.31
14	4.60	3.74	3.34	3.11	2.96	2.85	2.76	2.70	2.65	2.60	2.46	2.39	2.34	2.31	2.27	2.24
15	4.54	3.68	3.29	3.06	2.90	2.79	2.71	2.64	2.59	2.54	2.40	2.33	2.28	2.25	2.20	2.18
16	4.49	3.63	3.24	3.01	2.85	2.74	2.66	2.59	2.54	2.49	2.35	2.28	2.23	2.19	2.15	2.12
17	4.45	3.59	3.20	2.96	2.81	2.70	2.61	2.55	2.49	2.45	2.31	2.23	2.18	2.15	2.10	2.08
18	4.41	3.55	3.16	2.93	2.77	2.66	2.58	2.51	2.46	2.41	2.27	2.19	2.14	2.11	2.06	2.04
19	4.38	3.52	3.13	2.90	2.74	2.63	2.54	2.48	2.42	2.38	2.23	2.16	2.11	2.07	2.03	2.00
20	4.35	3.49	3.10	2.87	2.71	2.60	2.51	2.45	2.39	2.35	2.20	2.12	2.07	2.04	1.99	1.97
22	4.30	3.44	3.05	2.82	2.66	2.55	2.46	2.40	2.34	2.30	2.15	2.07	2.02	1.98	1.94	1.91
24	4.26	3.40	3.01	2.78	2.62	2.51	2.42	2.36	2.30	2.25	2.11	2.03	1.97	1.94	1.89	1.86
26	4.23	3.37	2.98	2.74	2.59	2.47	2.39	2.32	2.27	2.22	2.07	1.99	1.94	1.90	1.85	1.82
28	4.20	3.34	2.95	2.71	2.56	2.45	2.36	2.29	2.24	2.19	2.04	1.96	1.91	1.87	1.82	1.79
30	4.17	3.32	2.92	2.69	2.53	2.42	2.33	2.27	2.21	2.16	2.01	1.93	1.88	1.84	1.79	1.76
40	4.08	3.23	2.84	2.61	2.45	2.34	2.25	2.18	2.12	2.08	1.92	1.84	1.78	1.74	1.69	1.66
50	4.03	3.18	2.79	2.56	2.40	2.29	2.20	2.13	2.07	2.03	1.87	1.78	1.73	1.69	1.63	1.60
60	4.00	3.15	2.76	2.53	2.37	2.25	2.17	2.10	2.04	1.99	1.84	1.75	1.69	1.65	1.59	1.56
120	3.92	3.07	2.68	2.45	2.29	2.18	2.09	2.02	1.96	1.91	1.75	1.66	1.60	1.55	1.50	1.46
200	3.89	3.04	2.65	2.42	2.26	2.14	2.06	1.98	1.93	1.88	1.72	1.62	1.56	1.52	1.46	1.41
500	3.86	3.01	2.62	2.39	2.23	2.12	2.03	1.96	1.90	1.85	1.69	1.59	1.53	1.48	1.42	1.38
1000	3.85	3.01	2.61	2.38	2.22	2.11	2.02	1.95	1.89	1.84	1.68	1.58	1.52	1.47	1.41	1.36

Degrees of Freedom for Denominator

TABLE 3   Critical Values of the *F* Distribution   **Alpha = .01.**   (Source: The entries in this table were computed by the author.)

		1	2	3	4	5	6	7	8	9	10	15	20	25	30	40	50
							Degrees of Freedom for Numerator										
	1	4048	4993	5377	5577	5668	5924	5992	6096	6132	6168	6079	6168	6214	6355	6168	6213
	2	98.50	99.01	99.15	99.23	99.30	99.33	99.35	99.39	99.40	99.43	99.38	99.48	99.43	99.37	99.44	99.59
	3	34.12	30.82	29.46	28.71	28.24	27.91	27.67	27.49	27.34	27.23	26.87	26.69	26.58	26.51	26.41	26.36
	4	21.20	18.00	16.69	15.98	15.52	15.21	14.98	14.80	14.66	14.55	14.20	14.02	13.91	13.84	13.75	13.69
	5	16.26	13.27	12.06	11.39	10.97	10.67	10.46	10.29	10.16	10.05	9.72	9.55	9.45	9.38	9.29	9.24
	6	13.75	10.92	9.78	9.15	8.75	8.47	8.26	8.10	7.98	7.87	7.56	7.40	7.30	7.23	7.14	7.09
	7	12.25	9.55	8.45	7.85	7.46	7.19	6.99	6.84	6.72	6.62	6.31	6.16	6.06	5.99	5.91	5.86
	8	11.26	8.65	7.59	7.01	6.63	6.37	6.18	6.03	5.91	5.81	5.52	5.36	5.26	5.20	5.12	5.07
	9	10.56	8.02	6.99	6.42	6.06	5.80	5.61	5.47	5.35	5.26	4.96	4.81	4.71	4.65	4.57	4.52
	10	10.04	7.56	6.55	5.99	5.64	5.39	5.20	5.06	4.94	4.85	4.56	4.41	4.31	4.25	4.17	4.12
	11	9.65	7.21	6.22	5.67	5.32	5.07	4.89	4.74	4.63	4.54	4.25	4.10	4.01	3.94	3.86	3.81
	12	9.33	6.93	5.95	5.41	5.06	4.82	4.64	4.50	4.39	4.30	4.01	3.86	3.76	3.70	3.62	3.57
	13	9.07	6.70	5.74	5.21	4.86	4.62	4.44	4.30	4.19	4.10	3.82	3.66	3.57	3.51	3.43	3.38
	14	8.86	6.51	5.56	5.04	4.69	4.46	4.28	4.14	4.03	3.94	3.66	3.51	3.41	3.35	3.27	3.22
	15	8.68	6.36	5.42	4.89	4.56	4.32	4.14	4.00	3.89	3.80	3.52	3.37	3.28	3.21	3.13	3.08
	16	8.53	6.23	5.29	4.77	4.44	4.20	4.03	3.89	3.78	3.69	3.41	3.26	3.16	3.10	3.02	2.97
	17	8.40	6.11	5.18	4.67	4.34	4.10	3.93	3.79	3.68	3.59	3.31	3.16	3.07	3.00	2.92	2.87
	18	8.29	6.01	5.09	4.58	4.25	4.01	3.84	3.71	3.60	3.51	3.23	3.08	2.98	2.92	2.84	2.78
	19	8.18	5.93	5.01	4.50	4.17	3.94	3.77	3.63	3.52	3.43	3.15	3.00	2.91	2.84	2.76	2.71
	20	8.10	5.85	4.94	4.43	4.10	3.87	3.70	3.56	3.46	3.37	3.09	2.94	2.84	2.78	2.69	2.64
	22	7.95	5.72	4.82	4.31	3.99	3.76	3.59	3.45	3.35	3.26	2.98	2.83	2.73	2.67	2.58	2.53
	24	7.82	5.61	4.72	4.22	3.90	3.67	3.50	3.36	3.26	3.17	2.89	2.74	2.64	2.58	2.49	2.44
	26	7.72	5.53	4.64	4.14	3.82	3.59	3.42	3.29	3.18	3.09	2.81	2.66	2.57	2.50	2.42	2.36
	28	7.64	5.45	4.57	4.07	3.75	3.53	3.36	3.23	3.12	3.03	2.75	2.60	2.51	2.44	2.35	2.30
	30	7.56	5.39	4.51	4.02	3.70	3.47	3.30	3.17	3.07	2.98	2.70	2.55	2.45	2.39	2.30	2.25
	40	7.31	5.18	4.31	3.83	3.51	3.29	3.12	2.99	2.89	2.80	2.52	2.37	2.27	2.20	2.11	2.06
	50	7.17	5.06	4.20	3.72	3.41	3.19	3.02	2.89	2.78	2.70	2.42	2.27	2.17	2.10	2.01	1.95
	60	7.08	4.98	4.13	3.65	3.34	3.12	2.95	2.82	2.72	2.63	2.35	2.20	2.10	2.03	1.94	1.88
	120	6.85	4.79	3.95	3.48	3.17	2.96	2.79	2.66	2.56	2.47	2.19	2.03	1.93	1.86	1.76	1.70
	200	6.76	4.71	3.88	3.41	3.11	2.89	2.73	2.60	2.50	2.41	2.13	1.97	1.87	1.79	1.69	1.63
	500	6.69	4.65	3.82	3.36	3.05	2.84	2.68	2.55	2.44	2.36	2.07	1.92	1.81	1.74	1.63	1.57
	1000	6.67	4.63	3.80	3.34	3.04	2.82	2.66	2.53	2.43	2.34	2.06	1.90	1.79	1.72	1.61	1.54

Degrees of Freedom for Denominator (left vertical axis label)

TABLE 4

Power as a Function of δ and Significance Level (α). (Source: The entries in this table were computed by the author.)

δ	Alpha for Two-Tailed Test			
	.10	.05	.02	.01
1.00	0.26	0.17	0.09	0.06
1.10	0.29	0.20	0.11	0.07
1.20	0.33	0.22	0.13	0.08
1.30	0.37	0.26	0.15	0.10
1.40	0.40	0.29	0.18	0.12
1.50	0.44	0.32	0.20	0.14
1.60	0.48	0.36	0.23	0.17
1.70	0.52	0.40	0.27	0.19
1.80	0.56	0.44	0.30	0.22
1.90	0.60	0.48	0.34	0.25
2.00	0.64	0.52	0.37	0.28
2.10	0.68	0.56	0.41	0.32
2.20	0.71	0.60	0.45	0.35
2.30	0.74	0.63	0.49	0.39
2.40	0.78	0.67	0.53	0.43
2.50	0.80	0.71	0.57	0.47
2.60	0.83	0.74	0.61	0.51
2.70	0.85	0.77	0.65	0.55
2.80	0.88	0.80	0.68	0.59
2.90	0.90	0.83	0.72	0.63
3.00	0.91	0.85	0.75	0.66
3.10	0.93	0.87	0.78	0.70
3.20	0.94	0.89	0.81	0.73
3.30	0.95	0.91	0.84	0.77
3.40	0.96	0.93	0.86	0.80
3.50	0.97	0.94	0.88	0.82
3.60	0.98	0.95	0.90	0.85
3.70	0.98	0.96	0.92	0.87
3.80	0.98	0.97	0.93	0.89
3.90	0.99	0.97	0.94	0.91
4.00	0.99	0.98	0.95	0.92
4.10	0.99	0.98	0.96	0.94
4.20	...	0.99	0.97	0.95
4.30	...	0.99	0.98	0.96
4.40	...	0.99	0.98	0.97
4.50	...	0.99	0.99	0.97
4.60	...	...	0.99	0.98
4.70	...	...	0.99	0.98
4.80	...	...	0.99	0.99
4.90	...	...	...	0.99
5.00	...	...	...	0.99

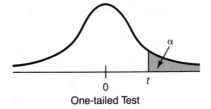

One-tailed Test

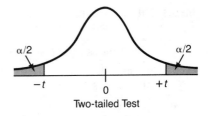

Two-tailed Test

TABLE 5
Percentage Points of the t Distribution. (Source: The entries in this table were computed by the author.)

			Level of Significance for One-Tailed Test						
	.25	.20	.15	.10	.05	.025	.01	.005	.0005
			Level of Significance for Two-Tailed Test						
df	.50	.40	.30	.20	.10	.05	.02	.01	.001
1	1.000	1.376	1.963	3.078	6.314	12.706	31.821	63.657	63.662
2	0.816	1.061	1.386	1.886	2.920	4.303	6.965	9.925	31.599
3	0.765	0.978	1.250	1.638	2.353	3.182	4.541	5.841	12.924
4	0.741	0.941	1.190	1.533	2.132	2.776	3.747	4.604	8.610
5	0.727	0.920	1.156	1.476	2.015	2.571	3.365	4.032	6.869
6	0.718	0.906	1.134	1.440	1.943	2.447	3.143	3.707	5.959
7	0.711	0.896	1.119	1.415	1.895	2.365	2.998	3.499	5.408
8	0.706	0.889	1.108	1.397	1.860	2.306	2.896	3.355	5.041
9	0.703	0.883	1.100	1.383	1.833	2.262	2.821	3.250	4.781
10	0.700	0.879	1.093	1.372	1.812	2.228	2.764	3.169	4.587
11	0.697	0.876	1.088	1.363	1.796	2.201	2.718	3.106	4.437
12	0.695	0.873	1.083	1.356	1.782	2.179	2.681	3.055	4.318
13	0.694	0.870	1.079	1.350	1.771	2.160	2.650	3.012	4.221
14	0.692	0.868	1.076	1.345	1.761	2.145	2.624	2.977	4.140
15	0.691	0.866	1.074	1.341	1.753	2.131	2.602	2.947	4.073
16	0.690	0.865	1.071	1.337	1.746	2.120	2.583	2.921	4.015
17	0.689	0.863	1.069	1.333	1.740	2.110	2.567	2.898	3.965
18	0.688	0.862	1.067	1.330	1.734	2.101	2.552	2.878	3.922
19	0.688	0.861	1.066	1.328	1.729	2.093	2.539	2.861	3.883
20	0.687	0.860	1.064	1.325	1.725	2.086	2.528	2.845	3.850
21	0.686	0.859	1.063	1.323	1.721	2.080	2.518	2.831	3.819
22	0.686	0.858	1.061	1.321	1.717	2.074	2.508	2.819	3.792
23	0.685	0.858	1.060	1.319	1.714	2.069	2.500	2.807	3.768
24	0.685	0.857	1.059	1.318	1.711	2.064	2.492	2.797	3.745
25	0.684	0.856	1.058	1.316	1.708	2.060	2.485	2.787	3.725
26	0.684	0.856	1.058	1.315	1.706	2.056	2.479	2.779	3.707
27	0.684	0.855	1.057	1.314	1.703	2.052	2.473	2.771	3.690
28	0.683	0.855	1.056	1.313	1.701	2.048	2.467	2.763	3.674
29	0.683	0.854	1.055	1.311	1.699	2.045	2.462	2.756	3.659
30	0.683	0.854	1.055	1.310	1.697	2.042	2.457	2.750	3.646
40	0.681	0.851	1.050	1.303	1.684	2.021	2.423	2.704	3.551
50	0.679	0.849	1.047	1.299	1.676	2.009	2.403	2.678	3.496
100	0.677	0.845	1.042	1.290	1.660	1.984	2.364	2.626	3.390
∞	0.674	0.842	1.036	1.282	1.645	1.960	2.326	2.576	3.291

TABLE 6   Critical Lower-Tail Values of T (and Their Associated Probabilities) for Wilcoxon's Matched-Pairs Signed-Ranks Test. (Source: The entries in this table were computed by the author.)

	Nominal Alpha (One-Tailed)						Nominal Alpha (One-Tailed)			
	.05	.025	.01	.005		.05	.025	.01	.005
N	T α	T α	T α	T α	N	T α	T α	T α	T α
5	0 .0313				28	130 .0496	116 .0239	101 .0096	91 .0048
	1 .0625					131 .0521	117 .0252	102 .0102	92 .0051
6	2 .0469	0 .0156			29	140 .0482	126 .0240	110 .0095	100 .0049
	3 .0781	1 .0313				141 .0504	127 .0253	111 .0101	101 .0053
7	3 .0391	2 .0234	0 .0078		30	151 .0481	137 .0249	120 .0098	109 .0050
	4 .0547	3 .0391	1 .0156			152 .0502	138 .0261	121 .0104	110 .0053
8	5 .0391	3 .0195	1 .0078	0 .0039	31	163 .0491	147 .0239	130 .0099	118 .0049
	6 .0547	4 .0273	2 .0117	1 .0078		164 .0512	148 .0251	131 .0105	119 .0052
9	8 .0488	5 .0195	3 .0098	1 .0039	32	175 .0492	159 .0249	140 .0097	128 .0050
	9 .0645	6 .0273	4 .0137	2 .0059		176 .0512	160 .0260	141 .0103	129 .0053
10	10 .0420	8 .0244	5 .0098	3 .0049	33	187 .0485	170 .0242	151 .0099	138 .0049
	11 .0527	9 .0322	6 .0137	4 .0068		188 .0503	171 .0253	152 .0104	139 .0052
11	13 .0415	10 .0210	7 .0093	5 .0049	34	200 .0488	182 .0242	162 .0098	148 .0048
	14 .0508	11 .0269	8 .0122	6 .0068		201 .0506	183 .0252	163 .0103	149 .0051
12	17 .0461	13 .0212	9 .0081	7 .0046	35	213 .0484	195 .0247	173 .0096	159 .0048
	18 .0549	14 .0261	10 .0105	8 .0061		214 .0501	196 .0257	174 .0100	160 .0051
13	21 .0471	17 .0239	12 .0085	9 .0040	36	227 .0489	208 .0248	185 .0096	171 .0050
	22 .0549	18 .0287	13 .0107	10 .0052		228 .0505	209 .0258	186 .0100	172 .0052
14	25 .0453	21 .0247	15 .0083	12 .0043	37	241 .0487	221 .0245	198 .0099	182 .0048
	26 .0520	22 .0290	16 .0101	13 .0054		242 .0503	222 .0254	199 .0103	183 .0050
15	30 .0473	25 .0240	19 .0090	15 .0042	38	256 .0493	235 .0247	211 .0099	194 .0048
	31 .0535	26 .0277	20 .0108	16 .0051		257 .0509	236 .0256	212 .0104	195 .0050
16	35 .0467	29 .0222	23 .0091	19 .0046	39	271 .0492	249 .0246	224 .0099	207 .0049
	36 .0523	30 .0253	24 .0107	20 .0055		272 .0507	250 .0254	225 .0103	208 .0051
17	41 .0492	34 .0224	27 .0087	23 .0047	40	286 .0486	264 .0249	238 .0100	220 .0049
	42 .0544	35 .0253	28 .0101	24 .0055		287 .0500	265 .0257	239 .0104	221 .0051
18	47 .0494	40 .0241	32 .0091	27 .0045	41	302 .0488	279 .0248	252 .0100	233 .0048
	48 .0542	41 .0269	33 .0104	28 .0052		303 .0501	280 .0256	253 .0103	234 .0050
19	53 .0478	46 .0247	37 .0090	32 .0047	42	319 .0496	294 .0245	266 .0098	247 .0049
	54 .0521	47 .0273	38 .0102	33 .0054		320 .0509	295 .0252	267 .0102	248 .0051
20	60 .0487	52 .0242	43 .0096	37 .0047	43	336 .0498	310 .0245	281 .0098	261 .0048
	61 .0527	53 .0266	44 .0107	38 .0053		337 .0511	311 .0252	282 .0102	262 .0050
21	67 .0479	58 .0230	49 .0097	42 .0045	44	353 .0495	327 .0250	296 .0097	276 .0049
	68 .0516	59 .0251	50 .0108	43 .0051		354 .0507	328 .0257	297 .0101	277 .0051
22	75 .0492	65 .0231	55 .0095	48 .0046	45	371 .0498	343 .0244	312 .0098	291 .0049
	76 .0527	66 .0250	56 .0104	49 .0052		372 .0510	344 .0251	313 .0101	292 .0051
23	83 .0490	73 .0242	62 .0098	54 .0046	46	389 .0497	361 .0249	328 .0098	307 .0050
	84 .0523	74 .0261	63 .0107	55 .0051		390 .0508	362 .0256	329 .0101	308 .0052
24	91 .0475	81 .0245	69 .0097	61 .0048	47	407 .0490	378 .0245	345 .0099	322 .0048
	92 .0505	82 .0263	70 .0106	62 .0053		408 .0501	379 .0251	346 .0102	323 .0050
25	100 .0479	89 .0241	76 .0094	68 .0048	48	426 .0490	396 .0244	362 .0099	339 .0050
	101 .0507	90 .0258	77 .0101	69 .0053		427 .0500	397 .0251	363 .0102	340 .0051
26	110 .0497	98 .0247	84 .0095	75 .0047	49	446 .0495	415 .0247	379 .0098	355 .0049
	111 .0524	99 .0263	85 .0102	76 .0051		447 .0505	416 .0253	380 .0100	356 .0050
27	119 .0477	107 .0246	92 .0093	83 .0048	50	466 .0495	434 .0247	397 .0098	373 .0050
	120 .0502	108 .0260	93 .0100	84 .0052		467 .0506	435 .0253	398 .0101	374 .0051

TABLE 7   Critical Lower-Tail Values of W_S for the Mann–Whitney Test for Two Independent Samples ($N_1 \leqslant N_2$). (Source: Table 1 in L. R. Verdooren, Extended tables of critical values for Wilcoxon's test statistic, *Biometrika*, 1963, **50**, 177–186, with permission of the author and editor.)

| | $N_1 = 1$ | | | | | | | $N_1 = 2$ | | | | | | | |
N_2	0.001	0.005	0.010	0.025	0.05	0.10	$2\bar{W}$	0.001	0.005	0.010	0.025	0.05	0.10	$2\bar{W}$	N_2
2							4						⋮	10	2
3							5					⋮	3	12	3
4							6					⋮	3	14	4
5							7					3	4	16	5
6							8					3	4	18	6
7							9				⋮	3	4	20	7
8						⋮	10				3	4	5	22	8
9						1	11				3	4	5	24	9
10						1	12				3	4	6	26	10
11						1	13				3	4	6	28	11
12						1	14			⋮	4	5	7	30	12
13						1	15			3	4	5	7	32	13
14						1	16			3	4	6	8	34	14
15						1	17			3	4	6	8	36	15
16						1	18			3	4	6	8	38	16
17						1	19			3	5	6	9	40	17
18					⋮	1	20		⋮	3	5	7	9	42	18
19					1	2	21		3	4	5	7	10	44	19
20					1	2	22		3	4	5	7	10	46	20
21					1	2	23		3	4	6	8	11	48	21
22					1	2	24		3	4	6	8	11	50	22
23					1	2	25		3	4	6	8	12	52	23
24					1	2	26		3	4	6	9	12	54	24
25	⋮	⋮	⋮	⋮	1	2	27	⋮	3	4	6	9	12	56	25

| | $N_1 = 3$ | | | | | | | $N_1 = 4$ | | | | | | | |
N_2	0.001	0.005	0.010	0.025	0.05	0.10	$2\bar{W}$	0.001	0.005	0.010	0.025	0.05	0.10	$2\bar{W}$	N_2
3					6	7	21								
4				⋮	6	7	24			⋮	10	11	13	36	4
5			⋮	6	7	8	27		⋮	10	11	12	14	40	5
6			⋮	7	8	9	30		10	11	12	13	15	44	6
7			6	7	8	10	33		10	11	13	14	16	48	7
8		⋮	6	8	9	11	36		11	12	14	15	17	52	8
9		6	7	8	10	11	39	⋮	11	13	14	16	19	56	9
10		6	7	9	10	12	42	10	12	13	15	17	20	60	10
11		6	7	9	11	13	45	10	12	14	16	18	21	64	11
12		7	8	10	11	14	48	10	13	15	17	19	22	68	12
13		7	8	10	12	15	51	11	13	15	18	20	23	72	13
14		7	8	11	13	16	54	11	14	16	19	21	25	76	14
15		8	9	11	13	16	57	11	15	17	20	22	26	80	15
16	⋮	8	9	12	14	17	60	12	15	17	21	24	27	84	16
17	6	8	10	12	15	18	63	12	16	18	21	25	28	88	17
18	6	8	10	13	15	19	66	13	16	19	22	26	30	92	18
19	6	9	10	13	16	20	69	13	17	19	23	27	31	96	19
20	6	9	11	14	17	21	72	13	18	20	24	28	32	100	20
21	7	9	11	14	17	21	75	14	18	21	25	29	33	104	21
22	7	10	12	15	18	22	78	14	19	21	26	30	35	108	22

TABLE 7 (*continued*)

	$N_1 = 3$							$N_1 = 4$							
N_2	0.001	0.005	0.010	0.025	0.05	0.10	$2\bar{W}$	0.001	0.005	0.010	0.025	0.05	0.10	$2\bar{W}$	N_2
23	7	10	12	15	19	23	81	14	19	22	27	31	36	112	23
24	7	10	12	16	19	24	84	15	20	23	27	32	38	116	24
25	7	11	13	16	20	25	87	15	20	23	28	33	38	120	25

	$N_1 = 5$							$N_1 = 6$							
N_2	0.001	0.005	0.010	0.025	0.05	0.10	$2\bar{W}$	0.001	0.005	0.010	0.025	0.05	0.10	$2\bar{W}$	N_2
5		15	16	17	19	20	55								5
6		16	17	18	20	22	60	...	23	24	26	28	30	78	6
7	...	16	18	20	21	23	65	21	24	25	27	29	32	84	7
8	15	17	19	21	23	25	70	22	25	27	29	31	34	90	8
9	16	18	20	22	24	27	75	23	26	28	31	33	36	96	9
10	16	19	21	23	26	28	80	24	27	29	32	35	38	102	10
11	17	20	22	24	27	30	85	25	28	30	34	37	40	108	11
12	17	21	23	26	28	32	90	25	30	32	35	38	42	114	12
13	18	22	24	27	30	33	95	26	31	33	37	40	44	120	13
14	18	22	25	28	31	35	100	27	32	34	38	42	46	126	14
15	19	23	26	29	33	37	105	28	33	36	40	44	48	132	15
16	20	24	27	30	34	38	110	29	34	37	42	46	50	138	16
17	20	25	28	32	35	40	115	30	36	39	43	47	52	144	17
18	21	26	29	33	37	42	120	31	37	40	45	49	55	150	18
19	22	27	30	34	38	43	125	32	38	41	46	51	57	156	19
20	22	28	31	35	40	45	130	33	39	43	48	53	59	162	20
21	23	29	32	37	41	47	135	33	40	44	50	55	61	168	21
22	23	29	33	38	43	48	140	34	42	45	51	57	63	174	22
23	24	30	34	39	44	50	145	35	43	47	53	58	65	180	23
24	25	31	35	40	45	51	150	36	44	48	54	60	67	186	24
25	25	32	36	42	47	53	155	37	45	50	56	62	69	192	25

	$N_1 = 7$							$N_1 = 8$							
N_2	0.001	0.005	0.010	0.025	0.05	0.10	$2\bar{W}$	0.001	0.005	0.010	0.025	0.05	0.10	$2\bar{W}$	N_2
7	29	32	34	36	39	41	105								7
8	30	34	35	38	41	44	112	40	43	45	49	51	55	136	8
9	31	35	37	40	43	46	119	41	45	47	51	54	58	144	9
10	33	37	39	42	45	49	126	42	47	49	53	56	60	152	10
11	34	38	40	44	47	51	133	44	49	51	55	59	63	160	11
12	35	40	42	46	49	54	140	45	51	53	58	62	66	168	12
13	36	41	44	48	52	56	147	47	53	56	60	64	69	176	13
14	37	43	45	50	54	59	154	48	54	58	62	67	72	184	14
15	38	44	47	52	56	61	161	50	56	60	65	69	75	192	15
16	39	46	49	54	58	64	168	51	58	62	67	72	78	200	16
17	41	47	51	56	61	66	175	53	60	64	70	75	81	208	17
18	42	49	52	58	63	69	182	54	62	66	72	77	84	216	18
19	43	50	54	60	65	71	189	56	64	68	74	80	87	224	19
20	44	52	56	62	67	74	196	57	66	70	77	83	90	232	20
21	46	53	58	64	69	76	203	59	68	72	79	85	92	240	21
22	47	55	59	66	72	79	210	60	70	74	81	88	95	248	22
23	48	57	61	68	74	81	217	62	71	76	84	90	98	256	23
24	49	58	63	70	76	84	224	64	73	78	86	93	101	264	24
25	50	60	64	72	78	86	231	65	75	81	89	96	104	272	25

TABLE 7   (*continued*)

N_2			$N_1 = 9$							$N_1 = 10$					N_2
	0.001	0.005	0.010	0.025	0.05	0.10	$2\bar{W}$	0.001	0.005	0.010	0.025	0.05	0.10	$2\bar{W}$	
9	52	56	59	62	66	70	171								
10	53	58	61	65	69	73	180	65	71	74	78	82	87	210	10
11	55	61	63	68	72	76	189	67	73	77	81	86	91	220	11
12	57	63	66	71	75	80	198	69	76	79	84	89	94	230	12
13	59	65	68	73	78	83	207	72	79	82	88	92	98	240	13
14	60	67	71	76	81	86	216	74	81	85	91	96	102	250	14
15	62	69	73	79	84	90	225	76	84	88	94	99	106	260	15
16	64	72	76	82	87	93	234	78	86	91	97	103	109	270	16
17	66	74	78	84	90	97	243	80	89	93	100	106	113	280	17
18	68	76	81	87	93	100	252	82	92	96	103	110	117	290	18
19	70	78	83	90	96	103	261	84	94	99	107	113	121	300	19
20	71	81	85	93	99	107	270	87	97	102	110	117	125	310	20
21	73	83	88	95	102	110	279	89	99	105	113	120	128	320	21
22	75	85	90	98	105	113	288	91	102	108	116	123	132	330	22
23	77	88	93	101	108	117	297	93	105	110	119	127	136	340	23
24	79	90	95	104	111	120	306	95	107	113	122	130	140	350	24
25	81	92	98	107	114	123	315	98	110	116	126	134	144	360	25

N_2			$N_1 = 11$							$N_1 = 12$					N_2
	0.001	0.005	0.010	0.025	0.05	0.10	$2\bar{W}$	0.001	0.005	0.010	0.025	0.05	0.10	$2\bar{W}$	
11	81	87	91	96	100	106	253								
12	83	90	94	99	104	110	264	98	105	109	115	120	127	300	12
13	86	93	97	103	108	114	275	101	109	113	119	125	131	312	13
14	88	96	100	106	112	118	286	103	112	116	123	129	136	324	14
15	90	99	103	110	116	123	297	106	115	120	127	133	141	336	15
16	93	102	107	113	120	127	308	109	119	124	131	138	145	348	16
17	95	105	110	117	123	131	319	112	122	127	135	142	150	360	17
18	98	108	113	121	127	135	330	115	125	131	139	146	155	372	18
19	100	111	116	124	131	139	341	118	129	134	143	150	159	384	19
20	103	114	119	128	135	144	352	120	132	138	147	155	164	396	20
21	106	117	123	131	139	148	363	123	136	142	151	159	169	408	21
22	108	120	126	135	143	152	374	126	139	145	155	163	173	420	22
23	111	123	129	139	147	156	385	129	142	149	159	168	178	432	23
24	113	126	132	142	151	161	396	132	146	153	163	172	183	444	24
25	116	129	136	146	155	165	407	135	149	156	167	176	187	456	25

N_2			$N_1 = 13$							$N_1 = 14$					N_2
	0.001	0.005	0.010	0.025	0.05	0.10	$2\bar{W}$	0.001	0.005	0.010	0.025	0.05	0.10	$2\bar{W}$	
13	117	125	130	136	142	149	351								
14	120	129	134	141	147	154	364	137	147	152	160	166	174	406	14
15	123	133	138	145	152	159	377	141	151	156	164	171	179	420	15
16	126	136	142	150	156	165	390	144	155	161	169	176	185	434	16
17	129	140	146	154	161	170	403	148	159	165	174	182	190	448	17
18	133	144	150	158	166	175	416	151	163	170	179	187	196	462	18
19	136	148	154	163	171	180	429	155	168	174	183	192	202	476	19
20	139	151	158	167	175	185	442	159	172	178	188	197	207	490	20
21	142	155	162	171	180	190	455	162	176	183	193	202	213	504	21
22	145	159	166	176	185	195	468	166	180	187	198	207	218	518	22

TABLE 7 (*continued*)

	$N_1 = 13$								$N_1 = 14$							
N_2	0.001	0.005	0.010	0.025	0.05	0.10	$2\bar{W}$	0.001	0.005	0.010	0.025	0.05	0.10	$2\bar{W}$	N_2
23	149	163	170	180	189	200	481	169	184	192	203	212	224	532	23
24	152	166	174	185	194	205	494	173	188	196	207	218	229	546	24
25	155	170	178	189	199	211	507	177	192	200	212	223	235	560	25

	$N_1 = 15$								$N_1 = 16$							
N_2	0.001	0.005	0.010	0.025	0.05	0.10	$2\bar{W}$	0.001	0.005	0.010	0.025	0.05	0.10	$2\bar{W}$	N_2
15	160	171	176	184	192	200	465								
16	163	175	181	190	197	206	480	184	196	202	211	219	229	528	16
17	167	180	186	195	203	212	495	188	201	207	217	225	235	544	17
18	171	184	190	200	208	218	510	192	206	212	222	231	242	560	18
19	175	189	195	205	214	224	525	196	210	218	228	237	248	576	19
20	179	193	200	210	220	230	540	201	215	223	234	243	255	592	20
21	183	198	205	216	225	236	555	205	220	228	239	249	261	608	21
22	187	202	210	221	231	242	570	209	225	233	245	255	267	624	22
23	191	207	214	226	236	248	585	214	230	238	251	261	274	640	23
24	195	211	219	231	242	254	600	218	235	244	256	267	280	656	24
25	199	216	224	237	248	260	615	222	240	249	262	273	287	672	25

	$N_1 = 17$								$N_1 = 18$							
N_2	0.001	0.005	0.010	0.025	0.05	0.10	$2\bar{W}$	0.001	0.005	0.010	0.025	0.05	0.10	$2\bar{W}$	N_2
17	210	223	230	240	249	259	595								
18	214	228	235	246	255	266	612	237	252	259	270	280	291	666	18
19	219	234	241	252	262	273	629	242	258	265	277	287	299	684	19
20	223	239	246	258	268	280	646	247	263	271	283	294	306	702	20
21	228	244	252	264	274	287	663	252	269	277	290	301	313	720	21
22	233	249	258	270	281	294	680	257	275	283	296	307	321	738	22
23	238	255	263	276	287	300	697	262	280	289	303	314	328	756	23
24	242	260	269	282	294	307	714	267	286	295	309	321	335	774	24
25	247	265	275	288	300	314	731	273	292	301	316	328	343	792	25

	$N_1 = 19$								$N_1 = 20$							
N_2	0.001	0.005	0.010	0.025	0.05	0.10	$2\bar{W}$	0.001	0.005	0.010	0.025	0.05	0.10	$2\bar{W}$	N_2
19	267	283	291	303	313	325	741								
20	272	289	297	309	320	333	760	298	315	324	337	348	361	820	20
21	277	295	303	316	328	341	779	304	322	331	344	356	370	840	21
22	283	301	310	323	335	349	798	309	328	337	351	364	378	860	22
23	288	307	316	330	342	357	817	315	335	344	359	371	386	880	23
24	294	313	323	337	350	364	836	321	341	351	366	379	394	900	24
25	299	319	329	344	357	372	855	327	348	358	373	387	403	920	25

	$N_2 = 21$								$N_1 = 22$							
N_2	0.001	0.005	0.010	0.025	0.05	0.10	$2\bar{W}$	0.001	0.005	0.010	0.025	0.05	0.10	$2\bar{W}$	N_2
21	331	349	359	373	385	399	903								
22	337	356	366	381	393	408	924	365	386	396	411	424	439	990	22
23	343	363	373	388	401	417	945	372	393	403	419	432	448	1012	23
24	349	370	381	396	410	425	966	379	400	411	427	441	457	1034	24
25	356	377	388	404	418	434	987	385	408	419	435	450	467	1056	25

TABLE 7   (*continued*)

			$N_1 = 23$							$N_1 = 24$				
N_2	0.001	0.005	0.010	0.025	0.05	0.10	$2\bar{W}$	0.001	0.005	0.010	0.025	0.05	0.10	$2\bar{W}$	N_2
23	402	424	434	451	465	481	1081								
24	409	431	443	459	474	491	1104	440	464	475	492	507	525	1176	24
25	416	439	451	468	483	500	1127	448	472	484	501	517	535	1200	25

			$N_1 = 25$				
N_2	0.001	0.005	0.010	0.025	0.05	0.10	$2\bar{W}$
25	480	505	517	536	552	570	1275

TABLE 8

Table of Uniform Random Numbers. (Source: The entries in this table were computed by the author.)

68204	38787	73304	44886	92836	43877	61049	49249	66105
61010	78345	75444	91680	33003	24128	97817	77562	62045
04604	93468	78459	27541	19672	14220	25102	42021	19252
36021	25507	64060	72923	58848	10374	63102	41534	92884
28129	43470	94097	16753	56425	75299	93688	75569	52067
09406	06584	46324	13981	06449	42604	13372	69040	95955
86423	81835	64226	20398	65772	91052	73496	14451	95967
13249	58525	81893	32894	68627	75644	45848	61511	90232
75454	17352	56548	39618	86705	50783	48388	82047	14660
06260	46176	99237	69874	84180	32005	66130	18055	99748
38507	92795	80672	00102	22980	69115	95653	05231	94996
03917	26795	59832	19014	96206	45413	76624	71219	65855
17927	32368	08177	31236	45401	26731	92256	99530	43998
26811	88937	37187	39762	29942	40091	65731	95955	23368
18480	28160	81908	30456	22462	15677	55642	67383	86884
37589	91842	76351	90585	45588	42858	37806	67969	50621
79903	34187	26952	75820	96335	90281	04269	85202	94965
46155	30200	75000	28570	47516	06744	72193	01258	85047
60916	73212	15853	28398	04721	69363	47071	65568	88519
34419	82840	88235	61966	86517	23966	45764	42177	17269
08692	26667	12941	14813	30815	26633	68184	80721	80505
92851	44185	90848	18341	77915	00177	64014	35490	02937
97909	07280	72167	10002	27374	92880	60055	94168	30742
28437	22027	07739	30905	33151	73567	82960	50104	67005
48165	28174	17909	11230	00929	54604	32435	54120	85199
99891	30913	06315	30201	72073	39589	62868	66339	15850
98022	13010	67970	99203	12536	88149	44387	20250	50798
91292	54688	47029	38970	77880	77295	11887	17628	93802
89081	34643	12988	12971	87742	57720	24438	64088	49496
32527	74239	20056	46668	94561	70111	92537	83562	11306
01870	21584	48574	09871	74453	24812	45770	95667	52377
84011	87542	96564	64256	64653	90025	61613	94168	83254
01568	29682	67489	62984	51901	30716	24513	46678	67991
40360	19206	40321	16004	64481	16130	03904	15811	19369
09392	39926	79590	23991	82492	13032	67337	54322	06058
77323	20500	52466	33008	84211	26357	79006	41178	35169

TABLE 8 (*continued*)

47590	01007	65376	18189	84040	39476	25383	45398	64917
29321	65783	71403	32894	32627	39067	47985	51485	27415
09530	05358	58722	31912	73356	65884	12883	36242	29646
65612	06843	72233	73352	66600	23237	71759	76881	19652
40355	85067	40788	40148	46099	48056	27858	58365	30202
24963	49571	82377	08687	73448	95484	15155	41780	71951
87273	44050	71961	48464	84084	65225	62846	11634	04853
31643	44756	12493	09024	74204	69949	67842	36141	08477
58326	55342	31419	80776	64028	59957	52969	71997	71477
02327	00460	39178	09511	92688	88585	99257	98752	39623
19377	49122	60591	79773	66289	89650	49298	13499	53623
95046	30203	47493	74395	45213	66739	45097	91670	62152
65013	71958	48360	70885	60313	44241	18740	05705	07488
86032	89018	97117	35656	20401	86438	87250	04717	67726
11799	15777	11548	45918	45706	88554	75315	70233	72575
17843	64809	00390	11980	66129	07197	36712	55062	61191
42770	65397	45010	06463	86242	06361	14293	36343	97628
02410	96933	57864	93197	88227	57139	66382	95768	60660
70939	20457	62468	68698	74875	61111	59083	09152	93625
85616	15100	26242	28677	74655	05679	56676	67224	75318
85515	33174	05496	78789	81297	73985	82120	94070	20529
73466	06254	88113	98367	22018	99372	70171	52705	61202
72255	50729	05681	37216	09363	02385	93098	09502	92589
08121	48330	86725	52922	90349	81934	14849	68005	06791
94005	85164	22994	58921	85943	67506	79730	85382	61568
09108	52299	25991	00940	22493	60987	93573	79469	97147
85687	31723	67907	55306	71748	85048	17690	04784	98470
26190	02164	95889	89712	89795	73001	82210	39357	23867
34208	07539	60907	60693	01965	43492	46688	28891	23410
13032	78798	21733	35703	71707	11931	93513	78339	74754
16801	05582	47975	25046	59220	08275	67901	94954	36662
88735	91500	41654	97225	61188	24527	35220	99794	56097
82127	17594	94217	55324	06134	25207	26758	08687	06929
29284	42271	45833	19481	56972	99042	45304	39832	40188
56300	60964	13751	72385	91180	42371	55924	95783	33096
33132	33229	39955	16779	99286	23392	24255	90856	60004
65296	94444	32091	90681	95823	73091	92912	85979	30232
11069	52931	26381	71830	50467	47783	25223	81796	97745
06720	69637	99670	58392	57943	75965	14740	74814	75598
62719	14295	16605	13146	36992	50560	50121	90278	98283
95556	36672	87202	92730	81961	38894	61358	44519	71529
12490	12304	28804	42772	27104	35518	67361	84159	52442
29865	28847	70904	96638	54226	44701	67589	27352	81078
74486	63507	92193	65022	09583	43615	59910	05301	69347
01878	56351	68618	84432	30948	65180	75446	95963	75619
65405	25720	09364	51333	03752	65756	51967	92469	47296
31711	35173	45290	49326	50368	63829	05640	26675	27367
41028	50367	01904	68068	02324	58723	96333	77032	47878
76916	55336	48767	76915	79711	05182	70489	10244	45078
16404	93068	91519	85895	34872	24701	60932	91141	33252
06776	51133	76482	14812	19777	19614	51100	52943	04068
76818	05839	26058	80972	43337	24203	72345	37967	88138
16916	64028	38968	02783	63049	12261	89587	88988	88834
33696	41621	16648	11837	08094	38217	32919	16625	91567

TABLE 8   *(continued)*

00143	56431	90537	95332	29879	29363	48055	86410	10594
15932	59628	00086	74633	81208	05470	56385	23601	70545
86111	14530	39958	36155	60613	73849	74842	31030	30448
46218	36313	62063	59326	93522	48983	50335	30178	42755
84153	32199	77166	63912	07984	55369	56520	14633	00252
81439	35471	29742	57110	13710	21351	29816	32783	69004
93229	82043	80136	97269	28858	03036	01304	51363	40412
78421	33809	92792	96106	95191	43514	08320	25690	76117
44265	86707	80637	44879	81457	06781	11411	88804	62551
89430	51314	76126	62672	31815	12947	76533	19761	93373
36462	19901	02919	29311	31275	83593	34933	95758	63944
55996	59605	51680	27755	06077	12797	67082	12536	64069
69338	43838	06320	63988	16549	27931	27270	94711	47834
40276	17751	72508	23027	70257	42812	87319	09160	02913
67834	93014	07816	93085	14552	10115	87740	44125	51227

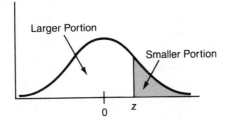

TABLE 9   **The Normal Distribution (z).** (Source: The entries in this table were computed by the author.)

z	Mean to z	Larger Portion	Smaller Portion	z	Mean to z	Larger Portion	Smaller Portion
.00	0.0000	0.5000	0.5000	.21	0.0832	0.5832	0.4168
.01	0.0040	0.5040	0.4960	.22	0.0871	0.5871	0.4129
.02	0.0080	0.5080	0.4920	.23	0.0910	0.5910	0.4090
.03	0.0120	0.5120	0.4880	.24	0.0948	0.5948	0.4052
.04	0.0160	0.5160	0.4840	.25	0.0987	0.5987	0.4013
.05	0.0199	0.5199	0.4801	.26	0.1026	0.6026	0.3974
.06	0.0239	0.5239	0.4761	.27	0.1064	0.6064	0.3936
.07	0.0279	0.5279	0.4721	.28	0.1103	0.6103	0.3897
.08	0.0319	0.5319	0.4681	.29	0.1141	0.6141	0.3859
.09	0.0359	0.5359	0.4641	.30	0.1179	0.6179	0.3821
.10	0.0398	0.5398	0.4602	.31	0.1217	0.6217	0.3783
.11	0.0438	0.5438	0.4562	.32	0.1255	0.6255	0.3745
.12	0.0478	0.5478	0.4522	.33	0.1293	0.6293	0.3707
.13	0.0517	0.5517	0.4483	.34	0.1331	0.6331	0.3669
.14	0.0557	0.5557	0.4443	.35	0.1368	0.6368	0.3632
.15	0.0596	0.5596	0.4404	.36	0.1406	0.6406	0.3594
.16	0.0636	0.5636	0.4364	.37	0.1443	0.6443	0.3557
.17	0.0675	0.5675	0.4325	.38	0.1480	0.6480	0.3520
.18	0.0714	0.5714	0.4286	.39	0.1517	0.6517	0.3483
.19	0.0753	0.5753	0.4247	.40	0.1554	0.6554	0.3446
.20	0.0793	0.5793	0.4207	.41	0.1591	0.6591	0.3409

APPENDIX D STATISTICAL TABLES

TABLE 9 (*continued*)

z	Mean to z	Larger Portion	Smaller Portion	z	Mean to z	Larger Portion	Smaller Portion
.42	0.1628	0.6628	0.3372	.93	0.3238	0.8238	0.1762
.43	0.1664	0.6664	0.3336	.94	0.3264	0.8264	0.1736
.44	0.1700	0.6700	0.3300	.95	0.3289	0.8289	0.1711
.45	0.1736	0.6736	0.3264	.96	0.3315	0.8315	0.1685
.46	0.1772	0.6772	0.3228	.97	0.3340	0.8340	0.1660
.47	0.1808	0.6808	0.3192	.98	0.3365	0.8365	0.1635
.48	0.1844	0.6844	0.3156	.99	0.3389	0.8389	0.1611
.49	0.1879	0.6879	0.3121	1.00	0.3413	0.8413	0.1587
.50	0.1915	0.6915	0.3085	1.01	0.3438	0.8438	0.1562
.51	0.1950	0.6950	0.3050	1.02	0.3461	0.8461	0.1539
.52	0.1985	0.6985	0.3015	1.03	0.3485	0.8485	0.1515
.53	0.2019	0.7019	0.2981	1.04	0.3508	0.8508	0.1492
.54	0.2054	0.7054	0.2946	1.05	0.3531	0.8531	0.1469
.55	0.2088	0.7088	0.2912	1.06	0.3554	0.8554	0.1446
.56	0.2123	0.7123	0.2877	1.07	0.3577	0.8577	0.1423
.57	0.2157	0.7157	0.2843	1.08	0.3599	0.8599	0.1401
.58	0.2190	0.7190	0.2810	1.09	0.3621	0.8621	0.1379
.59	0.2224	0.7224	0.2776	1.10	0.3643	0.8643	0.1357
.60	0.2257	0.7257	0.2743	1.11	0.3665	0.8665	0.1335
.61	0.2291	0.7291	0.2709	1.12	0.3686	0.8686	0.1314
.62	0.2324	0.7324	0.2676	1.13	0.3708	0.8708	0.1292
.63	0.2357	0.7357	0.2643	1.14	0.3729	0.8729	0.1271
.64	0.2389	0.7389	0.2611	1.15	0.3749	0.8749	0.1251
.65	0.2422	0.7422	0.2578	1.16	0.3770	0.8770	0.1230
.66	0.2454	0.7454	0.2546	1.17	0.3790	0.8790	0.1210
.67	0.2486	0.7486	0.2514	1.18	0.3810	0.8810	0.1190
.68	0.2517	0.7517	0.2483	1.19	0.3830	0.8830	0.1170
.69	0.2549	0.7549	0.2451	1.20	0.3849	0.8849	0.1151
.70	0.2580	0.7580	0.2420	1.21	0.3869	0.8869	0.1131
.71	0.2611	0.7611	0.2389	1.22	0.3888	0.8888	0.1112
.72	0.2642	0.7642	0.2358	1.23	0.3907	0.8907	0.1093
.73	0.2673	0.7673	0.2327	1.24	0.3925	0.8925	0.1075
.74	0.2704	0.7704	0.2296	1.25	0.3944	0.8944	0.1056
.75	0.2734	0.7734	0.2266	1.26	0.3962	0.8962	0.1038
.76	0.2764	0.7764	0.2236	1.27	0.3980	0.8980	0.1020
.77	0.2794	0.7794	0.2206	1.28	0.3997	0.8997	0.1003
.78	0.2823	0.7823	0.2177	1.29	0.4015	0.9015	0.0985
.79	0.2852	0.7852	0.2148	1.30	0.4032	0.9032	0.0968
.80	0.2881	0.7881	0.2119	1.31	0.4049	0.9049	0.0951
.81	0.2910	0.7910	0.2090	1.32	0.4066	0.9066	0.0934
.82	0.2939	0.7939	0.2061	1.33	0.4082	0.9082	0.0918
.83	0.2967	0.7967	0.2033	1.34	0.4099	0.9099	0.0901
.84	0.2995	0.7995	0.2005	1.35	0.4115	0.9115	0.0885
.85	0.3023	0.8023	0.1977	1.36	0.4131	0.9131	0.0869
.86	0.3051	0.8051	0.1949	1.37	0.4147	0.9147	0.0853
.87	0.3078	0.8078	0.1922	1.38	0.4162	0.9162	0.0838
.88	0.3106	0.8106	0.1894	1.39	0.4177	0.9177	0.0823
.89	0.3133	0.8133	0.1867	1.40	0.4192	0.9192	0.0808
.90	0.3159	0.8159	0.1841	1.41	0.4207	0.9207	0.0793
.91	0.3186	0.8186	0.1814	1.42	0.4222	0.9222	0.0778
.92	0.3212	0.8212	0.1788	1.43	0.4236	0.9236	0.0764

TABLE 9   (*continued*)

z	Mean to z	Larger Portion	Smaller Portion	z	Mean to z	Larger Portion	Smaller Portion
1.44	0.4251	0.9251	0.0749	1.95	0.4744	0.9744	0.0256
1.45	0.4265	0.9265	0.0735	1.96	0.4750	0.9750	0.0250
1.46	0.4279	0.9279	0.0721	1.97	0.4756	0.9756	0.0244
1.47	0.4292	0.9292	0.0708	1.98	0.4761	0.9761	0.0239
1.48	0.4306	0.9306	0.0694	1.99	0.4767	0.9767	0.0233
1.49	0.4319	0.9319	0.0681	2.00	0.4772	0.9772	0.0228
1.50	0.4332	0.9332	0.0668	2.01	0.4778	0.9778	0.0222
1.51	0.4345	0.9345	0.0655	2.02	0.4783	0.9783	0.0217
1.52	0.4357	0.9357	0.0643	2.03	0.4788	0.9788	0.0212
1.53	0.4370	0.9370	0.0630	2.04	0.4793	0.9793	0.0207
1.54	0.4382	0.9382	0.0618	2.05	0.4798	0.9798	0.0202
1.55	0.4394	0.9394	0.0606	2.06	0.4803	0.9803	0.0197
1.56	0.4406	0.9406	0.0594	2.07	0.4808	0.9808	0.0192
1.57	0.4418	0.9418	0.0582	2.08	0.4812	0.9812	0.0188
1.58	0.4429	0.9429	0.0571	2.09	0.4817	0.9817	0.0183
1.59	0.4441	0.9441	0.0559	2.10	0.4821	0.9821	0.0179
1.60	0.4452	0.9452	0.0548	2.11	0.4826	0.9826	0.0174
1.61	0.4463	0.9463	0.0537	2.12	0.4830	0.9830	0.0170
1.62	0.4474	0.9474	0.0526	2.13	0.4834	0.9834	0.0166
1.63	0.4484	0.9484	0.0516	2.14	0.4838	0.9838	0.0162
1.64	0.4495	0.9495	0.0505	2.15	0.4842	0.9842	0.0158
1.65	0.4505	0.9505	0.0495	2.16	0.4846	0.9846	0.0154
1.66	0.4515	0.9515	0.0485	2.17	0.4850	0.9850	0.0150
1.67	0.4525	0.9525	0.0475	2.18	0.4854	0.9854	0.0146
1.68	0.4535	0.9535	0.0465	2.19	0.4857	0.9857	0.0143
1.69	0.4545	0.9545	0.0455	2.20	0.4861	0.9861	0.0139
1.70	0.4554	0.9554	0.0446	2.21	0.4864	0.9864	0.0136
1.71	0.4564	0.9564	0.0436	2.22	0.4868	0.9868	0.0132
1.72	0.4573	0.9573	0.0427	2.23	0.4871	0.9871	0.0129
1.73	0.4582	0.9582	0.0418	2.24	0.4875	0.9875	0.0125
1.74	0.4591	0.9591	0.0409	2.25	0.4878	0.9878	0.0122
1.75	0.4599	0.9599	0.0401	2.26	0.4881	0.9881	0.0119
1.76	0.4608	0.9608	0.0392	2.27	0.4884	0.9884	0.0116
1.77	0.4616	0.9616	0.0384	2.28	0.4887	0.9887	0.0113
1.78	0.4625	0.9625	0.0375	2.29	0.4890	0.9890	0.0110
1.79	0.4633	0.9633	0.0367	2.30	0.4893	0.9893	0.0107
1.80	0.4641	0.9641	0.0359	2.31	0.4896	0.9896	0.0104
1.81	0.4649	0.9649	0.0351	2.32	0.4898	0.9898	0.0102
1.82	0.4656	0.9656	0.0344	2.33	0.4901	0.9901	0.0099
1.83	0.4664	0.9664	0.0336	2.34	0.4904	0.9904	0.0096
1.84	0.4671	0.9671	0.0329	2.35	0.4906	0.9906	0.0094
1.85	0.4678	0.9678	0.0322	2.36	0.4909	0.9909	0.0091
1.86	0.4686	0.9686	0.0314	2.37	0.4911	0.9911	0.0089
1.87	0.4693	0.9693	0.0307	2.38	0.4913	0.9913	0.0087
1.88	0.4699	0.9699	0.0301	2.39	0.4916	0.9916	0.0084
1.89	0.4706	0.9706	0.0294	2.40	0.4918	0.9918	0.0082
1.90	0.4713	0.9713	0.0287	2.41	0.4920	0.9920	0.0080
1.91	0.4719	0.9719	0.0281	2.42	0.4922	0.9922	0.0078
1.92	0.4726	0.9726	0.0274	2.43	0.4925	0.9925	0.0075
1.93	0.4732	0.9732	0.0268	2.44	0.4927	0.9927	0.0073
1.94	0.4738	0.9738	0.0262	2.45	0.4929	0.9929	0.0071

TABLE 9 (*continued*)

z	Mean to z	Larger Portion	Smaller Portion	z	Mean to z	Larger Portion	Smaller Portion
2.46	0.4931	0.9931	0.0069	2.78	0.4973	0.9973	0.0027
2.47	0.4932	0.9932	0.0068	2.79	0.4974	0.9974	0.0026
2.48	0.4934	0.9934	0.0066	2.80	0.4974	0.9974	0.0026
2.49	0.4936	0.9936	0.0064	2.81	0.4975	0.9975	0.0025
2.50	0.4938	0.9938	0.0062	2.82	0.4976	0.9976	0.0024
2.51	0.4940	0.9940	0.0060	2.83	0.4977	0.9977	0.0023
2.52	0.4941	0.9941	0.0059	2.84	0.4977	0.9977	0.0023
2.53	0.4943	0.9943	0.0057	2.85	0.4978	0.9978	0.0022
2.54	0.4945	0.9945	0.0055	2.86	0.4979	0.9979	0.0021
2.55	0.4946	0.9946	0.0054	2.87	0.4979	0.9979	0.0021
2.56	0.4948	0.9948	0.0052	2.88	0.4980	0.9980	0.0020
2.57	0.4949	0.9949	0.0051	2.89	0.4981	0.9981	0.0019
2.58	0.4951	0.9951	0.0049	2.90	0.4981	0.9981	0.0019
2.59	0.4952	0.9952	0.0048	2.91	0.4982	0.9982	0.0018
2.60	0.4953	0.9953	0.0047	2.92	0.4982	0.9982	0.0018
2.61	0.4955	0.9955	0.0045	2.93	0.4983	0.9983	0.0017
2.62	0.4956	0.9956	0.0044	2.94	0.4984	0.9984	0.0016
2.63	0.4957	0.9957	0.0043	2.95	0.4984	0.9984	0.0016
2.64	0.4959	0.9959	0.0041	2.96	0.4985	0.9985	0.0015
2.65	0.4960	0.9960	0.0040	2.97	0.4985	0.9985	0.0015
2.66	0.4961	0.9961	0.0039	2.98	0.4986	0.9986	0.0014
2.67	0.4962	0.9962	0.0038	2.99	0.4986	0.9986	0.0014
2.68	0.4963	0.9963	0.0037	3.00	0.4987	0.9987	0.0013
2.69	0.4964	0.9964	0.0036	:	:	:	:
2.70	0.4965	0.9965	0.0035	3.25	0.4994	0.9994	0.0006
2.71	0.4966	0.9966	0.0034	:	:	:	:
2.72	0.4967	0.9967	0.0033	3.50	0.4998	0.9998	0.0002
2.73	0.4968	0.9968	0.0032	:	:	:	:
2.74	0.4969	0.9969	0.0031	3.75	0.4999	0.9999	0.0001
2.75	0.4970	0.9970	0.0030	:	:	:	:
2.76	0.4971	0.9971	0.0029	4.00	0.5000	1.0000	0.0000
2.77	0.4972	0.9972	0.0028				

APPENDIX E

REFERENCES

Berndt, D. J., Schwartz, S., & Kaiser, C. F. (1983). Readability of self-report depression inventories. *Journal of Consulting and Clinical Psychology, 51,* 627–628.

Blanchard, E. B., Theobald, D. E., Williamson, D. A., Silver, B. V., & Brown, D. A. (1978). Temperature biofeedback in the treatment of migraine headaches. *Archives of General Psychiatry, 35,* 581–588.

Bradley, D. R., & Kjungja, L. (1982). Animated subjective contours. *Perception and Psychophysics, 32,* 393–395.

Bradley, J. V. (1963, March). *Studies in Research Methodology: IV. A Sampling Study of the Central Limit Theorem and the Robustness of One-Sample Parametric Tests.* AMRL Technical Documentary Report 63–29, 650th Aerospace Medical Research Laboratories, Wright-Patterson Air Force Base, OH.

Bradley, J. V. (1968). *Distribution-Free Statistical Tests.* Englewood Cliffs, NJ: Prentice-Hall.

Brown, J., Lewis, V., Brown, M., Horn, G., & Bowes, J. B. (1982). A comparison between transient amnesias induced by two drugs (diazepam and lorazepam) and amnesia of organc origin. *Neuropsychologia, 20,* 55–70.

Camilli, G., & Hopkins, K. D. (1978). Applicability of chi-square to 2 × 2 contingency tables with small expected frequencies. *Psychological Bulletin, 85,* 163–167.

Campbell, A., Converse, P. E., & Rodgers, W. L. (1976). *The Quality of American Life.* New York: Russell Sage Foundation.

Clark, K. B., & Clark, M. K. (1939). The development of consciousness of self in the emergence of racial identification in Negro pre-school children. *Journal of Social Psychology, 10,* 591–599.

Cochran, C. D., & Urbanczyk, S. (1982). The effect of availability of vertical space on personal space. *Journal of Psychology, 111,* 137–140.

Cohen, J. (1977). *Statistical Power Analysis for Behavioral Sciences* (Rev. ed.). New York: Academic Press.

Darley, J. M., and Latané, B. (1968). Bystander intervention in emergencies: Diffusion of responsibility. *Journal of Personality and Social Psychology, 8,* 377–383.

Doob, A. N., & Gross, A. E. (1968). Status of frustrator as an inhibitor of horn-honking responses. *Journal of Social Psychology, 76,* 213–218.

Eron, L. D., Huesmann, L. R., Lefkowitz, M. M., & Walden, L. O. (1972). Does television violence cause aggression? *American Psychologist, 27,* 253–263.

Fagerström, K. (1982). A comparison of psychological and pharmacological treatment of smoking cessation. *Journal of Behavioral Medicine, 5,* 343–351.

Fisher, R. A. (1935). *The Design of Experiments.* Edinburgh: Oliver & Boyd.

Goldstein, A. G., Bailis, K., & Chance, J. E. (1983). Do students remember pictures in psychology textbooks? *Teaching of Psychology*, *10*, 23–26.

Greenhouse, S. W., & Geisser, S. (1959). On methods in the analysis of profile data. *Psychometrika*, *24*, 95–112.

Harper, D., & Wacker, D. P. (1983). The efficiency of the Denver Developmental Screening Test with rural disadvantaged preschool children. *Journal of Pediatric Psychology*, *8*, 273–283.

Hays, W. L. (1981). *Statistics* (3rd ed.). New York: Holt, Rinehart and Winston.

Hicks, R. A., & Guista, M. (1982). The energy level of habitual long and short sleepers. *Bulletin of the Psychonomic Society*, *19*, 131–132.

Hindley, C. B., Filliozat, A. M., Klackenberg, G., Nicolet-Meister, D., & Sand, E. A. (1966). Differences in age of walking for five European longitudinal samples. *Human Biology*, *38*, 364–379.

Holmes, T. H., & Rahe, R. H. (1967). The social readjustment rating scale. *Journal of Psychosomatic Research*, *11*, 213.

Holway, A. H., & Boring, E. G. (1940). The moon illusion and the angle of regard. *American Journal of Psychology*, *53*, 509–516.

Hosch, H. M., & Cooper, D. S. (1982). Victimization as a determinant of eyewitness accuracy. *Journal of Applied Psychology*, *67*, 649–652.

Howell, D. C. (1987). *Statistical Methods for Psychology.* (2nd ed.) Boston: Duxbury Press.

Howell, D. C., & Huessy, H. R. (1985). A fifteen year follow-up of a behavioral history of Attention Deficit Syndrome (ADD). *Pediatrics*, *76*, 185–190.

Hraba, J., & Grant, G. (1970). Black is beautiful: A reexamination of racial preference and identification. *Journal of Personality and Social Psychology*, *16*, 398–402.

Huff, D. (1954). *How to Lie with Statistics.* New York: W. W. Norton.

Hunt, J. McV. (1941). The effects of infant feeding frustration upon adult hoarding behavior. *Journal of Abnormal and Social Psychology*, *36*, 338–360.

Jackson, J. M., & Padgett, V. R. (1982). With a little help from my friend: Social loafing and the Lennon–McCartney songs. *Personality and Social Psychology Bulletin*, *8*, 672–677.

Kapp, B., Frysinger, R., Gallagher, M., & Hazelton, J. (1979). Amygdala central nucleus lesions: Effects on heart rate conditioning in the rabbit. *Physiology and Behavior*, *23*, 1109–1117.

Kaufman, L., & Rock, I. (1962).The moon illusion, I. *Science*, *136*, 953–961.

Kennedy, D., Beard, D., & Carr, W. J. (1982). Differential recognition of the left vs. right side of human faces. *Bulletin of the Psychonomic Society*, *20*, 72–73.

Knehr-McDonald, P. (1984). Carelessness: Its relationship to cognitive style and problem-solving strategies. Unpublished Ph.D. dissertation, University of Vermont, Burlington.

Latané, B., & Dabbs, J. M., Jr. (1975). Sex, group size, and helping in three cities. *Sociometry*, *38*, 180–194.

Linn, R. T., & Hodge, G. K. (1982). Locus of control in childhood hyperactivity. *Journal of Consulting and Clinical Psychology*, *50*, 592–593.

Lord, F. M. (1953). On the statistical treatment of football numbers. *American Psychologist*, *8*, 750–751.

Lundberg, U. (1983). Note on Type A behavior and cardiovascular responses to challenge in 3–6 year old children. *Journal of Psychosomatic Research, 27*, 39–42.

McConaughy, S. H. (1980). Cognitive structures for reading comprehension: Judging the relative importance of ideas in short stories. Unpublished Ph.D. dissertation, University of Vermont, Burlington.

Neter, J., & Wasserman, W. (1974). *Applied Linear Statistical Models*. Homewood, IL: Richard D. Irwin.

Newman, S. E., Olson, M. A., Hall, A. D., & Hornak, R. (1983). Effects of encoding and retrieval contexts on recall. *Bulletin of the Psychonomic Society, 21*, 4–6.

Nurcombe, B., & Fitzhenry-Coor, I. (1979, October). Decision making in the mental health interview: I. An introduction to an education and research program. Paper delivered at the Conference on Problem Solving in Medicine, Smuggler's Notch, VT.

Nurcombe, B., Howell, D. C., Rauh, V. A., Teti, D. M., Ruoff, P., & Brennan, J. (1984). An intervention program for mothers of low-birthweight infants: Preliminary results. *Journal of the American Academy of Child Psychiatry, 23*, 319–325.

Obrzut, J. E., Hansen, R. L., & Heath, C. P. (1982). The effectiveness of visual information processing training with Hispanic children. *Journal of General Psychology, 107*, 165–174.

Overall, J. E., & Klett, C. J. (1972). *Applied Multivariate Analysis*. New York: McGraw-Hill.

Payne, S. L. (1982). Job-orientation stereotyping: Is it changing? *Journal of Psychology, 111*, 51–55.

Pliner, P. (1982). The effects of mere exposure on liking for edible substances. *Appetite, 3*, 283–290.

Robinson, B. E., Barrett, R. L., & Skeen, P. (1983). Locus of control of unwed adolescent fathers versus adolescent nonfathers. *Perceptual and Motor Skills, 56*, 397–398.

Ryan, T., Joiner, B., & Ryan, B. (1985). *Minitab Student Handbook*. Boston: Duxbury Press.

Saint-Exupery, A. de. (1943). *The Little Prince*. Tr. by Woods, K. New York: Harcourt Brace Jovanovich.

Sgro, J. A., & Weinstock, S. (1963). Effects of delay on subsequent running under immediate reinforcement. *Journal of Experimental Psychology, 66*, 260–263.

Smith, D. B., & Plant, W. T. (1982). Sex differences in job satisfaction of university professors. *Journal of Applied Psychology, 67*, 249–251.

Sternglass, E. J., & Bell, S. (1983). Fallout and SAT scores: Evidence for cognitive damage during early infancy. *Phi Delta Kappan, 64*, 539–549.

Stevens, S. S. (1951). Mathematics, measurement, and psychophysics. In S. S. Stevens (Ed.), *Handbook of Experimental Psychology*. New York: John Wiley.

Supramaniam, S. (1983). Proofreading errors in good and poor readers. *Journal of Experimental Child Psychology, 36*, 68–80.

Sutherland, R. J., & Linggard, R. (1982). Being there: A novel demonstration of latent spatial learning in the rat. *Behavioral and Neural Biology, 36*, 103–107.

Tukey, J. W. (1977). *Exploratory Data Analysis*. Reading, MA: Addison-Wesley.

U.S. Department of Commerce. (1977). *Social Indicators, 1976*. Washington, D.C.: U.S. Government Printing Office.

Velleman, P., & Hoaglin, D. (1981). *Applications, Basics, and Computing of Exploratory Data Analysis.* Boston: Duxbury Press.

Verdooren, L. R. (1963). Extended tables of critical values for Wilcoxon's test statistic. *Biometrika, 50,* 177–186.

Vermont Department of Health. (1982). *1981 Annual Report of Vital Statistics in Vermont.* Burlington, VT.

Wainer, H. (1984). How to display data badly. *American Statistician, 38,* 137–147.

Welkowitz, J., Ewen, R., & Cohen, J. (1982). *Introductory Statistics for the Behavioral Sciences* (3rd ed.). New York: Academic Press.

Winer, B. J. (1971). *Statistical Principles in Experimental Design* (2nd ed.). New York: McGraw-Hill.

Younger, M. S. (1985). *A First Course in Linear Regression.* Boston: Duxbury Press.

ANSWERS TO SELECTED EXERCISES

ANSWERS TO CHAPTER ONE PAGE 7

1-1 The student body would be considered a population when the interest is in being able to make statements about the opinions, behavior, and so on of the university's own students.

1-2 The entire student body of a university would be considered a sample when the interest is in drawing inferences about all university students in the country.

1-3 It would be a nonrandom sample because not every student in the population has an equal chance of being included in the sample.

1-4 Not all residents of the city are listed in the phone book. Transients, poor people, and especially women and children are underrepresented.

1-5 We could choose house or apartment numbers randomly from a city directory and then choose people within that house or apartment by using a random number table.

1-6 Average, mean, median, range.

1-7 The mean caloric intake of Americans living on social security could be of considerable importance.

1-8 Is the mean weight of a group of 30-year-old women who dieted consistently as teenagers different from the mean weight of a sample of 30-year-old non-dieters matched on weight as teenagers?

1-9 Categorical data: **(a)** the number of children in a sample who exhibit each of four different stages of moral development. **(b)** The number of people in a large office building using public transportation versus those using private cars to get to work. **(c)** The number of students majoring in each of ten undergraduate majors.

1-10 Measurement data: **(a)** Nearness-of-approach to a fear-arousing stimulus. **(b)** Heart rate during rapid eye movement (REM) sleep. **(c)** Score on the Beck Depression Inventory.

1-11 A personality construct of authoritarianism could be measured either as a relatively continuous variable (e.g., number of authoritarian items endorsed) or as a 3-point classification of authoritarian, neutral, or laissez-faire.

1-12 **(a)** We could be interested in the relationship between cognitive development as measured at age 2 and again at age 18—do subjects who do well at 2 also do well at 18? **(b)** We could be interested in the relationship between the number of times a subject rehearsed a list of words and the number of items correctly recalled at a later test.

1-13 **(a)** Do parents who receive counseling on adolescent problems respond more appropriately toward their children than parents who have not received counseling? **(b)** Do science majors perform better in a course on logic than social science majors?

ANSWERS TO CHAPTER TWO PAGE 16

2-1 **(a)** Nominal—hair color. **(b)** Ordinal—dominance ordering among a group of children. **(c)** Interval—the set of dates on which subjects complete an assigned task. **(d)** Ratio—the number of homework problems completed correctly for an assignment.

2-2 Salary is a ratio scale of income, but it is at best an ordinal scale of the contribution a person makes to the company.

2-3 It is a poor measure of learning unless we assume that the animal who suddenly went to sleep had forgotten all he ever knew about the task.

2-4 It is probably a much better index of motivation than of learning.

2-5 **(a)** Independent variables—good versus poor readers; male versus female. **(b)** Dependent variables—reading speed; score on a measure of anxiety.

2-6 The experiment examined the difference in legibility of handwriting (dependent variable) between left- and right-handed subjects (independent variable).

2-7 **(a)** Time to complete a task. **(b)** Weight. **(c)** Length of gestation.

2–8 **(a)** Pass–fail on an item. **(b)** Number of items correct on a 5-item test. **(c)** Number of convictions for DWI (especially if the highest category is $4+$).

2–9 **(a)** 9, 10, and 8 **(b)** 77 **(c)** $\sum_{i=1}^{10} X_i$

2–10 **(a)** 9, 2 **(b)** 57

2–11 **(a)** 5,929,657 **(b)** 7.7 **(c)** Average (mean)

2–12 **(a)** 3,249,377 **(b)** 5.789 **(c)** 2.406

2–13 **(a)** 460 **(b)** 4389 **(c)** 2.344

2–14 **(a)** $\Sigma(X + Y) = (10 + 9) + (8 + 9) + \cdots$ $+ (7 + 2) = 134 = 77 + 57 = \Sigma X + \Sigma Y$
(b) $\Sigma XY = 460$; $\Sigma X \Sigma Y = 4389$
(c) $\Sigma CX = \Sigma 3X = 3(10) + 3(8) + \cdots$ $+ 3(7) = 231 = 3(77) = C\Sigma X$
(d) $\Sigma X^2 = 657$; $(\Sigma X)^2 = 5929$

ANSWERS TO CHAPTER THREE PAGE 34

3–1 **(b)** Unimodal and positively skewed.

3–3 The problem with making a stem-and-leaf display of the data in Exercise 3-1 is that almost all of the values fall on only two leaves if we use the usual 10's digits for stems. The problem is not much better if we double the number of stems. Instead, use the units digits for stems and add a "catchall" category for high or low values.

3–4 **(a)** The scores for adults appear to be noticeably smaller.

3–10 It would be bimodal with one peak at 0 and another peak at about one pack (20) per day.

3–13 (1) Mexico has very many young people and very few old people, while Spain has a more even distribution. (2) The difference between males and females is more pronounced at each age in Spain. (3) You can see the high infant mortality rate in Mexico.

3–14 We use HI and LO categories to keep the stem-and-leaf display from straggling off at the ends.

ANSWERS TO CHAPTER FOUR PAGE 43

4–1 Percentile rank, 83rd percentile.

Instructions for Exercises 4-3 through 4-20. All percentiles and percentile ranks given for the following answers have been rounded and should be considered as approximate. The exact answer may differ by several points, depending upon how you group adjacent values, if at all.

4–3 44 **4–4** 52 **4–5** 38 **4–6** 39

4–8 13, median

4–9 10 **4–10** 97 **4–11** 51

4–12 Both $700 + 500$ and $500 + 700$ yield a total of 1200, but the first has an average percentile rank of 57, whereas the second averages 65.

4–13 86 **4–14** 64 **4–15** 2.93 **4–16** 65

4–17 61 **4–18** 1.0 **4–19** 2.93 **4–20** No

ANSWERS TO CHAPTER FIVE PAGE 49

5–1 Mode = 18; median = 18; mean = 18.9.

5–2 Mode = 10; median = 10; mean = 10.2.

5–3 Adults say "and then..." about half as often as do children.

5–5 The mean falls above the median.

5–6 1 9 10 15 15

5–7 Mean = 21.33; median = 21.

5–11 ADDSC: Mean = 52.60, median = 50, mode = 50; GPA: Mean = 2.45, median = 2.635, mode = 3.00.

5–12 The numerical codes for the levels of SEX and ENGL are arbitrary. The (mean $-$ 1) for SEX would be the proportion of subjects who were female.

5–13 The mode does not depend upon the relationships among the points on the scale, whereas the mean and median do depend upon such relationships.

ANSWERS TO CHAPTER SIX PAGE 70

6–1 Range = 30; variance = 20.214; $s = 4.496$.

6–2 Range = 16; variance = 11.592; $s = 3.405$.

6–3 The two standard deviations are roughly the same, although the range for children is about twice the range for adults.

6–4 The interval $\bar{X} \pm 2s_x = 9.908 - 27.892$ includes 96% of the scores.

6–5 The interval $\bar{X} \pm 2s_x = 3.39 - 17.01$ includes 96% of the scores.

6–8 2.381, 3.809, 1.428, 3.809, 2.857, 4.286, 4.286, 3.333

6–9 $-0.893, 0.536, -1.845, 0.536, -0.417, 1.012, 1.012, 0.060$

6-14 **(a)** Variance = 0.894; S.D. = 0.946. **(b)** In computing GPA we average over four or five courses and can thus balance out an extreme grade in one course with more moderate grades in others.

6-15 The range would not be affected. The standard deviation and the variance would be reduced because we have added a score that does not deviate from the mean.

6-16 The range would be unaffected, but the standard deviation and variance would increase.

6-18 Although we usually only draw one sample from the population, we would like to know that the statistics we calculate from this sample are like the statistics we would calculate if we had drawn a different random sample.

6-19 We want an unbiased statistic because we want one that is a fair estimate of the corresponding population parameter—that is, does not differ systematically from that population parameter.

=== **ANSWERS TO CHAPTER SEVEN PAGE 87** ===

7-2 For $X = 2.5$, $z = -0.92$, 18% of the distribution lies below $X = 2.5$; for $X = 6.2$, $z = 1.35$, 91% of the distribution lies below $X = 6.2$; for $X = 9$, $z = 3.06$, 99.9% of the distribution lies below $X = 9$.

7-3 **(a)** 68%   **(b)** 50%   **(c)** 84%

7-4 **(a)** $964.875 \leqslant X \leqslant 985.125$;   **(b)** $X = 985.125$; **(c)** $945.6 \leqslant X \leqslant 1004.4$

7-5 $z = (950 - 975)/15 = -1.67$; only 4.75% of the time would we expect a count as low as 950, given what we know about the distribution.

7-6 **(b)** 15.87%   **(c)** 30.85%

7-7 The answers to parts (a) and (b) of Exercise 7-6 will be equal when the two distributions have the same standard deviation.

7-8 $z = -1.28$; $X = \bar{X} - 1.28(30) = 111.6$

7-9 **(a)** $z = 1.28$; $X = \bar{X} + 1.28(400) = 2512$;   **(b)** $z = -1.645$; $X = \bar{X} - 1.645(400) = 1342$

7-10 **(b)** $z = (50 - 30)/7 = 2.86$. Only 0.2% of the time would we expect to find a result as large as this if the student is conscientiously sampling from a distribution with a mean of 30 and a standard deviation of 7. I suspect that he made up his data.

7-11 Multiply the raw scores by 10/7 to raise the standard deviation to 10, and then add 11.43 points to each new score to bring the mean up to 80.

7-12 **(b)** I suggested that she take the set of scores and empirically (i.e., by counting) determine the point that has 10% of the scores below it.

7-13 $z = (600 - 489)/126 = 0.88$. 81% of the scores fall below this, so 600 represents the 81st percentile.

7-14 $z = 0.675$; $(X - 489)/126 = 0.675$; $X = 574.05$

7-15 600 is at the 79th percentile, and the 75th percentile is 586.65.

7-16 The percentiles obviously depend upon the reference group.

7-17 $z = (66 - 52.60)/12.42 = 1.08$; 66 corresponds to the 86th percentile.

7-18 $z = 0.84$; $(X - 52.6)/12.42 = 0.84$; $X = 63.03$

7-19 $z = 0.675$; $(X - 2.46)/0.86 = 0.675$; $X = 3.04$

7-20 The answer using the normal distribution was considerably larger. The difference resulted from the markedly skewed shape of the distribution.

7-22 $z = 2.05$; $(X - 50)/10 = 2.05$; $X = 70.5$

=== **ANSWERS TO CHAPTER EIGHT PAGE 98** ===

8-1 Analytic—A mouse in a maze who is responding at random has a probability of .50 of turning left at a choice point. Relative frequency—A mouse who has turned left on 700 of the last 1000 trials has a probability of .70 of turning left this time (assuming no trend in the data over trials). Subjective—"I would give this experiment about a 70% chance of coming up with useful results."

8-2 **(a)** $1/1000 = .001$;   **(b)** $2/1000 = .002$; **(c)** $3/1000 = .003$

8-3 **(a)** $1/9 = .111$;   **(b)** $(2/10) \times (1/9) = .022$; **(c)** $(1/10) \times (2/9) = .022$;   **(d)** .044

8-4 **(b)**, **(c)**, and part of **(d)**

8-5 **(a)**

8-8 $(2/24) \times (3/24) = 6/576 = .010$

8-9 $(2/13) \times (3/13) = 6/169 = .036$

8-10 $.3278 + .1132 = .4410$

8-11 The probability that you are 20 years old.

8-12 The classification of the visual spectrum into about seven colors.

8-13 Political party affiliation; socioeconomic status as classified by Hollingshead and Redlich.

8–14 $10/1000 = .01$

8–15   **(a)** 200 people are above the 80th percentile. Therefore $p = 10/200 = .05$. **(b)** No one below the 80th percentile will be admitted. Therefore $p = .00$.

8–16 $z = (50 - 52.602)/12.422 = -0.21;$ $p(z \geqslant -0.21) = .58$

8–17 $z = (50 - 54.29)/12.90 = -0.33;$ $p(z \geqslant -0.33) = .63$

8–18 $p = 7/25 = .28$

8–19   Compare the probability of dropping out of school, ignoring the ADDSC score, with the conditional probability of dropping out given that ADDSC in elementary school exceeded some value (e.g., 66).

8–20   The unconditional probability is $10/88 = .11$. The conditional probability is .28. Students are much more likely to drop out of school if they scored at or above 60 in elementary school.

ANSWERS TO CHAPTER NINE PAGE 119

9–2 $r = .62$ **9–3** $r = .35$

9–7   **(a)** 4.67, 3.33, -4.67 **(b)** 4.67, 3.33, -4.67

9–8 $r = .99$,   .71, $-.99$;   three   possible   ways: 2 8 6 4, 6 4 2 8, and 6 2 8 4.

9–9   **(b)** $r = .74$

9–10   The correlation between I-131 and Verbal $= .2408$. The correlation between I-131 and Math $= .5501$. No. The large correlation is with Math SAT and not with Verbal, as reported.

9–12   The scatter diagram suggests that one or two extreme states are dramatically distorting the results.

9–13   In computing correlations each data point (state) counts equally; but because some data points are based on very small numbers of students, these states are overrepresented in the correlations.

9–14   I-131 × Verbal $r = -.04$;   not   significant. I-131 × Math $r = .26$; not significant.

9–18 $r = .80$ **9–19** $r = .44$

9–20   Yes. The coefficient (r) would still tell you how well a straight line fits, even if you think that a curved line would fit better. Often the fit of a straight line is sufficiently good for our purposes.

9–21   When we say that a correlation coefficient is reliable we mean that if we drew repeated samples from the same population the correlation coefficients for those samples would be of the same general magnitude. Correlations based on small samples are often unreliable because unusual data points can have an important influence on the correlation coefficient.

ANSWERS TO CHAPTER TEN PAGE 138

10–1 $\hat{Y} = 0.069X + 3.53$

10–2 $s_{Y - \hat{Y}} = 0.5796$

10–3   The incidence of birthweight < 2500 grams would be 8.36.

10–4   We would be extrapolating way beyond the range of the data on which the equation is based.

10–5 $\hat{Y} = 0.475X + 43.16$

10–6 $\hat{X} = 1.15Y - 17.65$

10–7 $\hat{Y} = 618.91$

10–8 $\hat{Y} = 635 = \bar{Y}$ **10–9** $\hat{Y} = 0.138X - 1.54$

10–10 $\hat{Y} = 0.885X + 0.941$

10–11   A one-unit difference in the SAT Verbal score is associated with a 0.885 difference in the predicted SAT Math score. The intercept has no interpretable meaning because a Verbal score of 0 is not a legitimate value.

10–14 $\hat{Y} = -0.0426X + 4.699$

10–15 $\hat{Y} = 8.38 - 0.778X_1 + 0.156X_2$

10–16   The best estimate of starting salary for faculty is $15,000. For every additional year of service, salary increases by $900 on average. For administrative staff the best estimate of starting salary is $10,000, but every year of additional service increases the salary by an average of $1500. They will be equal at $8\frac{1}{3}$ years of service.

ANSWERS TO CHAPTER ELEVEN PAGE 157

11–1   I set up the null hypothesis that last night's game was actually an NHL hockey game. On the basis of that hypothesis I expected that each team would earn somewhere between 0 and 6 points. I then looked at the actual points and concluded that they were way out of line with what I would expect if this were an NHL hockey game. I therefore rejected the null hypothesis.

11–2   **(b)** No   **(c)** I set up the null hypothesis that I was charged correctly. Therefore I would expect to receive about \$3.00 in change, give or take a quarter or so. The change that I received was in line with that expectation, and therefore I have no basis for rejecting H_0.

11–3 Concluding that I had been shortchanged when in fact I had not.

11–4 Concluding that I had been shortchanged when in fact I had.

11–5 The critical value would be that amount of change below which I would decide that I had been shortchanged. The rejection region would be all amounts of change less than the critical value—that is, all amounts that would lead to rejection of H_0.

11–6 I would adopt a one-tailed test if I wanted to detect being shortchanged but was not concerned about receiving too much money. I would not reject H_0 no matter how much excess change I received.

11–7 $z = (490 - 650)/50 = -3.2$. The probability that a student drawn at random from those properly admitted would have a GRE score as low as 490 is .0006. I suspect that the fact that his mother was a member of the board of trustees played a role in his admission.

11–8 We are not looking at a random sample of all students who took the GREs, but a selected sample of high-scoring students.

11–9 The distribution would drop away smoothly to the right for the same reason that it always does—there are very few high-scoring people. It would drop away to the left because fewer of the borderline students would be admitted (no matter how high the borderline is set).

11–10 I would draw a·very large number of samples. For each sample I would calculate the mode, the range, and their ratio (M). I would then plot the resulting values of M.

11–11 M is called a test statistic.

11–13 The alternative hypothesis is that this student was sampled from a population of students whose mean is not equal to 650.

11–14 Sampling error is variability in a statistic from sample to sample that is due to which observations happened to be included in the sample.

11–15 The word *distribution* refers to the set of values obtained for any observations. The phrase *sampling distribution* is reserved for the distribution of outcomes (either theoretical or empirical) of a sample statistic.

11–16 If α were to decrease, β would increase and power would decrease.

ANSWERS TO CHAPTER TWELVE PAGE 178

12–5 **(a)** $z = 3.86$; $p(z \geq \pm 3.86) = .0002$. We would reject the null hypothesis that these scores were drawn from a population with a mean of 100. **(b)** You would not reject the null hypothesis if you had been using a one-tailed test that $\mu < 500$.

12–6 It is not a random sample. (2) We have no definition of what is meant by "a terrible state" nor whether SAT scores measure it.

12–7 $z = 11.62$. We would reject the null hypothesis.

12–8 The sample sizes are considerably different.

12–9 $t = 2.18$ on 5700 *df*. We can reject H_0.

12–10 $H_0: \mu = 500$; $H_1: \mu \neq 500$

12–11 No, because we want to reject H_0 whenever $\mu \neq 500$. We cannot wait until we see the data and then decide which tail to use.

12–12 In this case it is not an important finding because the difference is so small. Even if $\mu = 503$ instead of 500, it makes no particular difference to anyone—it hardly qualifies as a sign of major improvement in GRE scores, especially because it is based on a selected sample.

12–13 $t = -1.47$. We cannot reject H_0.

12–14 There was a fair amount of variability and N was relatively low.

12–15 $512.3 \leqslant \mu \leqslant 537.7$

12–16 $500.3 \leqslant \mu \leqslant 505.7$

12–17 In Exercise 10-15 we knew σ but not s, and could solve for confidence limits using the population standard deviation. In Exercise 10-16 we knew s, although nothing was said about σ, and we solved for the confidence limits using s. In both cases the critical value of t or z was $+1.96$, but only because there were so many *df* for t (5700).

12–18 $\bar{X} = 101.82$, $s = 12.68$, $t = 0.82$ on 32 *df*. We will not reject H_0.

12–19 You did not know σ.

12–20 First we need to take a table of random numbers with a known variance. We would then draw many samples of 5 scores each. For each sample we would calculate the sample variance. When we had obtained several thousand sample variances we would plot their frequency distribution.

12–21 $t = (0.62\sqrt{8})/(1 - 0.62^2) = 2.85$
$t = (0.35\sqrt{8})/(1 - 0.35^2) = 1.13$

ANSWERS TO CHAPTER THIRTEEN PAGE 186

13-1 $t = 2.23$ on 14 df. Reject H_0. Conclude that physical guidance has reduced the amount of assistance required.

13-2 The physical guidance condition always came second, and improvement may reflect just the passage of time or delayed effects of imitation.

13-3 Half of the subjects could be run with the order of treatments reversed.

13-4 $0.068 \leqslant \mu \leqslant 3.666$

13-5 $t = 0.45$. We cannot reject H_0.

13-6 $t = -0.35$. Do not reject H_0.

13-7 The data in Exercise 13-5 suggest that the program was not successful. The data in Exercise 13-6 on the other hand would suggest that it may have been successful for some of the smokers but led other smokers to smoke even more. These two effects largely cancel each other out in the combined data.

13-9 $t = 1.39$ on 19 df. Do not reject H_0.

13-10 To answer this we need to know the critical value of t, which in turn requires knowing df, which requires knowing N. But we can use 2.00 as a critical value as a rough approximation. Then the required $N = [(2.00 \times 2.870)/0.333]^2 = 297$.

13-12 As the correlation between the two variables increases, the t will increase as well.

13-14 If subjects were asked to do a set of anagrams under one condition and then asked to do a second set under another condition, any strategies they learned in the first half of the experiment could carry over and influence the results of the second half.

ANSWERS TO CHAPTER FOURTEEN PAGE 202

14-1 $t = 1.44$ on 28 df. Do not reject H_0.

14-2 There is quite a substantial variance within each group.

14-3 By measuring the same subject under both conditions (as in Chapter 13) we were able to eliminate subject-to-subject variability.

14-4 $t = 1.60$ on 16 df. Do not reject H_0.

14-5 We use random assignment to try to protect against the possibility that people who are prone to having many cavities would be disproportionately as-signed to one of the groups, as could happen if we allowed friends to choose to be in the same group.

14-6 $t = 4.54$ on 16 df. Reject H_0.

14-7 $t = 1.52$ on 5 df. Do not reject H_0.

14-8 The differential dropout rate may be very important. Only half as many people were able to complete Program A as completed Program B.

14-9 $t = 0.59$ on 15 df. Do not reject H_0.

14-10 $-3.03 \leqslant (\mu_1 - \mu_2) \leqslant 5.34$

14-11 $-3.61 \leqslant (\mu_1 - \mu_2) \leqslant 14.11$

14-12 $t = 1.66$ on 86 df. Do not reject H_0.

14-13 $t = 3.77$ on 86 df. Reject H_0.

14-14 The ADDSC score can be used to create groups who later turn out to differ on GPA. In other words, ADDSC is a predictor of ninth-grade performance.

14-15 $t = -2.36$ on 8 df. Reject H_0.

14-16 $t = 2.13$ on 8 df. Do not reject H_0.

14-17 If the two sample sizes are equal, the pooled and unpooled estimates would be the same.

14-18 If the two variances are equal, the pooled (or unpooled) estimates would be equal to the common value of the separate sample variance.

14-20 Perfectly legitimate and reasonable transformation of data can produce different results. It is important to consider seriously the nature of the dependent variable before beginning an experiment.

ANSWERS TO CHAPTER FIFTEEN PAGE 218

15-1 (a) 0.250   (b) 2.50   (c) 0.71

15-3 $N = 98, 125, 169$

15-4 Power = .965

15-6 (a) $N = 15.21 \simeq 16$ (b) $N = 31.36 \simeq 32$

15-7 (a) $N = 38.72 \simeq 39$ subjects per group (b) $N = 84.5 \simeq 84$ subjects per group

15-8 Power = .30   **15-9** Power = .51

15-10 (a) Power = .22 (b) $t = 1.19$ (c) t is numerically equal to δ although t is calculated from statistics and δ is calculated from parameters.

15-11 The first one. Because he found a significant difference with an experiment having relatively little power, he must have been examining a fairly large effect.

15-14 He should use the Dropout group. (You can let σ be any value as long as it is the same for both calculations. Then calculate δ for each situation.)

15-15

Effect Size	γ	One-sample t	Two-sample t
Small	.20	289	1156
Medium	.50	47	186
Large	.80	19	72

15-16

Effect Size	γ	One-sample t	Two-sample t
Small	.20	121	484
Medium	.50	20	78
Large	.80	8	32

15-17 Not if the assumptions underlying the test are met.

15-18 Power would be equal to the probability of a Type II error when $\mu_1 = \mu \pm 1.96\sigma$.

≡ **ANSWERS TO CHAPTER SIXTEEN PAGE 246** ≡

16-1

Source	df	SS	MS	F
Groups	2	2100.000	1050.000	40.13*
Error	15	392.500	26.167	
Total	17	2492.500		

*$p < .05$

16-2 $t = -1.69$. Not significant; $t = -6.77$. Reject H_0.

16-3 (a)

Source	df	SS	MS	F
Groups	1	2.256	2.256	1.95 ns
Error	8	9.250	1.156	
Total	9	11.506		

(b) $t = -1.397 = \sqrt{1.95}$ (c) We need to ensure that the observations were independent.

16-4 (a)

Source	df	SS	MS	F
Groups	3	655.143	218.381	10.78*
Error	24	486.286	20.262	
Total	27	1141.429		

*$p < .05$

(b)

Source	df	SS	MS	F
Groups	1	51.572	51.572	1.23 ns
Error	26	1089.857	41.918	
Total	27	1141.429		

16-5

Source	df	SS	MS	F
Groups	2	1516.100	738.050	24.01*
Error	12	378.833	31.569	
Total	14	1894.933		

*$p < .05$

16-6 (a)

Source	df	SS	MS	F
Groups	1	1.260	1.260	0.87 ns
Error	10	14.532	1.453	
Total	11	15.792		

(b) t (unpooled) $= -0.883 = \sqrt{0.780}$
(c) t (pooled) $= -0.931 = \sqrt{0.867}$
(d) The pooled t.

16-7 $\eta^2 = 0.196$; $\omega^2 = 0.087$

16-8 (a)

Source	df	SS	MS	F
Groups	2	826.867	413.433	9.64*
Error	27	1157.662	42.877	
Total	29	1984.529		

*$p < .05$

(b) It does not compare good and poor readers—nor do we even know how well any of our subjects read.
(c) Whether or not words are capitalized influences reading speed.

16–9

Source	df	SS	MS	F
Groups	2	413.433	206.717	4.82*
Error	12	514.512	42.876	
Total	14	927.945		

*$p < .05$

There are still significant differences between the groups. Notice that most of the entries have been halved, including F, but not MS_{error}.

16–10 For Group 1 versus Group 2, $t = 2.77$. Reject H_0. For Group 1 versus Group 3, $t = 1.57$. Do not reject H_0.

16–11 I have somewhat more faith because it is a significant result produced by a less powerful experiment.

16–12

Source	df	SS	MS	F
Groups	2	6.581	3.290	3.93*
Error	85	71.191	0.838	
Total	87	77.773		

*$p < .05$

16–13 Because the groups differ not only because of the ability level of the student, but also because of the content of the course, it is difficult to know what the results actually mean.

16–14 $t = 4.4426 = \sqrt{19.737}$; $F = 35,242/1786 = 19.732$

16–15

Source	df	SS	MS	F
Groups	2	22.500	11.250	22.74*
Error	85	42.059	0.495	
Total	87	64.559		

*$p < .05$

16–18 $\eta^2 = 0.35$; $\omega^2 = 0.33$

16–19

Source	df	SS	MS	F
Groups	2	0.854	0.427	8.06*
Error	49	2.597	0.053	
Total	51	3.451		

*$p < .05$

ANSWERS TO CHAPTER SEVENTEEN PAGE 268

17–1

Source	df	SS	MS	F
Pay	1	3.828	3.828	10.43*
Sex	1	0.078	0.078	<1
P × S	1	3.403	3.403	9.27*
Error	16	5.875	0.367	
Total	19	13.184		

*$p < .05$

17-2

Source	df	SS	MS	F
Parity	1	28.9	28.9	6.08*
Weight	1	14.4	14.4	3.03 ns
P × W	1	0.1	0.1	<1
Error	36	171.0	4.75	
Total	39	214.4		

*$p < .05$

17–3 No, because 50% of the population of primiparous mothers do not give birth to LBW infants.

17–4 $F = 1.78$. Not significant.

17–5

Source	df	SS	MS	F
Site	2	356.044	178.022	6.07*
Delay	2	188.578	94.289	3.22 ns
S × D	4	371.956	92.989	3.17*
Error	36	1055.200	29.311	
Total	44	1971.778		

*$p < .05$

17–7 $t = 3.05$ on 36 df; $t = 3.00$ on 36 df; both are significant.

17-8 For Neutral versus A, $F = t^2 = 3.05^2 = 9.30$. Critical value $= (k - 1)F_\alpha(k - 1)$, $k(n - 1) = (2)F_\alpha$ $(2,36) = 2(3.29) = 6.58$. Reject H_0. For Neutral versus B, $F = t^2 = 3.00^2 = 9$. Again reject H_0.

17-9 $F = 4.35$ on 2 and 36 df. Reject H_0.

17-10

Source	df	SS	MS	F
Reputation	1	567.000	567.000	27.98*
Location	1	51.571	51.571	2.55 ns
R × L	1	36.571	36.571	1.80 ns
Error	24	486.286	20.260	
Total	27	1141.429		

*$p < .05$

There is a significant effect for Reputation but not for Location or the Interaction.

17-11 The Location effect in the one-way and the Location effect in the two-way have the same df, SS, and MS. However, the F is different because when we combine the groups into larger groups we inflated the error term. (*Note:* The one-way on four groups and the 2×2 produce the same error term.)

17-12 $\eta^2_{Age} = .09$; $\omega^2_{Age} = .09$
$\eta^2_{Condition} = .57$; $\omega^2_{Condition} = .55$
$\eta^2_{A \times C} = .07$; $\omega^2_{A \times C} = .06$

17-16 $\eta^2 = .29$; $\eta^2 = .01$; $\eta^2 = .26$
$\omega^2 = .26$; $\omega^2 = 0$; $\omega^2 = .22$

17-17 $\eta^2_{Parity} = .13$; $\eta^2_{Weight} = .07$; $\eta^2_{P \times W} = .00$
$\omega^2_{Parity} = .11$; $\omega^2_{Weight} = .04$; $\omega^2_{P \times W} = .00$

17-20 The two statistics would be in close agreement when the error term is very small relative to the sum of squares for the treatment effect.

17-21 Eysenck felt that older subjects would differ from younger ones on those tasks that involved higher levels of processing. He did not expect differences on tasks that required minimal processing.

ANSWERS TO CHAPTER EIGHTEEN PAGE 278

18-1 (a)

Source	df	SS	MS	F
Subjects	7	189,666.67		
Sessions	2	1,808.33	904.165	3.66
Error	14	3,458.33	247.024	
Total	23	194,933.33		

(b) There is no significant difference among the session totals.

18-2 (b) $t = 1.14$

Source	df	SS	MS	F
Subjects	7	130,793.750		
Sessions	1	506.250	506.250	$1.291 = 1.14^2$
Error	7	2,743.750	391.980	$= t^2$
Total	15	134,043.750		

18-3

Source	df	SS	MS	F
Subjects	9	60.000		
Time	2	27.467	13.733	5.02*
Error	18	49.200	2.733	
Total	29	136.667		

*$p < .05$

18-4 Compare Baseline with Training. $t = -2.98$. Reject H_0. Performance improved with training. Compare Baseline with Follow-up. $t = -0.54$. Do not reject H_0. After a Follow-up period, performance was not significantly better than it was during Baseline.

18-6

Source	df	SS	MS	F
States	9	46,737.445		
Years	6	1,987.203	331.200	19.70*
Error	54	907.653	16.808	
Total	69	49,632.301		

*$p < .05$

18-7 We tested the null hypothesis that the scores for each year represented samples from populations with equal means.

18-8 Because each state was measured on each year— that is, we would expect nonzero correlations between columns.

18-9 (a) $t = 0.34$. Do not reject H_0. Performance did not change during Baseline. (b) $t = 0.99$. Do not reject H_0. Performance did not change during the last three weeks of training. (Apparently it changed early in training and remained stable thereafter.)

18-10 $F = 0.1536$ $t = 0.3919 = \sqrt{F}$

ANSWERS TO CHAPTER NINETEEN PAGE 296

19–1 $\chi^2 = 11.313$ on 2 df. Reject H_0 and conclude that students do not enroll at random.

19–2 We cannot tell if students chose different sections because of the instructor or because of the times at which the sections are taught—Instructor and Time are confounded. We would at least have to offer the sections at the same time.

19–3 $\chi^2 = 2.4$ on 4 df. We cannot reject the H_0 that my daughter's sorting behavior is in line with my theory.

19–4 It generalizes only to the population of data that could be generated by my daughter. In other words we have only a sample of her behavior. We do not have a random sample of the behavior of people in general.

19–5 $\chi^2 = 29.35$ on 1 df. We can reject the H_0 that the children chose dolls at random (at least with respect to color).

19–6 $\chi^2 = 12.24$ on 1 df. Again we can reject H_0, but this time the departure is in the opposite direction.

19–7 $\chi^2 = 34.17$ on 1 df. Reject the H_0 and conclude that the distribution of choices between black and white dolls was different in the two studies. Choice is not independent of Study. We are no longer asking whether one color of doll is preferred over the other color, but whether the pattern of preference is constant across studies. In analysis of variance terms we are dealing with an interaction.

19–8 **(a)** It would test the null hypothesis that the mental health center at which a person seeks help is independent of the type of problem he or she has. **(b)** $\chi^2 = 10.305$ on 4 df. **(c)** Reject H_0 and conclude that the two variables are not independent.

19–9 **(a)** $\chi^2 = 5.153$, which is half of what it was in Exercise 19-8. **(b)** The sample size plays a very important role, with larger samples being more likely to produce significant results—as is also true with other tests.

19–10 $\chi^2 = 5.38$ on 1 df. Reject H_0 and conclude that achievement level during high school varies as a function of performance during elementary school.

19–11 **(a)** $\chi^2 = 16.43$ on 7 df. **(b)** Reject H_0. **(c)** Because nearly half of the cell frequencies are less than 5, I would feel very uncomfortable. One approach would be to combine adjacent columns.

19–12 We would be asking if the students are evenly distributed among the eight categories. What we really

tested in Exercise 19-11 is whether that distribution, however it appears, is the same for those who later took remedial English as it is for those who later took nonremedial English.

19–13 **(a)** $\chi^2 = 12.896$ on 6 df. **(b)** Reject H_0. The number of days required for delivery is a function of distance, but not in a neat and readily interpretable way.

19–14 To avoid confounding differences among Instructors with differences among times.

19–15 $\chi^2 = 0.658$. Do not reject H_0.

19–16 As sample sizes increase, with the same percentage in the cells, the power of the test increases.

19–17 $\chi^2 = 1.5$. Do not reject H_0.

19–18 Although there may be no significant differences between the percentages, the fact that 45% of the students feel that the course needs major improvements is an important result.

ANSWERS TO CHAPTER TWENTY PAGE 312

20–1 **(a)** $W_s = 23$; $W_{0.025} = 27$; **(b)** I would reject H_0 and conclude that older children include more inferences in their summaries.

20–2 **(a)** $W_s = 53$; $W_{0.025} = 68$; **(b)** Reject H_0 and conclude that subjects in the Lesion group take longer to learn the task, as the theory predicted.

20–3 $z = -3.15$; reject H_0.

20–4 $W_s = 53$; $W_{0.05} = 72$. Again reject H_0.

20–5 **(a)** $T = 8.5$; $T_{0.025} = 8$. Do not reject H_0. **(b)** We cannot conclude that we have evidence supporting the hypothesis that there is a reliable increase in hypothesis generation and testing over time. (Here is a case in which alternative methods of breaking ties could lead to different conclusions.)

20–6 **(a)** $z = -1.94$. Do not reject H_0. **(b)** We would come to the same conclusion. The answers agree well and would be even closer if N were larger.

20–7 **(a)** $T = 46$; $T_{0.025} = 52$. **(b)** Reject H_0 and conclude that first-born children are more independent.

20–8 $z = -2.20$, which agrees with our earlier conclusion.

20–9 The difference between the pairs is heavily dependent upon the score for the firstborn.

20–10 The Mann–Whitney test tests a null hypothesis that the scores were drawn from identical populations and is particularly sensitive to differences in medians. The t test tests a null hypothesis about means and assumes normality and equal variances in the population.

20–11 The Wilcoxon matched-pairs signed-ranks test tests the null hypothesis that paired scores were drawn from identical populations or from symmetric populations with the same mean (and median). The corresponding t test tests the null hypothesis that the paired scores were drawn from populations with the same mean and assumes normality.

20–12 The nature of the scale is important for the interpretation of the results but not for the choice of a statistical test on the actual numbers.

20–13 Because, by making assumptions about normality and homogeneity of variance, the t test refers specifically to population means.

20–14 $H = 5.124$. Do not reject H_0.

20–15 $H = 6.757$. Reject H_0.

20–16 $\chi_F^2 = 8.792$. Reject H_0—the truancy rate improved.

20–17 It eliminates the influence of individual differences (differences in overall level of truancy from one person to another).

20–18 We would not be able to take the relative magnitudes of the differences into account.

20–19 These are exactly equivalent tests in this case.

20–20 $\chi_F^2 = 9.00$. We can reject the null hypothesis and conclude that people don't like tea made with used tea bags.

≡ANSWERS TO CHAPTER TWENTY-ONE PAGE 316≡

21–1 This involves straight descriptive statistics, probably including boxplots of readability scores for items on each test.

21–2 They would use Pearson's r to correlate Denver test scores and scores on individually administered intellectual measures. The question might be taken to imply that some children had one measure of intelligence and other children had a different measure. In this case you could sort the children into groups and compute correlations for each group.

21–3 They could run a t test for two independent groups to compare the two groups. They could then obtain the correlation between the percent correct score and the reported level of use of study aids. (You should

recall that with two groups a t test and a one-way analysis of variance are equivalent tests.)

21–4 This is a 2×3 analysis of variance (Type of Cue During Learning × Type of Cue During Recall).

21–5 This is a one-way analysis of variance with three groups. They could also use protected t tests to compare individual groups if that is necessary.

21–6 He should run three separate t tests for two independent groups.

21–7 This is a more complex repeated-measures analysis of variance than the one we considered in Chapter 18. It is a 2×2 factorial design with Good versus Poor Readers and Easy versus Difficult Passages as the factors. Reader is a between-subject variable (different people are in the two groups) and Passages is a within-subject variable (the same people read both kinds of passages).

21–8 They should compare the two groups on locus of control scores, and maybe on Peabody scores, using t tests for independent samples. They could also correlate Nowicki-Strickland and Peabody using Pearson's r.

21–9 They could use a one-way analysis of variance on the MFFT score for the second administration. They should probably also run it on the scores for the first administration to check the experimental hypothesis that the groups started out together. (A more complex repeated-measures design also would be suitable [see Exercise 21-7], but I'd be inclined to stick with the two one-way analyses because of their ease of interpretation.)

21–10 This is a simple repeated-measures analysis of variance. The corresponding distribution-free test would be Friedman's rank test.

21–11 (a) He should run a 2×2 (Group by Abstinent versus Smoking) at each time interval. (b) We don't know whether the nicotine in the gum had any effect. It might be that having any kind of gum to chew was the controlling factor.

21–12 She could first find the mean rank assigned to each characteristic (for each sex and year). Because the raw data were originally ranks, I would probably be inclined to then rank the mean values. She could then calculate Spearman's r's between males and females for each year or between years within each sex. The correlations would be obtained for the ten pairs of scores (one pair per characteristic).

21–13 They should use a t test for two related samples. If they don't want to use a parametric test, they should use the Wilcoxon matched-pairs signed-ranks test.

21–14   They should use a Mann–Whitney test.

21–15   They should use a t test for related samples—the samples are related because Smith and Plant formed matched pairs.

21–16   They should begin with a one-way analysis of variance. Assuming that the F is significant, they could follow this up with a protected t test, comparing the two "theft" conditions. They could also correlate accuracy with confidence using Pearson's r.

21–17   This is a situation for a chi-square goodness-of-fit test.

21–18   This is another complex repeated-measures analysis of variance. The comparison of recall of the two lists (one learned before administration of the drug and the other learned after) is a repeated measurement because the same subjects are involved. The comparison of the drug versus saline groups is a between-subjects effect because the groups involve different subjects.

21–19   This is a t test for two independent groups.

21–20   They could use the Kruskal–Wallis test to compare the three groups and, if that was significant, use the Mann–Whitney test the way they would otherwise have used a protected t test.

INDEX

POWER

Effect Size (One sample)	$\gamma = (\mu_1 - \mu_0)/\sigma$
Effect Size (Two sample)	$\gamma = (\mu_1 - \mu_2)/\sigma$
Effect Size (Correlation)	$\gamma = \rho_1 - \rho_0$
Delta (One-Sample t)	$\delta = \gamma\sqrt{N}$
Delta (Two-Sample t)	$\delta = \gamma\sqrt{\dfrac{N}{2}}$
Delta (Correlation)	$\delta = \gamma\sqrt{N-1}$

CORRELATION AND REGRESSION

Sums of Squares

$$SS_X = \Sigma X^2 - \frac{(\Sigma X)^2}{N}$$

Sum of Products

$$SP_{XY} = \Sigma XY - \frac{\Sigma X \Sigma Y}{N}$$

Covariance

$$\text{cov}_{XY} = \frac{\Sigma XY - \dfrac{\Sigma X \Sigma Y}{N}}{N-1} = \frac{SP_{XY}}{N-1}$$

Correlation (Pearson)

$$r = \frac{\text{cov}_{XY}}{s_X s_Y} = \frac{SP_{XY}}{\sqrt{SS_X SS_Y}}$$

$$= \frac{N\Sigma XY - \Sigma X \Sigma Y}{\sqrt{[N\Sigma X^2 - (\Sigma X)^2][N\Sigma Y^2 - (\Sigma Y)^2]}}$$

Slope

$$b = \frac{\text{cov}_{XY}}{s_X^2} = \frac{SP_{XY}}{SS_X}$$

Intercept

$$a = \frac{\Sigma Y - b\Sigma X}{N} = \bar{Y} - b\bar{X}$$

Standard Error of Estimate

$$s_{Y-\hat{Y}} = \sqrt{\frac{\Sigma(Y-\hat{Y})^2}{N-2}} = \sqrt{\frac{SS_{error}}{N-2}}$$

$$= s_y\sqrt{(1-r^2)\frac{N-1}{N-2}}$$

SS_Y

$$\Sigma Y^2 - \frac{(\Sigma Y)^2}{N}$$

$SS_{\hat{Y}}$

$$\Sigma \hat{Y}^2 - \frac{(\Sigma \hat{Y})^2}{N}$$

$SS_{Y-\hat{Y}}$

$$SS_Y - SS_{\hat{Y}} = SS_{error}$$

SS_{error}

$$SS_Y(1-r^2)$$